"I finally got around to hearing our entire interview
on jazz and astrophysics. I think it is one of my
best ever—magnified and strengthened by our on-air chemistry.
Thank you again for your interest and your enthusiasm for what I do."

—Neil deGrasse Tyson, *Director, Hayden Planetarium,*
Department of Astrophysics at the American Museum of Natural History, NYC

"I have been along for this ride with Judy almost from the beginning
and I am constantly amazed at how her boundless imagination results in
some of the most fascinating conversations about jazz I have ever heard.
In fact, she is on par as a jazz radio interviewer with
public radio pioneers Marian McPartland and Dr. Billy Taylor.
She is carrying on that tradition in a way
that I have always been envious of.
The best always make it look (sound) easy."

—Felix Contreras, *host, NPR's Jazz Piano Christmas and Alt.Latino*

"Judy Carmichael's interviews for *Jazz Inspired* always bring out
the best in her subjects who readily share their affinity for jazz.
Over the years, she's "outed" many a celebrity as a closeted jazz fan,
for which this jazz man is grateful.
More importantly, Judy has shown how
the music can be a vital part of the creative process
for writers, comedians, actors, and other artists.
The only thing missing from this book is her infectious laugh.
You'll just have to imagine it."

—Lee Mergner, *Ja*

D1453131

"What we have loved, others will love,
and we will teach them how; instruct them how
the mind of man becomes a thousand times more beautiful
than the earth on which he dwells..."

—William Wordsworth

"Just go with truth and beauty and forget the rest."

—Bill Evans *(to Tony Bennett)*

"Being a jazz musician is an awful way to make a living,
but it's a wonderful thing to do with your life."

—John Eaton, *jazz pianist*

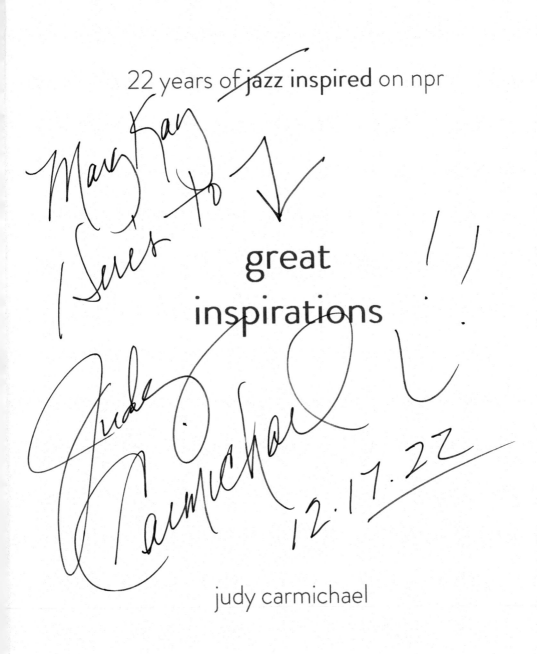

22 years of jazz inspired on npr

great
inspirations

judy carmichael

Mary Kay
(Seves to

great
inspirations

Judy Carmichael

12.17.22

C & D Productions
PO Box 360
Sag Harbor, NY
11963 USA

For information on booking a reading
or an event with Judy Carmichael,
contact Jamie Roche at:
piercemgmt@aol.com

or visit our website at
www.judycarmichael.com
www.jazzinspired.com

Cover design: Kathleen Lynch/Black Kat Design
kat@blackkatdesign.net

Interior design: Donna Lee McGullam

Photo credit, author bio pic: Judy Preiato

ISBN: 979-8-9864875-0-2
LCCN: 2022911670

Judy interviewing actress Blythe Danner for *Jazz Inspired*
onstage at the Tanglewood Music Festival in 2011.

For Kurt, Jamie and Evy.

Table of Contents

i   Introduction

1   F. Murray Abraham
Stage, film, and television actor.

7   Steve Allen
Host and co-creator of *The Tonight Show*, the first late night television talk show.

17   Jon Batiste
Bandleader for *The Late Show with Stephen Colbert*.

27   Tony Bennett
Singer and painter.

41   Alan Broadbent
Jazz pianist and composer.

53   Jimmy Buffett
Singer-songwriter.
and
Frank Marshall
Film producer and director.

63   Chevy Chase
Film and television actor.

75   Glenn Close
Stage, film, and television actress.
and
Ted Nash
Jazz saxophonist and composer.

85   Roger Corman
     Movie director, producer, and actor.

97   Blythe Danner
     Stage, screen and television actress.

107 E.L. Doctorow
     Novelist.

119 John Eaton
     Jazz pianist.

129 Robert Fairchild
     Ballet dancer, stage and film actor.

139 Béla Fleck
     Banjo player.

151 Renée Fleming
     Lyric soprano.

159 Dave Frishberg
     Jazz pianist, composer, lyricist and singer.

167 Frank Gehry
     Architect.

175 Jeff Goldblum
     Actor and jazz pianist.

187 Gil Goldstein
     Jazz pianist, accordionist, arranger and producer.

199 Christopher Guest
     Screenwriter, actor, director, and musician.

213　Don Hahn

Filmmaker, writer, painter, and musician.

225　Scott Hamilton

Jazz tenor saxophonist.

237　Fred Hersch

Jazz pianist and composer.

247　Penn Jillette

One half of the magic team of Penn & Teller.

257　Billy Joel

Pianist and singer-songwriter.

267　Darlene Love

Singer and actress.

277　Jane Lynch

Stage, film and television actress.

285　Seth MacFarlane

Producer, director, animator, actor, and singer.

297　Marian McPartland

Jazz pianist and composer.

309　John Musker

Animator, animation director, screenwriter and producer.

327　Willie Nelson

Singer-songwriter, actor, and author.

333　Arturo O'Farrill

Jazz pianist, composer, and arranger.

343   Paula Poundstone
      Stand-up comedian.

355   Paul Prudhomme
      Chef and cookbook author.

367   Robert Redford
      Stage and film actor, director, painter and founder of
      the Sundance Film Festival.

381   Hannah Rothschild
      British writer, philanthropist, and documentary filmmaker.

395   Nadja Salerno-Sonnenberg
      Classical violinist, educator, and author.

405   Roy Scheider
      Stage, film and television actor.

417   Diane Schuur
      Jazz vocalist and pianist.

425   Allen Toussaint
      Musician, songwriter, arranger, and record producer.

437   Neil deGrasse Tyson
      Astrophysicist, author, and science evangelist.

449   Loudon Wainwright III
      Singer-songwriter and actor.

459   Acknowledgements

461   About the Author

Introduction

When I was a young musician starting out in California, one of my first jobs was playing ragtime piano at Disneyland's Coke Corner, an outdoor café at the end of Main Street USA, the long walk that leads the hordes to the rest of the park. An average of 60,000 visitors a day passed by when I worked there in the late 1970s and early '80s. I stayed for five years, working five days a week, seven hours a day, sometimes two shifts in a row. The point: I met a lot of people.

The majority stayed for only a few minutes, anxious to move on to Space Mountain or a hunt for Mickey. But the comments from the ones who did stay were fascinating. Most Americans used me to shame or encourage their children to practice, although New Yorkers often expressed their hatred for Disneyland and their love for me. "You're too good to be working here!" they'd say. "Why aren't you in New York?"

A minority, usually people from other countries, respectfully listened, then had their children shake my hand and congratulate me. I was an anonymous girl in a silly 1890s red-and-white-striped costume—some kids even thought I was Audio-Animatronic—still, I was acknowledged for my music despite the over-stimulating atmosphere of smells, sounds, people, and the occasional Pluto-sighting. I even came up with a name for this phenomenon: "Picasso at a garage sale"—the ability to focus on something beautiful in spite of what surrounds it. I'm no Picasso, but I knew there was a different kind of attention being paid and there had to be a way to get others to that place of sensitivity and appreciation.

Back in the '90s I started thinking seriously about starting my own radio series to celebrate great artists, well-known or not, in contrast to so many media outlets that focus exclusively on famous people with a product to sell. My program would be about the artists, their work, their creative process, and their inspirations, not about a specific project. I would choose professionally creative people of all ages who had a broad view of their art and the world, people whose stories were illustrative and inspirational. The sad truth is that extremely young or extremely old creative artists are the ones most often celebrated even though most of life is the time in between. I also suspected that many creative people who *were* famous would welcome a deep conversation about their work, something beyond hawking their latest movie or recording.

Jazz is played very little on the radio so exposure to it is rare. Like other sophisticated music, jazz is usually introduced to someone by a friend or relative. Every jazz fan I know tells me about that initial recording their uncle or best friend played for them or rhapsodizes about the first time a date took them to a jazz club and it changed their life. An introduction to jazz is seldom accidental. Rather, it is the beginning of a love affair, launched with the help of a trusted matchmaker.

This general lack of exposure to the art form allows most people to think they hate jazz because they hear one thing they don't like and give up, knowing very little about the broad range of stylistic choices in jazz. People often tell me they hate jazz but love me, illustrating this point. I once asked a man, after such a comment, "Well, what *do* you listen to?" "Certainly not jazz!" he replied. "Something more like Louis Armstrong."

My inspirations range from classic movie musicals and literature to architecture, painting and industrial design. One of my most significant mentors was painter/designer Ray Eames. This wide range of interests was a driving force in my design of *Jazz Inspired*. I wanted the larger subject of inspiration and creativity to be the focus, not exclusively a discussion about music by musicians. I wanted a conversation between two professional artists about jazz and improvisation and how it inspires, an exchange that would bring the listener into this world and hopefully help them understand what is so special about jazz. I also thought a conversation about jazz inspiration would be a new way into a conversation with people who have been interviewed countless times and would welcome a different kind of exchange about their work.

As a starting point for our conversation, I ask each guest to choose five or more jazz recordings that most inspire them—a difficult task but a revealing one. The actor Roy Scheider talked about music's power to connect directly to our emotions. The novelist E.L. Doctorow discussed the rhythm of music and language. The filmmaker and actor Christopher Guest—that master of accents and improvisation—shared his thoughts about tone and risk-taking. Jazz became a new way for my guests to express their thoughts on creativity and gave them a deeper way of explaining it all.

I created *Jazz Inspired* in 1998 without the support of a radio station or network—an unusual way to develop a show in those pre-podcast days—so I had no budget to seduce guests with gifts, no staff to follow up, and no radio network to entice record labels with a promise of wider exposure for their artists. I taught myself to produce by listening to shows I liked and learning from people I admired. I attended public radio conventions, handed out CD samples of the show, and pretended I knew what I was doing.

Initially, no CDs came my way nor famous folks chasing me for a spot on the program. Additionally, although *Jazz Inspired* is carried by National Public Radio, it is not produced by them, so I raise the underwriting funds, find the guests, produce the show, and handle distribution. In the early years of *Jazz Inspired*, distribution required a $10,000 a year satellite upload. My production engineer, Kurt Heidolph, assembles it all. We're two people pretending to be fifty. Without the muscle of a big name behind me, the chase for my guests has been one of the most adventurous—and often hilarious—aspects of *Jazz Inspired*. The stories of these pursuits, which I've included here, give further insight into the creative people I've been fortunate enough to meet and have on the show.

The great gift of an artist's life is the focus on listening, seeing, and paying attention. Artists live in imagination and playfulness and have the desire to challenge themselves, to grow and create. This is something anyone can do—to choose to move forward creatively and be of value to something greater than one's own satisfaction, to *contribute*. I hope this book not only brings light to the process of creativity but inspires it.

Judy Carmichael's Jazz Inspired is in its twenty-second year on NPR stations. Ashlee Claud, General Manager of WVRU-FM in Radford, VA was the first to air *Jazz Inspired* in 2000. Years later she revealed that 2000 was her first year on the job, which somehow seems fitting.

The following conversations are the ones I found particularly surprising, inspiring, and meaningful from a wide spectrum of the world's most fascinating creative people.

— Judy Carmichael, March 2022

F. Murray Abraham

(b. 1939)

Film and stage actor. Multiple awards including two Obie Awards and the BAFTA, Golden Globe and Academy Award for Best Actor for Amadeus.

Interviewed in 1999

F. Murray Abraham became well known after winning multiple awards for his starring role as the Italian composer Antonio Salieri in the 1984 film *Amadeus*. We met a few years later at Knickerbocker Bar & Grill, a legendary Greenwich Village restaurant and jazz club where I frequently played and which happened to be around the corner from Abraham's apartment. Unbeknownst to me, he often came by to hear me play. One evening as I was walking past his table, he jumped in front of me, threw his arms around me, and announced, "Judy Carmichael, I love you!" I disentangled myself, recognized him, and said, "You're F. Murray Abraham!" Dramatically he exclaimed, "You *know* me?" "Of course, I know you! I love you, too!" Not surprisingly, we became fast friends.

Murray was one of the generous souls who agreed to be among the first people I interviewed for *Jazz Inspired*, and he delighted me by suggesting that we record our conversation onstage where he was performing later that night in the Off Off Broadway play *It's My Party and I'll Die If I Want To.*

JC: *Murray Abraham! You realize I can now say I've appeared on stage with F. Murray Abraham.*

FMA: Yes! Talking about the stage, this is a 99-seat house. We're in the basement of a church. And I share my dressing room back there with two other actors, and it's just about the same size as the first dressing room I ever had in a professional show, which was in L.A. about thirty-five years ago. And the difference is that that one had *six* actors in it. So I'm coming up in the world!

JC: *Well, I like being on stage here with you. Even with my own shows, I often prefer a theater to a concert hall. I love the theater atmosphere. They always say there's something special about being in a theater, and even for me, as a musician, I love what I get from performing in a theater. There's just something so warm and magical about it.*

FMA: Especially a theater like this, as intimate as this is. I think it's like the basic roots of theater. I believe that theater is not the first of the performing arts. I think it had to have been dance. It was pre-language. And of course, dance had to have music. And I have a feeling when you turn the lights out here, it's like a cave. It becomes very primitive. Anything can happen.

And then that idea that anything can happen is one of the reasons that the theater continues to thrive. And it's also that that's one of the direct connections to jazz because not only can anything happen, that's what you *want*, that's what you're there for.

JC: *Absolutely. I think that people always wonder what actors do before they perform. People always ask me, as a musician, what I do before a concert. I was especially pleased, and surprised somewhat, that you were willing to talk to me right before you go on tonight. I think that would surprise a lot of people. I think they think an actor's sitting in their dressing room meditating, getting in character. And that they don't want to see anyone. And here you are talking about jazz and saying, "Yeah, let's have a conversation before I go on stage and do something entirely different."*

FMA: That's really insightful, what you just said. The fact is, it depends on where you are in the performance and how much you've accomplished already. If this were early on in the production, I don't know if we could do this. I might need to get into it. But now it's under control, and I rather need to have this looseness, so I don't work too much on concentrating on it all. That can be distracting, but if you just jump into it, it sometimes is a lot more fun.

JC: And that seems like another similarity to jazz. You and I have talked before about jazz musicians we love, that they are the ones who just jump into it. I know you love Dizzy Gillespie. Now, there's certainly somebody who just jumped into it. You don't feel he was backstage meditating before a concert.

FMA: Can we talk about Diz? I say Diz, isn't that funny? It's ridiculous. I don't know him.

JC: But didn't he make you feel like you knew him?

FMA: Exactly. It was also said about Louis Armstrong. Woody Allen said that the man apparently had no enemies. What an extraordinary thing to say. Not only for that long life, but in a tough business like that. But I have a feeling it was the same thing with Diz because I know he got along with some tough guys. Miles loved him and he was tough, we all know that. And Charlie Parker. Charlie Parker was tough, and he loved him.

I'll tell you a story about Dizzy Gillespie. A long time ago I was in Washington doing a show, and he was in town in a club. I went to see him, and the set was such a big success that the guy who ran the place said, "Look, if you all wanna stay for a second set, Diz said he'll play. You don't have to pay another cover; just buy another drink, that's all." Everybody left, can you believe it? There were only ten of us who stayed. Diz comes out, looks out there, and you would think he'd get disgusted. Instead, he says, "Well, I said I was gonna play, so come on down, get right down here up front." He went on and he played for us. He did it. There was a line he said too, on the death of Louis Armstrong. He said, "Know him, know me." What a tribute!

Before we get off the subject of these famous people, I know a few stories, and one of them came from Charles Dunlap, an actor I worked with once. We did a film together, but Charlie is a serious actor, tough guy also. And I have a lot of respect for tough guys who make it, who rise above their backgrounds, myself included. Anyway, the point is, Charlie had a big success playing the part of a trumpet player. And the reviews were glowing, and one of the reviews said, "The guy can really play the trumpet." And he played four or five notes, right? And of course, as soon as that was published, there was word that among other first-rate trumpet players, Miles was coming to the show.

And he came down, sat in the front row, *right in the front row*! So, Charlie is trying not to be self-conscious. What happens is, he gets the trumpet when he's gonna play his bit, and he just picks it up, and puts it to his lips and blows. And of course, he does a clunker. Anyway, he finishes the show. And after it's over, they all came backstage. And Miles is in the dressing room not saying anything, but everybody's talking and eventually they all leave, and it's just Miles and Charlie. And Miles says, "Listen, man, when you pick up that horn, treat it with *respect*."

JC: Ah, yes. Rough. Well, you know, Miles said a great thing that applies to your art and mine. You know how people will tell you their feelings about a certain performance after they've seen you onstage? Well, someone came up to Miles after a concert and said, "Man, you really played great tonight." And Miles said, "Maybe you were just listening great tonight."

FMA: Wow! Thanks for that story.

4

JC: Great, right? And with this in mind, I want to ask you about working with an ensemble, which has to have similarities to working with a jazz band. It's got to be very similar in that you're doing the same play every night, but it's very, very different, depending on how you feel and how your fellow actors feel.

FMA: Absolutely. But I guess I'm trying to learn the lesson from that Miles story because I think that that judgment we keep passing onto ourselves gets in the way of the music. Whether the music is my kind of music, my acting, or yours. If you start evaluating what you're doing, I think there's something wrong with the transmission or with the muse that's not coming through. You really are looking for inspiration every single time. That's what a lot of people don't understand, you know? And those quirky things that certain musicians go through or certain actors go through, if that's what it takes then go ahead, man, I mean, go ahead.

JC: I agree. I had one of the old Count Basie guys tell me that at jazz festivals he would never listen to the musicians that were on before he was because he didn't want to be distracted. Because then he'd think, "Am I as good as that person? Am I not as good as that person?" Either way, he'd judge himself instead of just going out and playing the music.

FMA: But wasn't Basie good?

JC: I love Basie. I think about him just going out there and doing his thing no matter what. Did you ever hear Basie in person?

FMA: Never. But on the 88.1 jazz radio station, I heard him in a couple of concerts. And I also heard recently a tribute to Duke Ellington, and it was apparently a very famous recording of Duke out of Fargo, North Dakota. I mean, we're all very snotty about New York and Chicago. Jazz musicians … they're kind of heroes, you know.

JC: *Oh, I think so. I think it takes courage to play jazz and expose yourself, if you really stretch out with it. That's why I personally connect with stage acting because that seems tremendously courageous to me. You're completely exposed and out there.*

FMA: If you're gonna be playing, you *should* be out there, or as they say, "out." But it's true; otherwise, it's kind of boring. It's like a recording.

JC: *And people know it instantly. And they know it with acting too; don't you think? The audience knows if a person's just saying the lines and not connected to the character.*

FMA: But the problem I face as an actor is that I'm willing to try anything, any time, and a lot of actors don't like that. A lot of them get the show set, this is what we're gonna do, and they begin to expect a certain thing. And I'm not gonna give it to them, and they don't like that.

JC: *That's the same with jazz. There are musicians who will just play the same thing, and you'll see the other musicians just glaze over. They think the audience doesn't know, but they know on some level, the same way they do with acting. An audience member might not be able to tell you why a performance touches them, but they know when it happens.*

FMA: Absolutely. I think the improvisational quality is necessary because what you're talking about is not just change for the sake of change. You're really trying to find inspiration, you're trying to find something else about yourself, about the world, about this thing that's going on, a secret, a mystery; you really are. It's like getting carried away.

JC: *Well, Murray, I always get carried away when I get to see you!*

Steve Allen
(1921–2000)

Comedian, jazz pianist, composer, novelist,
and creator and original host of *The Tonight Show*.

Interviewed in 1998

Steve Allen was the original host of *The Tonight Show* so long ago that few people remember that it was he, not Johnny Carson, who invented the show. It was Allen who originated many of the bits used by subsequent late-night hosts, among them the man-on-the-street interviews and crazy character skits. And, unlike talk shows today, which are mainly promotional vehicles for stars with a product to hawk, Allen's *The Tonight Show* (originally called *Tonight Starring Steve Allen*) was an entertaining discussion of ideas and creativity.

Steve Allen was an accomplished artist in multiple disciplines and a fan of genuine talent. By his own admission, he'd rather have jazz great Art Tatum on the show than make small talk with the latest Hollywood starlet. Like Johnny Carson, Steve was intensely interested in his guests.

Men in particular loved him and talked at length about his influence. When I'd mention that I'd had the most fascinating conversation with Steve Allen on *Jazz Inspired*, men would get a far-away look in their eyes and rhapsodize on him at length. Because my parents were huge Steve fans as well—and watched all his shows through the years—I was aware of him from an early age.

My own big Steve moment came on my prom night in 1970 at the Coconut Grove in Hollywood, which by that time had lost the palm trees and become the "Now Grove," having been transformed by Sammy Davis Jr. into a swingin' black-walled space with groovy '70s décor. Steve was the

MC for the evening and consistently hilarious. At fourteen, I was already pondering a career as a comedic actress and listening to Steve that night it hit me: *He's a lot older than I am but still knows what I think is funny.* That impressed me then and impresses me now. It's significant that I don't remember my date or the main act, but I do remember Steve being great.

I talked with Steve in March of 1998, just two years before his unexpected death in October of 2000 from injuries he didn't realize he'd sustained in a minor traffic accident earlier that day. We met in his Van Nuys office, where the walls were lined floor to ceiling with files of jokes on every imaginable subject and where he had a small tape recorder at the ready to record ideas that came to him during our talk.

JC: *You're here with us on* Jazz Inspired *because you are certainly inspired in all kinds of ways creatively, but you're also a jazz player yourself and have been a presenter of jazz over the years.*

SA: Yeah, a lover of jazz, really.

Leonard Feather [jazz journalist] was once kind enough to refer to me as the best friend jazz ever had on television, but I never really thought I could claim that as something to boast about because I didn't have any philanthropic ideas in mind, I just loved it. If I liked bowling, you would have seen a lot of bowlers on my shows. It was that simple. I loved jazz, so naturally I booked all the great jazz players who were available. And if I was doing radio work, I'd play a lot of their great records.

JC: *I wish people had more jazz musicians on shows now, especially the talk shows.*

SA: Yeah, *The Tonight Show* and *Late Show with David Letterman.* They should, but that's like saying people should be better than they are. I don't think they will, because neither host has any particular interest in jazz. And again, it doesn't make me a better man, I just happen to love jazz.

JC: Also, when you had musicians on, you talked to them, which was different than now, where the host might get up and walk over to the guest musician and say hello, and pat him on the back, or shake his hand, but something I really liked with you is that you had the musician sit with you and talk about the music.

SA: Yeah, of course. In my mind, on any given night they were often the most important person on the guest list. I wouldn't be talking to some bimbo with a low-cut dress for twenty minutes about her new movie and then say, "Thanks a lot, Art Tatum. Good night!" I'd never do that.

In reference to the philosophical rationale for your show here, I recall one instance in which I was literally "jazz inspired" in writing a novel. It was my first novel. It was a million years ago. It was called *Not All of Your Laughter, Not All of Your Tears,* and I wrote it when I first went to New York, around 1951. It was very hot, it was summertime. I had a little room on 55th Street, just off Madison, someplace like that, and I was sitting there in my trousers with no shirt on—because the heat was so intense—at an old typewriter I had brought with me from Los Angeles, along with a small portable record player, although I had only one record. I figured I could buy all I needed in New York. But the one record was a great one; it was an MGM label Erroll Garner.

Do I have to say any more? Erroll Garner anything. The man never made a bad record or a second-rate record. Everything was a home run over the fence every time he sat down. And it was mostly ballads.

There were two separate Erroll Garners, as you know, two halves of his brain. One was a hard, wild jazz swinger and the other a ballad player. In an emotional sense, I really preferred the ballad Erroll. He was the most romantic piano player, the most sensuous, dreamy, magical piano player of them all. I would just put this record on, and I don't know how long it took to get through it—twenty-one minutes or whatever—and I would just stop typing and take a little sip of my beer and go over to the machine, turn the record over and play Side B. It really created a mood, and I floated on that mood in writing the novel.

JC: It's wonderful to think of Steve Allen—you've written so many songs, you've played, you've done so many things—that you go to New York with one record. That's a huge compliment to Erroll.

SA: Well, it was sort of a helter-skelter time in my life. CBS, by whom I was then employed, just gave me a quick rush: "We've got to get you to New York and get you on television." So I didn't have time to plan much, and I was traveling in my own car, so …

JC: But one record!

SA: Oh, yeah. And everything Garner ever recorded can do that to me. I also did some writing with Erroll in the old days.

JC: I didn't know that.

SA: Yeah. I would have done more sitting next to him, the way they portray songwriters in the movies, but it doesn't happen that way often in reality. In the movies, they're in the same room. The reason I didn't do more of that is he was too creative. He would play a beautiful melody for me, and it would knock me out and I'd say, "That's great, let me hear it again," and he could never play it again exactly the way. I'd say, "No, that's not the bridge you played." He'd say, "Oh, I'm sorry." He was simply creating something new every time he played it.

JC: That happened to me when I wrote my books of stride arrangements. Once I wrote them down, I had trouble playing them back because I'd started improvising. Has that happened to you?

SA: Well, since I don't read music, I don't have that specific form of the problem, but I have the same problem that Erroll had, although I don't put myself in his class in any way. But my brain just tends to start creating when I'm trying to play the same chorus over and over again. Since I can't read music that means I can't write my music on paper, so I put it on tape. We keep track of the material by the month, the January songs tape, the February songs tape, et cetera, and then we send it out to a guy who can't compose a note but can write down whatever he hears. And very often what I do is I'll just play one chorus of the song. Why play more of it? That's all there is to a song. You can do nineteen choruses, but Hoagy Carmichael did not write nineteen choruses of "Stardust."

JC: He didn't?

SA: [Laughs] He wrote one, so did Irving Berlin and everybody else. But I sometimes deliberately play two choruses on some tunes so I can judge at that early stage whether the first chorus or the second chorus was the better, or the prettier. That's my system. Something will   grab me about it and I just say on the machine, "Second chorus is better, write that one down."

JC: You're so prolific. I wondered how you managed it all. Even today, when I came in here, you had an idea for something and you turned on your tape recorder and said, "Here's the idea for Judy Carmichael."

SA: Yeah, I write all my books by dictation, too.

JC: When you think of a melody, are you one who runs right over to the piano and just says, "Here it is" into the recorder?

SA: Yes. First of all, because it's reasonable to do and it's a good system, but secondly, I'm not always near a piano. Maybe I'm on an airplane, at a swimming pool, or whatever. I probably lose—after creating them in my brain, whistling them in my car, or whatever—I probably lose about a hundred tunes a year, but nevertheless, we've kept track of almost 7000 of them, so the world, as Lincoln said, "will little note nor long remember."

JC: Yes, I think we're O.K.

Who were some of your favorite guests on the show? I specifically remember seeing this clip of Art Tatum.

SA: I was in an airport six or seven years ago and a guy said, "Mr. Allen? I don't want to disturb you, but I just want you to know I love your album with Art Tatum." Now to me, that's like saying he saw films of my fight with Muhammad Ali. I'm not qualified—literally, it's not modesty—I am not qualified to make an album with Art Tatum. It would be like adding a few touches to a Michelangelo painting.

I did some joke and he said, "No, I'm serious. I have it at home." I said, "You have an album?" He said, "You're on one of the tracks, yeah." Well, he was right. I got the name of the album and the company, and it was sort of a bootleg operation. There were a lot of really professional commercial recordings that Tatum did, thank goodness, but a lot of people—realizing that it was genius and that every time out he should somehow be kept track of—they would tape him off TV shows and radio shows. So this track was from the old *Tonight Show*.

Unlike today's talk shows, which don't book jazz people at all, or if they do, let them do one number if it happens to be a hit or has won a Grammy, we would have musicians play three and four tunes. We'd give about twenty minutes to Art Tatum. And then for a finish, if it was a piano player, we would roll out a second piano and then we'd do some four-hand stuff, just some standard, or the blues or whatever. So that's what this guy had on the tape that I heard. It was Tatum and me doing a tempo of *his* choosing. A *very* fast "Fine and Dandy." And I must say, something about the great rhythm section we were working with, and being inspired by him, I played at the top of my level, whatever that is, so I didn't disgrace myself.
We also did that with Basie and Duke Ellington, all the good piano players, and all the other guys too. I didn't sit in with everybody because sometimes I'd rather just sit there and listen, but it was a good showbiz kind of a thing to do.

JC: When you're working on a book, do you always listen to music in the background?

SA: Oddly enough, I used to when I typed, as I've mentioned, but I don't do it anymore because for the last twenty years or so I do all my prose writing, or fiction, by dictation. And of course, background audio would hang that up. But I often do get an idea for a song while listening to another song on the radio. I don't take so much as a chord or a note from what I'm hearing. That's stealing, that's illegal. You should get arrested for that. But something about a chord change or something the drummer does, whatever it is, in my car I'm suddenly going, "shoob-a doob-a doo." I turn off the radio immediately and make up a dummy lyric so I will later remember the melody.

JC: And you usually have your tape recorder with you.

SA: Oh, always, yeah.

JC: So, you can sing into that. I was asking too, because I would think for someone who has so much music in his head, so many ideas, that sometimes you might need silence. You don't need a time to sort of clear everything?

SA: There's no right way or wrong way. Simply because of the accident of doing several things for a living, I have learned that one part of my brain can be really consciously tired, if I'm writing a novel, let's say, and I'll do it for an hour and seven minutes and three seconds, and then I'm really tired. But I can then, as I pass through the living room, if I do, go right to the piano and do forty-eight minutes of composing, with no sense of exhaustion.

JC: And it refreshes you.

SA: Yeah, I guess it's because it's another part of my brain. It's probably just that simple. One part's tired, and the other part has just had a three-day rest.

JC: Talk about your "Buck Hammer" experience.

SA: I have always put the world on, ever since I was a child, so this is another example of that. I decided to have fun at the expense of the jazz critics of the world, some of whom were dear people who really knew what they were writing about and some of whom were faking it.

I've always been able to play pretty good boogie-woogie, and so can a lot of teenage kids who can't play any other kind of piano. When I was in the teenage period, which was in the late thirties, boogie-woogie was very big among all the White kids in America. I was one of the millions of White kids who loved that form, which of course originated by Black jazz players in the late 1920s.

Anyway, getting back to putting on the jazz critics. In the 1950s, I rented a recording studio and brought in a really good rhythm section. We made about a dozen boogie-woogie tracks. One was called "Tea for Two Boogie." Most of it was just traditional, different kinds of blues, and one was "Minor Boogie." And then, instead of putting it out under my name, I created an imaginary personage named Buck Hammer. And then I wrote scholarly liner notes, sort of like the jazz critic, Nat Hentoff. Very analytical, very scholarly, very sensitive to racial nuances and historical trends and all that stuff. No jokes.

JC: Whom did you credit for the liner notes?

SA: Everything was imaginary. We used a serious name, not a funny name, of course. Then we just floated it out in the marketplace, and the jazz folks loved it. The jazz critic for the *New York Herald Tribune*—a little popular paper then—said something I've never forgotten: "Hammer's death was a tragic loss to the world of jazz." The liner notes had alleged that after making this one album, being enticed to Nashville and recording this one set of stuff, the poor young man died. He was also depicted as something of a recluse, and a bit of an oddball. That he'd received a lot of offers from name people coming through his small town in Mississippi. Then there was another critic from *Downbeat* who gave it three and a half stars, which was a very high rating.

JC: So Buck Hammer was your "nom de boogie."

SA: [Laughing] Yeah.

Parenthetically, I learned something about piano playing in itself. One night at the London House in Chicago, Teddy Wilson, one of my idols, was playing there. I think this was after we had worked together on the Benny Goodman movie. I'd loved him since I was a teenager. Somebody sent him a little note telling him that I was in the joint, and he did that thing that musicians often do, "Hey, folks, let's get him up here and sit in for a number or two." Well, I didn't want to sit in because there was just a piano and a drummer and a bass, but he walked off and he said, "No, come on up." I just played two quick numbers, of course, which is all you should do in those situations, and one was a swinging blues thing and then for a finish I played a spirited boogie-woogie.

Boogie isn't hard, but it fools the audience into thinking you're playing something better than what you're actually playing. The audience indeed was fooled and went hysterical, and I sat down. Teddy came over to my table and said, "Hey, thanks," and I said, "Thank *you*, what an honor to even, you know, to be here tonight with you." He said, "I sure wish I could do that," and I thought he was kidding, so I laughed. He said, "No, I'm serious." I said, "About what?" He said, "I've never been able to play boogie-woogie." And I said, "But, Ted, your own kids could learn the left-hand thing." He said, "I can learn the left-hand thing as good as any of them but as soon as I try to add the right hand and funky ad-lib stuff, something about my brain can't go both those ways." One of the great piano players of the century, and he couldn't play boogie. And it was not that he just didn't dig it or didn't do it. He said that he was not able to.

JC: You could have told him, "I'm Buck Hammer, the famous, dead boogie player!"

Jon
Batiste
(b. 1996)

Pianist, composer, and bandleader for
The Late Show with Stephen Colbert.

Interviewed in 2019

Jon Batiste is an exuberant presence, whether playing music or talking about the importance of putting good energy and meaningful work into the world. His band, Stay Human, is named to honor the belief that human interaction during a live musical performance can uplift humanity despite the "plug in/tune out" nature of modern society.

Jon is a walking, grooving, musical bundle of joy. I'd witnessed his fabulous vibe in action many times on *The Late Show*. As a fellow high-energy musician, I know one can turn this on and *has* to turn it on during a show. I thought this might just be his stage persona, but when I finally met him, he was even more swinging in person than he is on stage. Music pours out of this man.

Like many New Orleanians, Jon comes from a long line of musicians. He joined his family band on drums and percussion at the tender age of eight and studied for years with his clarinetist uncle, Alvin Batiste, whom he considers a major influence. Jon went on to get his bachelor's and master's degrees from Juilliard in Manhattan but believes that his musical family and early life in New Orleans were equally important to his development, his attitudes about creativity, and his ability to move through life with joy and purpose.

Jon arrived exactly on time for our conversation, dancing through the door, softly singing a musical line as he gave me a hug, spotted the piano on the other side of the room and insisted I play something for him. I did, to shouts of "Stride on, baby!" When we finished our conversation, Jon practically sprinted back to the piano to match my stride with some of his own, stretching out on Eubie Blake, Scott Joplin, and Fats Waller. We'd still be jamming if I hadn't had to leave for another appointment.

JC: *Everything I've read about you mentions your desire to put positive energy into the world. How did this attitude develop?*

JB: I just think I've been blessed to feel things in a certain way. And the response to those feelings is generally to try to reconcile things that are separate and things that are kind of in a place of discontent. I have the gene, if you will, that makes me want to fix things. And that can be problematic. When I was younger, I discovered that you can't please everyone. But there's also a beauty to figuring out something that people thought you never could figure out or bring together. Things that you never thought could be possible. That's exciting to me.

JC: *And you think you were just born that way?*

JB: I think it's a combination of my nature and also the idea of growing and discovering things that you want to do as an artist and realizing that there has to be a point to it all. You have to define why you're making music for yourself. Otherwise, it's just an exercise or a hobby. Others can be entertained by it, but it doesn't have that depth. And that's the thing I thought long and hard about and really discovered. It's something you don't invent. You have to discover it.

JC: *Your new CD,* Anatomy of Angels: Live at the Village Vanguard, *focuses on your belief that the art of improvisation is often a spiritual process that creates moments* *that give the musician and listener a glimpse of another reality. I know you believe that music can bring us closer together and allow a fresh perspective. Did growing up in New Orleans influence these attitudes?*

JB: I think that New Orleans was an influence because the place is so infectious. The company you keep at a New Orleans party is different from the company you keep at any other kind of party. It's eclectic in a way that's unique, and the idea of a generation gap is nonexistent. I grew up playing in my family band and then playing in other bands when I was eleven, with kids my age and even younger, in *bars*. And that was normal.

JC: I love the attitude that music is fun and natural. It's not intimidating.

JB: Right. It's not an attitude that's reflected back from the audience enough, particularly when we're talking about jazz. People say, "I want to confess that I don't know a lot about this," like they have to offer a disclaimer before they have an opinion on the music. I've always found that a little sad, that people don't just listen to jazz or classical music and just *feel* it.

JC: This has happened to every jazz musician I know, myself included. People are always telling me that they don't understand jazz or, after they hear me, telling me that they thought they hated jazz, but they love me. Many musicians have told me they've had that same thing happen to them. Why is that?

JB: I think there's a change that occurred in culture. At some point sophisticated music was kind of intellectualized. Now it has no space in the popular culture, in the mainstream. And I think when that happened, jazz got relegated to the high-art space, which doesn't really give a lot of people access to it, those people who come from certain economic and cultural backgrounds. This attitude makes you feel as if you don't belong. And that's such an irony because jazz is all about the spirit of the audience and the performer creating a one-of-a-kind moment. So if you get people in a room who understand that, which people of all ages intuitively do, you don't have to explain jazz to them. They feel it.

But I don't think we feel jazz enough on a regular basis. And I think this is on the musicians too. I think a lot of musicians don't play in a way that's inviting to the audience, which is really sad. But it's also an opportunity. Every time I play, it's amazing how people respond. We just played in an open-air situation in California in a park for 5,000 people of all ages. There were kids coming up to the stage, dancing, and I saw elderly people sitting in lawn chairs watching us, recognizing the standards and nodding along. Then younger kids came up on skateboards, and I threw in references to hip-hop and R&B songs from today and put them in the context of jazz. All of these things are opportunities to bridge the gap.

JC: I love your emphasis on the experience that the audience has with jazz musicians. It's unlike anything else.

JB: It's easy to intellectualize something, but when you *feel* something it's hard to then theorize about it because you felt it. Maya Angelou said people never forget how you make them feel. The one-of-a-kind feeling that you can get from a jazz performance because it's so in the moment and so based on this dialogue between audience and performer, there's no other type of music that can give you that feeling. It's really cool to see people realize that for the first time.

JC: Right. After a concert people often say to me, "I haven't felt this way since I heard so and so." It's all about feeling.

JB: Definitely. It's a truly live music. It's a truly *alive* music. There's a sense of having to be there to truly understand it. I encourage first-time listeners to hear jazz live. A recording is great, but you can engage with it on a deeper level once you've experienced jazz in person and understand what this experience is all about.

JC: I enjoyed your new CD particularly because you captured what we're talking about here, and you discuss it in the liner notes, saying the CD isn't overproduced or edited. What they hear is what you played. And you talk about improvisation being a spiritual experience, which it is. I loved how you expressed it.

JB: Thank you. There's so much there to say. It's like church in a sense that there are these people who come together to focus on one common goal and it's a goal that's not a tangible thing. It's an experiential thing. We come into the club together and we settle into our space and we use the music almost as a form of launching us into this higher consciousness. And I wanted to commemorate that. It's almost impossible to share that experience with those who weren't there, but I think it's also possible to commemorate and share it with people and inspire them to come out and experience it when it happens again. And when people hear this album, they tell me, man, I could *feel* that something was happening.

JC: I felt it too. It's called Anatomy of Angels. *In the liner notes you said that somebody saw an angel onstage during your performance.*

JB: I loved that. My longtime drummer, Joe Saylor, who plays with me on *The Late Show* has been on most of my albums since I was nineteen. We all invite folks to the show, and he invited some folks who had never seen a jazz performance before. This was at the iconic Village Vanguard, which is a mecca for jazz. It's one of the oldest clubs, and it's been in that same condition forever and housed all of these great, live recordings. I told Joe's friends that they were in for a treat, and hopefully we'd give them something that lives up to that standard. And when they came backstage afterwards, one of them told Joe that they saw this almost glowing orb in the midst of the band. That was a powerful thing.

JC: With people filming everything these days, I'm glad you're talking about this because it points out how the audience can miss the essence of what we're talking about. I think about the fact that everyone taps into a concert from a different perspective. Some might be watching your cool hair as you nod into the music, some watch your hands, some watch your interaction with your musicians, some watch your feet tap. Some see a glowing orb! Everyone comes to this in a different way, and they miss all of that if they're concentrating on filming it.

JB: Everyone has different points of entry. And that's the key. You have to have a place that's cleansed from all distraction so everyone can reach a point of focus. And you have to come to it. It doesn't come to you. But once you let yourself be open to the experience of the music, and the community that's created through the music, then people are transformed in a way that's very beautiful. It's profound.

JC: Talk about Alvin Batiste, who I know had a big influence on you.

JB: It's hard to imagine where I'd be as a musician if I hadn't met him at the time I did.

It's really interesting to have a teacher who teaches you above your level of understanding at the time. Years after you stop studying with this person, you're still having epiphanies about things they told you.

I met him when I'd just started studying jazz, really playing jazz and being a musician as a professional, so I was about thirteen. At fifteen, I joined his band, and at seventeen, I studied with him. So from the time I was thirteen to seventeen, before I moved to New York, he was in my life. And once I came to study in New York, I'd still be thinking of things he told me. He was doing things then that people consider innovative *now*. His concepts and compositions are remarkable.

JC: I know you're a Thelonius Monk fan. Talk about Monk.

JB: A piano is an inanimate object. It has no life until you inject that life into it. Monk is a real, *real* individual in that he can make an inanimate object come alive. He has a way of playing one note that says so much about who he is. It almost defies science. It's not logical that he can play notes that sound like he's *bending* notes. It's a hammer hitting a string! I don't know how he's bending it as if it's a guitar. I listened exclusively to Monk for almost a year.

When I was about nineteen, I had an experience that I'll never forget. I heard his music at a jam session, not knowing it was his music, and the music represented a conceptual approach that I was working on at that time, apart from my knowledge of his music, which I knew nothing about. So once I heard that, I thought, wait, that's the thing I'm hearing in my head. I thought, wow, he's figured out what I'm trying to figure out *now*. It was like a kindred spirit. That's a beautiful thing to have discovered.

JC: One of the interesting things about Monk is how difficult it is to play his music and not sound like you're imitating him because it's so specific in how he played, so individual. I've even spontaneously played a note and come at it at an angle, sort of attacking it for a different sound, and immediately one of my musicians will turn around and say, "Monk!" just from one note! What I loved about hearing you play Monk is it's completely your own, which is especially fascinating since you share this conceptual connection with him.

Changing the subject, a bit: I'm curious about what singing has brought to you. For me, your singing has a lovely kind of innocence to it, which is wonderful in this day of American Idol, when everything is a huge production. When I first heard you, I thought of Randy Newman. He also has this beautiful innocence that's coming out of a tremendously sophisticated musician. When we talk about art, we're all trying to get back to that childlike spontaneity and truthfulness that we started with. The hope is that we take that original spark of talent, grow artistically, then somehow forget all that and get back to our original innocence. That's what I hear with you and Randy.

JB: Thank you. I love Randy Newman and he's an inspiration to me. I find that storytelling is really what singing does best. There's nothing like hearing someone tell you a story in song. To me, the most emotionally provocative singers are the ones who know how to tell a story, not necessarily the ones who quote-unquote "have the best instrument." That's not to say that I don't enjoy singers who have a marvelous instrument or that singers with a marvelous instrument don't tell stories. But for me, the aim is to really touch someone's heart. I'm not trying to show you what I can do, I'm trying to tell you a story that we can really key into from the heart.

JC: *I love that you chose to record "The Very Thought of You." It's such a beautiful song, and you had a different approach to it.*

JB: It's a beautiful story. It sounds to me as though he or she is daydreaming: *The very thought of you, and I forget to do* . . . It starts with him saying, I forget to do things, ordinary things, basic things. What state are you in when you forget to do those things? You're awake, but you're not present. You're somewhere else. So I wanted to create a musical palette that somehow felt like a daydream and lull you into a kind of meditative state before the vocals come in, setting the stage for the narrative to unfold.

JC: *I know it's important to you to have your music-making have a bigger meaning, and not in a grandiose way that so many artists talk about all this. They say, "Oh, my music means so much," which is just a complicated way of showing how narcissistic they are. And that's so tiresome.*

I feel that your music does something that the standards by those great composers were trying to do. They weren't writing songs about themselves but rather songs that spoke to the human condition. We can listen to those stories and hear how poets express the feelings that we're perhaps not able to articulate. When we hear a great singer or great instrumentalist, we're hooked into the story and feel less alone. We feel that somebody understands that state.

JB: Mood is something that's a universal language, just the way music is a universal language. We all like to hear stories. When you combine all these things, these elements of mood and storytelling and music, it's a superpower. It's the ultimate, because it speaks across generations, across cultures. You go into a room, and if you can set a mood, people know what to do. If you know how to set the right mood for the music or for the story to come together, that's everything. The great, great musicians whom I admire all knew how to create a mood. They carried an essence, a mood of their own, that people would then go to them for, to get that essence.

JC: *That's beautifully expressed. I read that those long choruses that Basie played upfront were to get the tempo exactly right, the mood exactly right. I always thought he did that for a nice opening for the rhythm section, but it was to get the tempo exactly where he wanted it. It also set the mood that brought everybody to the same place, then,* BAM, *the band came in.*

JB: Walter Page, Freddie Green, that whole sense of playing together is a real key to setting the mood. Musicians first have to align. They have to have a consensus as to what the mood is and what they're trying to accomplish.

JC: *It's like a sports team.*

JB: Exactly! You have to get the play, and everyone has to run the play, and that way you hopefully continue to advance in the game. In music there's no score, but if everyone isn't playing together, no one wins.

JC: *Talk about* The Late Show with Stephen Colbert. *I imagine that being a jazz musician is a huge advantage with this gig. I know basically how it all works, in that you have a rundown, you talk about who's going to be on, but at the same time, stuff happens. Most people don't know that you play during commercial breaks, that you're setting a mood, and, with Stephen—who's so deliciously in the thick of it and doesn't hold back—that you're "kinda keepin' the joy" in a time when we're all struggling to keep joy. I'd think your whole being would be helpful with that.*

JB: I just try to stay honest and keep something on the airwaves that's culturally significant—whether or not people understand it—and has an emotional depth. It's not just cookie cutter or functional, but gives people something to reference, maybe from nostalgia. There are songs that we play from different childhoods, whether it's Stephen's childhood or my childhood. And there are songs we play from a range of different styles of music that you wouldn't hear on TV.

It's great to talk to Terry Waldo, who may be one of the few people besides yourself who hears it when I reference ragtime or stride on the show. I remember playing Eubie Blake on the show and Terry calling me up and saying, "Man, did you just play Eubie Blake's music *for an entire night* on the show?"

JC: *And I saw your video doing "Memories of You," speaking of Eubie.*

JB: Yes! It's really just about providing those points of entry, for all different cultures, and also points of emotional uplift in a time of duress.

JC: *And music can do that. You talk about having conversations with an open mind, and I agree. Friends of mine say, "Well, I don't even go there" meaning they've given up talking to people who don't agree with them. I think it's incumbent upon us to have these conversations. But I've had to pace myself with the news. Now I listen to NPR in the morning and NewsHour in the evening—because they're balanced, not right or left— and in between, I listen to more music. Play more sports.*

JB: Balance! Balance is the key to us surviving. The focus is to not lose our humanity. The focus is always to maintain a sense of love and empathy and inner peace with whatever solutions we're also trying to come up with. If we lose sight of our humanity, we have an issue that's even greater than whatever we're facing. We have some very grave issues that we have to deal with, but I don't think it always needs to be done in spite of our humanity.

Tony Bennett

(b. 1926)

Jazz-influenced singer of the *Great American Songbook*,
and painter. Eighteen Grammy Awards,
forty-one Grammy nominations.

Interviewed in 2012

Tony Bennett is a rarity, an artist who has grown steadily in emotional depth while keeping his focus on the music he loves. Rather than record what might be considered more commercially popular music, Tony has stuck with the Great American Songbook, making some of the definitive recordings of our times.

Another unusual aspect of Bennett's career has been his continuing commercial viability. He has paired with popular contemporary artists for recordings and concerts—most notably his long tours with Lady Gaga—and never changed his approach or repertoire. Bennett was diagnosed with Alzheimer's Disease in 2016 leading to his final concert with Lady Gaga at Radio City Music Hall in Manhattan in August 2021. Throughout his career, Tony Bennett remained a classy, stylish, straight-ahead, jazz-loving interpreter of sophisticated songs, and thanks to him, younger generations have been introduced to the experience of listening to music of depth and poetry.

I have learned over the years that it can be easier to get big stars on the show if they're promoting a new CD or a movie. In Tony's case, his team agreed to give me time with Tony because I said we'd talk about *Duets II,* which had just been released. My plan was to talk a bit about that album but spend most of the interview discussing his creative motivations and how he has maintained his enthusiasm throughout his very long career.

Tireless as ever, Tony walked over to Nola Studios in New York, across from Carnegie Hall, to meet me after appearing on CBS *This Morning* at 8:00 a.m. Once in the studio, he said a few words, then focused on me and asked, "How long have you been doing this?" Something told him this wasn't a typical interview. I mentioned I was also a musician and played stride piano. He smiled broadly and replied, "Now *that's* a wonderful surprise!"

I said we'd be discussing *Duets II*—which would go on to win a Grammy—but if he didn't mind, I'd love to discuss his recordings with Bill Evans, which are considered classics.

"Your recordings with Bill Evans are my favorites," I said with enthusiasm.

"People with good taste always say that's the best work I've ever done," he replied.

I had him. All artists want to be appreciated for what *they* value in their work. These were not only my favorite recordings, they were Tony's as well.

We talked for two hours, during which time Tony was remarkably candid. Most musicians will play it safe when speaking of other musicians on record, but Tony surprised me. His opinions were polite and kind but not necessarily complimentary. He also expressed his frustration that jazz doesn't get the respect and financial support he feels it should.

TB: To me, the greatest music in the United States is what you do, which is jazz. And I am still very disappointed in the amount of sales that jazz albums make. They are treated like they're not commercially that successful. And yet they *are!* Newark has a great station, WBGO. I listen to it, and I hear a lot of jazz artists playing, and none of it sounds dated. It sounds like, "Hey! That's going to be good ten years from now, twenty years from now, or thirty years from now."

Too many jazz musicians were almost destitute towards the end of their lives because they didn't make enough money, and I think it's totally tragic. I think it really is the best music that there is.

In Europe and throughout the world, in Asia, they adore jazz, and can't wait for jazz festivals. We're the first country that has every nationality and every religion as citizens, which makes us a magnificent, creative country. It's great because we draw from different concepts and from each nationality. You'd think that that would be eulogized and respected by Americans, but there is a lot of bigotry in the world, and bigotry has the leaders of big corporations afraid to advertise jazz.

The greatest jazz artists, like Miles Davis, sold lots of records, but not as many as someone who's white and plays well, but not as well as Miles Davis. And yet sales are way down on jazz, and I don't understand that. I know that thirteen years from now, or fifteen years from now, jazz artists that are dead are going to be resurrected because the records, films, recordings, and television appearances are there, and people will say, "Look at what these people were doing at that age, during that time."

JC: I love you saying this. When I started this radio show, my hope was to bring jazz to more people, to help them understand and love it. Maybe people think they don't like jazz, but they don't realize that Tony Bennett, or someone else they admire, adores jazz and has all these jazz influences. I think you talking about the importance of jazz and expressing your thoughts on racism is helpful.

TB: The generation that I liked was Frank Sinatra, Count Basie, Duke Ellington, Woody Herman. And you know, it was great, the public really dug it. I came up ten years after that. It was big, because it couldn't be better, but it got into the hands of uncreative producers who really didn't make the right decisions. When great, creative producers heard someone as good as Count Basie, they would just say, "Do whatever you want." The good ones didn't tell him what to play or how to play it.

JC: Right. They'd know to leave him alone. You told me earlier that you welcomed the opportunity to introduce your duet partners on your new CD to the Great American Songbook. You also mentioned that Amy Winehouse was a big fan of Dinah Washington.

TB: Amy Winehouse was a *great* jazz singer. See, that's what people don't realize. You can't learn how to play jazz. Either you've got it, or you haven't.

JC: That feel.

TB: Yes, and improvisation. The *moment* is truly important to a great jazz artist. Just knowing what to leave out and what to put in or just make up. Jazz musicians are completely creative, and they should be respected as creative artists, but there's a lot of greed and power that moves jazz musicians into another class. Record companies think that jazz artists are foolish. They're *not* foolish. They're better than the artists that the companies promote. *Much* better.

JC: Lady Gaga is a jazz fan too. [This was recorded in 2012 before Bennett's first tour with Gaga in 2015.]

TB: She's a hell of a singer and a hell of a dancer and a very good piano player. She is an all-around performer, but she happens to like performing and she is a great performer, but boy, she knows how to sing. She improvises perfectly. She came up with things that surprised me, in fact on our record I was laughing and a lot of fans of mine were kind of critical about it. They said, "Why did you laugh so much on that record?" I couldn't believe what she was doing.

JC: People criticized your laughing? That's crazy!

TB: I said, wait a minute. She sings better than any jazz artist I ever knew, as good as Ella Fitzgerald or anybody.

JC: I can't believe that people would criticize your laughing and having fun. Those are the bits I love, because so often now, no one has that spontaneous, joyous feeling on a record. How about her scatting?

TB: She's a very talented person, and she can scat. But not everyone can do it. It takes someone to know how to do it, to scat, to swing, and she knows how to do it all. You can't get a singer that doesn't understand the art of a jazz improvisation and expect them to do it when they don't know how. It's not something that you learn at school. Like two and two is not four with jazz. Two and two is four and a half, or whatever. And it becomes a whole other way of looking at something. It's like the famous Fred Astaire line. He said, "If it doesn't swing, I'm out of here." If you don't have that feeling of swinging, it's not really interesting music.

JC: I agree. If it's swinging, it connects with you emotionally.

TB: It's also about the unexpected. Jazz musicians do the unexpected, so it keeps it interesting. You're doing something *interesting*. You're not boring the public. The audience is saying, "Wait a minute, look at what this guy is doing."

JC: What was it like with Michael Bublé?

TB: He's very, very good. What he is *going* to be is a very good performer because he understands a little about Dean Martin, a little about Sinatra, about all the different singers, and he's influenced by them. Then he takes it on the stage with his group. He's got great ears, and he is very influenced by and a great imitator of all these different performers, like Bobby Darin.

JC: It was interesting to me that you filmed all of these tracks, with each duet partner. What was it like being filmed while recording? Was it Faith Hill who wore a gown during the session?

TB: Yeah.

JC: *And you wore a tux?*

TB: Yes.

JC: *Does it change your focus, being filmed while recording?*

TB: Oh, yeah! Our cameramen won an award for the movie *Chicago.* So, we really got the best cameramen in the world to travel with us all *over* the world. Instead of the artists coming to us, we went to them. With Andrea Bocelli, we went to Pisa, Italy, to his home, and he had a great recording studio there. And after this record, *Stranger in Paradise,* we sat down with a great Italian meal that he gave us and the whole crew. The camera people, the crew that traveled with me, and my musicians.

We recorded everywhere. We went to London for Amy Winehouse, to New York for Lady Gaga, to the West Coast for Natalie Cole and K.D. Lang.

JC: *Was that fun, being in all these different spots with each artist in their own environment?*

TB: Yeah, it was great. I'd never recorded that way. You know, I just record in New York, and I am happy to be right here because I love living in New York. But this was different. We went all over the world to record this way, and each artist was in a different part of the world.

JC: *Many of our listeners might not know that a lot of times, when people do collaboration recordings, they aren't even in the same room. But because you recorded this way, you were looking at these people. You were right next to them, which had to change the energy of the recording.*

TB: Yeah, it was a great experience. Traveling around the world, making this album, and boy, I couldn't believe it when it came out! It just went to No. 1 on *Billboard.* And being eighty-five and having a No.1 album! And all the young people said, "How did you do that?" Just to know that it's absolutely platinum in every single country.

JC: And it corroborates what we were saying about these great tunes being appealing forever. The success of this CD is obviously due to you and these other artists, but the point you were making before is that starting with great material makes all the difference in the quality of the recording. And if these are platinum, it can't just be people of a certain generation who know these tunes buying the CD. A lot of other people are hearing these songs for the first time.

TB: That's what I mean about jazz artists only choosing great songs. They wait until they fall in love with a song. Something great like, "I Fall in Love Too Easily." You know, they hear it and say, "Hey, what a great tune! Let's do that!"

Great jazz musicians just have good taste, so recordings of these songs are lasting. For instance, when you hear Ben Webster sing a great standard—and I say "sing" because he sang by playing—you hear it and you just say, "Look at that. Look at how wonderfully he lays into that song."

JC: Talk about recording "Body and Soul."

TB: I met Johnny Green, who wrote "I Cover the Waterfront" and "Body and Soul." He was a wonderful, intellectual man. Highly intelligent. He had his own show on NPR. I just loved him because he was so caring. And at a time when absolutely no one knew I painted, he said, "I love your paintings." And I said, "Oh, you know I paint?" and he said, "I'd know your paintings anywhere." No one knew that I painted at that time. But he was so wide awake that he just gravitated to things. Whenever he saw something that was exceptional, he'd say, "That's really nice."

JC: That's one of the things about paying attention. I feel that most people aren't fully engaged anymore. They don't pay attention. Very few really listen. I always say, everyone has headphones on, but no one is listening.

TB: That's great!

JC: *I want to talk about tempos. Yours are just so beautiful. So many musicians seem to have slow, medium and fast tempos. But you have so many tempos in between. Talk about getting the right tempo for a tune.*

TB: My biggest influence was Count Basie. He just had the greatest time. It's hard to explain, but it was always just right.

JC: *When you're setting a tempo for a tune, with everything feeling different every night, do you have the tempo you want in your head and sort of feel it before you count it off to the musicians? Or are tempos decided before you walk onstage?*

TB: Well, I do that at rehearsals more than at the shows. But the show always changes a bit with each audience. One night they'll get something right away and you'll say, "Wow, we're right into this pocket." And at other times that's not there, so you feel it, and say, "Let's take this slower, let's take this next tempo a little slower," or "Let's move this up a little." Every night is a different performance. You never do the same show twice, you know.

JC: *You're fairly still in your performances. There isn't a lot of movement. Same with Basie. He was so cool. He would just point to the musician he wanted to take a solo rather than make a big gesture. Is this attitude something that you had from the very beginning, that you admired in other people like Basie?*

TB: That's a good question. Rosemary Clooney and I got a big break on an amateur show and we started selling millions of records, and when we'd run into the old-time performers, like George Burns and Jack Benny, who knew we were hot because we had these million-selling records, they gave us perspective. They would advise us and say, "Now, children, you're doing O.K., but it's gonna take you seven years before you become a consummate performer." And they were very accurate with that. You have to work, perform, and pay attention. The public will teach you what they like and don't like. And you learn quickly to take out what they don't like, and when it comes to what they *do* like, emphasize that even more.

It really took seven years. And I remember years later, when John Burr was my bass player, Bob Hope came out to see me at a show in New Orleans. Afterwards, John ran after him and Bob said, "Tony's finally become a consummate performer." It really takes seven years to learn what to do and what not to do, what to take out and what to leave in.

JC: I think now, with how fast things move, that performers expect their careers and development to happen very fast. When I was coming up, we didn't expect things to happen overnight.

I've seen you in person a number of times, but one concert, a few years ago, stands out for me. I saw you at a jazz festival where the audience was a bit revved up from the outdoor atmosphere, drinking all day and anticipating you. You could feel this great energy as we were sitting there listening to you and your band. It felt like the audience might get a little rowdy at any minute. Then, while you were singing, with your arm straight down at your side, you very subtly patted down with your hand, as if you were patting down energy, and you got them to contain that energy, which focused them to quietly listen to what you were singing. It was brilliant. Then, when the song was finished and they finally applauded, the energy was released. Was that move subconscious or planned?

TB: With every venue there are different acoustics. Different atmosphere. Sometimes the audience is noisy, and you have to find a way to get control of them. But that's what's so wonderful about it. You'd go insane if every night were the same show.

To some, I can't be a true, true jazz artist because I love performing. I love to entertain people. A lot of intellectual jazz artists think that's very corny. And I think they're very incorrect. If they don't like it, they shouldn't get into show business. Once you're in front of the public, you should entertain them. And the early masters, like Duke Ellington and Count Basie and all the greatest artists, loved entertaining an audience. They loved it. Today, there's more dissonance. Years ago, it was melody and harmony, and it stayed there and was very comfortable. Now there are artists that are getting more dissonant. A lot of the attitude of a lot of the jazz musicians is, well,

I'm very good and if you don't like it, I'm still gonna play the way I play. And they don't care whether the audience likes it or not. I think they should just stay in their rooms and play for themselves.

They're supposed to entertain the audience. People came to see them. They put down their hard-earned money. They're mostly working people who enjoy jazz and they should be given a performance. Billie Holiday used to entertain the audience, and no one, *nobody* ever sang better than that. You know, the audience makes you or breaks you. And if you don't care for them, they're not gonna care for you. If you care for them, they're gonna come right back at you and give you proper applause and you'll be accepted by the audience.

JC: That's so lovely to put it that way. If you care for them, they'll care for you. That's just really nice, to think of it that way.

TB: A lot of the audience has to save up for months to come see a performer. They have to get a babysitter, if they have children, and they have to take their wife out to dinner, besides paying for the tickets for the show, so by the end of the night, they're really spending an awful lot of money. It's terribly rude to put down the audience.

One of the things I really dislike, is when the door opens and the audience starts filing in and the musicians say, with distain, "Oh, here they come." To me, they should get out of show business. They shouldn't even be allowed on the stage. You're supposed to respect the audience. If you don't respect them, they're not going to respect you.

JC: I'm always having people say to me, "Oh, you love that energy you get from the audience." They don't understand that the energy has to be there from the start, from within. How do you keep that going?

TB: Well, you have to have energy. I learned that many years ago. My great friend, Frank Sinatra, the master—he was ten years older than I was—he always liked what I did. He gave me little instructions, when he was passing by me or something. And one time, during a big benefit in Los Angeles, he walked by me and said, "Keep your energy up." Just that simple.

It taught me, if you're going to do a show, if you're not energized when you walk out there, the audience is not going to be energized. The audience is going to be a complete reflection of where you're at. If you walk out with energy and try to give everyone a good show, they feel it right away. And right away they come right back at you. If you don't care, the audience isn't going to care. If you care, they're going to care.

JC: I have to ask, because you look so fabulous. I'm wondering how you're in such good shape. You play tennis, I know. Do you concentrate on taking good care of yourself?

TB: Yeah, I exercise three times a week. Eat very good food. I get a lot of good rest. I sleep well. Get up early. I love a full day. I enjoy being alive!

JC: Something that really has resonance for me, was your talking about Frank [Sinatra] making a comment—or somebody else you admired—saying one thing that changed or informed you. You were aware enough to listen to that. I think a lot of people aren't. Many people think, "I'm going to meet someone I admire, ask twenty questions and I'll get my answers." That's not how it works.

TB: That's right. It's about staying a perpetual student. I'm eighty-five, and I really have a lot more to learn. I'm not being egotistical. I'm just really saying there's a lot to learn. I paint also, and I paint every day, and it really teaches me. And a lot of people say, "You're great," but I know I have a lot to learn yet. Somebody like the great masters, like Rubens. You wonder, how could anyone be that good? It keeps you humble. It makes you realize you're doing all right but you're not Rubens.

JC: Do you paint at a specific time every day?

TB: Well, I love painting because you can start at twelve o'clock and what feels like minutes, you look at your watch and say, "Oh, my God, it's four o'clock!" It's completely time-absorbing.

JC: I have to ask you about two of my favorite recordings, your records with Bill Evans.

TB: Well, anybody with good taste, they always say that's the best work I've ever done. And it was because of Bill Evans. He was a complete genius. The reason that came about was because, a wonderful friend of mine— Annie Ross, another great talent—said she'd like to talk to Bill Evans about doing an album with me.

And so the album came about. It was wonderful because Bill said, "Leave your cronies home. Just you and I and the engineer, and let's make an album." And we did two days like that, two different albums, and once a television show in Canada. And the experience was just so beautiful because he was so highly intelligent. He really knew how to support *exactly* where I was at. He would just phrase something so it would lead me into the next section of the song, and it would be perfect. I would think, oh, my God, this guy, what a mind he's got.

JC: Was this something you spent a lot of time preparing for? You said you had two days, but did you rehearse a lot or was it fairly spontaneous?

TB: In fact, I couldn't believe how we wound up doing it. Bill would say, "What tune do you want to do?" and I'd say, "I like this song," and he'd say, "O.K." And then he'd sit down at the piano and start producing a concept for that particular song. I ran into the booth while Bill was doing that, and told the engineer, "Record this! Record what he's doing right now!" He did it for so long, the engineer said he couldn't, he'd run out of tape. In those days it was on tape. Bill's working it out was some of the best music I've heard in my life. It went on for hours, and it was frustrating that none of it got on tape.

JC: When I need to be inspired, these recordings are what I put on. They can make me cry.

TB: Yes, he was that good. I can't believe how he would sense the next phrase that I was going to sing. He'd support it. He'd bring it in with a beautiful little emphasis on where I was going. Being a great accompanist is a gift, a certain disposition. You can't explain it.

JC: I want to hear about your school, the Frank Sinatra School of the Arts.

TB: Well, that's doing great. Ninety-seven percent of our students actually graduate and go to college. It's a performing arts school, although we still teach some academics to get our students ready for college. But it's all of the arts. You could be a poet, a dancer, an actor, a singer, or a film maker. We have teachers that teach all these different subjects.

JC: Had you always wanted to have a school?

TB: Well, it's ten years now. My wife and I—she's really in charge—have a great situation, because now we're in fifteen schools all over the five boroughs, Staten Island, Brooklyn, Queens, the Bronx, Manhattan. And we have performing arts programs for fifteen different public schools. The dream is to eventually have every public school in the country have art programs so that there are more artists in the United States than anywhere in the entire world.

You should see the work some of our schools are doing. We visited one school in Brooklyn the other day. They're mostly Black artists and the work they're doing is unbelievable. The artwork, dancing, and performing.

JC: That's exciting, because as you know, the arts are often ignored in public schools.

TB: Yes, they're always cut. Teach the history of the world but cut the arts. You know the arts are *everything*. I learned that from Bill Evans: it's all about truth and beauty. This is what's great about jazz. You search for truth and beauty, and by doing that, something very creative happens and it makes the world more civilized, more human.

It's not just a matter of making money and always worrying about where the next dollar is going to come from and all that. It's *creating* something, and hopefully having it successful in a creative way so that you leave behind something of value.

JC: That's wonderful. I think that is the meaning of life: leaving something behind that's beautiful and truthful. And Tony, you are truth and beauty to me.

Alan Broadbent

(b. 1947)

Two-time Grammy-winning jazz pianist,
composer and arranger.

Interviewed in 2017

Alan Broadbent left his native New Zealand at the age of nineteen after receiving a scholarship from *DownBeat Magazine* to study at Berklee College of Music in Boston. He went on to work as pianist and arranger for Woody Herman's band, followed by stints with Nelson Riddle and Natalie Cole, studio work with Johnny Mandel and David Rose, and conducting and arranging gigs for everyone from Kristin Chenowith and Diana Krall to Scott Hamilton and Paul McCartney.

I'd been a fan of Alan since first hearing him with Charlie Haden's Quartet West and was thrilled to have the chance to talk to him in 2017 about his newly released CD, *Developing Story*, the culmination of a musical idea he'd had many years earlier for an orchestral jazz composition.

I started our conversation by reading to Alan something he'd written on his website:

> "It has been a life-long goal, through my orchestral arrangements and jazz improvisations, to discover in popular music and the standards, deeper feelings of communication and love."

I commented that this sentiment seemed especially important today, when so many people seem unable to communicate or spread love.

AB: Yeah, I kind of knew at a very early age how beautiful these tunes were. My dad had the collection of songs, sheet music, American songs. I was born in New Zealand, so growing up in the late '50s I discovered all the standards that I liked most. I'd separate and put them on the piano and run through them. I'd play the sheet music arrangement and there was always a certain beauty in the way that they were constructed. I also listened to classical music and played Chopin when I was a boy. But these songs did something to me as I was becoming more interested in composing in that style that was already thirty years old. When Jimmy Van Heusen wrote a phrase connected to the chords that were on the sheet music, I'd put it aside and say, "Yeah, for some reason that gets to me." For me, a revelation about these songs was when Dave Brubeck came to Town Hall in New Zealand in the early '60s on his world tour.

I'd never really heard jazz. Paul Desmond came out and leaned into the bell of the piano and they started playing "Tangerine." I knew "Tangerine" from my dad. It was one of the ones I liked because it had those intervals. But I only played the sheet music version, and Dave was playing these chords I'd never heard before, and Paul was just *singing*. And I got it right away. I knew the form, but I had no idea that this depth of feeling that was affecting me could be expressed in a simple song. That's how all that began my adventure into finding out how to play jazz and how to write songs.

JC: You were composing early on.

AB: I was trying to. At about the time that the Beatles took over the world, I was trying to figure out how Jimmy Van Heusen wrote "Polka Dots and Moonbeams" and how he went to A major in the bridge.

JC: I was just like you. I was thinking those same things instead of listening to the Beatles.

AB: And that whole thing, the '70s, the disco, Richard Tee, the whole synthesizer movement.

42

JC: You were missing all of that because you were thinking about Jimmy Van Heusen?

AB: Yeah, I couldn't relate. And Miles went into his Joe Zawinul thing, it had lost that feeling for me. I was still trying to figure out how to go to A major in the bridge.

JC: [Laughs] I'm laughing because I'm remembering when my older brother took me to see the movie A Hard Day's Night. *I was in elementary school and didn't exactly have my finger on the pulse of pop music, but my brother turned to me right before the lights went down and said, "If you start screaming, I'm leaving." The lights went down, and everybody started screaming, and I looked at him like he was God. How did he know everyone was going to scream?*

AB: Actually, I was seventeen then, and *A Hard Day's Night* was my big hit at the Embers Jazz Club in Auckland.

JC: You've always been hipper than I am. [Laughs] You wrote some string arrangements for Paul McCartney, bringing this all full circle. I laughed when that CD came out because it's called Kisses on the Bottom, *and I was the only one of my friends who knew that was referring to a Fats Waller tune and not something sexual. What was it like working with Paul?*

AB: Paul is a gentleman. Everything was basically laid out already with Diana [Krall], whom I had known since she was nineteen. They had the tracks all done, and it was Tommy LiPuma, whom I'd known through Natalie Cole years before, who called me, and Diana suggested that I just write these string arrangements. Johnny Mandel had done the original arrangements on a couple of the songs, but Johnny is Johnny. I could see where Paul felt that it wasn't apropos to what was trying to be said with this modest production.

JC: It was turning into Johnny Mandel?

AB: Exactly. So I found a way to color these things without imposing any grand ideas upon it all, but just taking what was there and enhancing the feeling of what was going on, and it worked fine. Paul was happy with it, and he was a real gentleman.

And there was a very touching thing too with my wife, Allison. There was no way she wasn't coming to the session and get to see Paul, but it was a closed session. She got all dressed up and sat in the green room while I did my thing. We were recording for a little bit when Paul comes up and very discreetly looks at me and says, "Alan, who is that woman in the green room?" I said, "Paul, that's my wife, Allison," and he said, "Oh, I thought so." I thought, *Oh shit, I'm in deep water.* We finish the take, and Paul goes directly out to the green room and introduces himself. Allison almost died. "Let's take a picture," he says. Here's what a gentleman he was: we take the picture, and then Paul shows it to Allison and says, "Is that O.K. with you?"

JC: *I love stories like this because they're so rare.*

AB: Yeah. That was a particular time in her life, with Woodstock and everything. I had no idea about that music.

JC: *But it meant something to her.*

AB: Exactly. Our connection was, we met at the Vine Street Bar & Grill in Hollywood, and we happened to connect with Mahler. That's when I said, "Hey, that's the gal for me."

JC: *I love that you brought me some Mahler. I don't often get to play Mahler on this show. Do you remember which track you sent me?*

AB: Oh, I do! But first, I think of my experience with the man. I was in Woody Herman's band for three years after Berklee. I was very young, and unfortunately the road kinda . . . well, I guess this is a little bit of a confession here. I discovered that I had a terrible disease with alcohol. After ten years of that horrific experience—ten years in L.A. trying to survive—I sobered up and went with Nelson Riddle.

I was going to a gig at Universal Studios with Nelson, and I was early. I heard this symphony on the radio. Now, I'd been listening to classical music since I was a boy—Bartok, Stravinsky, Ravel, Debussy. I had the scores to everything, and I thought it was all beautiful and special, and in a way, it comforted me. But at this moment I heard this music and thought, *this is the music I've been wanting to write all my life.*

Since I was early, I sat in my car and listened. It turned out to be Mahler's First Symphony. And there he was. I understood everything again, just like "Tangerine." And he was speaking to me across time, across a hundred years. This happened at a time in my life when I needed that—that person to pull me through as I was sobering up.

That's when I started collecting his scores. I began from the First Symphony, each movement, studied them, tried to figure out how he did this, the overwhelming beauty of the counterpoint. The orchestration of this was the first time in all the orchestra music I knew, the first time that when an instrument or instruments were playing, they weren't creating an effect. They were speaking, and I had to know how to do that.

At the time there were certain movements, certain symphonies, that were too dramatic or Teutonic for me because I just didn't understand. But then I found certain movements of certain symphonies that would just devastate me. This particular movement I brought for you is the andante moderato of the Sixth Symphony. The Sixth Symphony alone is very easy to understand, and when you follow it, all the counterpoint at the end is like watching fireworks over the Hudson. It's so unbelievably joyful.

The andante moderato, I can hardly listen to it anymore because I know it so well, and what it means to me. What Mahler went through. He lifts that thing off your back, just like Bird or Louis Armstrong. They take whatever your woes are, whatever's hurting you, they go through it with you, and they bring you to the other side. So for me, that's the greatness of Mahler. There are moments in Debussy that do it to me. A few moments in Bartok, but nothing like Mahler. Nothing as personal.

JC: Talk about the idea for your new CD, Developing Story.

AB: In my own humble way, when music comes to me, it comes unforced, and it's an idea, and it wasn't as if I was trying to copy Mahler or anything. It's just, I responded to the music with this thing. So it was a little eight-bar ditty or something I thought up. I kept working on it, adding some counterpoint, a little here, a little there. I was still trying to figure out how an orchestra worked. I knew the music of the young John Williams, movies that he did before *Star Wars* and everything. Also, the arrangements he did of *My Fair Lady* for Shelly Manne and Irene Kral are phenomenal. And he was only nineteen or something.

But I was still stuck with the piano. And for me, Mahler was the key to breaking away from the piano. I'd open up a page of Ravel, and it was so beautiful. The sunrise. But Mahler said, "No, no, no, no. Here you do this, you do that, and you combine that, and you get this." And it was like I could see the *science* behind the creativity. So it was just a matter of trying to figure out how to apply it to what I did.

I wrote an orchestra piece for a wonderful guy, Jack Elliott, in L.A., who had an orchestra he was trying to get together with young composers. It was a terrible failure. It was one of those awful times when I wanted to just sink in the chair and crawl away. Luckily, I was sober at the time, and it didn't drive me back to drink.

And I hung in there and just kept at it. I joined Natalie Cole's *Unforgettable* orchestra on tour in Europe and everywhere. And there I had access to all of Johnny Mandel's scores. And Marty Paich. They were in little bins backstage, and I'd spend time with them on the bus or wherever, just studying.

I was finally figuring out how to apply what I knew about the orchestra to popular standards. There it was in Johnny Mandel's arrangements. And it was Natalie who gave me my first shot at it with a beautiful song that Billie Holiday used to sing, "Crazy He Calls Me." She was throwing out some tunes to a couple of the guys in the orchestra, and I sort of raised my hand, "Natalie, me." And she loved it. And from there I began my first orchestral arrangements. I was already in my forties. So I was still trying to hone the craft, and I would always go back to what became *Developing Story* and just see if maybe I could do this or that with that idea. And I knew then that there is no way that an orchestra is gonna swing. You can't get sixty to eighty people to feel the pulse of jazz.

JC: It's hard to find a small group that all feel the same way. It's how we feel time. I've played with great musicians where we just don't feel the time the same way. We're just not right together. With an orchestra, it's a whole other thing.

AB: Although they have their own pulse. With a great conductor they can do it, but it doesn't have what Lennie Tristano called a "life force." This pulse that Bud Powell and Louis Armstrong had. That feeling you feel if you watch Louis Armstrong on YouTube do "Dinah" from 1933. His band is chunking along, and it's almost like he's in a boxing ring, and he's just testing out the perimeter, the bars, and he's bouncing against them, and he's throwing himself back into the middle of the ring. You can feel that in his time, where that rhythm section is going, and he's leaning on it, and then he's going forward. What he takes away, he gives back, and it's this constant feeling of the quarter note, his quarter note, with their quarter notes and that was revolutionary. Not too many people understand it. They go with his gravelly voice and imitate *that*.

JC: But they don't know what was really special about Louis.

AB: Exactly. The same with Billie Holiday. She said, "Take away my voice, and there's Louis Armstrong."

The one cat that taught us piano players to go beyond being a piano player and use your voice, singing on the piano, was Bud Powell. It was Bud who taught us beboppers that way of bending the time, being flexible with it. It's the flexibility with the time that makes it joyful, even in its saddest parts. You can play a ballad in jazz and make it just sort of lay there and be pretty. I can do that too, and it's fine, but the minute I start to play with some connection and engagement to the time, to the players—if they're willing— it takes it to another level.   And I can sense it in an audience. It separates jazz from every other kind of music. It's the art of rhythm.

I've been fortunate to get some wonderful reviews for *Developing Story*, but there are a few people who write about it, and it's obvious to me that they don't understand this other quality of music. They want to impose their own feelings on top of it.

JC: That's interesting. It was probably too much for them emotionally.

AB: Well, if you read some of the reviews of Mahler's symphonies in his time, they're dreadful, just dreadful. Mahler called those critics "our superiors." So now I think of those people as my superiors.

[Laughter]

But that's why I wanted to explain how a symphony works in the liner notes of *Developing Story*. For those of you who don't know how to follow a movement of a particular symphony, here's how I spell it out for you so that if you take this little idea that I gave you—that's taken me twenty-five, thirty years to work up—it becomes this little bit, and that little bit of it becomes a big bit at the end, and it might have different harmonies, so I hope it doesn't sound condescending to a lot of listeners.

JC: No! I loved it because it was short, illustrative and explained the journey you were about to take with this music and made me appreciate it more. And I'm a musician. I've seen orchestra concerts where the conductor says, "This is when the horses are doing the charge, and the strings do this," or something like that, and it gives people something to latch on to.

AB: You have to consider that the music that is played every day, what we call "The Military Industrial Entertainment Complex," is what people mostly hear, and they're being sold up the river by these people who consider themselves "artists" when in reality, the music is completely empty. If they weren't selling a million downloads a day, they'd feel they weren't a success. Their success is judged outside of themselves whereas real worth comes from within.

That's what I've been trying to do all these years, and I'm finally beginning to see the light. I spent years hearing what I wanted to be in my head and not *being* it. And so I took everything in very deeply when someone would be less than complimentary, and I'd want to say, "Wait twenty years. I know it's in there."

JC: I feel that way myself. I'm still hanging by a thread hoping someone understands. But that's what this is. We're all looking for a connection. When I hear you say that you went through your drinking and how obviously sad that was . . .

AB: Well, it was a problem for me. And it was sad for a lot of other people around me.

JC: I know. I've experienced that. My father was an alcoholic my entire life, and then he died when I was thirty. So I understand that effect. I've never personally had that issue, but the love of my life, my father, did. The people who are able to confront that, as you did, and have the courage to go to the depths, to walk in that valley of darkness and come back, are the ones who are reborn.

AB: The one thing I had was my love of music, and I saw myself destroying that. It was going down the tubes fast, and I managed to fake it. I spent the last ten years of Nelson Riddle's life with him as his pianist. But Nelson was a tolerant and loyal man, and he liked guys who could read and swing. This was way after Sinatra and just before Linda Ronstadt. During that period, I did everything with him. His television shows were my first experiences in Hollywood. But after the sessions Nelson would come out and the rhythm section would stay—me and Alan Stoller, a wonderful drummer—and a couple other guys. And he would bring us a couple of tunes that he had written, and the joy for him was just sitting there by the piano saying, "Let's try this one." O.K., we'd try it. "No, no, I don't like that one. Let's try this one." And finally, we'd get a take that he loved, and we'd be swinging away. The purpose being that in the '70s there might be a scene in the show where the guy's driving down Malibu somewhere, and he reaches over and he turns the radio on and there's a little combo playing, and that was us.

That was a joy for us. And to have Nelson sitting beside me. And now, to see all the clips on YouTube and everything. I knew *In the Wee Small Hours* and those things, but, my God, what a great, great musician.

JC: What about L.A.? I'm curious because I'm a girl who left L.A. as well.

AB: Well, I got off Woody Herman's bus, basically in '72, not knowing what the heck I was gonna do. I had $200 in my pocket. I managed to find a cheap place to rent, and I got this call to work with Nelson Riddle six months later. But for all the time that I was there, I never felt comfortable. I'm a jazz musician who loves the orchestra, but I'm first and foremost a jazz man.

And in LA, you have to be everybody's man. At about the time Nelson Riddle died, I tried my hand at synthesizers to try and earn a living, but I just couldn't do it. I could not make that transition because the piano meant everything to me. The way the eighth notes feel, the way the piano responds to my chords and my feelings. I spent most of the forty years that followed going out every weekend to Pasadena just to play with my friend Putter Smith and whatever drummer we could find. In L.A. you have to find your jazz place because it doesn't really exist. Even the clubs. There's somebody slurping spaghetti in front of you while you're playing "My Foolish Heart."

JC: Someone once asked me how my career would have been different if I started now in L.A. versus New York because it was very different for me then, and it got me thinking about this. And you talking about it is very significant because your experience was very similar to mine, even though we were pursuing a jazz career in a very different way. I've thought about this before, that if you're a person who is pursuing music in the way you talk about pursuing it, you take on projects that you feel resonate with you. I get to see your face while you're talking about these people that you worked with, and I see the delight and love on your face. I've tried to do some projects that had a lot of money attached, money I needed. I could not bring myself to do them because there was no connection. I wished I could feel it, but I couldn't do it. And not because of a moral reason. I psychologically couldn't do the gig. Then I started thinking about other people, people who'd say to me, "Well, so and so sold out," whatever that means.

AB: That's a quaint term.

JC: Right. I watched these people and I thought, no, they haven't sold out, they're just able to do it. I did take a gig once that I hated, and I got a splitting headache. It made me physically sick.

AB: Me too. Well, kind of the beginning of the end was when I was on a studio date and I was asked to play like Richard Tee, and they came out and said, "That's not Richard Tee," and this is when I'd look up into the sky and say, "There's gotta be some way I can be in New York."

JC: I knew a great pianist, a friend of mine with the fetching name of Hunky Page, who played in the Hamptons. He was just a great piano player, that old-style pianist who played in a beautiful restaurant, that kind of thing, great tunes, beautiful changes, studied with Lennie Tristano for a minute, even played a few gigs with Bird. And he said that one night somebody requested "Feelings." There's nothing like solo piano, where no one is really listening to you and you're playing for hours. You confront everything. You get sick of your own playing.

Anyway, he starts playing the tune and suddenly thinks, What if I died right now? What if I went out now and the last thing I did on earth was play "Feelings"?

He stopped in the middle of the tune. So now, whenever I start to make a wrong move, I think, What if I went out playing "Feelings"? *I can't do it.*

AB: In L.A., all the guys who are my age now are living on very comfortable pensions. But I'm still waking up every day thinking, *What am I going to do today? Where will I play? What will I play? Are the guys coming over to my house? Maybe I'll have a gig at Mezzrow, or somebody might call with a chart, or maybe I've got a new song in my head.* I'm still living the life.

JC: *That's beautiful.*

AB: All those times with Charlie Haden saved me. Charlie saved me from L.A. But any time we played in New York, it's the old cliché. I'd be in the cab coming from J.F.K., and I'd see the lights of the city and my heart would go boom, boom, boom, and it's like, *Why am I feeling this?* I was hoping I'd be able to honor that someday. Thanks to my wife, we had a situation where we could move here and say goodbye to all that.

Jimmy Buffett

(b. 1946)

Singer/songwriter, author, actor, and businessman.
Together with his Coral Reefer Band, Buffett
has recorded "Margaritaville" and other hit songs.

Frank Marshall

(b. 1946)

Five-time Academy Award-nominated film producer and
director often working in collaboration with his wife, the film
producer, Kathleen Kennedy. Marshall, Kennedy, and Steven
Spielberg founded Amblin Entertainment in 1991.
In 2018 Marshall received the Irving G. Thalberg Award
from the Academy of Motion Picture Arts and Sciences.

Interviewed in 2022

The New Orleans Jazz & Heritage Festival returned in April of 2022 with a bang after a two-year pandemic hiatus. This joyful moment was followed by the release of the documentary *Jazz Fest: A New Orleans Story,* which honors the festival's fifty years of celebrating New Orleans music, food, and culture. The film weaves together live performances and interviews from the fiftieth anniversary in 2019, along with historic footage from earlier days showing how the festival was created and how it grew to an eight-day event with five hundred bands.

Frank Marshall co-directed *Jazz Fest: A New Orleans Story* with Ryan Suffern. Jimmy Buffett and Quint Davis were the executive producers.

Jimmy Buffett and Frank Marshall met forty-two years ago at Harrison Ford's New Year's Eve party in Aspen, Colorado and became fast friends. Their shared love for music, guitar playing, and New Orleans made their collaboration on *Jazz Fest: A New Orleans Story*, a natural.

Well-known creative types with a new project to promote send their publicity team to work finding various ways to spread the word. I am often pitched to have these folks on my show but when I respond in the affirmative, the famous person involved is suddenly "unavailable."

The Buffett/Marshall PR team were lovely but complicated. As the back and forth dragged on, I decided to take a more direct route and called Jimmy's longtime man Friday and VP of his record label, whom I'd met years ago on a tennis court. That moved things along.

I talked to Jimmy the night after his concert at Jazz Fest while he was still in New Orleans. I was in Sag Harbor, New York, and Frank Marshall was floating around the Bahamas on Jimmy's new cruise ship, Margaritaville at Sea.

JC: Jimmy, you played Jazz Fest last night. Tell me about it.

JB: We played at 3:30 p.m., out at the fairgrounds, and it was quite inspirational, a lot of fun and very *hot.*

JC: It had to be very emotional. I find that every gig I do now is emotional.

JB: Very. The thing of it is, with coming back from this shutdown, it's like a boat in a storm: you've got to be very careful where you're going. We returned very slowly, and in fact, Frank played on our first gig at the Belly Up in California. We were a four-piece band playing for forty people. Frank pops up and plays with us occasionally and he popped up on that one. So that's how we started.

We had not seen each other as a band for almost two years, but we did a lot of Zooming and used that to play for fans who were on the front lines, and just fans in general.

We had three of us in Mike Udley's living room, and Mac McAnally and Eric Darken were Zooming from Nashville and we all just broke down crying. It was just that emotional. That's my road family. And to hear each other play just made us do it. I get goose pimples right now thinking of it. And those goose pimples have been there from that day till yesterday.

So we've come back slowly and stayed safe, until the last two days when everybody *went down*! We lost the Reeferettes, but most of all, we lost our tour accountant. That was a big loss. Listen, I don't care if you have four people or forty-five people, per diem is a big deal.

But this happening in New Orleans worked. If you have a wreck on the road or a flat tire and you need a spare, New Orleans is a great place to find a spare. Literally, in a day and a couple of phone calls, we got Allen Toussaint's son, who runs a band, to have his singers fill in for the Reeferettes, and Sonny Landreth filled in. Sonny was gonna do a couple of songs, so he said, "How many songs do you want me to do?" "Originally four," I said, "but how about eighteen?"

If you think about it, it was musicians in the beginning who gave people hope. And from that moment with forty people to yesterday with sixty thousand just havin' a ball, I came home after that and felt like I'd gone a couple of rounds with Muhammad Ali. I said, "I'm gonna lay down and have a little nap" and I slept for two and half hours in the afternoon. I've never done that. It just shows you the power of music.

JC: I think people don't realize how much the pandemic has affected them because we're all just trying to get through it. Then you get out there and the emotion hits you. But I want to hear more about you playing, Frank.

55

FM: This whole thing has been obviously unprecedented and an unbelievable experience. And we sort of had the same thing going on with the movie. The last time we were together was when we shot the fiftieth anniversary of Jazz Fest, which was three years ago. And then we all went along normally, finishing the movie, but then everything shut down. And I want to thank Sony Classics Pictures right now because we vowed together to wait until we could see and hear this movie in a movie theater. And they have been great about pushing back the release date.

I finally got to see it with an audience last month at South by Southwest when we had our world premiere and I had the same feeling that Jimmy had when he was standing up there on the stage that, oh my gosh, for the first time in two years, I'm experiencing a movie the way I used to. And people were up dancing in the aisles. This is the perfect comeback movie, the perfect cure for Covid, a perfect antidote. It's joy and happiness and celebration the way only music can bring it to you.

And I was so lucky to get to come up and have that experience musically at the Belly Up down in Del Mar. It was like a dam broke. Jimmy had to tell the audience what to do because they didn't know that they could get up or sing along.

JB: Like I said, we'd broken down in our rehearsal so I thought that might happen in the show but then the adrenaline hit me because I hadn't performed in so long and I shot out of there like a cannonball. I looked at Frank and said, "I'm way too far ahead." So I said, "Stop! We're gonna start again and I'm gonna explain some things to you." It was ten tables, forty people and it was like being a camp director. I told everyone they could dance, but they needed a couple of tiles between them; they had to stay on their tile. By the end of the show, you could see a compression of the jubilation of what I saw yesterday with an audience of sixty thousand. Forty or sixty thousand, it was exactly the same.

JC: What I think is so special about Jazz Fest is this combination of many different kinds of music and the unique energy that creates. Jazz musicians, like myself, who have done loads of jazz festivals, complain that jazz festivals over the years have evolved to include music that isn't jazz. But to me it makes sense that Jazz Fest is inclusive because New Orleans has always had a huge range of music. And jazz has many different influences too. New Orleans has always been—if I can say it this way—"bigger" than just jazz. It has more influences than any city I can think of. And this is something you captured so beautifully in this film.

FM: I think that's what's special about Jazz Fest. And that's what's so great when you go to the festival. There are sounds and smells coming from everywhere. And the city itself becomes a character in the movie. It was an exciting way to show the culture and the heritage all based around this music.

JB: Well, I am a product of all of that. That's where I started. I started listening to jazz because we would go to meet my grandfather's ship. He was a ship captain on a passenger freighter ship when I was a kid, and we would go to New Orleans to meet the ship when it came back from Buenos Aires. And I'll never forget being a ten-year-old kid and seeing a jazz band playing at the dock with confetti flying and champagne popping as the boat came in. He'd take us on the boat and then we'd go have lunch at Two Jacks. It was a family tradition, and music was part of it.

When I first realized that I was gonna do this, I started at a little junior college north of New Orleans in Poplarville, Mississippi, and graduated from the University of Southern Mississippi, not in collegiate terms but in terms of what bands I was in. The mecca was the Bayou Room on Bourbon Street which was a folk club right across the street from Pete Fountain's club and others. That music of New Orleans was there on the street, as well as all the burlesque and strip clubs. I was eighteen years old and as I confessed in the movie, I went there a virgin, and I did not come away one. New Orleans was Oz to me.

I hadn't seen the old clip of Quint Davis, the producer of Jazz Fest, marching in front of the band in the film and when I saw that I almost hit the floor laughing. I met Quint in 1973 when he had a hippie shop called The Love Shop.

And putting this all together is what Frank does so well, telling the story of New Orleans, the ups and downs over the centuries. I had friends who saw the film and had never realized the full history and they told me they cried. And what got us through? The music.

JC: Frank, you captured the joy, the energy and the pace of the festival and the city. Then you have this very emotional part about Katrina, which was so beautifully rendered. That captured one of the things that's so inspiring about New Orleans, that there are all these different types of people working together to survive. New Orleans has such a difficult history but somehow the city pushes forward, which you epitomize in that part of the film.

FM: Well, thanks, Judy. It's a perseverance. Quint and Jimmy say in the film that Jazz Fest had to go on. There was a movement in Congress not to rebuild after Katrina. But they knew they had to move forward with Jazz Fest. They didn't know who would show up, if anybody. Suddenly they got this call from the police department that people were lined up down the street. Again, there was a flood of joy and celebration because music is a universal language that brought everybody back together again. That's when they knew that New Orleans was back.

With my day job doing feature films, I know what I'm doing every day, I know every second we're shooting this, we're shooting that, it's planned. But what I love about making documentaries is, it's a journey of discovery. It's like having a treasure chest. And every once in a while, you find a gold doubloon. And the gold doubloon to me was that early footage of Quint Davis dancing in front of the band and George Wein with Mahalia Jackson at the first Jazz Fest. When you have things like that, that's what makes it so special for me to create a documentary.

JC: On the website of the New Orleans Jazz and Heritage Foundation they have the words, "We teach, we build, we celebrate." I'm always talking about audience development and that's something Jazz Fest does so well, featuring musicians young and old and drawing an audience of all ages.

FM: I think that's very important to the festival founders and to the foundation. Quint says that well in the movie where he says the festival is about heritage and culture and about looking back but it's also about looking forward and seeing what's coming.

JB: I know very well and very deeply that the Parrothead thing came out of my being a child of the Mardi Gras and taking what I learned in New Orleans. It wasn't planned, but it suddenly dawned on me one day when I saw the audience in Cincinnati, Ohio dressing up in Hawaiian shirts, that they were in costume, and I thought, it's just Mardi Gras. I grew up with that, marching in bands as a drummer and trombone player.

[Jimmy's fans wear tropical clothing and parrot hats at his concerts, inspiring one of his bandmates to coin the phrase "Parrotheads."]

And something that had deep meaning for me in the film was where Quint talks about the number of performers *created* in New Orleans because I was one of them. And I think, in my humble opinion, that what's lacking in the music business today is what you owe an audience as a performer, and that's something you learn here.

JC: Every New Orleans musician I know says they first played onstage when they were eight or nine.

FM: Like Jimmy said, it's a special thing for a kid to get a trombone in their early days and go out there and march and see what that's like. It opens up a whole new world of opportunity.

JB: And when you start performing at a young age it gives you a sense of time. It's something that's absolutely important if you're ever going to make a splash or just do it for fun. Everything runs in time in music. When you're on stage, you're managing time and you're managing energy. You're takin' 'em up and you're takin' 'em down. I read that audience last night, and I knew they'd been there three days. It was hot but they were still having a good time. But I knew the tanks were gonna get empty, so I cut two songs knowing I had to keep them at that high energy level because they needed it as much as I did.

It's timing and time. That's the most important thing I learned marching in those bands when I was a kid.

JC: Frank, I know your father was a jazz guitarist and record producer, but also, my sources tell me that you once had a job as a waiter/guitar player. Talk about this.

FM: Well, your research is very good. I was a waiter/dishwasher/folksinger back in the late sixties at a restaurant called The Randy Tar. The great thing about it was there was one in Aspen, so you were in Aspen in the winter, and one in Marina del Rey, so you were in the sun in the summer. It was very good because I'd wait on tables until about ten o'clock and then go downstairs to the bar and sit on my little stool and compete with the bartender and the blender. People weren't paying much attention. I did get to meet John Denver because he was down the road in Snowmass at a place called The Leather Jug. And when I think back on the difference between me and Jimmy and John Denver, they were writing songs and singing them, and I was just playing Peter, Paul and Mary and Gordon Lightfoot and that kind of stuff.

JC: You were a cover band! A cover band of one. Is this something that you keep up?

FM: Oh, yes. If I were talking to you from my house, you'd see a couple of guitars behind me. It's been a great way to relax. I love playing on the side. It's a great hobby to have. I grew up in this guitar family so anytime I went home I enjoyed playing with my dad or my brother. But I think it's probably better for the world that I chose another vocation.

JC: Do you remember the first jazz you heard?

FM: It was probably a guitar player named Howard Roberts who my dad had met. They became best friends and my dad produced him, so we had a bunch of his albums. So I'd say that the first time I paid attention to jazz was when I heard Howard Roberts.

[Frank's father, Jack Marshall, was a jazz guitarist and arranger and one of Capitol Records' top producers in the late 1950s and the 1960s. He's credited with the arrangement for Peggy Lee's recording of "Fever."]

FM: I want to say one more thing about time. Time and timing are also important in a movie and that's about editing. Without our editor, Martin Singer, we would not have this movie. All the little soundbites within the film must be perfectly placed or it throws you out of the movie. It's something we all learn. The timing of everything is what takes you on the journey both in music and in films.

JC: And in life!

Chevy Chase

(b. 1943)

Actor, comedian, screenwriter, producer and key cast
member in the first season of *Saturday Night Live*.

Interviewed in 2002

The late Hunky Page was a wonderful jazz pianist who played near my
home in Sag Harbor, N.Y., at the elegant American Hotel. Hunky was a
musician's musician whose talents drew celebrated musicians out of their
Hamptons getaways for an evening of fancy food and soulful music. One
of Hunky's famous fans was the comedian Chevy Chase, whom Hunky had
told me played jazz piano.

"Is he any good?" I asked.

"You should hear him."

Hunky had asked me to sit in several times, but I don't usually enjoy
that, so I always demurred. Then one night, in the dead of winter, I went to
hear Hunky with a friend. Only two other tables were occupied, one by
Chevy Chase and his wife, and the other by a young honeymooning couple
discussing which was more interesting, New York (his birthplace) or Los
Angeles (hers). Hunky's sophisticated playing and Chevy's presence in
this historic, almost empty little inn supported the groom's case for New
York hipness.

Eventually, Hunky asked Chevy to play. After prat-falling off the
piano bench, he dug into a gorgeous version of Bill Evans's composition
"Waltz for Debby," a surprisingly poetic contrast to his antics on the bench.
Hunky turned to me in his whimsical way and asked, "Judy, care to play a
tune?" This time I couldn't resist. When I finished, the groom turned to his

bride and without irony said, "See, honey, just like I told you, everyone in New York is talented!"

Chevy and I lost touch for years but finally reconnected in 2002 through his college band mate, Blythe Danner, who gave me his number.

"Hi Chevy. It's Judy Carmichael."

"JUDY! What took you so long to call? I thought you'd forgotten me."

Chevy is known for his sarcasm and irony, which does not always come across in print. To be clear, he does not do heroin, his wife is not a teenager, and he did not hang with Miles Davis in junior high school. Chevy started our conversation by falling over his chair when he entered the studio, so the show begins with noise, then silence.

JC: Chevy, you do realize we're on radio, and no one could see that pratfall except me.

CC: Really? This isn't television?

JC: Everyone knows your comedic work, but I doubt many know you're a jazz pianist. You and I met in the classic jazz situation.

CC: That's right. Does anyone out there know Hunky Page?

JC: They will now that we're talking about him.

CC: Hunky is one of the best and most interesting jazz pianists. He plays solo piano at the American Hotel in Sag Harbor. You and I met there, listening to Hunky. Hunky said, "Chevy, would you like to listen to this girl, Judy Carmichael? She plays stride." You sat down and played absolutely perfect piano. It knocked me out.

JC: I felt the same when I heard you. Hunky had told me you were going to play, but I guess I didn't expect you to play so beautifully. I was especially fascinated by your obvious influence from Bill Evans. I think that would surprise some other people as well.

CC: Well, there's a sensitive and warm side to me. There's a lot of woman in me. And a lot of heroin. Both of those things were in Bill. No, seriously, I knew Bill Evans back when I was in my late teens and into my twenties and even my thirties. And then sadly, Bill died.

I got to know him by hanging out in the clubs here in New York. The first time I heard him I was in high school. As opposed to listening to rock and roll, I listened to jazz. I just preferred instrumental music and didn't particularly care for the lyrics in rock and roll songs. It was all the same old stuff until I heard Ray Charles and the Beatles later on, when it started to get really interesting. Not to say there wasn't some great soul with Otis Redding and others.

My life was one of contrasts. On the one hand, I was in a private school up in Massachusetts, and I lived an upper-middle-class life, but I spent my time in the dregs of New York at the Vanguard, Five Spot, Jazz Gallery and all of the other jazz spots. Eventually I met Bill Evans. When I first heard him, I thought, *My God, this man is unbelievable!* And I called Miles Davis and he said the same thing.

JC: I guess you were already close with Miles by then. You were probably hanging with him in junior high?

CC: He was hanging. I was just there.

JC: Ah, I see. Seriously, how did you get to know Bill Evans?

CC: I got to know him as a fan, just the way I got to know Monk and Mingus and Coltrane. I was one of these young, WASPY-looking kids who would be there late at night after everyone else had left. I used to hold Danny Richmond's hi-hat in place at the Five Spot with Mingus, so people began to get to know me.

When I went to Haverford College, we got Bill to play there and I got to know him a little better. When I was at Bard College, we got him to play there too, so I got to know him a little better. It just went on and on to the point where I started driving him around. I'd drive him home to his house in Riverdale after gigs at the Vanguard. He gave me two of his cats that I had for about ten years.

When I became famous, it didn't particularly knock him out one way or the other, but he was a little more conversant with what I did and who I was. I was able to call him from California and say, "Listen, I'm trying to learn *Waltz for Debby,* but I can't read music. I play by ear." I'd put the phone on the piano, and I'd say, "How does this sound?" He'd say, "That's pretty good, Chevy. You have a good ear."

I remember once saying to Bill, "God, I'd give anything to play the piano like you." He said, "It's easy, Chevy." "Really?" "Yeah. Practice eight hours a day." I realized, jeez, I was driving cabs and writing comedy or whatever I was doing. But I certainly didn't have time to play eight hours a day.

JC: But you do take time to play a lot now?

CC: In the last few years I've been doing relatively little work in film and television. Basically, I've been concentrating on my three daughters—who are all teenagers—and my wife, who's also a teenager.

JC: That's convenient. They have the same interests. I think that was good planning on your part.

CC: The point is, you've got to stay creative. I think that that's what drove me to the piano. I'd say, about three years ago, I started playing piano four hours a day to get to the point where I could learn songs and finish them. Before that I just clowned around. As you know, I'd go to the American Hotel, maybe for dinner with my wife, and Hunky would be playing. He was always sweet, and he'd say, "Would you like to try a song?" He was always nice, but I felt ridiculous.

JC: But you have an incredible ear. Your voicings are beautiful. You've obviously listened a lot and worked hard at this. Do you have perfect pitch?

CC: I do. I think I got that from my mother. It's genetic. My kids have perfect pitch. Those who can tell one note from another. Though I don't know what perfect pitch means, really.

JC: That you can pick out the individual notes of a chord when you hear it and when you hear an "A" you know it's an "A" without having heard another note to judge its relative pitch.

CC: The voicings, I don't know what the hell I'm doing. I'm only now beginning to learn what makes that chord that chord. Why one's called a flatted fifth and or ninth or why it's diminished or augmented. Or why did I play that. It just falls into my fingers, and if it sounds good to me, I use it.

JC: In jazz we always talk about time. We talk about a musician having great time or great feel. That's the same in comedy. Timing is everything.

CC: They're very close. Jazz is a minute of music and a minute of time and a minute of music, as Bill used to say. And that's what distinguishes it from classical music and other forms. The improvisatory nature of jazz and the extemporaneous elements lend themselves to comedy. In fact, I always thought Thelonious Monk was the funniest pianist I ever heard. I thought he had a great sense of humor. If you were hanging out with him in the kitchen at the Vanguard, you wouldn't think he had a great sense of humor because he wasn't a guy who told jokes per se, but that didn't mean he wasn't funny. You listen to his voicings and his moods on the piano—you know that has to come from some kind of weird perspective. And sense of humor is perspective. My sitting down at the piano and improvising and playing about with chords and voicings and trying to get my right hand to work, that's not far from winging it in *Fletch* or *Caddyshack* or one of those movies.

JC: You have to practice to be able to improvise well; at least I do. I want to keep my technique sharp, so I have the physicality to accomplish everything I'm thinking while I play.

CC: How do you practice? Do you do scales?

JC: I do scales, and I also play some tunes and improvise with them. During practice I can take more risks than I would during a concert. I can fall off a cliff, start over, and get certain things under my fingers. That kind of practice makes me more fearless on the gig.

CC: That's what I don't do. That's the unfortunate thing of not having taken lessons. You get to a certain point where you say I wish I could do *that*—that kind of arpeggio or that kind of run that this guy just did, but you just don't know how to finger it.

JC: But you also bring something different to it. I only took a couple of years of lessons. I'm frustrated by that too, but we bring a different approach and new thoughts to it all because we weren't trained in the typical way. We had to figure out our own way forward.

CC: You're right. It really is about your heart anyway. When all is said and done, whatever I'm doing with the piano is going to come from a certain sensitivity in my heart. That's what jazz is about, ultimately.

There are great technicians, like Oscar Peterson in the old days. I used to think, *boy, that guy has got incredible chops.* He was an incredible technician. It was only twenty years later that I started to think that he was getting good. He started putting his ideas and *heart* together, so his solos were becoming more interesting. That's where I would like to get at some point before I die. To have the technique to say what's really in my heart. People like Peterson and others have often started with the technique and had to have their heart catch up to that.

JC: You and I are starting from the place of the heart. I feel the same way about my playing. But isn't that true with the best comedy too? If you're just telling a joke, you're telling a joke, but if someone is living it . . .

CC: I don't believe in jokes. I can't tell a joke very well. I forget a joke after it's been told to me. I laugh, but I don't come from that background. Nor did I ever do standup comedy, nor was I a comedian. I was a writer of comedy. My father is extremely funny. I learned from him what humor is. What makes me funny has little to do with jokes per se but with situation and physicality. The spontaneity of that certainly lends itself to jazz music.

There are times when I have to laugh at the way I'm soloing because I know I don't know what the heck I'm doing because I may throw in a clunk here and a clunk there. But then I think, *Hey, that's pretty funny, why don't I continue with these clunks and try to put them all together?*

How are comedy and jazz connected and interwoven? Well, the great standup comics, like Richard Pryor and Robin Williams, worked very hard. But standup comics in general work hard at getting and honing the jokes so the audience will laugh at a certain rhythm. The joke, then the laugh.

Then there are those who are more jazz-oriented. Richard Pryor, more than anyone, is the most jazz-like in terms of improvising standup comedy. He was just plain funny. He didn't tell jokes. He didn't come up with the same thing every time. He just performed.

The kind of humor I enjoy comes out of some sort of spontaneous, extemporaneous thought. What if this were to happen? How is this in some way inappropriate? The idea is to *not* be appropriate. I don't think being appropriate in jazz necessarily makes it any better. You're talking about an element of courage and making mistakes. In the same way that you're never more than a half step off in jazz at the piano.

The kind of comedy I like, and I do, is a continuum of get-outs, of making mistakes and getting out of it, and getting the laugh because of the error in an improvised, spontaneous fashion. The ability to do that comes from a talent that's been given you, a sense of timing, and an ability to read the audience and respond accordingly.

The getting out of it is the same thing that takes place in jazz. There are studied jazz musicians—most of the good ones are, like McCoy Tyner or

Bill Evans—but for the most part, when you listen to Jaki Byard, or musicians most people may not have heard as much about, you listen to them solo and you can hear them moving in a direction and getting out of it because a certain note was hit and it was a half-step off from where they may have wanted to go in a traditional sense, and so they make use of that and move to the next idea.

What amazes me about Bill Evans is that you always feel a sense of spontaneity. You feel a sense that he's never repeating himself. At the same time, he never makes a mistake. It's lyrically perfect. He'll begin with a certain phrase, something that seems out of sync with the time and out of sync from where he started. But then he'll complete it and bring it to its full resolution before he goes to the next thought. That to me is unbelievable. He is technically brilliant, makes no mistakes, and also draws out tears. There's so much heart to his playing. His voicings are so beautiful.

JC: That's improvisation at its highest level. Another thought I've looked forward to discussing with you is why there aren't more films about jazz musicians.

CC: Clint [Eastwood] has done it. Clint has tried with Charlie Parker and Monk. It's all about money. The question is, is there an audience for that?

JC: But there are great and interesting characters in jazz.

CC: Courtney Ross made a film about Quincy Jones. Probably cost her half of her capital, but it was worth it. There are some films made about some very innovative people, but nobody ever gets to see them. Where are you going to see them? On PBS? Maybe, if you could get on HBO. In the theater it's so rare, unless you're named Clint Eastwood.

JC: But those movies were successful.

CC: I don't know how successful, but with Clint, he could just go to Bob Daly and Terry Semel, the heads of Warner Brothers, and say, "Listen, I'm going to make this picture about Monk. It's not going to make any money for you, but I'll make you a $50 million movie in exchange." And then he'd go off and make some Western and make the studio $50 to $100 million.

A lot of people don't know that Clint is a jazz pianist. Warren Beatty is a jazz pianist. There are people that you wouldn't believe who play jazz piano. So when you say that people don't know that Chevy Chase plays the piano, there are more of us who dabble than you might think.

Great jazz musicians have worked very hard to get to where they are musically. You think of them as outlaws, or they might be Hells Angels on the side, or big tough outlaws, but in fact, they're sensitive and hard-working musicians. They're artists. It is remarkable how some of these people were viewed as outlaws, like Miles Davis or Mingus or Thelonious Monk. You wouldn't want to meet them in a dark alley. But these are artists, like painters.

Bill Evans played football. He was sort of a jock when he was in school. He played flute and violin and all that too. He didn't seem that way in the end, of course, because he'd taken so much heroin and everything else. It's unfortunate that people in that world were so driven to drugs and drinking. We lost so many so early. On the other hand, you think about how hard they worked to get to be the top masters of the game they're in. And they'd still make 150 bucks a week. That might drive you to buy a joint or two.

People who take drugs and those things are trying to escape some depression or some problem. So you can understand it. What reality are they trying to escape? You can understand someone thinking, *I've worked for twenty years, eight hours a day at something, and I'm one of the best in the world at it, and I can't even afford a Toyota.* That's depressing.

JC: It is depressing. And people don't realize that. They think that it's sort of romantic, that it's part of the whole experience to have that angst and be that poor. But jazz musicians want to make money and pay their rent like everybody else.

71

CC: The idea of selling out shouldn't offend anybody in the jazz world. The idea that Dave Brubeck can make a million bucks, or Miles. There were a few who could. They weren't seen as sellouts. It's the same in comedy. A guy goes from *Groove Tube* to *Mad Magazine* to *National Lampoon,* then gets to *Saturday Night Live* as a writer. Suddenly he's a huge star, and he's making movies and he's "sold out!" Well, that's not the case at all. The case is, hey, I'm making more money. It's not like the whole time that's what I was looking to be. It's the same thing in the jazz world.

JC: Who besides Monk has a great sense of humor in their music?

CC: Art Tatum.

JC: I agree! I've always heard the humor in Tatum's playing.

CC: Maybe Lennie Tristano didn't know he had a sense of humor.

JC: There are certain people I know who don't think of themselves as funny, and I find them terribly funny, even as storytellers. It's the same with certain musicians. I hear the humor in their music.

CC: I'm a funny guy. I'm a comedian, I suppose. But my music is not particularly funny. Just the mistakes. With Monk, he meant those mistakes to be where they were. They weren't mistakes. They were dissonances that ultimately made you chuckle.

JC: And Count Basie.

CC: And Count Basie had a sense of humor. And more particularly, he had that timing you speak of, for when to play what he was going to play, how spare to be, and how funny it might be. I think he was truly a funny man. A lot of these guys were truly funny people.

JC: What is your philosophy of playing? You've given this a lot of thought.

CC: There are no mistakes. You're never more than a half tone off.

JC: Easy for you to say. [Laughs]

CC: Well, with the kind of piano I've heard you play, Judy, a mistake stands out a lot more, but the kind of piano I play is *riddled* with mistakes, but you can't tell because I'm sliding into the next one. Well, actually, you *can* tell.

JC: But I'm not going to tell!

CC: [Laughs] I want people listening to know that just to sit at the piano on a daily basis, even for just a few minutes, can be the love of your life. I want kids to know that. I want anybody listening to us to know that. I've told people who are in all sorts of disparate lines of work, if you need to relax, sit at a piano. They say, "But I can't play the piano!" *Nobody* can play the piano. The fact is, you just listen to what your fingers are doing and let it take you somewhere. And sooner or later, you'll find that your heart rate is slower, your blood pressure has dropped. It's like doing yoga. It's a great gift to have a piano or a guitar. But pick up an instrument and play with it.

JC: I love that! Chevy, I'm so glad we finally got together.

CC: I kept waiting for you to call!

JC: Yeah, yeah, I never call, I never write . . .

Glenn Close

(b. 1947)

Emmy, Tony and Golden Globe winner and
eight-time Oscar-nominated actress.

Ted Nash

(b. 1960)

Jazz saxophonist, flautist, and composer.

Interviewed in 2021

On the 2021 CD *Transformation: Personal Stories of Change, Acceptance and Evolution*, the actress Glenn Close joined forces with the composer Ted Nash and the Jazz at Lincoln Center Orchestra on a series of Nash's compositions that integrate spoken-word segments curated by Close. Glenn Close was joined by Wayne Brady, Amy Irving, Matthew Stevenson and Nash's son, Eli who read their own writing or text chosen by Close.

This is the second collaboration for Glenn Close and Ted Nash, one that is especially personal as the spoken segments range from Ted Hughes' *Tales from Ovid*—a Close favorite—to a letter in which Nash's son comes out as transgender. Each piece focuses on change as positive, an attitude that Ted Nash and Glenn Close share and encourage others to embrace.

We taped our conversation on SquadCast, a platform that works much like Zoom and one I started using during the pandemic to record. Ted was in Manhattan, Glenn in Montana and I was in my home in the Hamptons. Glenn has admitted that initially she was a bit resistant to jazz. I asked her how she got past that fear.

GC: Instead of fear of jazz, I'd probably say I was intimidated by it. When I was at the College of William and Mary, we'd do poetry in English class which kind of gave me the same feeling of intimidation because I always felt that I didn't quite get it and there was always some smart kid who did. It kind of took away the joy of just reading the poem and having it resonate personally.

My transformation with jazz first started with getting to know the musicians. Then years ago, my daughter Annie and I were at Dizzy's [part of the Jazz at Lincoln Center complex] and Wynton Marsalis sat down with us and on a napkin explained the history of jazz, starting with the twelve-bar blues. He pointed out that there are twelve months in the calendar, twelve signs of the Zodiac, and twelve notes that jazz musician start with. It all came to life. And then, watching the musicians play, I was so inspired by the music but also how they tossed the lead to each other during the performance and gave each other a chance to improv. It's just awe-inspiring.

So now, to me, jazz is the sound of what it means to be a human being. Because we're complex, we're fragile, we're conflicted, and all the different sounds that come out of jazz are another way of explaining how we're wired as human beings. And now I can just relax into the music and feel like it's expressing all the complexities that are in me as an individual.

JC: That's beautiful. You make me extremely proud to be a jazz musician, Glenn.

TN: That was so beautifully said. I was surprised to hear you say that you were intimidated by jazz. You're in contact with all sorts of people at all sorts of levels of their artistry and for you to feel intimidated by this art form, one that feels natural to me, because I've done it all of my life, was kind of a revelation. But it made me understand that probably a lot of people feel that way and it's probably why we have limited audiences for this music.

JC: I put this on us, Ted. Jazz musicians need to take more time to bring people into this experience, to embrace them. At one of my concerts recently, I talked about "trading fours." I explained that with jazz we state the theme and then each musician does their variations on it. Sometimes we'll do a chorus where we divide it into four measure segments, so one musician plays four measures of their variations, and the next musician continues and improvises on that thought for four measure and the next does the same. After the concert, a man came up to me and said, "Thank you for explaining 'fours.' I've been listening to jazz for thirty years and never knew exactly what was happening when musicians did that." I thought I might have been over-explaining, but he was so grateful. That's what makes your napkin story so powerful. We must bring people to this. It's all about listening and knowing how to listen.

GC: Yes! And Wynton says it all starts with the blues.

TN: Wynton talks about the blues a lot. It's one of the most important aspects of jazz music. Blues is a form but it's also a *feeling*, so it's an integral part of the music. I think a lot of people don't even understand that jazz is largely improvised.

Judy, you've probably had this happen as well, where people will ask you after a concert, "Was what you played all written out?" That lack of understanding explains why people can be intimidated or confused by jazz. I don't think we have to constantly explain it to the audience, but we *do* have to engage people by being engaged in the music ourselves and being honest and truthful and responsive.

Judy, you talked about listening, but a lot of people don't listen to each other when they're playing.

GC: A lot of actors don't listen to each other!

JC: Glenn, I would think that something that draws you to jazz is this aspect of listening. The greatest actors are great listeners. And that's certainly true for musicians, especially jazz musicians.

GC: In my acting, I *reflect*. I receive and give back. It's all what I get from another actor. But I have to say, we only did three performances of *Transformation*, and listening to what Ted chose of the best of those performances, I know that if we'd done a longer run, that the speakers and the musicians would have been even more eloquent because we didn't know all the timing that was possible. We would have become an absolute unit if we'd had more time. Listening back, I can hear what would have been possible.

TN: We had so much to get together. By the sound check, we were still trying to figure stuff out. By the second performance, I was still figuring out how to give you and Wayne [Brady] more space around your words and how to conduct the band so they could respond to you in the right way.

GC: While listening back on the recorded tracks, I could hear the evolution in the way everyone responded to each other. You can hear the musicians responding to the spoken words. If we'd done more performances each would have been beautiful in a different way, but it would have evolved. We would have been more cognizant about giving each other space.

JC: What's interesting to me is the musicality of speech working with the rhythm of the music. It's a different kind of acting partner.

GC: And also, with poetry and other things that people hear for the first time, we need to know exactly what we mean as we're saying it or else the audience isn't going to get it. It's why I luxuriate in eight performances a week when I'm doing a well-written piece because it's infinite what you discover. We're all on the wing, which is another exciting aspect of this album. We're all on the wing. But we have the same intent, which is to tell these stories.

TN: Talking about communication is so important. With musicians I think that sometimes they don't realize how important it is to communicate to both the musicians around them and to the audience. Actors are trained to do that, and some do better than others, but musicians forget that a lot. We can learn so much by watching people like you, great actors and how they communicate and how they take the words and make us understand deeply what they mean. We *can* move people with our music if we understand that.

GC: Sometimes you do a stage performance where you think, *Oh, my God, I was bad tonight.* And somebody will come backstage and say, "Oh my gosh, that was one of the best things I've ever seen." And you learn to say, "Thank you." You don't say, "Oh, my God, I was horrible!" You're struggling within yourself to find this seamless connection but in that struggle and in the words that you have to say, you're communicating something. And sometimes the *struggle* communicates something despite yourself.

JC: What I find interesting along those lines—and Ted, I know you've had this happen too—is when I think the whole band has had a great performance and we walk offstage, and I say that to my musicians. Then the guitar player says his amp had issues and the saxophonist says he was struggling with his mouthpiece, and you realize you've all had a different experience of the same moment, exactly what Glenn is saying. Then there are those nights when it's perfect for everyone in their own way and you walk off and look at each other and say, "Yup, it was great" and you all know it.

Ted, I'm curious about the process of putting this composition together. The two of you got together with a clear intent on what you wanted to create and the message you wanted to put forth, but how exactly did you write the music to the words?

TN: As Glenn and I worked on the material, we had a general idea of the larger themes of transformation that related to our personal stories. A lot of these connections were made through Glenn's association with these people who lived through transformative experiences. We didn't know how the pieces would be read so I couldn't have someone read something in advance and write to it. There was a lot of flexibility during the rehearsals. Wayne Brady came in and said we should get rid of all the music I'd written to accompany his reading. He preferred just the rhythm section. I had to be flexible and willing to eliminate all this music I'd spent hours on to support what Wayne wanted. So the process proceeded like that.

Once I had the poetry and the words everyone would speak and started to write, I used something I learned from Glenn. I asked her about her process. She said it isn't so much about a certain method but rather that she uses her imagination, so I did the same thing. I read the words then closed my eyes and imagined what the music should be. Then I used the keyboard to capture what I was hearing in my head. And then during the rehearsal process it was about adjusting and fitting things in with the rhythm of the words and getting the timing together.

JC: Talk about "Preludes to Memnon."

GC: It's a poem I have loved my whole life because I get very comforted by nature. And we're all aware of the leaves falling off the trees in the autumn, the war of atoms that goes on to make a leaf be detached from a branch and float down to the ground. To me, it says everything. "The maelstrom has us all." We are part of the maelstrom. We're fragile, we're conflicted, that's who we *are*. And the more you're aware of the maelstrom, the more I think you can arm yourself to be able to negotiate your way through it.

JC: Ted, I wanted to talk to you about one of your inspirations that brought about a personal transformation. Talk about hearing Charlie Parker.

TN: I was a classical clarinet player going into high school and that was really what I thought I was going to do. My uncle and my father were studio musicians, but they came out of a jazz tradition. When I first heard Charlie Parker playing some blues, I instantly knew that that was what I want to do. That was a transformation. I didn't understand about improvisation, but it was just this sound and this feeling and the freedom that is part of it. It was frustrating, though. I was fourteen and practicing a lot and I know my teacher would step out of the room and kiss his wife and say, "I don't know about this kid."

Then, suddenly, I was sixteen, and I could just do it. I worked hard but didn't know if it would come together, and then suddenly it did. It's like learning any language. There's a moment where it magically comes together. But I didn't know that would happen.

JC: Well, my teacher told me I'd never amount to anything.

GC: And I flunked my audition for Yale.

JC: We're all such failures!

[Laughter]

JC: Is that true or are you saying that to make everyone feel better?

GC: Absolutely. I think I still have the rejection letter.

JC: You should frame it! Now I want to talk about your piece "Rising Out of Hatred."

GC: The way we came to this was Eli Saslow, the Pulitzer Prize-winning journalist who co-wrote the movie I did called *Four Good Days*. He came to the set while we were shooting and told me about his book *Rising Out of Hatred*, the story of Derek Black, a white supremacist, and his transformation away from that doctrine through his college friendship with Matthew Stevenson, an Orthodox Jew.

At first, we asked Derek if he would come and write a piece about his own transformation. He came back to us and said he was too nervous about security. So I suggested we go to Matthew. He then wrote that beautiful piece, Ted added the music, and Matthew came and presented it in person. And to show you the good will and generosity that came into these three performances, Matthew, of course, could not perform on Friday, so I called my friend Christian Slater, and he flew up all the way up from Florida to do that Friday-night reading. He did it beautifully and Matthew came back for the final Saturday.

JC: That piece and their story touched me deeply. It took a long time for Derek Black to turn into a white supremacist, so it wasn't going to be a short process to bring him away from it.

TD: Yes. If you think about exposure to diversity, there are many places in this country, and all over the country, where people don't have enough exposure to diversity, so they don't even understand about other people.

GC: If you take off our skin, we're exactly the same. We have the same blood, the same organs, the same muscle. And that's what art does. If you look at a great piece of art, it doesn't have anything to do with your color. It has everything to do with how your brain is wired, how you react to something. There are certain notes in a certain order that will always elicit the same responses, and the same thing is true with words.

The thing that I loved and was very proud of about our evening was that a lovely young man walked out onstage, nobody knew who he was, and it turned out to be Eli Nash. Or Matthew Stevenson comes on, you knew he was Jewish because he had a yarmulke on, but nobody knew who he was. But people might have seen him with that yarmulke and come to an immediate judgment of who he was, never knowing what he'd accomplished. And that element of introducing not only people's stories but who those people are themselves was extremely important to the presentation of this piece.

JC: And for you, Ted?

TN: The one that's the most meaningful to me because it's deeply personal is the "Dear Dad Response" and of course, "Dear Dad Letter." That's very important to me because it's about my son, Eli, and his talking about transitioning and my response to that.

I wanted to create music that was simple, like a child growing. At the very beginning of the piece, it's like a nursery rhyme, just a simple little melody.

Then each time it's played, another layer, another depth is added, and the work becomes more and more complex, just as we do as we grow up. There's so much growth and transformation involved with the complexity of being a baby, then being a child, and then being an adult, as is the case with my son Eli being born a girl and becoming a man. "Dear Dad Response" is my response to "Dear Dad Letter" his telling me about his experience with his transition. Once he made this commitment, he felt more comfortable with himself. He became more open, more loving, and more affectionate. There's a lot of optimism in this piece and it reflects that.

Roger Corman

(b. 1926)

Academy Award winning director and producer of independent films whose works include the original *The Little Shop of Horrors*.

Interviewed in 2020

Roger Corman has been called "The Pope of Pop Cinema" and is celebrated as a trailblazer in the world of independent film. He is known for his cycle of low-budget cult films adapted from the tales of Edgar Allan Poe along with many other horror classics, including *The Little Shop of Horrors* and *The Man with the X-Ray Eyes*.

In Hollywood, Corman is equally celebrated for mentoring and giving a start to many young directors and actors, from Francis Ford Coppola, Ron Howard, and Martin Scorsese to William Shatner, Bruce Dern, and Jack Nicholson. In 1964 Corman became the youngest filmmaker to have a retrospective at the Cinémathèque Française as well as exhibitions at the British Film Institute and the Museum of Modern Art. In 2009 he was awarded an Honorary Academy Award for what was described as "his rich engendering of films and filmmakers."

I met Roger Corman years ago—I had played a recital in the home of a mutual friend and met Roger during the social period afterwards. I was immediately struck by his focus, enthusiasm, and complete engagement in the moment. Our conversation ranged from music and psychology to horror films and children's books. When friends found out I was going to interview Roger, the comment I heard most often was something like, "I thought you were cool before, but getting Roger Corman puts you on a whole other level." People love Roger.

Roger and I recorded our conversation in his office in Los Angeles March 4th, seven days before COVID-19 shut down the world, a lucky bit of scheduling on our part. We discussed a movie he's been working on, various trips he had scheduled before the pandemic struck, and finally jumped into recording. At ninety-four—at the time of this interview—Roger was as energetic and motivated as ever and just as busy. He's an inspiration on every level.

JC: *Roger, I have to say right away that I'm very excited to find out that originally, the main character in* The Man with the X-Ray Eyes *was going to be a jazz musician. There are jazz musicians out there hearing this right now, myself included, who are unhappy that you didn't stick with this premise.*

RC: Well, what happened was, I came up with the idea of a picture about somebody who had X-ray eyes, and generally, on my films, I write a brief outline of the story and then work with a screenwriter from there on. I thought of different ways to do it, and the obvious one was a scientist who's doing some sort of visual research. And I thought, *That's too easy. I really need something more interesting, more offbeat.*

JC: *Of course, that's jazz.*

RC: Jazz, mainly for the reason that I've always been a fan of jazz. I did at one time go to various jazz clubs, and I was aware that there was a certain amount of drugs floating around with jazz musicians. So I thought the character should be a jazz musician who's taken too many drugs which have an effect on his brain and his eyes, and he can now see through things. I started writing the story, and I was halfway through it when I thought, "You know, I really don't like this story. It's too weird." And I finally thought, "I'm going to go back to the original idea, simply a scientist who's doing research, visual research."

JC: You mentioned that you used to go hear a lot of jazz. When you were making some of your films, the jazz scene was huge in Los Angeles. Talk about some of the clubs that you went to and going out and hearing jazz.

RC: Hollywood was the center of entertainment and there were a number of jazz clubs around there, plus others in different parts of the city, but generally, you went to Hollywood to hear jazz.

JC: You have such great jazz in so many of your films. Talk about Machine-Gun Kelly. *That movie had a wonderful jazz soundtrack.*

RC: I've always felt that the music should reflect the time of the picture, so for *Machine-Gun Kelly* I did a little bit of research and found that Jimmie Lunceford's band was one of the biggest pop bands in the country at that time. My composer was Gerald Fried, who's gone on to be a major composer and worked on *Mission Impossible* and *Star Trek*. I told Gerald that I wanted a jazz score in the style of Jimmie Lunceford, an original score with some of the stylistic elements of the Jimmie Lunceford Band, which would bring the mood back to the period.

JC: Something that strikes me too with your films, is that jazz works so well because there's a drive in it that suits the tension you build cinematically. Even with your horror films, where people think of those as moving forward slowly, like, "Oh, my! What's creeping up? It's dark, there's something in that closet." But there's still a drive and tension that I think makes jazz work very well. Am I imagining this?

RC: No, you're not. I was trying to build tension in the horror films, as you say, with "something in the closet." It would be somebody walking down a hallway and what I was looking for was a tension between the person going to the closet and finding out what the secret is, and at the same time the person thinking, "I gotta get out of here." It's the idea of putting those two things together by using the jazz or other types of music to start a little slow but then build higher and higher and higher until you hit with the climax when the door to the closet is open.

JC: Much has been written about your quick shooting schedules and low budgets. It occurred to me that certain kinds of constraints can be great inspiration for creativity. It's certainly the way it is for most jazz musicians. All the recordings I've done have had small budgets, and if we get it in the first take, that's the take we use. Much of what a jazz musician records can be improvised, so we don't want to run through the song too many times because we'll lose the original freshness. I wondered if there's an equivalent to your movie making process. At this point you could go out and get a bigger budget if you wanted, but I suspect that there's something about this way of filmmaking that you love and are inspired by.

RC: You're right. The earliest pictures I did generally had ten-day schedules. You mentioned *The Wasp Woman* and *Machine-Gun Kelly*. Those were both ten-day schedules with budgets of about $60,000 or $70,000. You were moving fast on the set, and there was an energy building up within the crew and cast because we knew we had to move fast, and I think that lent something to the picture itself.

JC: I would think it would. And you know you have to be on your mark. I've always thought of you as the watercolorist of filmmakers because a watercolorist grabs opportunities and develops from there. It's fast or you miss your moment.

And Roger, you know we have many connections, but here's another: Fred Katz! The only jazz class I took in college was a jazz appreciation class at Cal State Fullerton, and Fred Katz was the professor.

Talk about Fred's score for The Little Shop of Horrors. *And talk about a short shoot! This was the shortest. The whole film is obviously so original, fresh, crazy, and hilarious.*

RC: Well, what happened was, I had an office at a rental studio in Hollywood, an independent studio, and I was having lunch with the studio manager, and he mentioned that they built a fairly good office type of set and nobody was coming in to the studio and it was just sitting there, so I said, "Well, if I can move very fast before somebody comes in and rents the set or it's torn down for another picture, I'd like to play around and gamble with something I built here around this set."

I made a deal with him to take the set for a week. I rebuilt the set slightly to become the flower shop. We rehearsed the actors for three days—Monday, Tuesday, and Wednesday—then we shot the picture in two days, Thursday and Friday, plus a little night shooting. The whole *Little Shop of Horrors* was conceived as just sort of a joke, just fooling around with what we could do with a small amount of money. It was supposed to be a comedy horror film, and it did very well. And I think the actors were laughing and improvising a little bit but staying very close to the script because you couldn't make too many experimental jumps. And shooting on a two-day schedule. I remember we started shooting at 8 a.m. on Thursday morning and at 8:30 p.m. the production manager said, "We are hopelessly behind schedule." [Laughs]

JC: There are things I caught this time that I didn't catch the first time I saw it, little inside jokes and puns. And as I was watching this film, I was thinking of the challenge of making something funny that's also scary, because it is scary! Every time that guy gets next to that crazy plant, I'm afraid his finger is going to be chopped off. Seymour keeps giving blood from his hand to it, and all that tension is built, but at the same time it's ridiculous and funny. How do you do that?

RC: It was difficult to carry out the original conception, but the three days of rehearsal enabled us to work together with the cast to develop when we knew we wanted the horror moments, when we knew we wanted the laughter, what the timing was and where we'd build up the tension. Also, it started with the idea that there is a connection between laughter and horror. With horror you start by building up a sense of suspense and with laughter, the beginning of the humor, and then with both, you build and build and build, and then wham, you hit with the horror and then the scream of the audience or you hit with the actual punch line itself and you get the same reaction, but it's laughter.

JC: I'm fascinated with that juxtaposition of joy and horror. They always talk about that in writing and especially with certain novelists, who are so good at illustrating the tragedy and comedy of life. Right when the worst thing happens, something silly follows, which happens all the time. Speak to that.

RC: Well, to a certain extent, children's books or children's tales involved horror, in other words, most fairy tales, like *Little Red Riding Hood…*

JC: Is horrific!

RC: Exactly! These stories build up to a sense of horror, and I think it has to do with helping little kids deal with the world around them. They're beginning to realize that when they were three years old everything was all fun and games, but now they're beginning to realize there is more to the world. I think the fairy tales unconsciously were designed to prepare little children for the complexities, and to a certain extent, the horror that they're going to face as they grow older.

JC: Bruno Bettelheim talks about this.

RC: Yes!

JC: He wrote that fascinating book, The Uses of Enchantment: The Meaning and Importance of Fairy Tales. *It discusses how you connect with different fairy tales at different times in your life, then see them very differently, depending on where you are in your age and development.*

You also famously have a great nose for talent. You've launched the careers of loads of people who have gone on to tremendous success. I'm curious what these people have in common. It's not just talent.

RC: Well, there's a number of different things. I've probably been more extensively involved with young directors but also with some young actors. The directors were people like Francis Coppola, Martin Scorsese, Ron

Howard, and Jonathan Demme. The first two actors who started with me were Charlie Bronson in *Machine-Gun Kelly* and Jack Nicholson in a whole number of pictures we did together. He once commented, "You're almost the only guy who's hiring me." And I said, "That's because they don't know, but eventually they *will* know."

JC: What did you recognize in Jack?

RC: Jack had a great ability to play a dramatic scene and bring the full drama out of it but give it an edge that very often brought a little bit of humor with the drama. It was a unique quality he had and still has.

JC: Sometimes, if it's about playing somebody who's evil or frightening, it's even scarier if there's that little bit of humor. It's like, "Wait a minute, are they laughing and they're about to cut my throat?"

RC: Yes. There are many examples of this, but one example of somebody who was maybe known a little bit but not much was Richard Widmark. And in one scene, he plays a maniac killer, and he pushes an old lady in a wheelchair down the stairs and he laughs.

JC: Wasn't that his mother?

RC: Yes. And it made him a star. Everybody remembers that scene, and immediately he jumped to star status.

JC: That was just an incredible scene, because you knew he just didn't care. He not only didn't care, he was laughing as he pushed her! Which is really frightening.

There must have been something that all of these people had in common beyond talent. Was it focus? Was it hard work? Was it all of those things?

RC: All of the above. For instance, Bob De Niro was the most thoroughly prepared actor I've ever worked with. His first film was a picture called

Bloody Mama. It was a story of the Ma Barker gang, a woman who ran a farm during the Depression. She lost it because she couldn't pay the mortgage, so she and her sons roam through the South robbing banks. I thought we were shooting in Arkansas, so De Niro went to Arkansas on his own, a week before shooting, just to hang around bars and talk to people to get a feeling of the way they spoke. And I've talked to people who worked with him later on in his career and they say, "He's still that way. He puts immense preparation into the role."

JC: I think many people, especially pretty people, think, "Oh, I can act." But you're talking about the hard work of it, the focus. I'm thinking of the people that I know you've influenced and helped early in their careers and they all seem extremely intelligent. They weren't just people reading lines

RC: I agree. With actors—and even more so with directors, writers, and so forth—I think you have to have a certain level of intelligence to really read the script, to understand the character in the script and how that character can be portrayed.

JC: And the capacity for empathy and looking at life through the character's eyes. What do you feel you've given to these people? What would you like to think that these people learned from you when they were working with you?

RC: Well, first I would say they would have been successful if they had never met me because they had the ability. They were good to start with, and then I did help them to a certain extent—probably more the directors than the actors—because directing is what I did, writing and directing too.

I have taught certain things, particularly with the directors. The directors knew before they did their first picture that they were going to spend a morning with me, and we were going to have "the talk." It almost became a joke. Before he directed his first picture, *Grand Theft Auto,* Ron Howard came in with a notebook and said, "All right, I've heard about the talk. I wanna take notes as you talk."

JC: I had always thought that most directors were inspired by a story, but I see you being inspired by all kinds of things, whether it's a title, a location, or the most recent thing you and I discussed about an island you saw after a hurricane. Is that common for lots of directors?

RC: I think it is. Essentially, I get inspiration from the world, from the things going on all around.

JC: I'm fascinated by people who start in different directions in their careers and wind up somewhere else. Your degree is in engineering. You seem to have always been very clear on how you wanted to put your projects together. I'm wondering if you think that your engineering study contributed to the way you approach putting these projects together or if that was already your personality.

RC: I think it was really within my personality, but I also think the engineering did help, particularly when we were shooting very rapidly, because one thing I emphasized to young directors is the importance of pre-production planning. If, as with most of my early pictures, I had a ten-day schedule, I didn't want to go on to the set not fully prepared and waste part of the ten days trying to figure out where the camera goes.

So I put heavy emphasis on pre-production planning, particularly writing out and sketching your shots, knowing that you're never going to follow your sketches a hundred percent. You'll follow maybe eighty or ninety percent because something you planned doesn't work. Or you get a better idea while shooting and you use that. But if you've got everything sketched out you have the skeleton in place, so you don't have to waste time. The worst thing a director can do . . . Well, come to think of it, there are many bad things a director can do.

[Laughter]

RC: But one of the worst is to come on to the set and say, "Where am I going to put the camera?" You should have figured that out in advance. I mentioned Ron Howard earlier. Ron, of course, had been an actor before he became a director, and I told him, "You have to know your plan and come onto the set the first day and say, 'The camera goes there, and this is what's going to happen.'" Two things take place. One, you get off to an efficient start, and second, the crew knows that you've—as we used to say—done your homework. I remember on Ron's *Grand Theft Auto*, it took place in a house we had rented in Brentwood and a woman who played his mother on the TV show was in the first shot and I was wondering what Ron would do.

He came in very cool, and he said, "We're working. The camera will be on the dolly with a 30 lens. We start at this point. We follow the actress dollying and panning with her as she goes. She sits down and she picks up the telephone and we cut to a close-up at that time. I'm gonna get some coffee; let me know when you're ready." And I thought two things. Ron absorbed totally what I had said, but also, as an actor, he was able to play the role of a director knowing what he was doing.

JC: Tomorrow I'm going to be teaching a class on listening skills at California State University San Marcos and talk about jazz musicians as great listeners. I've had many actors tell me that they think of acting as reacting and that takes engaged listening. You're a great listener. Speak to that a little bit because I think this is a great time to encourage everyone to listen better.

RC: Well, good acting is partially, as you say, "reacting." So you're listening to the other person and you're in the scene, and you're interacting with the other actor and what he is saying inspires you to say your lines. As you say, I've been a small-time actor, generally. Almost always, I've done my acting with directors who started with me and they hire me back for a couple of days just for the fun.

JC: As well they should.

RC: I was playing a scene in *Philadelphia*, directed by Jonathan Demme, who started with me. I'm on a witness stand and I'm representing for a law firm that's been accused of something, and the head of the law firm is Jason Robards. We played the scene. It was fine. And then Jonathan came up to me and said, "In the midst of it, just take a quick move with your eyes and look to Jason as if you want encouragement that you're saying what he wants you to say."

Now the lawyer on the other side was Denzel Washington. He was not aware of what Jonathan had said to me, but I was speaking to him in the scene and I glance at Jason, as Jonathan had instructed. Jonathan said, "Cut! Now we'll pull the reverse. Now we'll be on Denzel Washington." And when Denzel spoke his lines, I was saying my lines off screen. When I came to that point, he looked to Jason Robards. He had noticed this quick look of my eyes and integrated it into his own performance. So he looked to Jason also.

JC: Talk about being engaged! That's acting, listening and paying attention on the highest level.

Blythe
Danner

(b. 1943)

A multiple Tony and Emmy Award-winning
film, stage, and television actress.

Interviewed in 2002

I had been a fan of Blythe Danner for years and became an even bigger one
after spending time with her. When I mention to friends that I had her on
the show, both men *and* women enthusiastically say they love her.

Blythe is unusually lacking in the typical movie star vanity. She
walked into the NPR studios in Manhattan for our initial conversation
makeup-free due to a stye in her eye that she didn't want to irritate. Even
so, when my publicist asked to get a picture of the two of us, Blythe happily
agreed. "I'm not looking my best, but sure, O.K." I can't imagine anyone
else in the public eye giving that response.

Blythe's jazz connection came to me when a friend called and said,
"Turn on Channel 4! Gwyneth Paltrow is being interviewed and just said
her mom (Blythe) used to hang out with Bill Evans! Did you know Blythe
Danner is a jazz fan?" I hadn't known, but with further research, discovered
she'd sung in a jazz band in college with Chevy Chase as her drummer. The
pursuit was on.

Blythe has appeared twice on *Jazz Inspired*, once in the studio and
nine years later, when we taped on stage as part of the Tanglewood Music
Festival in Lenox, Massachusetts. Fans of Blythe's stage work associate her
with the music of Stephen Sondheim, notably her starring role in a 2001

Broadway revival of his musical *Follies*, but at Tanglewood, she delighted the crowd by singing a Dave Frishberg tune and delighted *me* by joining me in a duet.

After twenty years of interviews, I've noticed that my most knowledgeable guests are also the least likely to pontificate. Blythe frequently asked my opinion on the musicians we discussed and called the next day to make sure her thoughts on Bill Evans were well expressed. She wanted to exchange ideas rather than show off her great knowledge of jazz.

JC: Everyone knows you as a great actress, but they may not know you as a jazz singer

BD: Well, probably only the people who heard me in 1965 at the Baggy Knees, a nightclub in Vermont. It was the only professional gig I ever had. At Bard College, I sang a lot. And once I sang at a little club off of Gramercy Park which I'm sure isn't there anymore.

JC: And you had an illustrious band at Bard.

BD: Oh, yes. We had a great jazz flutist and Kenny Shapiro on piano—who actually taught me how to sing jazz—and Chevy Chase on drums.

JC: Did you think you'd go on to have a professional career as a jazz singer?

BD: I think it was my dream, way down deep somewhere. I was planning on being a nurse, but I hated the sight of blood. So that was nipped in the bud. I spent a year in Berlin as an exchange student, but right before I left, I fell in love with Boch and Harnick's *She Loves Me*, Sondheim, and *West Side Story*, which changed my life because then I knew I wanted to do that. So I always thought if I went anywhere, it would be to musical comedy. After Bard I had a burning desire to sing jazz, but the idea of being alone and sort of isolated at the microphone terrified me. I just didn't have the confidence.

JC: With acting, you don't feel alone because you're acting with someone else?

BD: Exactly. It's like, when they ask me if I'm interested in doing a one-woman show, I always say, absolutely not! I want to look in somebody's eyes. To me, acting is *reacting*. I like to inhabit and hide behind a character. Anything where you stick out like a sore thumb, I'm pretty uncomfortable doing.

JC: That's interesting, because a lot of singers I know think of themselves as a character when they're singing, but you still want to be working with another person.

BD: I think had I pursued jazz I would have found that too. You do inhabit the character, or certainly the song. But at that time, when I was young, I was afraid of doing that.

JC: Did your love of jazz and singing jazz influence you when you were studying acting in college? Did that have a big influence on how you approached roles and characters?

BD: I never would have thought that at the time, and I wouldn't have thought of it for many, many years. But I did a Pinter play, *Betrayal,* on Broadway in 1980. I'd graduated from college fifteen years before that. And it was while I was doing *Betrayal* that I realized that what you're saying is true. The director, Peter Hall, said to me, "You're giving a very jazz performance." I thought, what the heck does he mean?

But I realized that I'd always been working that way. And yes, the jazz probably informed that. Night after night, doing the same play, you are quick to look for something new, as a musician improvises a song to change and keep it fresh. I think most actors work this way, but not consciously.

And particularly with Pinter. With music, you have the clear parameters of the song to start with, but with Pinter, it's the pauses and the silences that are those very strong parameters. And then, as you do in jazz, you have the structure of the melody, which is the jumping-off point into kind of a free-fall. And you don't have lots of long speeches with Pinter. So much is informed by the pauses and the silences, and you can interpret those both physically and vocally. You're unconsciously doing that, but it gives you lots of freedom.

I had the great pleasure of working with Raul Julia and Roy Scheider in this production. Raul and I had so many love scenes and so many sexual, sensual scenes. So we just played with it every night. It was like throwing a ball. I'd throw the ball to him, and then all of a sudden, he'd catch it completely differently and throw it back. Meaning that the words would just, perhaps, *quicken*. Or he'd take another pause. Well, in Pinter, you can't take *another* pause, really, but within your line, you can do whatever you want, basically. Maybe the silence would be longer. It just gave us so much to play with. It was so exciting. And then you'd go off on sort of a riff. It was just wonderful.

JC: I always think of Harold Pinter as the Thelonius Monk of playwrights. And how you describe Pinter reinforces that thought. No matter who plays Monk, it's still immediately recognizable as Monk, and I think it's the same with Harold Pinter.

BD: And when you hear Thelonius Monk, probably more than any one pianist, you know immediately who it is.

JC: Perhaps if you'd started out as a jazz instrumentalist, you might have kept playing jazz because it's all about that interaction with the other musicians, unless you're a soloist. As you describe what you did with Raul Julia, it sounds like two musicians jamming.

BD: That's what it feels like. As I said, I didn't really discover it until then because I hadn't been conscious of that. And I was singing jazz all through college, so I'm sure that informed my acting.

JC: Do you listen to jazz when you're working on a character?

BD: Well, I listen to jazz as matter of my daily sustenance, basically. I love classical music too, so I listen to a lot of that. So, yes, depending on the character and depending on the play. I haven't really thought about that, but it is funny, when you're working on a role how you gravitate towards certain music. And such different music.

I was doing Tennessee Williams' *Streetcar Named Desire,* and every night before I went on, I would always listen to Joe Williams, specifically '63 at Newport, because it was so out there.

You might think I'd listen to New Orleans jazz. For me, it doesn't have so much to do with the time and place of where the character lived; it has to do with the inner *spirit* of that character. Nico Psacharopoulos, our brilliant Greek director who ran Williamstown for years, always said, she's a fighter, strong, don't play her like a little disintegrating, crumbling flower, which a lot of times she is so interpreted. So Joe Williams somehow got that fight going for me every night.

JC: *This is part of your process.*

BD: Yes. I do this for almost every play. Just having done *Follies,* before I'd go on, I'd listen to someone like Mark Murphy. And, well, Bill Evans is my secret, great love. I mean, all of our group was highly enamored of Bill.

JC: *What is it about Bill's playing that speaks to you so deeply?*

BD: He was trained to play classical music—Chopin, Ravel—so he had a great classical sense underneath, but he just had so much pain and beauty, just so deep.

I first heard him in Montreal. I went with a girlfriend who lived up there. I said, oh, my God, Bill Evans is in town! We have to go, because Kenny Shapiro, who had played piano with me in college, would always talk about Bill and we'd listen to him a lot. To hear him live, I just sat there and wept.

And his manager came over and said, "You really dig Bill. Would you like to meet him?" So I did meet him that night and started a friendship. We'd go to hear him at the Vanguard. He just goes deeper than anybody else I've heard. He always had his head way down by the keys, and I'd ask him about it, and he'd say, "I hear things I can't hear when I'm sitting up straight.

He was very bright and very articulate. There was just a sadness about him. I didn't know him well enough to ever ask him about that, but I had an affinity for him and for his essence, and that came across so strongly in his music.

JC: That's how I feel about your acting. I remember my first time seeing you and having an immediate emotional connection the same way you speak of this with Bill. I think a lot of people, in any art form, are afraid to go to that place. And that's what I'm struck with with your work and with Bill Evans.

BD: That's the highest compliment you could give me!

JC: Musicians always mention Bill's beautiful voicings. But I've always been struck by his direct connection to the heart, which for me, you have too. And that little bit of sadness.

BD: Even in my comedy?

JC: Yes, which makes it especially interesting to me. Were your parents musical?

BD: I grew up in a very musical household. My father was a banker. He was actually known as "The Singing Banker" in Philadelphia. He did a lot of oratorio work. He was singing outside once in Philadelphia, and he was hitting a high C or something, and a fly flew into his mouth!

JC: [Gasps] Is that true?

BD: It's true. And he had to decide whether to spit it out or swallow it, and he swallowed it and continued.

JC: Now, *there's* a trooper!

BD: [Laughs] I grew up with a lot of oratorio work and a lot of religious music and lots of Oscar Hammerstein and things like that. My parents weren't at all into jazz. I was going to George School, a Quaker School in Bucks County, Pennsylvania, and the wonderful man who headed the music department played us some jazz and talked about Dave Brubeck. Dave came up to the Lambertville Music Circus, and I went over to hear him and really got into it. I actually started singing a little jazz then because the pianist at a little jazz club in New Hope asked me to come by. That was my first jazz singing.

JC: *Again, thinking about character and emotion. You grew up listening to classical and jazz music, something that comes from a complex emotional base, which had to inform how you viewed the world and ultimately how you viewed characters and what you brought to them. I think about young actors who have grown up with pop music, which is not very complex emotionally.*

BD: It's interesting you should say that because some of the kids I worked with recently have surprised me by being into jazz. I don't know how common this is, but I do know a number of interesting kids who love jazz, who are interesting actors.

JC: *Someone who is drawn to acting—as opposed being drawn to being a movie star—would be somebody who is, by definition, interested in an emotional life and character. So, I would think they would be drawn to music that is more complex.*

Do you feel that you're more confident now about your jazz singing than you were when you were a college student? Could you ever see yourself singing jazz somewhere?

BD: Well, over the years, I've sung a little bit at the Williamstown Cabaret. I also really love Sheila Jordan. And I would be so blatant as to go and copy some of her stuff. She did "Falling in Love with Love" and goes off on a couple of great choruses. I actually had the nerve to copy her for a Williamstown Cabaret, and her daughter walked up to me afterwards and said, "My mom is Sheila Jordan." I should have given her credit!

JC: *Hilarious! What are the chances? But did you enjoy yourself? You didn't feel so alone?*

BD: I loved it. I think being older, after all these years of performing, you've got to let that old stuff go. But I think people who really do it have a whole wonderful act going, and I don't think I'd enjoy that part of it.

I've been asked to do a talk show and I always say, "Never!" It's very different from acting. Just because you act, people think you're very open and not shy.

JC: *I completely understand. You're thinking about character. And you're spending your time on that, not sitting there chatting it up.*

BD: Where can you hide?

JC: *That's why we love radio.*

BD: We *love* radio! No makeup!

JC: *Exactly! Why do you think there haven't been more movies about great jazz musicians? Why isn't there a great movie about Bill Evans?*

BD: I think you and I know about Bill, but the average man on the street doesn't.

JC: *The average person didn't know who John Nash was and they made* A Beautiful Mind. *Do you think it's hard to capture that kind of artistic essence in a movie? The jazz musician or painter is often portrayed in a clichéd manner.*

BD: Suffering drug addict?

JC: *Yes.*

BD: It's hard to portray the complicated story of an artist, a jazz musician, because it's so multi-layered and internal. As Americans, we don't have that much patience with that kind of process. If we did, jazz would be much more popular. *'Round Midnight* was a wonderful movie, though, so they managed it there.

JC: Talk about appearing in Follies.

BD: To me, Sondheim was so attractive. I wanted to play the role in *Follies* so much because my introduction to the theater—besides Chekhov and *The Seagull*—was going to *West Side Story* as a young girl and just being completely blown away by that.

In our production that we did last year, I was sorry that more people didn't understand what the director was getting at because I thought it was a profoundly beautiful production. I didn't agree—and most of the people I respect didn't agree—with a lot of the reviews that wanted it to be more razzle dazzle.

Sondheim isn't a bit afraid to go way down deep and plumb the depths of human feelings without any sentimentality. People, when they go to the musical theater, are for the most part hoping they'll experience more sentimentality. I think they're afraid when they see how Sondheim really pierces the heart. I think people don't want to see that. Other productions of this musical haven't gone there. They haven't had the courage to go there. I was disappointed that that wasn't perceived in a deep way, and I was very disappointed in most of the critics. People I really respect were just knocked out by it. People who came back from the original production, which was in 1971, said, "You got it right. We didn't know that you had to go there. That very, very, deep, dark place."

The audiences responded incredibly. Unfortunately, the show wasn't supported well by most critics. But it was one of the most fulfilling things I've ever done, and again, it felt like jazz some nights. Judy Ivy said it once, that you don't even need the dialogue. His lyrics are so strong and so beautiful, you can have the whole piece just with his music.

JC: I feel this is the same thing that you were saying about Bill Evans. Sondheim goes to that place where so few are willing to go. I loved it, as you know. The audience the night I saw it just went crazy.

BD: Stephen Sondheim *wrote* from that place but had never had a production go there so completely.

JC: I know you're a Dave Frishberg fan and also love Blossom Dearie.

BD: There is an intimacy in both of them. They both tell a story and are very exposed. And they're both so funny. But there's always that little jabbing pain underneath, which makes them so fascinating.

I was asked to go on *The Tonight Show* years ago to promote something I'd done, and I said I'd do it if I could sing. All of a sudden, I got very courageous. I met Frishberg through a friend, and he actually came to my house to rehearse. He was going to accompany me doing "Peel Me a Grape." And then they said they didn't want me to sing, even though they hadn't heard me, so we never did it. But I don't know where that came from. I guess since Dave said he'd play with me I got this burst of courage.

JC: I'm starting a movement to have Dave Frishberg accompany you and for you to sing on The Tonight Show!

BD: Now that's really weird because this is completely the opposite of what I said to you before. Here I'd be using *singing* as a crutch.

JC: I think you should do this!

BD: No, I'll stick with how I've been doing it. Very minimal. Leave them asking for more, right?

E.L.
Doctorow

(1931–2015)

Internationally acclaimed novelist whose books include *Welcome to Hard Times, The Book of Daniel, Ragtime,* and *Billy Bathgate.* His books have been published in thirty languages, and many have been made into movies, among them *Ragtime,* which also became a Tony-winning Broadway musical.

Interviewed in 2000

E.L. Doctorow and I met on a tennis court in Sag Harbor in the mid-1990s and became a doubles team for a while—he the tall terror at the net and me the whirling dervish covering the rest of the court. One of my great thrills was occasionally being included in his longtime weekly men's doubles game with the late writer Peter Matthiessen and one of several other celebrated writers, playing on Peter's court in nearby Sagaponack, another gorgeous Hamptons village. These men were great players but much older than I, so I was included not for my riveting repartee (they provided plenty) but for my spry legs and forehand crosscourt.

I'd just moved to the Hamptons full-time and knew very few people, so this was a heady introduction to it all. Doctorow was an early supporter of my idea for *Jazz Inspired* and generously agreed to be in my initial group of thirteen interviewees. Once the show took off and I was looking for other guests, he was also the person who said, "Judy, have you noticed that all you have on your show are old, white guys?"

"All I know are old, white guys," I replied.

"Branch out."

I spoke with E.L. Doctorow in 2000, shortly after the publication of his novel *City of God* in his home in Sag Harbor. He said he'd only do the interview if I could tell him the jazz connection in *City of God*. I plowed ahead, read the book, and called him with my theory. My interpretation, although different from his and not what he expected, was one he liked even better, so he agreed to our conversation.

JC: From what you've told me, music has been a part of your life forever.

ED: I grew up in a very musical household. My mother was a fine pianist. As a girl, she paid for her music lessons by playing the piano for silent movies. Her father and brothers would sit in the row behind her and make sure no one bothered her. She'd look at the screen and rattle off Schubert or Chopin, depending on what was playing on the screen, improvising as she went.

My father was not a musician, but he was something of a musicologist. He owned a record shop during the '30s and into the '40s on Sixth Avenue between 43rd and 44th Street, in the old Hippodrome building. He sold records—78 RPMs in those days—along with sheet music, musical instruments, and then radios. We'd wander around that store after it closed on a Saturday evening and toot on the saxophones and bang on the drums. We were very proud of him because he was so knowledgeable, and he had stock that no one else in the city had. Not a few of the great artists of the day—Arturo Toscanini, Vladimir Horowitz, Arthur Rubenstein—patronized his shop and bought records from him.

There were always records in the house because music was such a part of the family life. At the age of sixteen, my older brother Don formed a little band, and they used to rehearse in the front parlor. They got themselves a job at a Borscht Belt hotel up in the Catskills by lying about their age. Since my brother's name was Don and his fellow band organizer was named Irwin, they called themselves Don Irwin and His Musical Cavaliers. I, unfortunately, was a very unsuccessful piano student. Usually, people were quite relieved when I finished my practice.

JC: Was your mom your piano teacher?

ED: No, I studied at a place called the Bronx House on Washington Avenue in the East Bronx. My saintly teacher was a woman named Lisa Elman, the sister of the famous violinist Mischa Elman. While Mischa Elman went around the world concertizing, poor Lisa had to deal with wretched little students like me. Anyway, to everyone's relief, I gave it up after five or six years.

This was during the Depression when nobody had any money and my father barely kept the store going. But there were always a lot of books in the house and a lot of music. It was what we would call now an enriched childhood. Because of my father's knowledge and his love of all kinds of music, we had this richness around us. He would bring home not only records of great opera performances but jazz records as well. I remember in particular one album that excited me terribly. It was an album of boogie-woogie with people like Jelly Roll Morton, Meade Lux Lewis, and Albert Ammons.

I remember putting these records on, and already being something of an aspiring writer, I would imagine this music as introducing some radio drama that I was about to write. In those days, radio always had musical introductions or musical interludes to allow for transition between scenes. Whenever I was excited by music, I always thought of it as the possible beginning of some radio show.

JC: But you never pursued it?

ED: No, I would wait for the idea to come, but it was never as exciting as the music was, so I would just go out and play ball.

My father brought home a large 78—or maybe it was an LP—of the original Benny Goodman Carnegie Hall performance of *Sing, Sing, Sing,* which was very ambitious and symphonic in its scope. We would listen to that over and over.

We listened to jazz and swing along with everything else. I was also listening to Bartok and Shostakovich. I was listening to Prokofiev. I was listening to Aaron Copland. It was all the same. It was all one fluid response to exciting, great music. It was an amazing thing for a kid to be exposed to all this.

JC: How old were you when you appreciated how great it was to have this kind of upbringing?

ED: I was probably between twelve and sixteen. I had some friends who were serious piano students, and I'd go away to summer camp and see them stop what they were doing so they could practice. It was kind of a shaming experience for me because I had given up the piano. On the other hand, I did very well in the annual Gilbert and Sullivan operetta at the end of the camp season.

JC: I'm fascinated that you didn't suffer from what so many kids do when their parents love a certain kind of music and encourage them to listen to it. Often the kids hate their parents' music, but it sounds like you were thrilled with what your father liked.

ED: I was very lucky that way. They were educated and enlightened parents. Then, of course, there are certain cultural conditions to consider. World War II started when I was about ten years old. My brother Don was eight years older than I and went off into the Army. We were all very conscious of the role musicians played in providing moral support for the troops overseas. We heard stories of orchestras like Glenn Miller's going all over to support the troops.

In those days recordings of Black musicians were known as "race records," and my dad valued them and had a wide stock of them. He also had collections of folk music that had been recorded by Alan Lomax and his father.

A few years ago, when I was at the Century Association, the club in New York City, I was approached by John Hammond and he said, "Your name is Doctorow, isn't it? Are you any relation to *Dave* Doctorow?" "Yes, he was my father." "Let me tell you a story," he said. "When I was a young man and didn't have a dime, I used to go to your father's shop and sit in the listening booth and listen to these records and be desperate to take them home. And I would confess to him that I didn't have any money, and he'd say, 'Take the records anyway; you'll pay me when you can.' That was your father, Dave." Imagine hearing that from John Hammond!

JC: Who would become one of the most important record producers of jazz and popular music, discovering Billie Holiday, Benny Goodman, Basie, Bob Dylan, Bruce Springsteen, and on and on.

Your 2014 novel City of God *has lyrics from different tunes printed throughout the book. As a musician, it's impossible for me to read these lyrics without hearing the tunes in my head. But the way you juxtaposed them within the story, then interpreted them, was fascinating to me. It really made me look at the lyrics differently.*

ED: I'll tell you what interested me. I'd been listening to jazz for many years. The idea I had was, what if it were possible to do with words what a jazz quartet does with the music? They state the theme, and then each of the members of the quartet goes off and does the variation or the riff. And then they all come back together and play together a little bit and restate the theme. What if I could do that verbally? I would set the lyrics down as the equivalent of the original theme and then do four separate verbal riffs on the original theme. And that turned out to work in terms of this novel I was doing. I gave these interludes the heading "The Midrash Jazz Quartet," Midrash being the collection of interpretations in the Middle Ages provided by the rabbis for the more difficult or cryptic passages in that book of the Bible.

JC: It made me look at those lyrics as I never had before, since I've only heard them with music.

ED: Popular song lyrics are often very powerful. They're quite short. And in that brevity is some compaction of energy in some way. Some lyrics are quite mysterious. If you look at the original lyrics of "Me and My Shadow," they are very strange—this idea of a doppelgänger walking along the street with this shadow in this empty city. Or a song like "Dancing in the Dark," which is the basis in this book for these musicians to go off on these philosophical bents. I have the greatest regard for the lyrics of some of these standards. They're not quite poetry. They're something else. But it is a great, great art.

I learned a little bit about lyric writing as a result of working with the people who put together the musical version of my novel *Ragtime*. For all my love of music—jazz, popular, swing—I came to ragtime rather late. It was actually in the early '70s. I remember particularly listening to a very classical interpretation of Scott Joplin rags by a pianist named Joshua Rifkin.

Ragtime became a possible metaphor for the entire action of the book. And it meant things to me privately. That book, like all my books, I dig out of my brain. I just imagine the brain as a rag bin. And you pull out these little bits of cloth and sew them together and there's your book. But people said that the rhythms of the sentences and the flow of language in that book actually attempted to reproduce a ragtime piece. I don't quite believe it, although it's certainly flattering.

What I did do is divide that book into four parts, and a rag is in four parts. In the way it plays off personal lives against historical forces, you could make the claim, I suppose, that the historical forces are the basic stride or the inevitable irrepressible beat, and the attempt to escape history is the syncopated right hand.

JC: That's interesting.

ED: Well, it's interesting, but I don't know that it's accurate.

[Laughter]

JC: City of God *is like a jazz solo to me in that seemingly unrelated ideas are juxtaposed in such a way that makes all the ideas more powerful and propels the whole novel forward.*

ED: When you start writing a book, you want it to keep going; it has to generate itself after that first impetus that you get. And certainly, the references to music had that generative power, that evocative force that brought me to new words, new lines, new ideas. So that all worked nicely.

JC: *Novel writing is a solitary art form. What was it like being involved with* Ragtime *the musical and being part of a collaborative effort?*

ED: I came to appreciate all the kinds of talents and arts that go into that kind of group composition, sort of like people building a cathedral. It's really an amazement when any one musical works. There are so many disparate elements and probably one more element than can reasonably be handled.

At any rate, the lyricist in that show, Lynn Ahrens, was awfully good. First of all, Lynn had to have the skill of knowing where a song should go, which I suppose she decided with the composer, Steve Flaherty. Then the songs had to move the story along, which they did beautifully. In the third place, there's the wit and concision of those lyrics. And in the fourth place, as one of the singers told me, Lynn's lyrics are very easy to sing. She wrote words that were "singable." A great lyricist, in addition to all the other concerns, has to write a line that can be sung by a singer.

JC: *It had to be great to have people talking to you about your story, actually interacting with you. If you do a book tour, people are telling you that they love your book, of course, but most people reading your book aren't getting the opportunity to say to you, "Mr. Doctorow, I love your book," because they're off reading it alone. It's not like my playing music where people respond in real time.*

ED: That can be an advantage, actually.

[Laughter]

ED: One of the things I realized when I got involved in this production was the great advantage of writing novels. You don't have to be there when someone's reading your book. When you're doing a show, you're in the theater with people watching, and you know exactly how they're reacting. You get the good and the bad.

JC: *You don't always know what people are thinking from their reaction, though. But you do definitely know if people are applauding or they're not.*

ED: It's not always comfortable.

JC: *They're applauding you at home, Ed.*

ED: And we haven't talked about author's paranoia here.

JC: OK, *tell me about author's paranoia.*

ED: It works this way. You've published eight or ten books. Someone will come over and say, "Mr. Doctorow, my favorite book of yours is such and such." Then you think to yourself, what about the *other* ones? Do they mean *nothing* to this person? Or someone will make a hyperbolic remark and write, "Doctorow is one of the three best writers in America," and you think, who are the *other* two?

JC: *I thought you were going to say that people come up to you and say, "I really loved so and so," and it's not something you've written.*

ED: That has happened to me. Someone congratulated me for writing *Slaughterhouse Five,* which was written by Kurt Vonnegut. I accepted the congratulations. You can always tell when someone's read your book in talking to you about it and the degree of response there and sincerity. It's very easy. I'm sure, as a practicing professional musician, you can more or less tell the same thing.

JC: Yes. And people have complimented me for things I haven't done, and I too accept the compliment.

ED: People can be very funny. Someone will raise their hand in the audience after a reading and ask, "Mr. Doctorow, what was your purpose in writing this book?" Asking this sincere question. So, I say, "Well, my purpose was to *finish* writing this book."

JC: [Laughs] What role does music play in your novels?

ED: There's a lot of music in all the books. In *Billy Bathgate,* as Bo Weinberg is being taken by tugboat out to New York Harbor with his feet in a bucket of cement, where he's going to be deposited for whatever sins he's committed—at least in the mind of Dutch Schultz—and as he's waiting for death, he begins to sing *Bye Bye Blackbird.* And that was actually picked up for a while in the movie and then it wasn't used, which astonished me. I thought it would be immensely powerful to see Bruce Willis on this heaving tugboat deck in the black of night singing *Bye Bye Blackbird.* But it didn't happen.

JC: This will come as a shock to you, Ed, but sometimes in movies, they make the wrong decisions.

ED: That's what I've heard.

JC: On another subject, do you listen to music when you're writing?

ED: No. Writing a novel is really an insane undertaking. It's an act of extended concentration. And it's very wearying. You can't go at it halfway. I, for instance, always face a wall when I'm writing. I won't face a window. I'll arrange it so that the only way out is through the sentences.

When you write a novel, there are things that are very supportive. For instance, reading poetry. Reading a good poet is, I think, almost more useful to me than reading a novel during the year or two or three or four I might be working on a novel. I don't know why exactly. Nobody can top the poets. So, if you're reading Yeats or Robert Frost or contemporary poets, there's always a new understanding of what language can do. These are bright little bursts, almost little epiphanies, as you see the possibilities that can be derived from a line that mixes Anglo Saxon words with Latin-derived words. You study the poets, and you realize that they can describe things as nobody else.

JC: As musical as you are, I would think that music would distract you from your writing.

ED: It would. When you're not working, you can, of course, pick up on music. That's useful. Certainly, listening to the Scott Joplin rags was a profound encouragement to the creation of *Ragtime*.

The sources of whatever energies you have can be various. You can use something someone says on the street because novels are a big kitchen sink form. It includes everything, all the different vocabularies. A journalist can't tell you what someone is thinking; they can only cite their actions or quote their remarks. But the novelist can go right into someone's mind. A novelist uses everything, including legends, myths, history, confessions, mutterings of poor mad people in the street. It's all data. It all has equal status in the novelist's eyes. And certainly, music has been quite important to me.

JC: It must be exhausting. Does the music fill you back up?

ED: It gets rather selective. Just as you understand there are certain books or poets you can read who were important at a certain moment during your work—and you don't even know why—so there are very circumscribed sets of musical sources for you at any given time that inspire you. For instance, one day my wife played for me a recording of a brilliant Romanian pianist named Dinu Lipatti, who died very young several years ago. It was this Schubert thing that just got me down at the toes and just rose up to the top of my head. So I found myself listening to Dinu Lipatti consistently, regularly.

JC: I'm struck by a similarity to playing jazz that I thought about when you were talking about the actual process of writing a novel. A jazz musician is out there like a watercolorist, grabbing opportunities that happen and capitalizing on the moment. It's very fast. You have your ideas, and you have to put them out there, and you have to elaborate on them. With a novel, you're constantly polishing and adding layers, more like painting in oil.

ED: That's the key part of it. You do end up editing yourself. You don't do that immediately perhaps, but eventually you discover the premises of your book. And you have to deliver on those premises. That's where the editing comes in. That's when the polishing comes in. It's definitely not a performing art. It's not time-driven. Some books take years.

But there is something, I suppose, that is equivalent to the musician's improvisation. At the beginning of things, you're writing to find out what you're writing and unless you're open, as opposed to already knowing where you're going, it's not going to work. So, in that sense, while the jazz musician knows certain intervals or things that he can always drop in there, nevertheless there's a lot of total spontaneity and self-discovery in the performance of it. That's what's similar, and that's what is so exciting.

I was trying years ago to explain the process. I came up with an image that people seemed to like. Writing a novel is like driving a car at night. You can only see as far as your headlights extend, but you can make the whole trip that way.

JC: That's beautiful. Now I know you love horn players. Who are your favorites?

ED: You have to say first and foremost Louis Armstrong. If you listen to those early recordings now, they are irrepressible. There is such vitality in them and such musicianship, so much so that it makes me think—and I know it's controversial—that the earliest jazz might turn out to be historically the best jazz. Now I happen to very much like Lennie Tristano, for instance, and Thelonious Monk, somewhat. But the sheer joy of the music is quintessentially what we associate with Louis Armstrong and those early records of his.

It is possible, if you want to talk theory, that the great creation in any art form comes at the very beginning. For instance, Shakespeare wrote at the beginning period of what we think of as Elizabethan theater. There were a bunch of guys who suddenly wrote this way. And he was the best. And it was gone. It was all over. And it may be true that the true genius of jazz— I'm not talking about the greatness of individual musicians, I'm talking about an invention—that the great creative genius of the invention of jazz has never been topped. Given your repertoire, maybe you have a little of that feeling, too.

JC: What I connect to in what you're saying is that some of the pure joy did seem to go out of the playing with some of the later musicians.

ED: Something nervous happened. Something responsive perhaps to the times. Music got fractured and bitter and a little bit atonal. And very "statemental."

To this day I'm surrounded by musicians and fortunate enough to live among them. My wife Helen sings with the New York Oratorio Society. My daughter Caroline has recorded a couple of CDs and is a performer in the folk country genre. It's quite possible that all these people have these musical gifts and exercise them just to keep me away from the piano.

JC: [Laughs] And I hear your grandchildren dance.

ED: Sometimes I'll say to them, they're three and five, "We're going to dance now, kids. Do you want to listen to Brahms, Schubert, or Judy?" And they'll say, "Judy! Judy!"

John
Eaton
(b. 1934)

Jazz pianist, historian, and Steinway Artist.

Interviewed in 2015

John Eaton grew up in Washington D.C. and spent much of his professional life there with long associations at Wolf Trap and the Smithsonian, and with occasional forays into politics, playing at the White House and once, memorably, at the Supreme Court. John is one of the last of a generation of pianists influenced deeply by early jazz greats, Fats Waller and Art Tatum, as well as later pianists like Bill Evans and Erroll Garner. John is also an educator and hilarious raconteur, making our conversation one of my most enjoyable.

     For reasons that I've never fully understood, I was enthusiastically supported by Black musicians when I first came on the scene, but by only a handful of White musicians, John being one of them. John's friendship and encouragement helped keep me going when I was feeling mostly alone in those early years. This conversation gave me a wonderful opportunity to revisit that time and some of the events that shaped both his music and mine.

JC: *Listening to your playing again and immersing myself in your choices for today brought back all these great memories of Hanratty's, our old place of employment on the Upper East Side. Talk about your memories of that time.*

JE: You and I were actually competing for the same gig. When Dick Wellstood, the regular pianist, was off, Hanratty's would bring in other players. I heard about this, may I say, *girl* pianist, a fabulous stride pianist who had been hired and was drawing more business than any of the guys. My god, twenty-five, twenty-seven years ago. Of course, we're not allowed to say "girl" anymore.

JC: I debuted there in '82. I remember it specifically because that was my big New York debut. Knowing we were going to talk, I've been thinking not only about your great playing but also about the fact that that place was specifically known, at least in my memory, as a place for "two-handed" piano players. That's what they called us. That was unusual then—people who didn't need a bass player.

JE: Well, in the early '80s for a place to feature solo jazz piano, and particularly solo jazz piano with a traditional bent, was unheard of. It was really Wellstood who got it all started because Hanratty's had somehow acquired an upright piano, which they had in the bar in the front. William F. Buckley, the right-wing writer, was a friend of Dick's, and he alerted Dick that there was this employment opportunity. And Dick went down, and the job was his. And the thing evolved into a real piano room where they had the piano in the back, a real grand, where you and I played.

JC: Is that where we first met?

JE: No, we met at the Kool Jazz Festival in Waterloo Village in New Jersey. And that was another, by today's standards, improbable presentation, all those greats on one stage. There was Ralph Sutton, Dick Hyman, Art Hodes. And you and I were the young people.

JC: We were the outliers, you from D.C. and me from California. This is all coming back to me, looking at your choices to play today. The music that's inspired you has inspired me. When I came on the scene, everybody was surprised that I was this young girl playing stride. Now I meet young people who are playing it as part of their repertoire. They don't focus on it in a big way like I did, but they're still playing stride, whereas none of my contemporaries were when I first played Hanratty's. It's encouraging that pianists know this music now a little better than when I was coming up.

JE: Well, sweetie, you really were a pioneer—are a pioneer. You don't *look* like a pioneer, otherwise you wouldn't get any gigs, but in the context of that time, there wasn't anybody playing what you played—and you were a woman. And you're a lot younger than I am, so you were much younger than the other people who played there. And you were the only woman they hired.

JC: *I was thinking about how much you educate while you perform. You don't walk on stage and say, "This is a master class," but I love how you talk about the music and give a little history and context. You're known for presenting composer evenings. It'll be a Gershwin evening or a Cole Porter evening. How do you entice a younger person into this world of the Great American Songbook? We know why we love it, but what do you say to the uninitiated?*

JE: Rule No.1 is, you have to play it for them. And Rule No. 2 is, don't trash their music. Don't draw any odious comparison between new music and old music. Just let them hear it. And you may have noticed that there's a larger and larger young audience honing in on this music, and that's because as we've gone along with our respective careers, another generation has emerged. They don't have the loyalties to the '60s or the issues of the '60s. So it's all right to like Gershwin. Thirty years ago, it wasn't cool to admit that you liked Gershwin. Or Fats Waller.

Whatever I do in terms of talking is something I do naturally. And playing is important. Let them hear the music because that's what really persuades.

JC: *I don't think you have to say a lot, but you do have to create an environment that invites people into the music, something that I think some jazz musicians have lost.*

JE: You have to establish a rapport with the audience. And when all is said and done, it appears that I'm a teacher. I've done after-dinner banquets for corporate groups and that kind of thing, and I'm always astonished when somebody comes up to me when I'd presumed that I was doing an entertainment, and they say, "We learned so much from you tonight!" Of course, that wasn't the purpose of the thing. It was supposed to be after-dinner entertainment. The teaching thing just sneaks in there.

JC: I think that's a great point because I think that people want to learn. It's a funny thing to say but I think that learning gets a bad rap. Like, "Oh you're going to force me to learn something?" But people want *to learn something.*

JE: Yeah, they like to feel that they're on the inside of how it's done. And you're quite right, there's a prejudice against education. I don't know why, whether it's an American thing.

JC: Talk about Willie "The Lion" Smith. Nobody has mentioned him in ages. I'm a big fan, and you brought me "Echoes of Spring," which I adore. He was like two different pianists, one when he was playing fast and bombastically and another when he was doing gentle things like "Echoes of Spring."

JE: I met "The Lion" when I was in college. He came up with a band, and he played in my fraternity.

JC: I love to think of "The Lion" at Yale!

JE: I was captivated by his playing, and a lot of that, of course, was personality. But there was something so compelling about his playing that it rubbed off on you. Duke Ellington, after his first visits to New York, came away similarly captivated, and it's been said by more important people than me that Duke Ellington's style in part came out of "The Lion." Then Thelonious Monk's style came out of Ellington, so there's a line of descent there.

JC: You also brought Fats Waller's recording of "Carolina Shout," which is my favorite version. When I learned that tune, I listened to every recording imaginable then put my own together. Why is Fats' version special to you?

JE: Well, it was one of the first, if not *the* first, jazz piano recording I ever heard. I think that when I was ten or eleven, my parents bought me a collection of jazz pianists' records. I remember that that recording in particular knocked me out. He not only captures the spirit of what James P. wrote, but he puts his own spin on it.

JC: What kind of musical education did you have?

JE: I was a hopeless student. My first teacher gave up on me after a year. I was six years old, and she told my mom, "He will end up playing in a nightclub."

JC: Like that's a bad thing? Well, maybe if you're six . . .

JE: Actually, she was very loyal to me. My last teacher when I was a teenager, at fourteen or fifteen, was Ruth Crawford Seeger, who was a very famous pioneering woman classical composer. Her stepson was Pete Seeger. She taught me for a year and gave up, and then my father threw in the towel and said, "This is silly." Because I wouldn't practice. And that's the curse of people who can play by ear, they really don't want to do the other thing. And I didn't study seriously until I'd already embarked on a career and I discovered Alexander Lipsky, who was a famous classical teacher. And he worked with me for twenty-five years. I started with him when I was about twenty-four, relatively late.

JC: How old were you when you got your first gig?

JE: First professional gig? Probably nineteen. I was still in college.

JC: So you were already gigging, but you'd been playing by ear and learning the standards and all that?

JE: Well, I was headed for a career as a college English teacher. That wasn't really who I was or what I wanted to do, so I started gigging at night when

I was in graduate school. Then I kept fooling myself and saying, "Well, this is just a sideline." Then I went in the army, and when I came out, I was determined to do what I've done ever since. And I've never regretted it.

JC: I remember having one of my moments of, "How can I keep this going? I love the music, but how am I going to make a living?" and I remember telling that to Max Morath, the ragtime pianist and historian. And he very casually said, "Yeah, every five years or so we all have a moment when we think we're going to quit. Then we don't. So just don't even think about it."

It was such great advice, especially because he was so casual about it. If he'd gone, "Oh, yes, you're right. It's terrible. You're never going to make it. You won't be able to pay your mortgage," or something like that, I would have panicked. But he said, "Eh, don't worry about it," and I just sort of went forward. Did you ever have those moments?

JE: Well, now that you've brought it up, Dr. Carmichael, I would say, yeah, there is that five-year reassessment. When you've lost a gig, when your career isn't going anywhere, when you haven't had any reviews. At one point, I was tempted to go into the seminary and become an Episcopal priest. Then a friend of mine, who *is* an Episcopal priest said, "You're out of your mind! You don't want to do that. You were born to do what you do." Well, all that Max Morath was saying, and all that you and I know, is that the music business, the entertainment business, is an unforgiving business. It's an awful way to make a living, but it's a wonderful thing to do with your life.

JC: What a beautiful way to put that.

JE: And I just thought it up, too!

JC: I like to say things like that to entertainers and musicians out there listening because I think we're in this together, and I think a lot of times people don't think that way. I had a lovely thing said to me by a singer, Maud Hixson, who lives in Minneapolis. She said she loves to read about me playing in various places around the globe, because I travel so much. She always feels it's like she's receiving a little ping, like a submarine signal, that I'm out there, and letting her know that she can go forward. That I give her courage to keep going. I think that what these people are saying is that every minute there's a musician somewhere in the world who's discouraged, who's thinking, "I can't keep doing this." So they need to be reminded of why we originally started doing this and remember their initial joy. That can be burned out of you with the slog of trying to make a living at it.

JE: Well, the bottom line is that we love what we do, and many people who are making a living doing what they're doing, hate what they're doing or are indifferent to it or do it only because it's a job. We have not only a job but a calling. Maybe it's built into the order of things that we constantly have job insecurity.

JC: Now talk about your singing.

JE: [Laughs] My great friend, Mark Russell, the political satirist, described my singing as a cross between Fred Astaire and Walter Mondale.

JC: Oh, my word! What does that mean exactly?

JE: It was for a laugh.

JC: Well, it got one from me!

JE: Anyway, I talk-sing. But I discovered that people want to hear the words, and whatever it is that I do, I was able to get away with it. I even sang at the White House. And I sang at the Supreme Court.

JC: At the Supreme Court! Talk about being afraid of being judged!

JE: They loved it! It was the only 9-0 decision in decades.

JC: I'm not surprised.

JE: Thank you, dear. But it's not in a class with your singing. I loved your record. You really sang. I talk-sing. I was one of the few popular artists or musicians who ever appeared at the Supreme Court. They have two or three concerts a year, and generally it's either chamber music and/or opera singers because several of the justices are real opera buffs. So I opened the show. Everybody else on the program was a well-known opera singer. I sang "One for My Baby." And they loved it. Some of the people in the audience, the very select Washington audience, were somewhat appalled that a saloon song was being sung at the Supreme Court.

JC: It's one of the great things about the music that we do, as opposed to some contemporary music. Listening to the greats we've heard, it really is about the communication, to even just one person. Audience numbers don't matter. If you go to a Taylor Swift or Beyonce concert, it's about the spectacle of it as well as the music.

JE: That's the difference in the experience you're describing. Whether it's just you in the audience or hundreds of other people, you'll take something away from the experience that will stay with you for a long, long time. Perhaps forever. The spectacle is all outside you, and when it's over, it's over. And that's very different from a true musical experience.

JC: I always compare it to People *magazine versus great literature.* People *magazine gives you that quick burst of energy because you're looking at a bunch of beautiful people having fun. It's a little harder to dive into a Nabokov novel. But if you do, it makes you think. It makes you smarter, and it stays with you. And I think that's the difference with music that is more sophisticated or complex. Sophisticated music continues to feed you in a deep way, and it's different every time you hear it. That's pretty remarkable.*

JE: I'm reminded of something that Zero Mostel's wife, Kate, once said to me. He used to come to hear me when I was playing at the Carriage House in Georgetown. You think of Zero Mostel as being somebody who's so famous that he's somehow above the system. And his wife said to my wife, Penny, when she and I were just married, "Listen, honey, the only time you've got to worry is when they're out of work." We assume it only happens to us, but it happens to the most famous actors and performers. Deep down, this is who we are, this is what we were meant to do, and somehow, we were fortunate enough to have done it. The other thing is, let's face it, we give people joy, pleasure—that's our role. And we get paid for doing it. Or we get paid nothing, as the case may be. But I've never regretted it. Never ever.

Robert
Fairchild
(b. 1987)

Former New York City Ballet principal dancer and
Tony Award-nominated stage and film actor.

Interviewed in 2017

Robert Fairchild starred as Jerry Mulligan on Broadway in *An American in Paris*, the most honored musical of the 2015-16 season. Robert first saw Gene Kelly in the film *Singin' in the Rain* when he was in fourth grade, an experience that inspired his ambition to sing and dance onscreen. He studied jazz and tap growing up, but at fifteen, his older sister, Megan Fairchild—currently a principal dancer with New York City Ballet—encouraged him to attend a summer camp at the School of American Ballet to polish his classical technique. To everyone's surprise, Robert fell in love with ballet and eventually joined his sister at New York City Ballet. After starring in *An American in Paris* in New York, Paris and London, he set his sights on a broader career path that includes acting and singing in movies, bringing him back to his initial dream of being a modern-day Gene Kelly.

    I saw Robert in the London run of *An American in Paris* in May of 2017 and fell in love with every aspect of his performance. With a little research, I discovered that he's a passionate tap dancer—he didn't tap in the stage version of *An American in Paris*, so this was a surprise—and jazz fan, making him a perfect *Jazz Inspired* guest. Perfect, but impossible to reach.

    Coincidentally, a year and half later I was approached about having Leslie Caron—Gene Kelly's co-star in the film version of the show—on *Jazz Inspired* to promote a limited run of the film of the London production of *An American in Paris,* the same production I'd seen. I had no idea if she'd be right for *Jazz Inspired* but thought, "She's Leslie Caron! Say yes!" After many aborted attempts at scheduling, the film's publicist apologetically explained that Leslie wouldn't be able to do the interview, but would I have any interest in Robert Fairchild?

Robert is tall, handsome, spectacularly fit, and seems completely unaware of the effect of it all, making him even more appealing. As I opened the door to my Manhattan studio and welcomed him in, he said, "I think we should hug, don't you?" We discussed our both being from out West, where you meet more huggers than you do in the East. We hugged, laughed, and jumped into the conversation.

JC: Talk about Gene Kelly. He was a huge early influence for you. I love that you grew up watching old movies. Me too!

RF: Yeah, my mom would take me to Blockbusters—when there *was* a Blockbusters—and we'd get one popular movie, and she'd get one old Hollywood musical. That's how I was introduced to Gene Kelly. The first thing I saw of his was *Singin' in the Rain.* He had just passed away. My mom bought me the VHS version for a Valentine's Day present, and I was hooked. My sister got me into dancing, and Gene Kelly made me want to be a dancer.

Also, there's something about him as a role model for so many guys growing up my age in a small town. I grew up in Salt Lake City, and to see a guy who loved to dance was everything. It made me feel like what I wanted to do with my life was acceptable and that there was some guy out there who was just nailing it.

JC: Did you know you wanted to dance when you were very young?

RF: Yeah. I'd put on performances with my sister. She'd come home with routines, and I'd be doing them in her old costumes behind her. I was always obsessed with dancing and performing. I started dance classes when I was four, but as soon as I could walk, I was moving around.

JC: I think wanting to dance in that environment would be very hard for a young man or for a boy. Were you bullied?

RF: Yes. If you're not Mormon and if you don't play football, you're kind of the odd man out. I didn't tell anybody I danced, let alone did ballet. The only thing that they knew I did was hip-hop. That's the only thing I felt wouldn't get made fun of. I stuck out like a sore thumb. But I had a big dream, and no matter how much I was teased, nothing ever stood in the way of that. And I owe so much of that to Mr. Kelly for giving me the power to believe in myself, and that he made it cool, and that he was . . .

JC: Very masculine.

RF: So masculine, so athletic.

JC: Was that part of it too?

RF: Yes. He was a dancer, and he was a *guy*. There was just so much there to soak up as a little kid.

JC: When I saw you in London, I was struck by that same super-masculine aspect to your dancing, along with the grace, which I loved. As a straight woman, I was delighted to see a male ballet dancer as the romantic lead I believed, if you know what I mean.

RF: I know exactly what you mean. I'm glad you felt that way. No matter what role you're playing, you have to become the character. So no matter what your sexual orientation, you're inhabiting the role. You have to dive into being that person fully. And to be able to do that with your body and your physicality is so important, because ninety-three percent of all communication is done through body language.

I took an acting class, and the teacher kept saying over and over that there was this study from some university that said this. He was talking about how we tell stories in pictures and film and that it's less about the voice and more about moments and pictures. It was really fascinating. And as a dancer! God, you've got ninety-three percent of all communicating possibilities.

JC: You mentioned a specific Gene Kelly track for me that you really love.

RF: It's "I Like Myself." It's the song he sings when he's roller skating and tap-dancing in his roller skates. I just think the lyrics are so simple and beautiful: "Can it be, I like myself? She likes me, so I like myself. If someone as wonderful as she is can think I'm wonderful, I must be quite a guy." It's really heartfelt and special and sweet, about a guy with low self-confidence who gets attention from the person that he's interested in, which boosts his self-esteem to believe in himself, that he must be a good guy. It's just a sweet, sweet message.

JC: I love that you chose that song because Gene Kelly was the person who helped you like yourself.

RF: Oh my God, yes! That's so interesting. Full circle there.

JC: Now I want to ask you about tap because I'm such a huge tap fan. Is it usual for someone to be able to tap and do ballet? I know dancers take all kinds of classes, but you're really passionate about both.

RF: Well, tapping is how I started, when I was four. I think it was just cheaper to enroll in tap, jazz, and ballet, so that's how I ended up doing more. But tapping was my first love. It was my closest connection to Fred Astaire and Gene Kelly, and I wanted to be just like them. So getting the opportunity at New York City Ballet to tap in *Slaughter on 10th Avenue*, and in a Fred Astaire tribute we did called *Not My Girl,* it made me realize I had this dormant dream, this big passion. And since leaving ballet, I've had more opportunities to tap. God, it's so much fun!

JC: *Is it something you practice all the time to keep it up?*

RF: Tapping is like riding a bike. However, when you get more detailed, obviously, it's so complex, it's like a mind game. Your feet are going so fast and it's so rhythmical. What I love about tap is that you're a musician. And there's this famous quote from Balanchine, the founder of New York City Ballet: "See the music, hear the dance." Some of my favorite ballets that I got to dance at City Ballet were ones that were tap dancing with ballet slippers. Just like a rock skipping on the water, traveling fast, fast footwork. And I was like, "Why do I love these ballets so much?" And I realized, "Oh, my God, it's because it's like tap dancing with ballet shoes!"

JC: *I think of you as a jazz guy. Everything I've read about you reinforces that thought, especially that you like it when things go wrong.*

RF: I do!

JC: *That is such a jazz attitude. Early in my career I asked an older musician what I should do if I'm in the middle of a concert and I hit a wrong note. He said, "Well, that's a great thing about jazz. If you hit a wrong note, you just hit it over and over and over again, and then it sounds right."*

RF: [Laughs] I love that! At New York City Ballet, you never do a perfect performance. You can't go out there and try and be perfect. You have to go out there and *play*. There has to be a sense of curiosity and a sense of play. And I remember when I was watching one of the greatest ballerinas, Jenifer Ringer, doing *Brahms-Schoenberg Quartet*, second movement. And it was Balanchine choreography, and there's a part where she's supposed to step up, do a double pirouette, and put her leg out behind her in arabesque and grab the guy's hand. It's a blind catch, and they didn't meet, they didn't catch. So she ended up doing something else in the moment that—forgive me, Balanchine—was even more beautiful than the original choreography.

It was in the moment, it was spontaneous, it was alive, it was, "This didn't happen, *but this did!*" And I thought to myself, "Don't get upset when you mess up in performances because Plan Bs are so interesting." You're doing pirouettes, and maybe you fall out of them, and then all of sudden, the body takes over.

Once, in a performance of *The Nutcracker*, all of a sudden, my body took over when I started to fall. I did a chassé to the right, and I posed, and then I turned back to center, and it worked. And the audience clapped. My sister, who's in the company as well, was watching the performance, and she was like, "Oh, my God, only Robbie could get away with falling out of a pirouette and making it look exciting and for the audience to start clapping." It's all about what you do in the moment because that's really dancing. I love that uncertainty.

JC: I love that you have that attitude because I don't think that's how people usually look at ballet. They look at how perfect is it.

RF: I'm a rare breed in that regard. You use technique to tell the story. When it becomes *about* technique, I'm not interested. But when it's about technique that furthers the story, that's the key. Why are you on stage? What are you saying? That interests me more than somebody doing the set perfectly right. I want to see how they use it to convey something.

JC: That's also a very jazz attitude. This surprises people who aren't jazz musicians, but the big thing that the jazz guys say all the time to instrumentalists is, "tell a story." Jazz musicians look down on musicians who use their great technique only to show you they have great technique. What's the journey you're taking with this song? What's the message? Especially without the lyrics. I love you saying it that way because I don't think this is how most people look at ballet.

RF: No, not at all.

134

JC: In some ways, my favorite part of An American in Paris, *when I saw it in London, was when you leaped on the stage from the wings. You flew through the air. I know it's a showbiz thing, but I loved it. I came with a ballet dancer from the Royal Opera House that night, and even he gasped, along with everyone else. Out of nowhere, there you were. How do you do that? Technically, is that an easy thing that looks hard? Is it difficult?*

RF: It's definitely the moment in the show where I try and pull out everything I can because that's like the dancer's version of their high C. Or like their big money note at the end. And so you gotta pull it out. It was a chassé and a step, step, and then launch yourself! And just to get to dance to Gershwin's score, something that was made so long ago but feels so inspired. It was not difficult to do because of the music.

JC: The music launches you.

RF: Yes, it's swelling. It's been swelling for eight bars. And then you can just feel it, and then you get to physicalize that.

JC: It's one of those things that when it's done well, like anything on stage, you feel you're a part of it. We all felt like we flew through the air and leapt on stage. We're all fantasizing that we could do that too, and you made us feel we could!

RF: Oh, thank you! Wonderful.

JC: I think of the energy and commitment that it takes to dance at that level. And now you sing and act, so you're upping the game. And to do that many shows a week takes it all to a nuclear level.

I want to talk about what one does in ballet to maintain physically. It all looks so effortless, so I don't think people realize the profound effort it takes to actually do it and sustain it throughout the run. I still have people say to me, "You don't practice anymore, do you?" So I know that people are often naive as to what this takes.

RF: Your whole day is planned around maintenance and preparing for the show that night. And even though I went down to six shows a week, that still means one show every day. And staying at the top of my game and taking ballet class. There are moments in the show where I'm so exhausted that as soon as I get off stage, my dresser has laid out a towel and I fall down, lay on my back, and rest, because I don't have a lot of time to recover.

JC: During the show?

RF: Yeah, to get my energy back and calm myself for a second. The next moment after that specific part is the hardest singing for me in the show. So after I calm myself, I do stretches and vocal exercises backstage that my singing coach gave me right before I go back on. It was no joke, the amount of work and the amount of constant prepping.

JC: And to keep your focus. To never let yourself fade off and think, "I'm tired," because then it's all over, right?

RF: Exactly. Especially when you do two shows in one day, people are like "O.K., just pace yourself." I'm like, no! As soon as I start thinking about pacing myself, I think about what I have to do after this, and it makes me even more tired. So I just have to stay in the moment and do it.

JC: How many shows would you do if you were doing a ballet?

RF: You'd do two shows if you were doing a full-length ballet like *Swan Lake*. You do two shows a week. Out of a four-week season maybe you'd get three shows.

JC: So, it's a huge difference. And you're not singing on top of that. Broadway actors often have vocal cord issues because of overuse, and these are people with fantastic training. And you're thinking of that for the entire body.

RF: It's crazy. Just thinking about it, I must be a little nuts.

JC: You've shifted your career with this. This was a great experience, an exhausting experience, but it's completely changed how you view everything. I would think it's changed your dancing as well.

RF: Yeah, I can't go back to just dancing. Something in me has awakened, and it's all about telling the story and figuring out how many ways I can, with my body, with my voice, with all of it, so that no matter what role or opportunity is brought before me, I'm ready. The one thing I don't have now is a ballet season where I can look at the schedule and see what I may or may not be dancing. I don't know what's next, so I just have to stay at the ready.

JC: Do you like that uncertainty or is it making you nervous? Or both?

RF: I feel alive. I feel like this is exactly where I'm supposed to be.

JC: I read something you said that I loved. In an interview you did about playing Jerry Mulligan in An American in Paris, *the interviewer asked, "Aren't you intimidated?" And you said, "Well, should I be?" [Laughs]*

RF: That's so funny. If you watch the movie, there's no one who's gonna do it like Gene Kelly did back in the day. When you've got someone like that, it's just perfection, and we're not making this to do a carbon copy. This is all different—different songs, some of the same songs, completely different choreography, a little alteration of the story. So you're paying tribute to the incredible property that is *An American in Paris*. And we're doing an updated version.

I think the reason for telling the story now was to do none of the rainbows and daisies and that colorful version you could do in 1951. But since we're in the 2000s—we started doing this in 2013—we could push the story closer to the dark side of World War II and really get into the nitty-gritty. It's a beautiful, heartfelt, romantic tragedy about all these artists trying to find love and pursue their art when they feel completely derailed. That's the reason we're telling this story again. So when people ask me, "Are you intimidated doing the role that Gene Kelly did?" I say, "No. This means I get to be closer to the man who inspired me."

At one point, three months into the run on Broadway, I was in a trash can icing my legs, and realizing that I'd had this dream. I wrote an essay when I was in fourth grade that said, "My special place is on Broadway because there's this guy named Gene Kelly, and he's just like me, and I wanna be just like him someday, and I also wanna be in a movie." So here I am getting to fulfill this childhood dream. And it's not about what can I do with it but like, "Oh my God, I get to be a part of his legacy!"

JC: *I feel that artists embrace change to stimulate their creativity. People say to me all the time when I try something new, "Weren't you afraid?" Well, yeah, but I did it anyway. And I think it's even more of a risk for people who are already known. For you, it's everyone asking, what's this ballet guy doing, thinking he can take on Broadway? In a way, you have even more risk, but you did it anyway.*

RF: You never know how far you can go if you don't jump. Of course, there's fear. But you think, "Oh, the possibilities!"

Béla
Fleck

(b. 1958)

Grammy Award-winning banjo player.

Interviewed in 2011

Béla Fleck enjoys many styles of music and has explored most of them with his banjo, an instrument not usually associated with a panoply of possibilities. He has collaborated with a broad range of musicians—everyone from Yo-Yo Ma to Chick Corea—and he has won fifteen Grammy Awards and been nominated in more categories than anyone in Grammy history. Béla has an almost scientific strategy for studying and mastering different musical styles, and this approach, combined with his passion and curiosity, allows him to continually nourish his artistic growth and bring banjo music to a wide audience.

JC: Why has the banjo gotten such a bad rap?

BF: It's kind of what happened to the banjo after the Jazz Age, when it became predominantly thought of in a Southern, country kind of context. And things like *Hee Haw, The Beverly Hillbillies,* and *Deliverance* didn't help because the instrument was associated with cheesy humor or inbred folks playing the banjo out in the mountains. It's ironic that the banjo has gotten this rap as being this very Southern, White instrument when it actually comes from the slaves. It comes from Africa, and it played a big part in the beginning of jazz.

But I happen to love the Southern, White part of the banjo as well. I got into the banjo because I heard that kind of music. When I heard Earl Scruggs playing, it was like the voice of truth. Like a lot of people in jazz when they hear Louie Armstrong or Charlie Parker, it's like the voice of truth: "Oh, my God, what is that? I gotta find out what that is."

I didn't have a background in folk or country with my family. We were Upper West Side, New York City kids. But that sound just galvanized me. Fortunately, my grandfather got me a banjo when I was fifteen, and I just loved the sound. I was surrounded by '60s and '70s music, jazz, the Beatles, and all the great stuff that was happening when I was pretty young and starting to learn to play the banjo. So I wanted to play all of that too. I thought you should do music that relates to you, not just the music that's typical of the instrument. That's kind of my whole story, right there.

JC: What kind of banjo did you start out with? There are different kinds of banjos.

BF: That's true. In early jazz music, we're usually talking about a four-string tenor banjo, and then as we get into some of the ragtime stuff, you've got the plectrum banjo, which is also four string, but it's tuned differently. I don't know as much about those banjo styles as I do about the bluegrass and the old-time style. The first one I got was like a Kay banjo, which was the cheapest starter banjo you could find. My grandfather found it at a garage sale up in Peekskill, N.Y., where he lived when I was a kid. Up to that point I was playing guitar.

JC: You're virtuosic. You've obviously played and played and put a lot of work into it. But what were your early years like in terms of inspiring you?

BF: Just Beatles songs. You'd buy a Beatles book, and it would have the little chord symbols up on top. I wasn't studying. You know how when a kid is interested in something, but they're not really doing it? I was one of those kids until I got the banjo. I was a dabbler with the guitar. I took some lessons from a guy upstairs in my building who was like a lead guitar player, and he taught me the blues scale positions, which was kind of interesting, but I didn't want to sit around and practice that stuff.

When I got the banjo, it was a whole different story. I couldn't put it down. And everything that I'd learned about the guitar came in handy. I was already using my fingers and pressing down strings and playing those little blues scale things. Oddly enough, every guitar player plays these blues scales, but very few banjo players play them. So even the idea of the blues scale moving up and down the neck in positions was something that came in handy and that wasn't typical to bluegrass banjo players. They tend to play out of chord positions and build around that. So then I just found teachers and took private lessons because there was no real schooling for it. But I was always interested in the hot guys and the fancy guys, the more virtuosic cats.

Bluegrass banjo had some pretty amazing guys over the years, from Earl Scruggs kind of creating the style of the three-finger rippling, rolling style all the way up to Tony Trischka, a guy from Syracuse who became my teacher. And he was the most modern guy out there. He was playing with jazz musicians and playing in keys that weren't normally used, and he had an amazing—still does—style of playing. He had this primitive thing, which I always thought was a great part of the banjo, but he also had a lot of imagination, a lot of technique. He changed the whole concept of what you could do with a bluegrass kind of banjo.

After a couple of years, I imitated him so well that people said they couldn't tell us apart. I thought I was doing really good until one day it occurred to me, "Oh, there already is a Tony Trischka, and I'm not gonna become a *better* Tony Trischka." So I had to start throwing away a lot of the things I'd learned from him that I loved and look for areas that he hadn't pursued. And though he was playing with jazz musicians and playing a lot of music that hadn't been done on a bluegrass banjo, he hadn't really looked at it— I always say this and people laugh—as a musical instrument. Like if you learned the violin, you'd learn all your scales, all your modes, and you'd would learn the classical repertoire. If you learned the saxophone or the piano, you'd learn to play all of these scales and arpeggios if you're gonna be a jazz musician or a learned musician. But banjo players didn't approach it that way, but I decided I would.

So I just started working my way through those things, figuring them out for myself and sort of mapping out the banjo neck and how to accomplish these things. The bluegrass banjo tuning isn't really made for that so it's harder to accomplish. Because it's a fourth, a major third, and a minor third. And then the first string and the fifth string are the same pitch. It's just not set up for scales the way a violin is, or even a guitar, where there's some continuity from string to string. The great thing about the violin or the mandolin or the cello is, if you know the distance from one interval to the next, it's gonna be consistent with any string you go to, because all the strings are tuned the same distance apart. But with the bluegrass banjo they're all tuned a different distance apart, so you have a lot more to consider.

JC: *More mental acrobatics going on.*

BF: Exactly. Also, the range is such that under your hand, there's only a ninth or a tenth at the most in one position. So that means a lot of shifting has to be done to have any range at all. And you have to use the open strings to get any kind of longer arpeggios, which means you can only play certain arpeggios till you start to learn to use the notes in between to shift. I'm getting real technical here.

JC: *It explains why more people haven't done this on the banjo.*

BF: Right. Well, I think it was evolving in this direction, and people like Tony Trischka were the step up to me. And then I've taken it the next step. And now there are some guys coming along that are gonna take it the next step. Like when Earl Scruggs showed up with a three-finger style, nobody had done anything like that. There are arguments that there was a guy who did it before him, but he was the great musician who found a way to do it that was so compelling. There are so many stories of people who, once they heard Earl Scruggs, they had to stop what they were doing and become a banjo player.

JC: Now, obviously, you've heard all the banjo jokes, you've heard people saying, "Why aren't you doing this on guitar?" I'm sure you had people say, "You'll never make a living on banjo."

BF: I had famous people tell me that. Ricky Skaggs said, "You need to learn to play pedal steel so I'll hire you in my band, and you can also play a little bit of banjo." I was like, "No, I'll stick with banjo." My banjo teacher before Tony Trischka said the same thing. "Man, I just have to tell you," he said. "This is not necessarily gonna go well if you expect to be a banjo player for your life. You're really good, but it's not easy." And I just kept my head down and said, "Just let me do my thing."

JC: I came out of ragtime, and I remember when I first got into jazz having a jazz musician say, "I'm really afraid you're going to like jazz too much" because he could see the future and where I was going. If you love it, it doesn't mean that you're going to make a great living or it's going to be easy, but I think it does give you this passion and determination, which is so important.

BF: Right. And when people come up to me and say, "Well, how can I do this?" I go, "I can't promise that you can make a living at it, but it'll be a great part of your life if you follow your passion."

JC: Your career has been very creative. You've done so many different kinds of things. I can't imagine that that's from you just sitting around and thinking, "Gee, it'd be fun to do this." There's a lot of planning to this, and challenge.

BF: Well, you try to be intelligent about stuff, and you apply that to your playing. You listen to yourself realistically and assess your playing and go, "Boy, I don't really sound like Charlie Parker. I don't have that going on, but this is good. Now, what can I do if I want to sound more like that? Or how can I put more space in my playing, or how can I use the banjo's strengths better?" Then you try to apply your intelligence to it, and you try to come up with a lesson plan for yourself of like, "O.K., well, if I'm not leaving enough space, let me make up some exercises with a bunch of space with them, and I'll just play those for the next few months whenever I'm sitting around with a banjo, and by the end of that, I'll start doing that when I'm really playing."

So with touring and playing with different musicians, having a great idea is great, but if you're not willing to do all the work and commit to that idea for the next couple of years, you won't make much progress. It'll just be a cool idea, unless you have a staff that does it all for you. Maybe Yo-Yo Ma has that. I don't know. Maybe somebody has that.

JC: *I don't know who they are.*

BF: Me neither. I have to go learn the music. I have to study it. I have to find the people. I have to make a recording. And then it means making deadlines, working really hard. I work really hard, and I enjoy working really hard. But I get off on trying to think of something that I haven't done, figuring out how to do it at the highest possible level and then going out and doing it. I did this classical banjo album called *Perpetual Motion*. Peter Gelb at Sony Classical had all this success with the *Titanic* theme, so he had a lot of money and they signed me up. I was on the jazz label and the classical label. And what they always want people to do on the classical label is stuff people know. He was trying to think of things for me to do. "Why don't you do the concert concerto on the banjo?" I was like, "I don't have the range of the guitar. It's just gonna be less."

We eventually started talking about the idea of doing a real classical banjo album. And where most people, like my pal Edgar Meyer, who's a great classical soloist, might have said no to what Gelb thought was a good idea, I said yes because I didn't know the music and I wanted to spend time on it. Like doing an album of Bach on the banjo. Bach, Chopin, tunes that everybody's heard a million times, which would seem like a cheeseball move if you were a violinist. It'd be like playing the hits. But for me, because I was a banjo player, it was gonna teach me all this stuff about music that was sort of in my head, but I didn't know how it worked. So I spent a year working on this stuff on a banjo, and then I recorded it and did the whole classical kind of recording where you're edited to get a great version of it, and then I went out and toured. And that's when you really learn to play it.

It seemed when I first talked to him about it, I thought, "Maybe this is sort of a cheesy thing to do," and while we were doing it, it was so hard. But I'm so proud of that record.

JC: What first attracted you to jazz?

BF: It was later that I started doing the real studying on jazz. I'd always heard that Charlie Parker was supposed to be good. So I got this Charlie Parker record, and I was like, "Whoa!" There was something about Charlie Parker rhythmically. And he was so in time, he was so aggressive rhythmically. I think of it now as like Bach, these endless, perfect lines spun out. So I tried to play them on the banjo, and I couldn't figure out any of it. I didn't have any of the tools to transcribe. But I'd always listen to those records, and there was a tune, "An Oscar for Treadwell," that I particularly loved.

So I started to transcribe the solo, and eventually I got the first measure. I was kind of excited about that, but I couldn't do it. So I put it away and went on learning the banjo every other way I could. And every few months I'd pull it back out and listen to it again and try to figure out a little more and get frustrated and give up because I didn't have any of the tools. I didn't know my way around the neck enough to have any shot at playing what he was playing. But as the years went on, at a certain point I was able to transcribe the first chorus. And I discovered that his language fit my tuning on the banjo very well because he uses a lot of chromatic stuff. He uses a lot of scale patterns the way Bach often seems to. And it taught me a lot of things about fingering on the banjo that were really, really interesting.

The other big turning point for me was hearing Chick Corea's "Spain." Let me put it this way, when I listened to Charlie Parker, I wasn't sure I'd ever be able to do it or that the banjo really would ever be able to do that. But when I heard Chick Corea play "Spain," the way he's playing the Fender Rhodes, it was a little distorted, lots of short stabby notes, and I thought, "Maybe that kind of way of playing might work on the banjo to play jazz." So immediately I tried to do the same thing. I got the record. I tried to learn it. I couldn't learn it. [Laughs]

JC: I love you saying these things, that you tried, worked at it and still couldn't do it. You came back to it, though, and you kept working. People say to me all the time that it's all talent. Music is such a mystery to people, they just think it's magic, like this stuff just happens.

BF: We know that's not true. It takes work. Especially if you're trying to figure it out on your own. Eventually I could play the song "Spain." I couldn't play the solo, but I could get little phrases of it. And every time I'd learn a little phrase, I'd go, "Well, that's not that hard. I know what that is, that's just a Dorian scale," and then, "Oh, that's just a little chromatic filling line. That's just a little chord pattern. Why doesn't it sound that way when I play it?"

So I learned that there was something about the way Chick played and the way Charlie Parker played that was rhythmically so powerful that they could basically play anything they wanted to and it would sound right, like the voice of God in their hands. And Earl Scruggs, I realized he had the same thing that these guys that I liked had. They were all very rhythmically developed musicians, and I thought, "Well, if you're gonna play the banjo, you're probably gonna have to play it in a very rhythmic way."

JC: What was it like recording with Chick Corea?

BF: It was humbling and exciting and a learning experience. He's one of those guys who just speaks the voice of truth when he plays. Everything he plays, it's like, "How could you play something so perfect and so spontaneous?" It could be a lesson plan. It was funny because I feel like I'm a poser or a dilettante. Bruce Hornsby is a good friend of mine, and we talk about being jazz dilettantes. We're like, "We love it so much! We think it's so great." And yet we haven't spent the kind of time to play it. Sometimes, because I do so many different things, I haven't put in the time on jazz itself that I've just put into music overall.

When I talked to Chick about it, I said, "You know, I'm not really like a jazz musician." He said, "I know what you are. You play whatever you wanna play, and I'll figure out how to make it work." So he looked at me as a challenge. Like, "O.K., Béla, he doesn't know all these rules and stuff, but that'll be fun for me. I'll figure out how to make whatever he plays work. I'll add harmony and different things to it to make it work." Meanwhile, my challenge was to try and be more of a jazz musician and try to understand more of those kinds of rules to play with Chick. Luckily, we had that rhythmic thing in common. And eventually, his compliment to me, which I found to be a great compliment, was, "You know, banjo's really a lot like piano." I was like, "Yes! That's what I'm always trying to get people to see." That the banjo can be a very piano-like instrument. You don't have to think of it as a rural thing or connect it to the backwoods of Kentucky. It's just a musical instrument and at times it has a piano characteristic.

JC: And you got that from Chick Corea.

BF: Yeah, it was a nice thing for him to say. The other thing I have to say about Chick is that he's so talented. Sometimes I'd practice all day because I was gonna be playing with him that night. And he *didn't* practice all day. And so I'd think, "Oh, here's this song with some chord changes, and I'm gonna come up with some cool stuff to do it, and I'm gonna surprise Chick with some cool stuff that I've figured out to play on this song." Big mistake, because it was like stirring up a nest of hornets. Once I threw something new at him . . .

JC: He went crazy?

BF: Exactly! It happened in his head instantly. *Oh, if he does that, that means I can do this, this, this, and this!* All of a sudden it was like an explosion of piano ideas.

I think the proudest I am about my whole experience with Chick is that I instigated him to do some things that he hadn't done before. Not so much how I play, because I always felt humbled by his ability. And the piano is such a big wonderful instrument. The banjo will never have the possibilities that the piano has. But we sure had a great time, and I'm really proud of the record we made together.

Also, I like to take my time making records, and I even have my own studio so that I don't have to rush. My musicians and I can spend a day on a track if we want. I can cut in the morning, do some editing, and everybody can come back and listen to it later on. And then if we wanna fix anything, we can do it. So Chick and I had five days planned to record in LA. We hadn't rehearsed at all, and we get there and the night before the session, Chick says, "You know, I think we can record *and* mix in this time." And I was like, *"Are you crazy?"*

JC: We jazz guys are used to that. Boom, boom, boom. We come in and do it.

BF: I know. But I don't know how to do any of this stuff, and these tunes were hard. I'd never played any of this stuff with him. I can see doing it quick if you've rehearsed and if you're good at that idiom. I could do a bluegrass record in a day with most people. But with Chick, it was like the biggest record I'd ever gotten to do with a heavy jazz cat. It was really fast.

We'd do the first take and he'd be like, "I think that was pretty good." I'd be like, "No, Chick. *You can't do this to me!*" So where I'd normally play a tune for an hour with the band, with the Flecktones or whoever I'm playing with before we record it, we just really got to it. Chick would say, "We like to do things once or twice."

JC: That's a very jazz way.

BF: Right. And he'd say, "If we do twenty takes, then we're gonna have to go study them all and figure out which ones are the best." The problem with Chick is that *every* take is great for him. For me, it takes three or four takes to get up to speed. So we compromised. We'd do like four takes. Which for me was like insane to be playing the most challenging music I'd ever played. But it ended up really good.

So in a way, it was along the lines of the other things I like to do, throwing myself into Africa and playing with people I've never met, and just turning on the tape machine. It was about letting go of control. And at the end, Chick said, "You know what? I think I've been rushing through records a little bit. I think I'm glad we took the time, and I think the record is better because of it."

Renée Fleming

(b. 1959)

Internationally acclaimed lyric soprano. First classical artist
to sing "The Star-Spangled Banner" at the Super Bowl.
Four Grammy Awards.

Interviewed in 2005

Renée Fleming is celebrated world-wide for her sumptuous voice and
compelling stage presence in opera, concerts, recordings, theater, and film.
In 2012 she was awarded the National Medal of Arts, America's highest
honor for an individual artist.

Less well known is Renée's love for jazz, something I discovered
through the jazz pianist Larry Ham, a mutual friend who once mentioned
being part of Reneé's jazz group in college. When Renée released her jazz-
inspired CD *Haunted Heart* in 2005, I grabbed the opportunity to interview
her during her publicity tour.

I thought I was meeting Renée on my own, but when I arrived, I
found a long line of journalists anxiously awaiting their Renée moment. I
know very little about opera, so I was already a bit tense, but following
twenty people who know a *lot* about opera made me more so. I'd never
experienced this sort of crowded journalistic crunch and couldn't stop
thinking of Hugh Grant in *Notting Hill,* waiting to see Julia Roberts's movie
star character on a press junket and nervously blurting out that he was from
Horse and Hound.

Finally, at the front of the line, the press agent took my arm, looked me in the eye and announced firmly, "You've got fifteen minutes." "I need at least forty," I countered. "You've got fifteen." I figured once I got in the room, they'd have to drag me out.

Renée was sitting in front of a large window that gave her spectacular, cinematic backlighting, wearing a powder blue scarf that perfectly enhanced her beautiful green eyes. I'd felt I'd put in real effort by not wearing jeans.

Renée is shy and controlled, but I got her laughing and she loosened up. Forty-five minutes later, she said, with obvious surprise and relief, "Thanks, Judy. That was fun."

JC: What kind of music did you listen to as a child?

RF: Well, everything. My parents were both high school vocal music teachers, so I heard a lot of classical music. My father conducted several different church choirs, so I grew up singing all that repertoire. I discovered and started writing my own music when I was about twelve and wrote for about ten years. Then I just stopped, inexplicably.

Because I was the oldest child, there were no older siblings listening to popular music, and I came to pop music late, in middle school. The first time I heard Top 40 music, I was in art class. The teacher played it on the radio, and it was a revelation to me. It wasn't until high school that I found music on my own, and I began to explore a bit. Joni Mitchell's *The Hissing of Summer Lawns*—which came into my hands from a girlfriend in another art class—was incredibly influential. And my father always listened to jazz, so I had a little of that exploration from him. My taste is a little formed by him because he was the only one who wanted to do recreational listening. My mother, when she came home from teaching music all day, really wanted a break from it. But my father listened recreationally to classical and jazz.

JC: What kind of jazz?

RF: He was interested in singing groups, Dave Brubeck, George Shearing. I can't remember everything I heard, but there were lots of different things.

JC: What kinds of things were you writing?

RF: I think my first song was called *Stargazer*. I performed it in the sixth grade. I continued writing all through college as well. I also wrote some classical music and some art songs that I performed. I guess it was kind of a precocious thing to do. I think I needed it. I was so shy. Communication was not easy for me. I'm so grateful that my children have a better time of it. That was a way for me to express myself. I think that's why I stopped in my early twenties, when I became better at talking.

JC: Did you listen to jazz differently from classical music?

RF: No. I never questioned genres. We never discussed it. It was all music. Growing up singing in as many choirs as I did, I also was enormously influenced by my teachers. I was fortunate enough to go to schools that had very highly developed and sophisticated music programs. One reason I wrote music was to be able to take guitar class in middle school, and I mastered that instrument pretty well. I played a lot all through high school, accompanying myself. I wrote music for the guitar as well as the piano. I had a terrific musical upbringing and training.

JC: I've had a number of people who grew up with classical music tell me that they were specifically told not to listen to jazz. That it's somehow bad for you. Why do you think that happens?

RF: I don't know. It could be a generational thing. It could be the way they were brought up in more of an elitist household, at least as far as the arts are concerned. Parents might have been afraid that if their children discovered pop music, rock and roll, or jazz, they would turn away from classical music.

The truth is, what we all understand now, if the seed is planted at a young age, whether it's taking your child to the opera or the ballet or to any of the arts, as much as they whine and groan and complain, the seed is planted. Even if they leave it in their teens and twenties, they will often return to it later when their sensibility and maturity enables them to develop a sophistication and appreciation for the finer arts. I think it's important to plant that seed and allow children to go wherever their imaginations take them artistically.

JC: You sang jazz when you were in college, at SUNY Potsdam, something I don't think a lot of people know.

RF: I sang first with a big band, then with a trio every weekend for two and a half years. Different players would come and guest with us. We became a very popular hit in our little college town, every Sunday night at Alger's Pub. I learned an enormous amount about performing through that experience. I came out of my shell. I became less inhibited. I was forced to communicate with an audience, which I had absolutely no clue how to do. I did not come naturally to that. I was never a natural extrovert or a natural performer. It was an incredibly formative experience for me.

JC: A jazz audience is very different from a classical audience.

RF: Well, this was actually a college party audience so you could barely hear us from the talk, but they all felt it was the place to be so we must have been doing something right. At the end of my four years, I was able to perform in a master class for Illinois Jacquet. We formed a fast friendship, which existed until he passed away a year ago in 2004. That was a really enlightening experience because he was the first person to say, "You could do this professionally, and I would encourage you to tour with me. I'd love to introduce you to the world of jazz as a singer."

At that point I hadn't made any decisions about what I wanted to do because of course, as a student, I was being classically trained and enjoying that. But at that time, I was more interested in singing jazz. It was a crossroads because at that point I was too afraid to move to New York on my own. I felt too young, too immature, too frightened. So I went to graduate school instead, and it became the road not taken. It was more circumstantial than not, I think.

I'm thrilled with what I'm doing. In fact, it suits me better. It suits my personality better. And I love it. But there's a part of me that has remained a passionate fan of jazz.

JC: *Who were your models with jazz? Did you listen to a lot of jazz singers or jazz instrumentalists? Or both?*

RF: I first came to be passionate about Sarah Vaughan. She was my first real love in this music. But I explored everyone. I listened to everybody.

JC: *Why Sarah?*

RF: It was her sound, her style. I felt she really interpreted the music. It just appealed to me. It's a matter of taste more than anything. I always felt she was the baroque performer and Ella Fitzgerald was the classical performer. She had a much more Mozartian style, if you can connect the two in some odd way. Eventually I came to appreciate Shirley Horn, who was my next great love. Recently, I'm a huge fan of Kurt Elling. I love his ballads disk from a couple of years ago; I almost don't go anywhere without it. I also listened to a lot of instrumentalists. I was fanatical about Pat Metheny through my college years and offshoots of Wayne Shorter and Weather Report. And lots of artists from the ECM label, because I studied in Germany and I was exposed to a lot of that. I heard Jaco Pastorius live in a tiny basement bar in Munich when I was a student there. I had a tremendous exposure to this music. It really inspired me in my classical work.

JC: In what way?

RF: First of all, being able to improvise for those two and a half years and being compelled to improvise and sing scat. All of that freed me up. I always had good ears, but it really developed my ear to a much higher level. It lent itself perfectly to the bel canto repertoire in which I sang many, many roles. In bel canto, as well as in Handel, and probably Mozart too—although it's not the fashion to do it that way now—artist singers improvised. Even if the parts were written out, they were still able to put their own creative stamp on this repertoire. Since then, we, as interpretive artists, remain exactly faithful to what the composer has written. In Baroque and some classical music, singers were expected to completely personalize the roles they were singing, writing cadenzas and, in essence, flights of fancy, just like a jazz artist. Taking the aria as a chart and making it their own. It's a different style of music but the exact same process and the same skill. I really have used it.

When I first sang Handel, it was in Paris a number of years ago with William Christie, who's been the director of Les Arts Florissants all these years, he said, "I want you to sing it like jazz." And I said, "You're kidding, right?" I had this preconceived idea of Baroque music and particularly Handel as this pristine, perfect world and that I needed to get out of the way and sing with no vibrato, with as pure and white a sound as possible. He said, "Absolutely, not. I want you to make us cry in the aisles. I want you to make us swoon. I want you to use your vibrato as an expressive tool and swell and bend the line." During the whole rehearsal process, I kept saying, "Are you sure? I'm going to get crucified for this. I'm going to get killed." And he said, "No, this is absolutely correct." Within the realm of my own daring and my own courage, I went into that world a little bit.

JC: And he knew you loved jazz?

RF: Yes, he knew I would understand. Those were formative years for me, when I sang jazz, and they have, no question, made my classical style more personal.

JC: With a classically trained singer, I'm always curious about what it's like listening to someone like Billie Holiday or some of these jazz singers with a lot of dirt in their voices. Is it hard for you to listen to it?

RF: No, I love it, actually. In fact, I was kind of fortunate because when I made *Haunted Heart*, I had a cold, so there's a lot of dirt in my voice too, but it's appropriate. I said, "Oh, good, I don't have to work to get away from a purity of sound." Having said that, sometimes I go to a Broadway show and I'm mortified, not just about the singing but also the speaking because you can hear either that someone is not well or that they're in the process of doing damage to their voice or any number of things. There are times where I can go and be disturbed by that because I'm a singer and I know exactly what's happening. But with someone like Billie Holiday, who's no longer with us, I'm just thrilled to hear that incredibly recognizable, within one note, voice. And that unique sound with her life experiences and pain in that sound. I'm a huge fan of hers. I'd never think all singers have to be held to our standard of purity, by no means.

Some of our favorite voices were not perfect voices or beautiful voices. In fact, probably the most famous singers in recorded history have had voices like that. In a funny way we identify with them almost more for their imperfections. They also developed as more interesting artists because they were never able to rest on the laurels of a perfect voice.

I really love listening to different things and understanding why certain things are enormously popular and certain things aren't. Why do people find an operatic voice—particularly a soprano voice—so hard to hear? Certain soprano voices with a big vibrato. That operatic sound that children love to mimic. And other people love it. They're fanatical about it.

JC: When I hear great operatic singing, I'm thinking it's not only what I do in terms of being an instrumentalist but it's the use of whole body in a deep way. You're feeling it inside of you and bringing it out, whereas I'm starting with an instrument that's outside of me and bringing it into my fingers.

RF: Yes! And for every voice type in classical music, there are voices that would appeal to anyone. There are voices that are so beautiful and so pure that they make music that is universal. And then it's making sure the public is exposed to it to see if they like it and not make preconceived judgments about it.

JC: It all comes down to exposure.

RF: That's why your show is so interesting. It marries these different worlds.

Dave Frishberg

(1933–2021)

Jazz pianist, vocalist and songwriter.

Interviewed in 2007

Dave Frishberg was a unique voice on the jazz scene. A humorous, sensitive chronicler of our times, Dave was that rarest of talents: a literate, intelligent, contemporary lyricist who poetically revealed the human condition in all its joy and melancholy. A Frishberg tune is the perfect, cheeky addition to any jazz set, which has made him one of the most popular composers with singers as diverse as Blythe Danner and Mel Tormé, not to mention Diana Krall, Michael Feinstein, Rosemary Clooney, Shirley Horn, Anita O'Day and the countless others who have recorded his songs.

I met Dave in my early twenties when he agreed to give me a piano lesson, which is more accurately described as an afternoon hang where Dave listened to me play, then played himself and expanded on my ideas with some of his own. The lesson was a generous gift of time and talent that has stayed with me ever since.

This interview was one of the few where I flew to the guest to tape our conversation, in this case, in Dave's beautiful home in Portland, Oregon.

JC: *Do you think of yourself first as a singer/songwriter or as a pianist?*

DF: I've always thought of myself as a piano player first. I still kind of think of myself that way. Then as life took me along with it, I became a piano player who summoned up the nerve to sing his songs in front of people. That's the way it's felt, just to the nerve to do that. Both the courage and the *gall*. [Laughs]

JC: Had you sung growing up? People ask me constantly if I sing. People assume that if you're a pianist, maybe if you're a female pianist, that you sing. But before you were singing, did people always ask you if you sang?

DF: Not really. People always ask me if I give lessons.

JC: They do ask us all the same questions. You started writing before you were singing, so you weren't thinking of writing for yourself?

DF: It was the farthest thing from my mind. I just became interested in songs. Songs are one of the things that attracted me to become a pianist. I just loved songs. I wasn't crazy about learning to be a classical player. I never did study that realm at all. But I liked songs. I liked pop songs. It came easy to me to play the piano.

JC: You're talking about "pop songs" of another day. You're talking about what we now call "standards." Talk about loving those songs and getting drawn into the idea of writing lyrics and songs like that.

DF: One thing that's important to remember is that when I started to get into the professional piano playing business and looking for jobs, the biggest credential you had to present was your repertoire. The idea was you had to know a million songs. Do you know all the songs? And the songs meant every song that ever was. That was the deal. That was always one of my goals as a beginning pianist, the learning of the material. Learn songs, and then you can get gigs. That's number one.

Number two, when I got to New York as a professional player, most of my gigs were with singers, rehearsing them, preparing them for their auditions, helping them learn material. That got me acquainted with a lot of sheet music and also with a whole repertoire of songs that I'd never considered before, because they weren't necessarily jazz vehicles that were interesting to me in an instrumental way. I began to hear all these songs, and I began to realize that some of them were better than others. Then I began to pay attention to which composers I liked and what I liked about them. And then I began to feel that I could take a crack at this. That's how I began to get interested in writing songs.

JC: The actual leap to singing, though, is a huge one. I think as jazz musicians we've seen and heard so many bad singers and great ones too, that it makes it even more daunting for us to dive into singing.

DF: Daunting is right. Except when I dived into singing, it was in a very confidential way. I think I dived into singing because I started writing. Instead of handing my songs to anonymous demo singers to try to get them to publishers, I'd have to make the demos myself because I knew how they were supposed to go. That's when I began to sing my own songs. That's when I began to take courage in the fact that my voice could do it. I never bothered to learn how. It was never my intention. But I had worked with a lot of singers. I'd been around singers. And gosh . . . I can *hum* and sing around the house.

JC: [Laughs] What would be the biggest thing you've learned from singers, in terms of your own singing? You have such a distinctive style.

DF: I know that musician singers have always appealed to me. Like Bob Dorough, for instance. Or Nat Cole. I like the way musicians handle vocals. I guess I've liked the way jazz musicians handled vocals. Fred Astaire's voice always appealed to me. I've always enjoyed that conversational way of singing that musicians have. Also, I like the way they handle rhythm and time. So that's what influenced me in singing.

I have no idea what I'm doing. I took a few lessons with a guy years ago, and I made a tape of it. And I've been using that tape to warm up on for thirty years. Just that tape in a hotel room. I know that I'm not still singing correctly. My voice is disappearing as I grow older. I'm not able to hold notes for as long as I used to. I run out of breath quicker. There's a huskiness and a deepness to my voice that didn't used to be there.

As far as singers who impressed me vocally, I'd have to say Barbara Cook. She absolutely kills me. Every time I hear her, I have to wonder, *who's that?*

JC: And you're a Peggy Lee fan.

DF: Peggy Lee is to me the acme of pop singers. I loved the attitude she brought to it. It was always understated. She's one of the very few understated jazz singers, if you stop and think about it. Also, the economy of her stage presence always knocked me out. She didn't have to do anything except move her wrists. She didn't do any rhythmic movements. She seemed very, very in control of what she was doing, yet lost in the material.

JC: Talk about Bob Dorough.

DF: Bob Dorough is unique. *Nothing like him has ever been seen before.* [Laughs] He's a big influence on my whole life, really. It's interesting to think of the musicians who have been very influential on my life in subtle ways: Bob Dorough and Al Cohn. And I know that I'm not alone in this. Bob was an example to me musically. He's so musically gifted, a real musically gifted freak. He's also a very thorough and conscientious musician. He doesn't know how to write a cheap note. Or play a cheap note.

I've always admired how industrious he is and how ingenious he is. Also, he's a very spiritual character, outside of his music. He affects people in that way too. There's a magic about Bob. To me, he's a guy who says yes to life. Speaking as a guy who says no to life, it's something I look at with much awe and respect.

JC: How do you say no to life? I don't believe that.

DF: Yes, you do, Judy. Bob and I are polar opposites.

JC: O.K., you're right. What about Al Cohn?

DF: When I got to New York, I began to meet musicians in the big leagues, people who I had been following since I was a kid reading *Downbeat*. I was always curious about Al Cohn because all the saxophone players in *Downbeat*, when asked who their favorites were, Al Cohn's name would always be included. I couldn't figure out why. Why was he such a big star? When I finally met him and began to work with him, play with him, and began to be associated with him, I was hooked too. They called him Mr. Music, which was a perfect way to express it because the music just radiated out of him. And if he came into the room, even if he didn't have his horn with him, the band played better. [Laughs]

And personally, he was such a great person, so generous and warm. And funny. And intelligent. Brilliant. I was honored to even know him. He always said the right thing and did the right thing. And he was always a model to me of how an artist should conduct himself, comport himself . . . while drinking quite a bit of Scotch every day. But you never knew it!

JC: I love you talking about how these role models conducted themselves and their commitment to the work. Now talk about your songwriting process, which I suspect is very different from the way much of pop music is written today, which is written specifically to sell units and make money.

DF: There are a couple of ways of being a songwriter, and my way might be different from that of others. Songwriters today are really kind of groove-makers. A lot of the music that they generate is engendered in the beat and in the time and in the groove and how it's "swinging," to use the term that we used to use. And that seems to be the driving force behind just about all the music of the younger people, no matter what the category.

I don't approach songwriter that way at all. I don't even think of a groove. That may account for my relative lack of popularity in the corridors of power in the music industry. I approach it, as some songwriters do, almost as more of a journalistic endeavor. It's something I want to use to communicate with people. That's the dimension of songwriting that interests me more than groove. Not that I don't enjoy the groove, but I don't write songs for people to dance to.

JC: *And you love words.*

DF: Absolutely! That's very interesting to me too. I never really thought about being a lyric writer. The first thing that attracted me about songs was how cleverly they were composed. Lyrics came later. And it's gotten to the point that I don't trust anyone to write the lyrics for me. If I collaborate, it's always as a lyrics writer with someone else doing the music. I want to be in control of those words.

JC: *I think audiences still love thoughtful lyric writing if they're exposed to it, but they don't get enough of it.*

DF: You're right. A lot of what people hear today, the lyrics are really masked and overpowered by the music. The lyrics are beholden to the groove. Take someone like Bob Dylan. Dylan especially. There's a case where people *are* listening to the lyrics, but they're not listening to the music, which is lucky because there's very little music there to listen to, to hold on to.

That was Dylan's gimmick, to put it in an awkward way. If he had a gimmick, and I'm not sure he did, but his gimmick was himself. In my estimation he wasn't much of a composer or a song constructor, but he had this great gift for words that kind of just poured out of him. I don't really think they meant much. But they were constructed by Dylan in such a way, in such a beguiling and clever and entertaining way, that you kind of convinced yourself that they were meaningful. But I defy you to find anything meaningful about the song "Blowin' in the Wind," which really is not meaningful. It certainly doesn't answer the question of why some guy is gonna walk down some road.

JC: You mean the answer isn't blowing in the wind?

DF: I doubt it.

JC: I once said to a friend, "You know, I never understood any of those lyrics when I was growing up," and she said, "You didn't do a lot of drugs when you were younger, did you?" and I said, "No." And she said, "That was the problem."

DF: Absolutely. Drugs make you very open minded.

JC: How did you develop your piano style?

DF: I was imitating my heroes. I think we all do. And you try to imitate as close as you can. Pete Johnson, Albert Ammons—those were the people that I wanted to sound like. I had the notes down and the feeling down, but I didn't have the chops, the chops to make it buoyant. That changed to trying to copy Al Haig and Bud Powell. And that changed to trying to copy Horace Silver. I spent a lot of time on that. And then I found two guys that I couldn't imitate. Jimmy Rowles and Duke Ellington. They could touch a piano, and I couldn't get that same sound. But I was so impressed with what they were doing that I just soaked myself in their music. And often while I'm playing and my thoughts stray, as they do, I often wonder, would Jimmy like this? Or, does this do justice to Duke Ellington?

JC: That's beautiful. How has your music changed, especially in the last few years?

DF: I'm trying to play simpler. Trying to be less pianistic in some ways while improvising, so that I'm not driven by reflex so much.

JC: A musician's life is so interesting. The travel. The people we meet. We get to go into a town as a musician, not as a tourist, so immediately we connect in a different way.

DF: You know, the real reason I wanted to be a musician is because I liked to hang around with jazz musicians. I like their company. I always compare it to going into athletics in the old days before it was about money. And today music is about money. It would have been crazy for anyone in my youth to think they were going into music for the money. But today it's easy to see that that could be the prime motivating thing. You tell your folks you're going to be a singer/songwriter today, and they're thrilled. Ka-ching, ka-ching!

JC: And they back the band!

DF: Exactly. And that's why the music sounds the way it sounds.

Frank
Gehry
(b. 1929)

A world-renowned architect whose major buildings include

the Guggenheim Museum in Bilbao, Spain,

and the Walt Disney Concert Hall in Los Angeles.

In 1989 he was awarded the Pritzker Architecture Prize,

considered the highest honor in his field.

Interviewed in 1999

Frank Gehry was already an architectural rock star back in 1999 when I asked him to be one of my original thirteen guests on *Jazz Inspired*. He immediately said yes without even asking me anything about the show, an extremely generous gesture considering his insanely busy schedule. He had a line of people at his Santa Monica office waiting to see him the day we got together, each ready to claw me out of the way to get their Gehry moment.

I met Frank in 1989 right before he won the prestigious Pritzker Prize, often called the "Nobel Prize of architecture." Through a fortunate set of circumstances, I was included in the group that accompanied Frank to Japan, where the Pritzker Prize was being awarded that year, to attend the ceremony and the series of events celebrating his win.

Although this excursion included many memorable moments, one that stands out begins with Frank looking down at a white grand piano he'd spotted in the gleaming, cream-colored lobby of our hotel, an elegant space located at the bottom of the series of circular walkways. Frank spied me across the hall as I exited my room, dolled up in a chic white dress for the fancy dinner our group was attending that night. The lobby and atrium were white, the piano was white, my dress was white. Frank, with his artistic eye, couldn't resist.

"Judy, there's a piano! Look at this scene! You have to play!" He grabbed my hand and almost dragged me down to the piano. "Play a Fats Waller tune!"

The marble floor and the funnel of floors above us created fabulous acoustics. Soon heads were leaning over every balcony, and a crowd gathered around us. Ever since, whenever I see Frank, he doesn't say hello but rather, "Let's find a white piano!"

By the time we sat for our interview, he'd had second thoughts about his jazz cred, and the first words out of his mouth were, "What am I doing here?" Frank feared that he didn't, as he put it, "know enough about jazz." But he'd supported my music for years so I knew that while in his own mind he might not be a jazz maven, he was on some level a jazz lover. In addition, Frank is fascinating, funny, droll, and profound. I knew we were destined to have a great conversation.

JC: *So, Frank, welcome to* Jazz Inspired.

FG: What is it that I'm doing here?

[Laughter]

FG: I'm the least jazzy person you know.

JC: *Oh, you're more subtly jazzy. I think jazz musicians are the cool guys, and you're definitely a cool guy.*

FG: I play intuitive architecture. And I think I play off the beat. Is that jazz?

JC: Absolutely. And I think your buildings also seem very alive. They always seem to me like they're moving.

FG: Well, it's about motion, a lot of it. In the old days they had decoration. And since I'm a modernist I can't do decoration, so I've got to find something to put *feeling* into the building, and motion is one way. It's an old idea, actually, because the Greeks did it in their sculptures. Anyway, I've played with that. And it works . . . sometimes. When it works, it's great.

But I start a thing, I guess, like I fantasize jazz musicians do. Where I get the program, I understand the problem, I understand all the issues, and I have the language. And then I start. I don't know where I'm going, but when the answer reveals itself in sort of a normal structure, then I kick it off. And I guess that's when I play off the beat. I try to find the way to stay away from a normally structured environment.

JC: Which is exactly what I think the best jazz musicians do. Because if they're just playing right on the beat, the music is predictable and boring and doesn't have that wonderful fluid motion.

FG: You don't know where you're going when you start. You have a tune that starts you off.

JC: Yes, and you have a commission, a building to be built. I also think working with an office of architects is like playing with a gigantic big band.

FG: Everyone wasn't here this morning and I said, "How can I play this stuff if we're not all here at the same time?" So I did think of my architects as a band today, strangely enough.

JC: The challenge is getting everyone to work in concert to realize your vision but still remain open to their input to contribute to the whole. It's similar to my band improvising their ideas but within the constraints of my stylistic requirements because it's my band realizing my musical vision.

FG: It's hard. I find some people can do it and some people just can't.

JC: Yes, but that's about choosing the right people to be in your band.

Something that strikes me about your buildings is that every time I go into one of them my view of it changes. It seems completely fresh and different with each visit. Jazz musicians change the way they play a tune each time they play it, and the audience hears it differently each time because they're listening differently, depending on their mood or level of engagement. Somehow you accomplish this in your buildings.

FG: That's the humanity of it. That's what makes it accessible to people because I've given them these entrées. I liken it to a handrail. You know when you're walking down steps, you need a handrail . . .

JC: Right.

FG: And when you go into a building that's strange for the first time, you need some kind of emotional handrail. So I give people that basic *thing* in some form or another. I can't tell you exactly how I do it, but that's always there. And then they can play off the beat. Then they can do their own readings and become part of it. And you do the same thing when you play jazz. You give them a tune that's recognizable and improvise from that.

JC: And if it's too abstract, the listener has nothing to hold onto, no handrail.

FG: Exactly. Like when Ella would sing, and you'd recognize the tune and words, and then she would take off and scat. The handrail's the tune, and I do the same thing in architecture.

JC: Talk about your Hollywood experience.

FG: I used to hang out in Hollywood at a bar where Kid Ory, the trombonist from Louisiana, played. There usually weren't many people in the bar, so he'd do his set, then come over and have a drink with me. I loved talking with him, so I'd go back fairly often, and we'd have these conversations.

And then, when I did cardboard furniture in '72, I met Duke Ellington and his sister because they were involved with the people who were my partners with that. My partner's son—you may know him, a kid named Brooks Kerr—used to play sets with Ellington. So the Duke came to Brooks' house and sat on the cardboard furniture and we'd talk. It was great. And I would go to the Rainbow Room and hear Duke.

Also, when I was in high school, I had this job to run the senior dance or whatever it was, and I had to get the entertainment, so I got Oscar Peterson. I remember, he was nineteen years old.

JC: You hired Oscar Peterson to play your high school dance? You are a cool guy, Frank!

Now, I want to talk about the Concord Pavilion because I have a special place in my heart for that place. I played my first jazz festival there. Did you listen to jazz while you were designing that? I read that when you designed the Experience Music Project in Seattle, Paul Allen (the late cofounder of Microsoft) asked you to listen to a lot of Jimi Hendrix when you were working on that.

FG: Yes, he did. And I did listen to Jimi Hendrix. And Purple Haze. I did all that.

JC: Did you design the Concord Pavilion specifically for jazz festivals?

FG: Yes, it was designed for jazz and classical. So it had to work for both. But the energy of the place was supposed to be for jazz. Louie Bellson, the jazz drummer, was on the committee, and his wife used to come to these meetings.

JC: Pearl Bailey?

FG: Yes, and a lot of others too. Ray Brown?

JC: Bass player. See Frank, you know more about this than you think.

FG: I probably do. [Laughs]

JC: I think so. Who did you listen to when you were younger? Besides your hiring Oscar Peterson, of course. You could have been a jazz promoter, Frank. This whole architecture thing could have been put aside.

FG: Ha! Well, I love Fats Waller, and somehow in my memory banks I think I interviewed him for the high school paper, but it may have been a dream. But I did interview Ellington for this high school thing.

JC: So, you were meeting all these fabulous people in high school. Was this because you had a big interest in jazz?

FG: Well, yes, because I'm a right-brained person so I have trouble with music, and I used to *love* it. I learned to play *Pinetop Blues* on the piano by listening to the records.

JC: Then you do have some musical talent. You did it right from the records?

FG: And I learned to do the walking boogie bass. I could still do it if you had your white piano here, Judy.

JC: We will have to do a subsequent interview with the piano in the studio and talk about blues and boogie piano playing, Frank!

And didn't you play guitar? I read somewhere that you played a little guitar.

FG: That's a terrible story. My mother was a violinist when she was a kid, and she wanted me to get into music when I was in grade school. At the time we lived in Timmins, Ontario, way up north of Toronto. There wasn't much music going on, so they got me guitar lessons on the Hawaiian guitar.

JC: You were the "Don Ho of Toronto?"

FG: Yeah, sadly. And so I learned to play the Hawaiian guitar, but they didn't teach me music with notes. It was a number method. I could play "Aloha." And I actually played it on the radio once.

JC: *So, you are a* performing *musician!*

FG: Oh, yes. My checkered past.

JC: *Your checkered past as a musician! Talk more about your creative process. I know you and I have discussed the similarities to my process with music. Talk about your design sketches, which are very jazz-like to me.*

FG: Well, my sketches *are* very jazz-like, I would think. But nobody can read them. But when the building is done and you look at the sketch, then you say, "Hey, this looks like the building."

JC: *If somebody's listening right now, and they've never seen a Frank Gehry building, and they keep hearing me say it's jazz architecture, how would you describe your buildings?*

FG: I go blank when you ask me a question like that.

JC: *Well, in terms of what you try to accomplish that's different from other architects. I think of the open-ended quality of your buildings, like what I hear with a great jazz solo. It's very alive, even after the solo is played.*

FG: I try to engage people's feelings, so that's an important issue for me. Depending on the project, depending on what *kind* of project and what's important. Like I'm doing a little building in Scotland, a tiny little 2,000-square-foot club for cancer patients. And the first models of it got too fancy. It has to be just right. It has to have a feeling that these people are not being pushed into some architectural extravaganza to suffer. So it has to be comfortable.

So I worry about the appropriateness of the moves I make for the issues that I'm dealing with. For instance, at M.I.T. I'm doing a building for scientists—computer scientists, and people in linguistics, philosophy, and artificial intelligence. There are seven different groups. And the building has to be connective so that these different groups have meeting places. I created an interesting group of buildings that kind of look like a Léger Circus painting.

It's like a group of different objects where the conference room looks like a separate building and the café is kind of a separate building. Each building sits around a courtyard, like people, like sculptures, and that creates the place where the scientists can go for their interaction. Their laboratories look out over this sculpture garden where the connectivity happens. I spend time worrying about these kinds of issues. Then, of course, we have budgets and stuff like that to worry about.

JC: Well, it's very different from what I do in that regard. You have a client.

FG: With money. And they have a limited amount of money.

JC: And jazz musicians never deal with people with money. [Laughs] We just hope for the best.

FG: You're just out there!

JC: We're laughing, but there still are those similarities in our process.

FG: I think every artistic endeavor has the same thing: You have a set of constraints, and they're important, because we use them. If you're an artist, you use those constraints to your advantage. You manipulate the situation somehow and then express your creation. You solve those problems, but then you make it into something else. And that's the game we're in. And I think that's the same for you.

Jeff
Goldblum
(b. 1952)

Actor, jazz pianist.

Interviewed in 2020

Jeff Goldblum is a distinctive presence regardless of what role he plays, from his early portrayals in *The Fly, Jurassic Park,* and *The Big Chill* to more recent turns in *The Grand Budapest Hotel* and the long-running TV series *Law and Order: Criminal Intent.* Since 2014 Jeff has brought his talent and enthusiasm to a new pursuit as a jazz pianist/singer, with a semi-regular club gig in Los Angeles along with festival and concert dates in other parts of the world.

A challenge when interviewing a celebrity is going beyond their professional charm and the answers they've repeated endlessly in previous conversations. I suspected that Jeff's upbeat, energetic persona was authentic, but was afraid I wouldn't be able to get beyond it to something deeper. Then I read an interview he'd done where he described what he called "the joys of conscientious discipline" and his passion for learning. This was my entry into something interesting.

I carried out a long, involved pursuit of Jeff for *Jazz Inspired* when he released his first CD, *The Capitol Studios Sessions,* in 2018. To my surprise, we finally set a date. Thrilled with this big "get," I flew out to California to tape, only to have the interview cancelled the following day. A year later, I went through a similar back and forth with his second CD, *I Shouldn't Be Telling You This*, ultimately receiving a firm no. A few months after that, I received an email from his new publicist pushing hard for me to have Jeff on the show. Yes, this is often how it goes. I said yes but prepared for a last-minute bail. Happily, that didn't happen.

Jeff and I taped at NPR West in Culver City, California. Although he'd just finished an interview for NPR's *World Café* and was scheduled for Conan O'Brien after our talk, he was demonstrably excited about sharing ideas with another jazz pianist. Jeff grabbed my hand for a firm shake when I walked into the studio and told me how much he loved my version of "I Got Rhythm," mentioning specifics that made it clear he'd watched that YouTube clip multiple times. It was also obvious that he'd listened to *Jazz Inspired*. He knew the focus of the show and came prepared with a list of songs that had inspired him. Like the greatest talents I've been fortunate to meet, Jeff was completely engaged, prepared and all in.

Jeff and I are both loaded with energy and the combination was like a couple of happy, hyper puppies. We eventually sat down to record, following the recording engineer's not so subtly pointing at the clock. When we finished the interview, but continued to gab away, the engineer politely threw us out to make way for the next interview. Jeff and I walked out the door, arm in arm, singing a duet on a Peggy Lee tune and would probably still be there if Jeff hadn't had to run off to Conan.

JG: I have two kids, a four-year-old and a two-year-old, Charlie Ocean and River Joe. Charlie Ocean is just starting to take piano lessons—the Suzuki Method—which I had to look into 'cause I didn't learn that way. He's just a couple of weeks into it. He's playing "Twinkle, Twinkle, Little Star." I'm trying to encourage him to practice and learn how to make that part of his daily life. But his fingers, they wanna be kind of straight.

JC: *Yeah, that's how kids do it.*

JG: Yeah, but I still do that too. I must say, if I went back and retooled, I'd do the fifth finger especially. I've got a callus right there on the side of it because I think I kinda karate chop the keyboard.

JC: I have a callus there too, on the same finger! I never noticed that. That's interesting. Well, I only took a couple of years of piano lessons and I'm a bit horrified that my little finger sticks out when I play right-hand runs. People who have had loads of training, curl their fingers. My little finger sticks out like I'm holding a cup of tea!

JG: Well, you're elegant. You're classy.

JC: You think that's what it is?

JG: Yes, you're classy. You can't help yourself.

JC: I like your interpretation of this, Jeff. Not bad technique, class. Thank you for that. Now, tell me how you fell for jazz.

JG: That first piece that got me into jazz was "Alley Cat." I think it was a little stride-y. That's what got me wanting to practice more and got me a little bit better.

JC: Being engaged in the music when you're young is so important. How do you keep your kids enthusiastic about playing? It can't just be finger exercises; it's got to be something like "Alley Cat" or "Twinkle, Twinkle, Little Star." Something fun.

JG: That's right. Well, I'm leaving it to the teacher. Like, my dad was a doctor, and the conventional wisdom is, you shouldn't treat your own family. Likewise, I don't think I should teach him. He's got this good teacher at Suzuki, and they just came up with this "Twinkle, Twinkle, Little Star" idea, a song which I guess we'd sung to him. And they do this ear training. They blindfold them and sing the melody and ask, "Is that lower or higher?"

JC: That's great. A lot of teachers don't do that. It's just, "Play those notes." And something that you said, I want to quote you to you. Many people I've had on the show— especially people who teach in colleges—talk about the challenge of helping their students realize that developing a skill takes time. They all want it fast. You said that when you were fourteen, you were taking lessons and didn't want to practice because you hadn't yet learned "the joys of conscientious discipline." I loved that phrase.

I talk about this when I do master classes, especially with younger people. They know they have to practice with sports. Somehow that is associated with play, fun, joy. They know if they play soccer, they need to practice kicking endlessly because they know it's more fun to be better. And you're better if you practice. Somehow, they seem to miss that with music.

What was the breakthrough for you? How did you realize that joy? You mention in a number of articles that I've read that you get up in the morning, work out, then play piano, and that there's joy in that discipline.

JG: I know that now. I didn't then. Our teacher came in, taught me once a week, and I'd dread him coming because I hadn't practiced, and it would be John Thompson or some of those things.

JC: We all had those John Thompson books.

JG: Yeah. And I guess, there was that cliché of—not that I knew this then—but people would say, "Oh, while all your friends are out playing baseball, why do you wanna get cooped up and play piano?" Your mom is making you play, da, da, da—all that stuff. I just didn't get it. I didn't get anything about how you have to cultivate the garden within a twenty-four-hour period, put in some time, and not just go through the motions, but do kind of a session of getting your mojo working in some way—which I now know about—and keep learning more every day.

That occurred to me when my teacher gave me "Alley Cat," when he gave me a piece of music I liked. And I went, "There's something in me that gets jazz. It's just something in my blood." It's the syncopation that I kinda got exposed to then that I just loved. And then I was like, "Hey, I don't know about practicing, but I'm gonna sit however long it takes to be able to do this." I definitely feel you have to have focused practice and a consistent routine to develop a high level of skill in music or anything else.

I suppose if you wanna tap dance and you see Fred Astaire, you go, "I love that so much." If somebody told me right now that it would take 100,000 hours for the rest of my life to do that, maybe I wouldn't. But you have to love it. You have to go, "I gotta do that so here I go." I still do that. And then of course, over the years, I've done that with acting and with other things, and I'm still not only practicing it but developing it and figuring out how to practice so that each day's session will be as fruitful as possible, acting-wise or whatever.

I have these lines that I'm doing for *Jurassic World*. I have a nice part in the next dinosaur movie that we're going to film in a few months in England, and I'm working on the script. I'm kind of a morning person so each day I get up early and I have a fresh kind of an approach with it. And with memorization—just like musical memorization—it's nice to cram and it's nice to go through things repetitively and by the time you do your fifth rendition of something, something's developing. Then it's nice to take a break, of course. And the test of that is, if it's in your system, is when you come back to it freshly, you can just sit and see what's there.

Even if I'm on the road, I make sure that I get a piano, 'cause that's one of the morning things that I make sure I do wherever I am. Either I get a keyboard that I set up in my room, or if you go to these hotels, I pester the concierge and I go, "Is there a piano that I can play?" Or I say, "Is there a practice place nearby?"

JC: I think that discovering your own way to practice and making that a habit is essential. I hope that people who listen to this show learn their own ways to practice discipline and explore their creativity. I think everybody is creative. They don't have to be a professional. My hope is for everyone to take a moment in the day to focus on being creative and think, "This is going to be my moment to write something in a journal or do anything creative."

JG: Or even meditate or work on their relationships or their own character and see what they need to improve. Whatever you're working on, however you're growing yourself. It's a case-by-case basis, but you'll figure out how you need to do it. Oftentimes, it's a balance, with a strict kind of treating yourself like a new puppy and going, "Here is what you need to do." And being tough on yourself, but then being kind to yourself too, and saying, "Well, play, now just play." You can't just make yourself do something perfect right away. You have to do a little of this and a little of that.

Ask yourself what you're really interested in. It's such an amazing thing, how you grow, the nature of growth. You can't dig up the seed and see, "Hey, how's it doing?" You gotta trust that nature will take its course. The thing is, we're part of nature, of course, and part of the system whereby in a twenty-four-hour period you just have to touch the piano. You have to do some touching or see what happens, and then you sleep, and you wake up and something has changed.

This morning, I played better than I'd ever played before. Something had grown; something had stuck. And then you put some more time in, and then twenty-four hours later, something else has happened. And there's a joy in that. And then you go, "Hey, I get how this works. I'm gonna put in the time." But you have to be patient. And then of course, you really can't assess the results until decades have gone by, and then you go, "Hey, maybe I got something." But really, you do it for the pure joy, at least partly, for the pure joy of non-result-oriented process activity, where you go, "I just liked the practicing. I like to keep learning. I like to keep growing."

JC: When you're doing your different gigs, you interact with the audience, and it's all about having fun. A lot of actors are shy. Were you ever shy?

JG: Well, yes. There are parts of my nature, yeah, that we could call shy. And there are still seeds of that. It's still a thrill to kind of break through the nervousness or the danger of something, first to think, "Hey, I wonder if I'll be able to do this," and then "Gee, I did it again," or "That still works."

JC: I see a pattern here. For you, it's all about growth, self-improvement, and confronting the things you're afraid of, but also, you're a real advocate for joy. You talk to your audience and bring them into the experience of the performance and your enjoyment of it. I hope that will encourage some of the people who hear you to go to another jazz concert.

JG: You're absolutely right. I do enjoy myself. And many people who come to our gig have never heard jazz before. And you feel a little responsible. "Hey, we're the first. You've never heard *Blue Minor* before?" We're introducing them to this.

JC: Aren't you thrilled to introduce them to this? When I have somebody say I'm their first jazz, it's an honor.

JG: Yeah. And I love it so much. It's not like I'm performing so much as kind of sitting side by side with my musicians and going, "Look, dig this, let's listen to this." And of course, I'm hosting and introducing them to each song and at each moment with, "Listen to what Joe Bagg is doing, and listen to what Kenny Elliott and Alex Frank and John Storie and Scott Gilman and James King are doing. Wow!" I'm thrilled by it myself. And I play with them, and of course, they're improvising and doing something different, and I see the other musicians go, "Oh! Oh!" and they're delighted by each other and it just kills me. It's devastatingly, excruciatingly pleasurable.

I think part of my joy is the gratitude and the sense of how lucky we are to be able to be here, just to be on this planet. And then to be one of these people who's playing music, and what that is, it's, oh, boy, that's really sweet stuff!

JC: You give the audience permission for that too, because I think a lot of times they're inhibited. They have to feel comfortable enough to let go. They're nervous too. They don't know what's going to happen. Performers always complain that audiences in England are restrained, which I've found as well, but only at the start of the concert. I play a lot in England, so I handle this going in. I'll walk out on stage and say, very seriously, "I know you English people are so uninhibited that concerts can get kind of wild, like a rock concert. Please just don't do that. This is serious music. Please hold back." They all start laughing and know it's safe to let go. And then they just open up and it's great. But it's a permission thing.

JG: Oh, that's good! [Laughs] And I know there were very few women jazz instrumentalists when you were coming up. I'm very moved by that. I'm very inspired by it.

JC: Thank you. I appreciate you saying that. It was hard for women, so I think a lot didn't go for it.

JG: Imagine all the talent that we lost.

JC: Talk about recording "Little Man, You've Had a Busy Day" from your new CD. Talk about what it meant to you. It really touched me.

JG: Thank you. It's a lullaby that I'd known for a while, had sung to my kids. As I said, I have a four-year-old and two-year-old. My whole life has opened up in a whole other way these last, almost five years. So this was a song I sing to the kids when we put them to bed.

JC: It's so sweet and moving.

JG: Well, it touches me. Touched me to do it originally and just thinking about it, yeah, it's sweet.

JC: I'm a huge Fred Astaire fan, which is one more thing that we have in common. He was one of my original inspirations. And you were directed to listen to him.

JG: Well, I've always loved him. I love his tap dancing. I love his singing. Alex Frank—who's helping me with my piano and singing—said, "Here's who you should model yourself after. You'll never be able to do what he does. You can only aspire to what he did. Fred Astaire. So many of those great composers said if there's one person who could introduce their new song, they would want it to be Fred Astaire because he sings the melody and he *acts* it. He communicates it better than anybody, and he's just great. Alex said, "You've gotta listen to, "Steppin' Out" that he does with Oscar Peterson." I don't know that album. I've gotta get it. So I'm in the middle of a growth spurt, hearing all these things, but I love Fred Astaire.

JC: Being an actor, a storyteller, must influence your playing and approach to lyrics.

JG: I guess so. I mean, I have my own particular history over the last few decades and how I've worked on things and continue to work on things. Like I've said, I practice all the time. And so I do "Little Man, You've Had a Busy Day" every day, for instance. I do it once, make it a part of this routine that I go through in the morning. But it keeps changing. It keeps developing. And it takes a while sometimes. Everything is a work in progress. So, when we recorded, I was at a certain stage with all of it. I investigated and developed all these songs and developed them more because we've played them live. And I've sung that live and on a TV show here and there. But just for my own enjoyment, I sing it every day, along with the record, and it changes. I have imagined a new imaginative step on the journey through what it means, what it could mean, how each line kind of comes out and gets rendered, and it's really fun to keep doing that.

JC: It seems like it would be the same as doing a stage show. The lines are the same, but the performance should be different every night.

JG: It should. It does. It has been. I've done long runs of things, and it's not until that last show on the last week of the eight-week performance, the eighth performance of that week, the last show you're gonna do, that I go, "Ah, I know what I'm gonna do with this now. I'm gonna try for some new thing." Even though the lines are the same, you can have an inner journey, an improvisational journey, of thinking and feeling about it.

JC: The greatest singers told a different story with the lyrics every time they sang the tune because they're in touch with where their emotions are that day. I would think it's exactly the same for an actor.

JG: Right. You don't know who you're gonna be that day. You're different every day, biorhythmically and in every other way. When we were kids, I had a 45 of Peggy Lee's "Is That All There Is?" And that just killed me. I just loved her. And it's her 100th birthday this year. And Alex, who knows everything about everything, said, "You know, she had some kind of vocal challenge that caused her to not be able to do much of a vibrato." And so she had to learn to sing in this kind of straight way, which I kinda love myself.

JC: And with her, it's all about the space and the swing and that feel. It's not about long-held notes and vibrato.

JG: No.

JC: You believed every word that woman sang.

JG: And she was a great songwriter too.

JC: Yes. Another question: Do you like to be alone when you practice? Do you mind if people are around?

JG: Both. Sometimes the only place to practice when I'm on the road is in lobbies, and oftentimes people are coming in and out. I don't mind it, depending on what I'm doing.

Being "private in public" is one of the things that our acting is. It's a cornerstone of the acting credo because you gotta shoot scenes in movies sometimes on Fifth Avenue in New York, and you haven't rehearsed, and you don't know what it is, so you gotta work it out and find it while other people are gawking at you, and while the other actors are looking and going, "Uh-oh, I don't think he's got it yet."

In a similar vein, sometimes actors go, "Oh, don't be in my eye line. When the camera is rolling, I want to imagine as easily as I can that I'm in the camera-less place that I'm supposed to be depicting, and if the crew is back there, I don't wanna see them." Another actor, who I really like—and I sort of aspire to this credo myself—said, "Oh no, no, that's not me, do anything. As a matter of fact, try to distract me. You won't be able to do it."

JC: I can perform in those kinds of situations because I worked at Disneyland for five years.

JG: I know that about you! We have a Disney connection too! I'm doing this show, *The World According to Jeff Goldblum*, which is on Disney Plus. But *you* were at Disneyland!

JC: *The Disney training was fantastic because for starters, I was wearing a turn-of-the-century outfit, so right away you have to give up who you are.*

JG: Right! There's something good about that.

JC: *And kids would sneak up and push me. I'd stop playing and they'd say, "Mom, she's not Audio-Animatronic. She's not Great Moments with Mr. Lincoln." And every now and then, kids would squirt ketchup on me, just to see if I'd stop playing. Thanks to that, I can do anything now, although I try to avoid ketchup coming at me.*

JG: Right. But now you can't play as well *unless* somebody's squirting ketchup on you.

JC: *Exactly. It's required.*

JG: I'm gonna try that. Tomorrow morning. Forget we had this conversation. I want you to be surprised when I sneak up while you're practicing . . .

JC: *"When did you last see Jeff? Wasn't it with a ketchup bottle in his hand?" Very funny!*

Now listen, I want to keep you here for another hour, but we should talk about The World According to Jeff Goldblum *before we wrap up. You're paid to be curious. How wonderful is that?*

JG: And I don't even have to pretend to know anything that I don't.

JC: *Because you're learning about it.*

JG: Yeah. I'm learning and saying, "Here, come with me and let's see if we can learn something." If you're interested, like I am, this is not dissimilar from my music. I'm going, "Hey, I'm a work in progress. I'm not pretending to know anything. I'm not trying to impress you. I'm just trying to take us both on a little adventure of learning and experience."

JC: *No judgment. That's a great message. Also, I want to give you a big compliment.*

Full-time jazz musicians can be very resentful of super-famous people who form a rock band, jazz group, whatever, and get into playing the part and say things like, "Oh, now I'm on the road and this is so hard. I'm a cool musician." They amplify all of the clichés. Most jazz musicians are hanging by a thread, as you know, so it's spectacularly irritating to have that pushed in your face by someone who doesn't depend on this for a living. You don't do that.

I especially appreciate that your attitude is, "Come on, baby, we're going to have some fun!" You put out a very clear message that you're grateful to be doing this, want to have fun and learn about jazz by surrounding yourself with great musicians whom you respect and bring your audience into the experience. Thank you for that, Jeff.

JG: Wow, you're so welcome. Well, the gratitude is all on my side. And let's stay in touch. I can talk to you for hours.

JC: *We'll make a plan!*

Gil Goldstein

(b. 1950)

Three-time Grammy-winning jazz pianist, accordionist, arranger, composer and producer.

Interviewed in 2008

Gil Goldstein has worked with some of the biggest names in the music business—everyone from Sting, Justin Timberlake and James Taylor to Gil Evans, David Sanborn and Esperanza Spalding. He loves these disparate stylists and brings equal passion to each project. Gil epitomizes what you want in a collaborator: enthusiasm, emotional engagement, and complete lack of pretense.

Many people tear up on *Jazz Inspired*. Get people talking about their art and what's inspired it, and you touch their heart. Gil is *all* heart, so it wasn't surprising that he couldn't talk about his love for the arranger Gil Evans without tears running down his face. It's the only time I've interrupted an interview to grab a box of Kleenex for a guest.

JC: *What first inspired you to play the accordion?*

GG: I came to accordion from watching Lawrence Welk. The accordion was the star on that show. It was the coolest instrument, had little rhinestones on it. So I fell in love with the accordion early on, probably at two. My dad says I was always saying, "I wanna play accordion." And also, when I grew up in Baltimore in 1950, that was the instrument people started on. It was something parents could afford. I guess they were fifty or eighty dollars. An accordion wasn't a big investment like a piano. Anyway, I started playing the accordion. And then I stopped for many years when I started to feel that it wasn't hip, which was sad because it is my root instrument. I rediscovered it about twenty years ago, and I still love it.

JC: I've had musicians talk about the range of things that you can do with an accordion, in terms of arranging.

GG: I think it's the best. The reeds are labeled clarinet, bassoon, and oboe. They don't really sound like that, but they're different registers. And the accordion meshes perfectly with strings, with woodwinds, with brass. It's the perfect—I don't know how to say it—*accompanimental* instrument. Is that a word?

JC: We're making it a word. Because of the sound of it, the timbre of it?

GG: I honestly don't know why. It seems to be kind of a sponge when I'm playing with strings. I did a record last year where I overdubbed arrangements for Abbey Lincoln. I had a great idea for a really weird combination of instruments that didn't sound so great. There was a cellist coming in, so we replaced the four voices that I wrote for with two accordions, me playing both, with two cellos. And it sounded so good. You can't tell where the accordion starts, and the cello leaves off. It's one sound. It's the same thing with woodwinds. And somehow, I feel like it's my beginnings as an arranger, to work on the accordion. You have the palette of an orchestra when you're working with the accordion.

JC: That must have helped you in terms of how you think musically. It seems like it would be a good core or base instrument to start with, to help learn about music.

GG: I think it is. Another thing that's different than the piano—I started playing piano when I was about nine, and I started playing accordion when

I was five—is that the accordion really has the breadth you don't have with the piano because you can hold a note for twenty, thirty seconds, and you can end a note. You can go deep, it can stop, and it's a little harder to do that on the piano.

The other thing that you can do on the accordion that's incredible, which I just discovered not long ago, is you can just rock your finger for vibrato. We all do that on the piano. You wanna make a little vibrato. On the accordion, you actually *can* vibrato because it rocks the thing that goes over the reed, and it really does create a vibrato. So that was always my dream. In college, when I would study classical piano, my teacher—he was a great teacher, Dr. Stewart Gordon, at the University of Maryland—would say, "Gil, you can rock your finger as much as you want; it's not gonna affect the sound." I always envied cellists and violinists because they could really put that into a sound. They can vibrato and change the amplitude of the sound. Judy, I'm gonna get you playing accordion!

JC: I think it's a great instrument, and I always like that aspect of being able to—no one can see me doing this, but I'm acting like I'm playing an accordion—to be able to sustain the notes the way you're talking about, because that's the thing we miss with the piano. Anyway, talk about your song "Snowbound," because you say you play bass accordion on it. I don't know about bass accordion.

GG: Well, I didn't know about it either until I found one in a store in Nyack, north of New York City, which I don't think is there anymore. Actually, this leads to a funny story. The great pianist, Don Grolnick worked with James Taylor for many years. I was touring with Pat Metheny when Don was on the road with James, so we were always in the same place with our tours overlapping. They were doing smaller venues and recording a live record. Don heard me play accordion because I played a lot of accordion with Pat. One day he called and said, "James has always wanted accordion in the group" and I was like, "Yeah, man, this is gonna be great!" And then Don said, "So can you tell me a good place where I can get one?" [Laughs]

Don was a great accordionist, so I recommended the Nyack place, where he bought a very nice Bell accordion. I became very good friends with the guy who owned the shop after Don bought his most expensive accordion. One day I went up there to buy some accordions for myself and he had a bass accordion, which I didn't know anything about. It's a bit of a paradox because the bass accordion is only the right hand but it's in a very low register and doesn't have a left hand. It doesn't have any buttons. You just hold the strap. They used to use them in accordion orchestras; they'd have three bass accordions. It's a great sound.

I got to play with Jim Hall, who is a total inspiration and who I stalked from when I first moved to New York. I knew he lived at a certain address, so I'd just hang in the neighborhood. I was trying to bump into him. Eventually I got to meet him and play with him for many years and it was great. So I told him that I'd gotten a bass accordion. He called me up and had me play it for him over the phone and then he wrote a song based on the sound of the bass accordion.

JC: *I love that! Talk about Gil Evans.*

GG: It's hard to talk about Gil Evans without getting a little teary, because . . . [Starts crying] Yeah, so here we go. Take two.

JC: *I feel that way about Gil Evans too, and I didn't know him like you did.*

GG: He was also a very, very sweet guy, and very smart and very . . . He had all the qualities that made me say, "That's what I wanna do." I always felt like, "Gil Evans . . . I'm not gonna understand that for a while." I'd listen to the records, and I'd go, "It's a little too much for me." It's like, "I can't even start to understand what he's playing."

Another inspiration for me, obviously, was Bill Evans. He was somebody that when I went to the University of Miami in 1973, I had an idea about. I eventually wrote a book about this idea, about a line going through a solo that connects, kind of a pitch access thing. And I said, "Gee, I noticed that in Bill Evans' solos, but I wonder if he's thinking that when he does it."

So I called up information. I knew he lived in Riverdale, and he picked up the phone and he said, "Hello." And I went, "That's Bill Evans." I could hear it in his voice. And I said, "O.K., hey, I'm Gil, and I'm a student at the University of Miami." And he went, "O.K.," and I asked him the question, and he gave me a totally clear answer.

"Of course, I know that happens," he said, "and I'm trying for that to happen, but I can't consciously think, I can only hope that it occurs." And I said, "That's fair, you're not thinking, 'I gotta connect a C to a B and then go down.'" And he said, "But I've trained myself to hear like that." And I said, "But what do you think of when you play?" He goes, "Well, I try to create a motif and then develop it." And I thought, "What a simple thing. Really? That's it? God, maybe he needs more." I almost felt sorry for him for a minute.

JC: *I'd say he did pretty well with that, Gil. [Laughs]*

GG: But if you think about that, and you hear him play and you go, "O.K., he came up with this little idea. And now he's varying it. Oh, he's displacing the rhythm." I don't know if you know the video he did with his brother, called *The Universal Mind*.

JC: *I've cried when I watch that, because it's profound on so many levels. The psychology of his brother asking him the questions and Bill answering very clearly. So clear and so honest. I think that that tape should be shown to everyone, on so many subjects, not just on piano. Because of the honesty of it. And what his brother keeps trying to get him to say . . . to make it more complicated.*

GG: Explaining the concept of creativity.

JC: *It's about this simple thing. He has an idea. He tries to get a motif and develop it. That really is basically what we're all trying to do.*

GG: Right. And he just happened to realize that he could put it into words like that and clarify it. But also, the thing that he said in there about learning, in general. He said, "I see students who try to learn too many things at once. You really have to say, 'All right, I'm gonna work on this and work on the rhythm.'" And to me, it's like you said, it's something that everyone, in every discipline should watch, if they're an artist or an actor. It's really the nature of learning and the universal mind. I loved that he started it with that. You remember, it starts with him saying, "The universal mind. We have to contact it so that if we contact it, then the listener recognizes it. If we didn't contact it, there's no communication."

JC: *And it's so beautiful because of the honesty on intent. He was brilliant enough to be able to illustrate this idea, which is very difficult to explain. He illustrates somebody playing who is not being honest, who's just using unrelated ideas beyond their ability rather than working within their vocabulary and doing what they know. They say to writers, "Write about what you know," and it applies here. Play within your vocabulary and say something meaningful. If you're using unrelated ideas beyond yourself, it has no meaning and doesn't connect to the universal mind.*

GG: Exactly. It was what he also used to say, "You have to find the true solution to the problem, truth for you. This is my solution; this is my rhythm that I choose to play. And that you feel totally that it's an honest musical choice. And he could recognize also in himself when he'd say, "That's not honest. I'm going to reject that."

JC: *You've written for the Carnegie Hall Rainforest concerts for Sting, James Taylor, and Billy Joel. How do you arrange for such different artists?*

GG: That's a little bit different than the arranging I do when I work with somebody like Dave Sanborn or Michael Brecker or Chris Botti. I feel like I have to develop a completely unique style for all those people. It's like it's custom-made. Now, saying that, this is usually pretty fast, how it comes together for the Rainforest, and I don't have much interaction with the musicians. But I did play with Sting with Gil Evans many years ago in Perugia. We did a concert together, so I knew he loved Gil Evans. I had to write an arrangement of *Moon River* for the last Rainforest concert, so I tried to make it sound like Gil Evans. And when it was over, he went, "Sounds like Gil. Not you, the other Gil."

JC: *But that's what he wanted.*

GG: That's what I thought he wanted. And it's another funny tie-in with that story because the opening song for that Rainforest concert was *That's Amore*. They had originally called me just to play accordion, and then they said, "Oh, by the way, we need some arrangements. Would you have time to do some arrangements?" I said, "Yeah." And then they said, "Also, do you conduct?" I said, "Oh, yeah, I'm kind of a conductor." So then I was the conducting accordionist arranger. I conducted *That's Amore* with the accordion at Carnegie Hall. I still love *That's Amore* for some reason.

JC: *That's fantastic. Talk about from Lawrence Welk to Carnegie Hall. How hip is this?*

GG: Exactly. And who conducted from an accordion at Carnegie Hall? Not many people.

JC: *Talk about Pat Metheny.*

GG: Well, I was very lucky to go to the University of Miami at the same time that Pat was there, in 1973, I think. It was also a time when Jaco Pastorius was in Florida. So, it was really an eye-opening year in Florida. And I heard Pat play the first time in a classroom, on my third day of class. And he played with the same intensity he does today. It might have been even a little bit more forceful, because he had just discovered it. And the same was true for Jaco, that almost in the beginning, they played it even more like, "I'm trying to get this out and prove this theory."

It was like, "Wow, this is a whole new language." And again, with Pat and with Jaco, I said, "Someday I hope to." I get to work with Pat a good deal but not enough. I wanna work with him more. Jaco, I never got to really work with in his short life. But I'm a big fan of his music. About ten years ago, I decided that whenever I do a project, I'm gonna include Jaco's music, 'cause he's an incredible composer. Whether he's playing it or not, the music itself is so strong. And he didn't write that many songs, I guess he only wrote about thirty or forty songs, but they're so . . . I don't even know the word . . . they're really so modern, for lack of a better word. And Pat, too, he was writing songs and continues to write songs that you can find some roots in it, and then it goes into a whole new language, and it's like another example of somebody really finding their voice and being able to state it very truly.

JC: Which do you prefer playing, accordion or piano? Because we've talked a lot about accordion, but you're a monster piano player.

GG: Unfortunately, with piano, in the last couple of years, I've had it overshadowed a little with accordion, but my love for piano tends to come back from time to time, and I'm in a piano phase now. One of the things that I'm always afraid of with piano, though, is that I go to a place, and have to play a strange instrument. With accordion, it's always my old friend, so that's a little bit hard for me. Now, you have to deal with that all the time.

JC: But that's all I know. So, at the same time as you're saying this, I'm thinking, "If I got hooked into playing the same piano every time, I'd be less tolerant. I don't like it, but you're right, I'm used to it. But if I had a choice like you do, I'd probably want to play the accordion, because I'd know I've got my old friend with me.

GG: Sometimes it's very difficult for me with piano concerts, playing live. In the studio, I'm very particular about certain pianos, and there's been a couple pianos that I totally loved, and I feel like I almost couldn't play what I played without that piano. So I'm very dependent on the sound of an instrument, and I'm almost helpless when I get behind an instrument that

I feel like I can't really communicate with, even if it's a great instrument, but just not my style of great piano.

JC: We haven't talked a lot about that on this show, and I think about that a lot. You're making me feel better, because very often I'm in situations where the piano just isn't working, especially with stride. If it's a piano that I can't play soft, it's a problem. A lot of them, if they're not regulated right, you either hit them hard, or you have to lay into it and push the keys down slowly. But if you're hitting them percussively like I do, there's no control. And I really have trouble getting a decent softer sound. I'll wind up using the soft pedal just to try to get some dynamics.

GG: I know. I have a confession in that I almost always use the soft pedal, because to me, if it's not a great piano, then I think, at least I have two of the three strings. It's like two-thirds as bad.

JC: You're making me feel better. Seriously, I always feel horribly guilty about doing this. It feels like a cop-out if I'm using a soft pedal.

GG: I feel guilty, too. I have a funny story about the first record I did for Blue Note. Michel Petrucciani used to live in my neighborhood in Brooklyn, and we were friends. He listened to one of the early takes of the record, and he goes, "Man, you use the soft pedal a lot." He could hear the soft pedal. He goes, "Now you took it off, now it's on, now it's off." And he said, "That would have sounded completely different if you didn't play it with this soft pedal." And I went, "You're putting me on, aren't you?" And he goes, "No. I could hear it."

JC: How do you play accordion with a pianist or another chordal instrument? Although you play with guitar all the time.

GG: I personally really like playing with other chordal instruments. I always wanted to play with Jim Hall, and I always wanted to play with guitars. My first inspiration and my first gig was with Pat Martino and it was like, "That's what I like. I like being with another chordal instrument."

The last thing that I did at the University of Miami was a Jazz Forum that Pat did there for the students. I played a duet with him, and I said to my piano teacher, "Hey, I'm doing a thing with Pat today at the Jazz Forum." He goes, "I don't like guitar and piano together." And I went, "You don't like guitar and piano? That's my favorite stuff. Bill Evans and Jim Hall, that's what I live for." And I decided right at that moment . . . I did a total reverse psychology of his teaching. I went, "That's gonna be my thing." He just made me confirm my love for it, 'cause I went, "What's not to like?" It's two beautiful instruments that have a chance to cooperate."

JC: Talk about someone hiring you. Say I'm hiring you now to arrange something for me . . .

GG: Is this a real job offer?

JC: I knew you were gonna ask me that. How would you do it? You talk to somebody, find what they want, brainstorm on where you want to go?

GG: Yeah. I do a little bit of research if somebody asks me to arrange for them. And I start listening to their records. Also, with the age of concept records, a lot of people would say, "O.K., James Moody is gonna do a Sinatra record for Warner Brothers; that's gonna be his first record." So I go, "O.K., great opportunity." I know Frank Sinatra, but I hadn't really studied Sinatra. So I read an autobiography and start listening to all the records and then start listening to James Moody and trying to find where's the place that they're gonna meet. I feel very lucky to do that, to come into contact with so many great musicians, singers, and instrumentalists.

JC: Talk about this project with Juliette Greco, Le Temps D'Une Chanson (The Moment for a Song).

GG: She's a great French singer. She was one of Miles' French girlfriends who had a lot of photos done, and I'd seen her in that. But I didn't know half the story. She was there with Jean-Paul Sartre, and she was very into that whole scene as a thinker and a poet, and she's on the same level as Edith Piaf in France; she's a national treasure. And coincidentally, when I started playing music, my parents, they weren't musicians, but my dad liked French music, so I always heard French music, and there was a lot of accordion records and French-style music. So somehow in the back of my head I have that sound connected with the accordion.

It seemed pretty natural, but I like to think that I'm pretty natural to every style. I like to think of myself as someone who can absorb a style and reinvent it in my own way. I play with guys that play with Paco De Lucía, I played with a lot of the Brazilian musicians, and I feel like, "I can understand this style." And it makes me feel like I can broaden my base of music. I shouldn't necessarily be a jazz musician, I like improvised music and I love jazz, but it's not my natural thing that I should be drawn to.

I don't mean to be racist about myself, but I just feel . . . not that I should be doing Yiddish music, but I just feel like, "Gee, we're born into a time and a place, and maybe there is a music that we should play, I don't know. Still, I think in the end everybody has to outgrow where they're born into. There's so much stuff out there that I wanna know it all, I don't wanna leave anything out. And I arranged for Richard Bona, who grew up in the Cameroon, in a small village, and I feel totally comfortable. Even though I'm from Baltimore.

JC: I think that's your gift, that you really do love all these things. You're musically curious. And you've created a career where you capitalize on that gift. A lot of people are unfocused and don't get anything done if they have that personality. They're just dilettantes. But you really love it all. Every time we've talked, it's been, "Let's play together." Or, "I wanna do a two-accordion project." You mention loaning me an accordion and I know it's actually gonna show up. You're that enthusiastic all the way from going from Juliette Greco to Judy Carmichael to Sting.

I've been a fan of yours for so long, I'm thrilled that you took this time. And I'm really looking forward to the piano-accordion project.

GG: Well, something that I haven't explored on the accordion is stride. And with accordion, there's something that's really very natural to stride, because the buttons are really set up for that. There's a row of the bass notes, and then there's the chords there.

JC: So this is going to take you in a different direction?

GG: I'm already thinking of some things.

JC: I know it's going to take me in a different direction, too. It's bringing out the inner accordion lover in me.

GG: That's what we try to do. You do that with stride, which you love. And I do that with the music that I love. We try to bring it to people and say, "Check this out."

Christopher Guest

(b. 1948)

Screenwriter, composer, musician, director, actor, and comedian. Along with Martin Short, Billy Crystal, and Harry Shearer, Guest was hired as a one-year-only cast member for the 1984-85 season of *Saturday Night Live*.

Interviewed in 2004

Christopher Guest is a favorite among Hollywood insiders, a unique presence in a town in which everyone *thinks* they're unique, but many are just another pretty face. More than anyone, Guest is the one who people in the business are most impressed with when I say I corralled him for *Jazz Inspired*.

Guest has been distinctive in a broad range of comedic and dramatic roles on Broadway and in television and film, playing everything from Count Rugen in *The Princess Bride* and Dr. Stone in *A Few Good Men*, to a memorable year on *Saturday Night Live* with Billy Crystal, Martin Short, and Harry Shearer.

The performance style that Guest finds most exhilarating is the improvised tour de force he displayed as Nigel Tufnel, the lead guitarist of the heavy metal band, Spinal Tap, in Rob Reiner's *This Is Spinal Tap*. Guest honed this "mockumentary" style in his own films, *Waiting for Guffman, Best in Show, A Mighty Wind,* and *For Your Consideration*, which he directed and co-wrote. An interesting addition to Guest's CV is his dual British/American citizenship as the 5th Baron Haden-Guest, which surely gives him a leg up when it comes to the various British accents he's employed in multiple roles.

My experience with Christopher Guest was surprising, unusual, and hilarious. I'd originally read an article that referred to Guest and his wife—the actress Jamie Lee Curtis—as the coolest couple in Hollywood. The article also discussed Guest's improvisational filmmaking style, which he feels is similar to jazz. Guest starts with a plot and the characters, then has each actor improvise their lines as they work their way through the story. Jazz musicians start with a tune, they and their instrument are their character, and they improvise their way through a song. Guest is also a musician, so he was perfect for *Jazz Inspired*.

For years, I asked around to see if anyone I knew could get to him. Word had it that he didn't like to be interviewed and could be an unresponsive interviewee. In the midst of my pursuit, a screenwriter acquaintance asked me to a dinner in her East Hampton home that she was calling "Five Great Women." The conversation was mainly about the movie business, and at one point, the woman seated to my left, Jean Guest, launched into a discussion about her son Chris and his latest movie.

"Wait, do you mean *Christopher Guest*? I'm dying to have him on my show! I didn't realize he's your son!"

She turned away, stabbed a carrot with her fork, and firmly replied, "I can't help you with Chris."

"No, no, no!" I feebly replied. "I wasn't asking for help!"

Rule No. 1: Never ask a new friend for help with Hollywood people. For that matter, don't ask an *old* friend for help with Hollywood people.

Rule No. 2: Never say what you're thinking with Hollywood people.

Meanwhile, out in Santa Monica, a close buddy of mine was taking her morning walk through a beautiful area of that town called Rustic Canyon, right by the dog park that inspired Guest's movie, *Best in Show*. I knew that Guest lived in this area but didn't know that my pal had taken matters into her own hands and decided to deposit my *Jazz Inspired* press kit in the Curtis/Guest mailbox.

I was on tour when my assistant called and exclaimed, "You have to listen to this! This just came in on your voicemail!"

"Hi, Judy. This is Jamie Lee Curtis. We obviously have a friend in common. I've read your material and love the theme of your show, but I'm not the right person for you; my husband is. His name is Christopher Guest. Call him. Here's his cell number."

I called him the next day, told him the concept of the show, and this man who everyone said would be resistant to this sort of thing, said, "Sounds like fun. Sure."

Coolest couple indeed, but a challenge. Guest gives very little feedback, is often monosyllabic, and has essentially dispensed with all the conversational niceties the rest of us use to facilitate fluid conversation. He's completely engaged, fiercely intelligent, and expects the same from you. He also periodically threw me an improvisational line to see if I'd go down that path, which I did. At one point, our conversation went like this:

Me: "Does it bother you ..."

He: [Cutting me off] "Yes."

Me: [Waiting a few seconds] "Hmm...interesting. That bothers me too."

Rob Reiner famously hosted a dinner honoring Christopher Guest that was attended by a hundred of Guest's closest friends. Reiner's first words from the podium were, "How many of you have asked yourself, at some time or another, 'I wonder if Chris likes me?'"

I survived the *Jazz Inspired* interview, enjoyed it, and afterwards even received a final surprising tribute to my efforts on my voicemail.

"Hi, Judy, Jean Guest here. I just heard your interview with Chris. He obviously liked you a lot. He usually doesn't talk that much."

Christopher Guest and I met at the NPR studios in Los Angeles in 2004, when he was in the midst of filming *A Mighty Wind*.

JC: How do you equate your moviemaking process with jazz?

CG: There are some similarities. I think that in jazz there's obviously a melody or a song, and players are given the chance to take off from the melody. You start out in a certain key. People can take off from there. My films are somewhat different because there is no script. There is no dialogue written down. But there is a story, and that's in some way the analogy to having a tune. Everyone in a scene will know the point of a scene—where the scene has to begin or end—but getting there is up to the individual actors. I guess that's the connection.

JC: How do you work with your actors? You obviously know what they're capable of, but do you tweak their characterizations?

CG: First of all, these are people who I know can do this work. There are very few actors who can do this in the first place. This is not something you can really learn how to do. You can perhaps learn how to do it better or get better at it. You can't show up and do it. I give them a lot of leeway. I have a lot of trust in them because I know what they can do. I write a character for them, and I give them the background for their character, where they grew up, the facts associated with the character. But then it is up to them to go from there. There is no rehearsal. They show up after I've talked to them about these characters, prior to filming. We show up, and the camera starts rolling. It's totally pure in the sense that what you're hearing being said is being said for the first time.

JC: One of the things that really appeals to me about your films is the commitment of these actors and how honest emotionally the films wind up being, which speaks to me as a musician and as an artist. It's even more moving because these are characters who aren't just doing something funny; it's really about the character and coming from a deeper place. I find it more real than a typical documentary that becomes less real because the people know they're being filmed. These actors are coming from an honest place. They seem to stretch out in an amazing way, like a jazz musician. Certain musicians, if they really get into a jazz chorus, can go to the edge emotionally and take the listener to that same place, which is the way I feel watching your films.

CG: I think that's true. They go to places you really can't imagine prior to writing the story. It does come down once again to picking the people I'm lucky enough to have—Eugene Levy, Catherine O'Hara, Fred Willard, Parker Posey. They have tremendous courage. You need to have courage and not feel restrained in any way. In the same way that you would hope that a musician wouldn't have any boundaries and that would be the ideal thing. I think the actors really enjoy this process more than some more conventional films, which are a little bit more restrictive.

JC: Fred Willard in Best in Show *is what I'd call a great chorus. It's Paul Gonsalves at Newport. He just keeps going and it's so funny. Do you think that was a surprise to him?*

CG: Well, I can't speak for him personally. I only know that when I do that—go off on an improvisational tangent—I couldn't tell you afterwards exactly what happened. I couldn't tell you more than a couple words of what happened.

JC: Don't you think that's what is happening when you're improvising music? I think it comes from a similar place.

CG: Yes, I think you're right.

JC: What jazz did you first listen to?

CG: As a kid I first listened to Charlie Christian and then got deeply interested in the well-known jazz players, like Jim Hall and later Larry Coryell. I used to go to the Village Vanguard to listen to Kenny Burrell. I was just obsessed with the sound of that bebop guitar because it was a very specific tone. But I have a wide variety of interests, and there are a lot of other guitarists that are favorites. Ry Cooder is a favorite of mine.

JC: What were your earliest experiences with music?

CG: My first instrument was a clarinet. A B-flat clarinet.

JC: Why were you drawn to that?

CG: I wasn't.

JC: It was handed to you?

CG: No, it wasn't handed to me.

JC: It was thrown *at you?*

CG: [Sighs] I was taken to a music school. My mother said, "What would you like to play?" I said, "Drums, definitely drums." She said, "No. What else?" "Trumpet would be cool." She said, "No trumpet." Just the noise, I guess. "What else do you have here?" *"The clarinet."* I remember making a face. The *clarinet* [said with distaste]. No offense, but it's not what you want to hear. So I played the clarinet for a while.

I went to a high school in New York City called Music and Art, a school for training classical musicians. But pretty soon it was evident that I was drifting off into another area. So the next instrument was the guitar and then the mandolin after that.

JC: But those instruments were your choices, right?

CG: Yes.

JC: Does your music refresh your moviemaking process and your moviemaking process refresh your music or are they organically mixed?

CG: Well, they probably are, if I would think about it, but I don't. I need to play music and I need to hear music. I need to hear different voices. I don't mean in a Joan of Arc way.

[Laughter]

I collect guitars, and each one represents a different sound. When you pick up a different guitar, it will make you play a different way. When I do characters in movies, I hear, as a musician, the voice of the character. I am improvising in that voice. I have to like the voice. If I pick up a guitar that I don't like the sound of, I'm not going to be motivated to play. There are certain instruments you can't put down. So, in that sense there is a connection.

JC: You have such a wonderful ear for accents and a great eye for detail. Do you remember as a child being a big observer and consciously taking notes, as if you were building a file cabinet of behaviors?

CG: I remember as a kid in New York that the city was a great place to observe people. There are so many people on the street. That's one of my earliest memories of being very conscious of the way people spoke and the way they walked. I was maybe six or seven. I'd sit in the window and watch people, and then I'd imitate the way they walked.

JC: That, in its own way, is a jazz thing to me, because certainly jazz musicians are listening to different kinds of music, picking up different ideas and making it all their own and putting them into their own voice, like you're talking about. How long did you play clarinet before you escaped?

CG: A long time. I guess I played for about eight years.

JC: A long time! Well, we'll move on to a less painful subject. Folk music is close to your heart. A Mighty Wind, *which you're working on now, is about folk music.*

CG: I played bluegrass starting when I was fourteen or so. It was interesting to me because the technique required to play it was so different than for other kinds of folk music. The film I'm doing is about folk musicians from the '60s who are trying to make a comeback. I've written some songs with Michael McKean and Harry Shearer and Eugene Levy for this film. This is a different kind of music. It's not technically challenging. It's of a period, and it's very specifically geared for comedic purposes.

JC: On another subject, some musicians can play jazz and classical, but most . . .

CG: Can't.

JC: Exactly. Do you find it's the same in making movies for you, that you can be in a play and you're doing the same lines every night and . . .

CG: No. It's true about music. I think there are very few classical players who can jump over. It's nice when they take the chance to do it. There's a record that Yehudi Menuhin did which was kind of fun. I remember as a clarinetist, when I was in school, and someone said, "We're just gonna jam." I said, "Great, where's the music?" and they said, "No, no, we're just gonna play." And I said, "What are we gonna play?" and they said, "We're just going to play, and you'll play along." I had only read music. "Well, what would I play?" That was obviously my problem, that I couldn't do this, but the minute I picked up a guitar, that wasn't an issue. I could just go. For some reason, the training with clarinet had narrowed my scope. I could read and play the music, but the idea of just playing something else, I couldn't do that.

JC: You haven't mentioned playing the piano, but in This Is Spinal Tap *there's a wonderful scene where you're composing a tune, that D-minor tune. Did that scene just come to you?*

CG: I'm not really a piano player. But I play a little piano, and I write on the piano sometimes. I'd been working on this tune which, if you separate from the joke context, is actually O.K. I kind of like the melody of it. I only had the tune, but the words were all improvised. I just sat down and that's what happened.

JC: I'm struck by the musical choices we talked about playing today, your favorites. They're all very emotional. You said "Giant Steps," which is an up-tempo kind of thing, but the other ones are romantic, wistful and a bit melancholy.

CG: I think I *am* melancholy.

JC: Is that the kind of music you put on at home a lot of the time?

CG: No. I think I have a pretty eclectic collection of things. I often wonder what you'd hear, if you went into somebody's CD carousel in their car. Mine goes from Tal Farlow to Ella Fitzgerald to bluegrass to the Chieftains. It's just a wild mix of different sounds.

JC: Do you like that variety, skipping around from one style to the next?

CG: Yes. But I listen to one CD then another. I don't generally get through six CD because I'm not driving to Argentina.

JC: Well, I figured with the traffic in L.A. you'd have the time.

CG: You have that right.

JC: I was asking because I'm a very energetic, up-tempo kind of musician, and I've been playing more ballads lately, and I think it's because I'm actually happier. I've noticed in my own life that I don't think I was ever happy enough to play ballads. Ballads would make me more unhappy. I'm fascinated that you say you're melancholy and you're drawn to that type of music. Do you go in the opposite direction to get you into a different mood?

CG: I'm also drawn to the idea of a slower tempo because for a guitar player—and it's true certainly in jazz—it seems that people fall into certain patterns when you play fast. Then everything starts to sound the same. There are obviously people who don't do that, but it's harder because you have to think faster. And you tend to rely on tricks that you know. To play slow is really hard.

I guess I base my judgments of someone's playing on the slow songs on the record rather than the ones they play fast. If you can play slow and get me, then it's really magical. In slow songs it tends to be more chordal than it is single notes. Then it starts to meld in with something like the way Bill Evans plays. With a great guitar player playing slowly, the voicings start to be very similar, and that's very intriguing to me, hearing those close voicings.

JC: *Also the tone. People who allow themselves to play slower are comfortable with the spaces between the notes. They're going to a different emotional place. Again, I think about your films. These actors are comfortable going to that deep place.*

CG: It's definitely slower. I'm intrigued by dialogue with real-time speaking as opposed to conventional films, which are cut to a rhythm of the way people talk. It's not the *real* rhythm of the way people talk. It's manipulated. In my films, they go on and on for quite a long time. That interests me. Maybe that has a connection to the slower songs, people who aren't afraid of that space.

JC: *What about John Coltrane?*

CG: His sound is so evocative and so different that regardless of the speed or the tempo it is very haunting to me. Right from the beginning that really grabbed me. Right from when I was fourteen or fifteen, that was a very powerful sound.

JC: *Who are your favorite jazz singers?*

CG: Ella Fitzgerald's voice is so remarkable in its tone and musicality that it's hard to beat that. Obviously, there's Sarah Vaughan and so many great singers, but Fitzgerald is the one that did and still does touch me.

JC: *Really? Because she's not a singer people would mention for bringing out that emotional quality we've talked about. She's a virtuoso and has a gorgeous voice, but she's not Billie Holiday.*

CG: That's true. It's more polished. But it's the tone of the voice. I recently bought the entire set of songbooks that she did, about twelve CD's. It's a stunning body of work. The ballads are the ones that really kill me.

JC: *Are there any male singers who have that same quality? I ask because nobody mentions the men.*

CG: You're right. That's interesting, isn't it? I bought a set of Mel Tormé stuff from the very beginning of his career. He does a version of "I Cover the Waterfront" that is staggering.

I got to know him a little bit. I had this inclination or intuition that he could improvise as a talking improviser, and I invited him to do a scene with Spinal Tap in a TV show that we did about ten years ago. I got his number, and I called him up. He said, "Hey, man, how are you doing? I love the movies, man." And I said, "How would you like to do a scene with us for this TV show?" And he said, *"Let's swing."* He shows up the next day. He sat there and then took off. It was as if he was born to do that. It was swinging, and it didn't miss a beat. And it was funny, and it was perfect, and it was great.

JC: What sort of scene was it?

CG: We were sitting in a delicatessen. The joke was that we all meet in a deli every morning to talk. We thought it would be funny if Mel Tormé was there. He was incredible. There were things he did that were just remarkable.

JC: What about him made you have that sense?

CG: When I cast my films, I don't audition anyone, because there's no written script, there's no words. I just talk to them. You can tell in three seconds. I had seen Tormé on TV, and I had a feeling that it was gonna work.

JC: Were you doing this kind of improvising when you were a kid?

CG: Yes, I was improvising right away. I didn't know what it was. In New York City, unlike Chicago, which had *Second City*, there wasn't anything like that. I just didn't know any better. I just did it with friends.

JC: Tell me about Miles Davis, another of your favorites.

CG: I wasn't initially drawn to the trumpet, other than when I was kid, and I thought it would be fun to play the trumpet because it was loud. To listen to Miles is not like listening to other trumpet players. There's something so complex emotionally and raw. To refer to him as a technical virtuoso wouldn't have anything to do with what he did. There were obviously other players who could play around him, but that wasn't what this was about. I was drawn and repelled by the naked pain of it. I couldn't take very much of it because it was so painful, but there were times when I needed to hear that.

JC: Who are some of your other favorite musicians?

CG: Béla Fleck is a banjo player, which you wouldn't associate with jazz. He's been playing a long time. He's done many records that go off in different directions and that perhaps start with a bluegrass foundation, but he's so technically accomplished that he's gone off in wild areas. I was lucky enough to play with him once in Nashville. His mind, it's just extraordinary. He's done a classical record. He plays jazz. He plays all kinds of music. It's just miraculous to me.

JC: You keep up your bluegrass playing. That's more improvisational. Do you do that with your mandolin and guitar?

CG: Yeah. I enjoy it. This is the kind of schizophrenic world I live in. I have a three-level house, and in the basement, or first floor, I have a recording studio. I have twelve guitars in the basement, one of them is my favorite jazz guitar. On the middle floor, I have two acoustics and a mandolin. On the top floor, I have an acoustic guitar and a mandolin. Depending on what floor you're on, you pick up that guitar and you're in that world.

JC: Do have any recordings of yourself playing?

CG: The irony is that my career took this turn in my early twenties when I was interested in comedy and in combining comedy and music. So the music I tend to do is funny. Well, it's not the music itself being funny, per se, but when you combine it with the funny lyrics we do in Spinal Tap, it's funny. If you take away the lyrics, Spinal Tap is just a heavy metal band. It's even more convoluted because the playing I do as the guy in Spinal Tap is not the kind of playing I would choose to do. It's very over the top and stupid, basically, which I find funny.

But the answer is no. I'm sure I have something at home, but to find it, well, I'll talk to you in a few years.

JC: Did you think this is just a casual, little thing, Chris? This is one of those shows that's going to take years of production, so you have time.

CG: No, I imagine 2005, 2006, something? A couple of years to get this together?

JC: Exactly. This is big. A friend of mine compares my production schedules to the making of Ben Hur. It's an enormous, complicated project. Although nobody has been killed . . . yet.

CG: Good. That's encouraging.

JC: If you look outside, you'll see I parked right behind a chariot.

CG: Really?

JC: You didn't see that out there? That was my car.

CG: I hate to tell you, but they put a boot on that chariot.

Don Hahn

(b. 1955)

Filmmaker, writer, painter, and musician. Two Oscar nominations, two Golden Globes and numerous other awards.

Interviewed in 2020

Don Hahn produced *Beauty and the Beast* in 1991, the first animated film to receive a Best Picture Academy Award nomination, as well as receive more nominations than any animated movie in Oscar history. In 1994, he went on to produce *The Lion King*, the top-grossing traditionally animated film of all time. Don writes, paints, plays music, makes films and feels each activity keeps the others fresh and interesting. Throughout our conversation, he returned to the theme of honoring the people he most admires, those who have remained creative throughout their lives and continually evolve in their view of both their art and the world.

 Don's most recent project is his documentary celebrating the life and genius of the lyricist Howard Ashman, who along with Alan Menken wrote the music for *Little Shop of Horrors, The Little Mermaid, Beauty and the Beast* and many other shows. This was only my second interview conducted during the pandemic and my first done virtually.

JC: *How did you go from a music major to filmmaker?*

DH: I was a music major in college, but I wanted to study all kinds of things. I took journalism, history of religions, and all these other courses because I was curious. And that's always stayed with me. I've never thought of myself as a "producer." In fact, it's taken me ten or twenty years to figure out that I can be all the things that I want to be. That sounds really corny, but it's true. And I tend to spend a lot of time reinventing myself because I get a little bored with things and I love the variety of it all. I love to be able to make movies, then go paint, then go play some music, and then go *listen* to some music.

I think we're sometimes so pressured by our school system. There's a lot of amazing things about it, but it's wrong to say that you *have* to be a dentist or *have* to be anything specific. I don't believe that. The people I've admired in my life were amazing artists *and* great tennis players. They had multiple hyphenates to them. I really idolized those people. Walt Disney is one of them, and Jim Henson and Johnny Carson. I have this kind of curiosity about me that wants to get into all those areas.

JC: I think it refreshes the brain to pursue different things to keep yourself creative.

DH: It does with me. Like when I'm making a film or documentary. Documentaries are small, three or four people, so they're not like an animated film with 600 people and too much money. When you're doing a documentary, stopping to paint or stopping to study the Arts and Crafts movement and John Ruskin or something like that, it refreshes you and it completely takes you off of what you're doing, so when you come back to it you suddenly go, "What the hell was I thinking?" and you have fresh eyes about it. I love that feeling. So I'm always in too many places at once but that's how I live my life and I enjoy that a lot.

JC: I think it's especially great to talk about this at this moment in time and hopefully inspire people to do things they don't usually do. I've had a few people tell me they're bored. I'm stunned by that. I'm not talking about people who are in tragic circumstances right now, but people with money who say this. When the pandemic happened, I immediately thought, when am I ever going to have a year at home? I travel constantly, so this was an opportunity to do new things rather than obsess on what I don't get to do. You mentioned the contrast between working on an animated feature and a documentary. Talk about that.

DH: I was really seduced by animation when I was much younger. I came out of school ready to perform in orchestras and be a player and a teacher, but animation seduced me because I was also an artist. When I went to Disney, that was kind of my university, because animation could stretch any muscle that you have. You could do music, you could stretch your artistic muscles, storytelling muscles, acting, any of that stuff. And it's also highly collaborative which I loved. And so, for gosh thirty-five or forty years, I loved doing animation. But eventually, I reached kind of a burn-out factor, and a lot of that was just wondering if there were other chapters to my life and feeling like the world doesn't need me to do another animated film.

I also felt a little moved by the political situation—and by some of the things that are happening in the world—to focus more on social issues and use my filmmaking skills to tell stories about people who don't have a storyteller, to talk about the disenfranchised and people who need a voice. So that all got me into documentaries. I don't know anything about documentaries but for the last ten years I've tried to learn them, and I've now made more documentaries than I have animated films. And I *love* it!

It's such a different thing. Instead of 600 people and four years—like you have with an animated feature—with a documentary, it's six people and forty minutes. You're doing it really fast. And animation is highly planned. Every drawing and every scene, because of the expense, is highly planned. The documentaries aren't. They're like putting a jigsaw puzzle together without the picture on the box. You're trying to piece together all these disparate elements. And I love that. What happens is, you pick out a story, like the Howard Ashman documentary, and after you're working on it for a while, it starts to tell *you* what the story is. And I just love that feeling.

So for this point in my life and career it's been great. And I'm gonna keep doing it because telling these stories helps me feel better about my role on the planet. We just told a story for PBS about a teacher in Long Beach, California, who teaches these inner-city disenfranchised kids, and teaches them through literature and has them reading Anne Frank and Shakespeare and all these things. To interview her and tell her story, it opens my eyes to the fact that there's a whole world out there of people I never knew. And the privilege to sit down with those people is stunning to me. I admire animation still. It's amazing. But I love what I'm doing now.

JC: *It's wonderful to bring others into the life of these people and help us understand and appreciate them, which I felt with* Howard. *Here's Howard Ashman, whom people may know as a great lyricist, but for me what was so beautiful about that film was your revealing the core of who Howard was. Here was a person with enormous talent, unusual talent, who had to find his own, unique way to realize and utilize it all. You showed us that talent isn't the only thing, and persistence isn't the only thing. Even as an artist myself, with my own story, this was fascinating. I told you earlier that I cried at various times during the film because you revealed the beauty of this individual and what he went through to accomplish all that he did.*

DH: You know what's funny is I thought I knew Howard when I set out to make this film, and I'd been thinking about it for a while. I talked to his sister and his mate, Bill. But when I dove into it, I realized that I didn't know him at all. You peel back the layers and you start to discover. And what I found interesting about him was that inner life, the life that nobody sees. We all kind of wear a mask in public and have our public persona, but the life behind that, the life that Howard lived, was interesting. I also felt like, here's a guy who spent his career writing these beautiful songs for Disney but he's unconventional. Here's this Jewish kid from Baltimore who's gay and goes to Indiana University and moves to New York and opens his own theater? Like, who does *that*? So those were the things that just blew me away.

And *Little Shop of Horrors* comes from a 99-seat theater that Howard opened in this kind of abandoned building in Manhattan and you just go, *wow!* The artistic bravery and heroism that that takes was inspiring to me, and I wanted to show that. I wanted to show his process so that if you're watching it, you'd see why he was so good. See him working with John Musker, Ron Clements, see him working with orchestra, and then you start to see, oh, *I get it.* He was Ursula (the sea witch in *The Little Mermaid*) before Ursula was Ursula. He was Mermaid, he was Belle, and he embodied those characters before anybody ever came onboard on those characters. That was extraordinary at the time I was working with him thirty years ago, but looking back now, you just go, oh, that's a really unique human being.

JC: I love that you had the bits of him directing the actors singing their part. That was interesting for me, even as a professional musician, but I think for people who don't know this process, that would be particularly fascinating. He didn't have the spectacular voice of the people playing these parts, but he knew what the character should convey, and you show that.

DH: I think he was humble and didn't see himself as a singer or maybe even an actor, but he was both those things. I don't know if he read music or did the standard things a professional musician would do, but he got it all and was so tuned in and so learned about musical theater. For instance, he was able to say, "Well Gaston in *Beauty and the Beast* is the opposite of the Beast. He's ugly with a heart of gold, and Gaston is handsome with the heart of a pig." And then he'd say, "Well, Gaston's really like Miles Gloriosus from *A Funny Thing Happened on the Way to the Forum.*" And we'd all go, "Yes, Howard." And then we'd go home and look it up and think, *who the hell was Miles Gloriosus?* We'd have to do our homework just to keep up with him.

JC: You sent a couple of fantastic demos of Howard and Alan Menken. Talk about the original concept of the Genie being a Fats Waller type of character, which I love, of course, being a stride girl.

DH: Well, a demo tape is kind of a what a sketch is to an artist. You're trying to get something raw down on a piece of paper. Once Howard and

Alan had workshopped an idea, they'd record with Alan playing and Howard singing. And those demo tapes were kept and are just a treasure. Some go back thirty years. It's a way to workshop a song. So there might be several demo tapes showing a progression on a single song. And then when it was well enough along, Howard would send those into us.

There was a day when I got a demo with "Belle" and "Be Our Guest" from *Beauty and the Beast*. It was probably the happiest day of my life. But Howard was hesitant about sending it in because he thought no one had asked for a four-minute opening number in *Beauty and the Beast* and he feared they'd be laughed at by everyone involved.

So he had all this brilliance but also all the insecurities that we all have about our art. Are people gonna like this? Is it worthwhile? And I think that was so humanizing when you hear about those stories.

JC: Did Robin Williams, who did the voice of the Genie, listen to this? I know that a lot of actors don't want someone else's interpretation of a character.

DH: All the actors listened to it because it was such a guide track for them. Some actors don't like to hear a line reading or performance reading because they want to bring only themselves to it. But to learn these songs you really have to understand what the intent is.

Howard did another thing that's amazing. He always did these unusual mashups like, let's take Hans Christian Andersen, the precious Danish storyteller, and put it with reggae music in the Caribbean. Let's take '50s girl group rock and put it with a Roger Corman movie. So those kinds of mashups were also really interesting. You had to listen to those tapes to understand how unusual it was.

In the case of the original *Aladdin*, it was conceived as kind of a Fats Waller/Cab Calloway meets a Hope/Crosby road movie. And it's funny because when it went to Broadway it actually turned into that. So the

Broadway version of *Aladdin* is very much like the original Howard version of it. And there's no question that Robin Williams was brilliant in that role and really made that movie.

JC: I hear from one of my spies that your mom played stride piano.

DH: Yes, she did! We grew up in a musical household. She played the organ in church, and at home we always had a piano. She was one of those people who could sight-read beautifully. She was a real woman of the midcentury, kind of a stay-at-home mom, but in retrospect I realize that she had these amazing skills, brilliant skills. She never went to a music school but just through her love of music played that good old-fashioned stride piano. And of course, we listened to Lawrence Welk all the time and Jo Ann Castle. Did you ever think you'd do an interview where Jo Ann Castle came up? [Laughs]

JC: No, but I knew we'd go in some interesting directions!

Earlier you talked about being curious, and in my notes about you I circled the word "curious." I think it's essential for an interesting life to remain curious and to be interested. And to grow up in a household with parents who aren't necessarily super-talented but who are engaged and creative is a great gift. It wasn't until years later, thinking back on my childhood, that I realized that all my friends wanted to come to my house. My parents weren't professional musicians, although they were very talented musicians, but mainly, they were more fun than the other parents. So something was always happening at Judy's house. And you obviously benefitted from the same sort of situation, one that reinforced a certain creativity and curiosity.

DH: Absolutely. I didn't know it at the time, but I was lucky. I was even influenced a little bit from that pre-television generation where everybody played an instrument. At the holidays everybody got around the piano, grabbed a songbook and sang. I had a grandfather who played cello—born in the late 19th century, so another generation—but everybody had an instrument, everybody had a hobby. You'd express yourself that way whether it was cooking or dancing or painting or whatever. And I just thought that's what everybody did.

JC: It was back when being creative was something people aspired to. I almost hate to verbalize that idea, but this show is about inspiration and I want to inspire people. There are loads of studies now proving that studying music as a child changes your brain, making you better at math, better at abstract thinking. We know there's a huge connection between animation and music, and not just that music is part of animation, but there are all those animators who are either musicians or freakish fans of music.

DH: Totally. I was listening to the interview you did with David Silverman and he was talking about that.

JC: He brought his tuba to the interview and we played afterwards!

DH: So here's a guy who's a brilliant animator and directs *The Simpsons* and various things and he also plays a tuba that's hooked up to a propane tank so you can have flames coming out of it. How great is *that*?

JC: [Laughs] Talk about working with Richard Williams, the animation director of the 1988 film Who Framed Roger Rabbit, *one of my favorite movies. I've heard great stories about him, and I know that he played cornet and you sat in with his band.*

DH: I did. I was young and coming up and went to London to work on *Roger Rabbit*. Everyone had said, oh Richard Williams, he's tough, he's eccentric, he's difficult, he's a screamer, he's never finished a movie. So I went in with a bit of trepidation and I ended up just loving the guy because he was demanding. He set the bar high. He was funny as they come, had the greatest stories ever. He was one of the best trainers and educators that I've ever seen because he was a missing generation. There were Walt Disney's "Nine Old Men" [Disney's name for the core animators he hired in the 1920s and 1930s] and my generation. Richard was a missing link, kind of in the middle of that. And he would pull in these old animators and have them lecture and teach and film them and transcribe their lectures. And he also played cornet and was a huge Dixieland fan. He had a band called Dick's Six that played at the Grosvenor House most every Sunday. I'd go listen, and every once and a while his drummer would ask me to sit in. And Dixieland for a drummer is really fun. It's not brain surgery. It's just a joy.

I think that Dick and I bonded through that experience because we could have conversations away from animation and just talk about music once in a while. I really admired him, just the commitment to excellence and brilliance in every area of his life. He had so many interests in reading and art and painting and Dixieland. His was a life that I really admired.

JC: Something I certainly got from your movie Howard *and from everything you're saying about the people you admire is that these are people who know a lot about their art and continue to learn and have passion. We need passion now more than ever. People need to come out of themselves and think about putting good into the world. It's like where you've said your life is going now, wanting to tell stories that count and illuminate these great individuals for the rest of us.*

DH: It's hard because that requires a lot of self-study and introspection. I remember that Joe Grant, who wrote *Dumbo*, told me, "You know, Don, it has to be an obsession." So even more than passion it has to be an obsession. And I think that takes a while for anyone to discover. And then there's the hard work part.

I had a vibraphone teacher in college who said, "Transcribe this Charlie Parker solo and bring it back and play it note for note." So I would do these solos and come back and play them for him, and just that rigor of listening critically to another artist's solos was so eye-opening and eventually you assimilate all of that. But I was crazy about it. You have to be obsessed, which is the only way I would have been able to do that. And that obsession changes through your life, which is a good thing. You can constantly reinvent yourself, and that creates an interesting life.

JC: *I love something that you said in an interview, "How can you create the illusion of a life unless you have a life? Live a big life that you can own." That's just so beautiful and so true.*

DH: And it's also messy. A big life you can own is chaotic and sloppy and dirty and full of failure, but *yeah to all that!* How else do you learn and grow if you can't fall on your face a few times? And I'm a master of that. I don't know what I'm doing. I've been surrounded by great people my whole life and my success relies on them. But I've been excited about getting to work with them because they inspire me.

JC: *And you don't have to be a professional. Sing! Be good, be bad, just go enjoy it. You don't have to be famous.*

DH: Well "famous" is fugitive. It comes and goes *so* quickly. Especially now, it lasts about two weeks and that's it. The fame you build inside yourself or with your family and friends is so much more critical. Like, to me, you're famous with all my friends and I've never met you before, and yet you are. All the people you hang out with—the Roger Allers of the world or Eric Daniels and Margie—are good friends and I think, well, you're kinda famous in my family, I just didn't know you. So that's the kind of fame I like.

JC: *That's what counts. And I want to finish with what I found so inspiring at the end of* Howard. *You captured so beautifully how he just kept going and kept writing on his deathbed. It could have been maudlin, but it wasn't. It was sad, but I've thought about Howard a lot, especially now when we're in a pandemic, with our own challenges, but here's a man with AIDS who just keeps going almost as if he's ignoring that he's dying. He was only forty in 1991 when he died.*

DH: Alan Menken and Howard's sister told me something that I didn't realize, that Howard didn't want to be defined by his disease. I think that's an important point. He felt like, yes, he had the disease, yes it was during a time that it was incurable, it was a death sentence, but he wanted to be defined by his work. So he never stepped out in directions that would make him an AIDS activist or anything that would make him defined by that horrible disease. He wanted to be defined by his music and his lyrics and his work. So even when he was in his hospital bed writing songs, like "Prince Ali" from *Aladdin*, he wanted to use the days he had left on earth to write.

That's a kind of artistic heroism that I don't have. But I think we can take inspiration from that. When times are so hard that you're dealing with a death sentence, something like AIDS or cancer or a pandemic or all the things we face, you can still look ahead and work on the thing that brings you joy and brings life into your body. That's what Howard did and that's really inspiring.

Scott Hamilton

(b. 1954)

Swing and mainstream jazz tenor saxophonist

Interviewed in 2009

Scott Hamilton came to prominence touring with Benny Goodman in the 1970s and released his first recording in 1977 when he was just twenty-three years old. He surprised critics and fans alike with the depth and maturity of his playing and went on to become an international jazz star at a time when that achievement seemed almost impossible for most jazz instrumentalists.

Scott and I entered the scene around the same time, so it was interesting to compare notes on our shared experiences and discuss how the jazz world has changed over the years. Scott is one of my favorite musicians and favorite people. We seldom see each other due to our respective touring schedules, so I was delighted when we were both booked for the 2009 Ascona Jazz Festival in Switzerland and I had the chance to interview him.

SH: I started coming over to Europe in 1976 or 1977, not long after I arrived in New York. I think I left New York five times in those years to work with Benny Goodman in Little Rock, Arkansas, or Grand Rapids, Michigan. I started traveling internationally in 1978, going to Japan and then Europe for the festivals in the summer. And then everyone I knew began to travel to Europe on a regular basis. I think the traffic started to get heavier in the early seventies when the French started to bring over a lot of

American musicians. In those years, it was different in Europe than it is today. Every town that had a post office had a jazz club.

I remember doing a tour with Chris Flory, Chuck Riggs, and Phil Flanigan one year, and we didn't leave Holland. We were in this very small country for six weeks, and we played a different club every night. It was a terrific scene. And when we were doing those gigs there were always nine or ten American groups traveling around Europe at the same time. Dizzy Gillespie was doing it, and Art Blakey's group, a lot of people who ordinarily would never play clubs. Also, a lot of places in Europe had government money to help the clubs and they were able to pay fairly well.

JC: Did you find that people listened differently in those clubs?

SH: I always found it to be the difference between clubs and concerts rather than the difference between Europe and America. It was always said that European audiences were more attentive and respectful of jazz musicians.

JC: But you didn't find that to be true?

SH: I don't know. I suppose a lot of it was the type of places we were playing. By the time I got to New York, most of the club gigs I did were in jazz clubs where we were a known quantity. At the clubs I was working, the audience came because they knew me and they wanted to see me, which was so different from any experience I'd had before that, where basically I was the most unpopular club attraction in New England.

JC: You're reminding me of the first time I did a concert in New York. I'd been doing all these concerts in California where no one listened, same as your New England experience. So here I was on a concert stage in New York, and one of my friends told me that when people applauded, I kept saying, "Thank you, thank you, thank you," because I was so stunned anyone was listening. My friend said, "Pretend like you're used to it. Don't make it so obvious that nobody's ever applauded for you before."

SH: [Laughs] It really is a good way to come up, don't you think? Because you still have to show people who hate you a good time.

JC: Exactly.

SH: Chris Flory and I had our own groups back in Providence when we were just starting off. But when I came to New York in '76, Chris came at the same time. We both moved there together from Providence. The first gig that I got—Michael's Pub, on West 55th Street—Chris got hired the next night. We walked into the best job in the world, and we got to stay for six weeks. Hank Jones on piano, Milt Hinton on bass and Ronnie Cole on drums.

They were going to be the house trio while they moved several horn players and singers in and out. Billy Butterfield had been booked there the week I started. And Billy was needing a little help. I was young, cheap and unknown. But there had been a couple of articles about me in the *New Yorker*. Whitney Balliett, their jazz critic, had written a thing, and there'd been a couple of things in jazz journals. So they knew that they could put me in there and get a certain amount of business. And it worked out well. I played with Billy for a week, and then Johnny Hartman came in, and Chris was on the job by then too. We played with Johnny, and after that Carrie Smith came in for a week. We actually did a couple of weeks just the five of us, just sax and guitar.

It was fabulous. Every night from nine to one we were playing with Hank Jones and Milt Hinton and learning all kinds of things. Afterward, we'd go out to Eddie Condon's and Jimmy Ryan's and hang out with everybody in the music business. People we'd been listening to all our lives. It was very exciting, very exciting.

JC: Talk about Dave McKenna because I know you love Dave. We all love Dave.

SH: Of all of the musicians I've had a chance to work with, Dave occupies a space maybe the most special. He's very, very important in my life, his playing and him too. I love him. I really do. My favorite thing about Dave is the way he came about. I've always heard stories from his family about how one day they all came home, and he was playing the piano. They hadn't even known that he could. And also, the way that he learned. He learned by listening to the radio and figuring it out himself.

Other people have talked a lot about Dave's technique. It is amazing, and it's unique. But I don't hear many people talk about Dave's touch. I don't think I know of a pianist who's capable of playing the melody of a ballad with . . . I don't know how to describe it. It's just investing it with that much feeling and that much uniqueness of sound. Bill Evans is somebody who comes to mind as a guy who had that kind of intensity in his ballad playing. But to me, of all of the many things that Dave does, maybe this is the thing that affects me the most.

JC: Talk about playing harmonica. By the way, I'd read that you played the harp and took that to mean harp, as in angels in Heaven kind of harp. Happily, you set me straight before this interview, explaining to me that the harmonica is sometimes referred to as a harp.

SH: If I'd played the kind of harp you were thinking of, I'd probably still be playing it! I started playing harmonica when I was a kid. When I was eleven or twelve, all of my friends were getting into rock 'n' roll bands, and that was the thing to do. If you wanted to be with your friends, you went in that direction. So I did. I listened to the radio and got into this and that. But at one point I heard some records by Paul Butterfield and Mike Bloomfield and those guys. I got very turned on by that.

I also saw the J. Geils Band in Providence. They played on Thayer Street in Providence when I was about thirteen. They had a fabulous harmonica player in that band. They were very, *very* exciting. This was before they got popular as a rock 'n' roll band. They were mostly playing blues at that time, but they were really exciting. I started playing around with the harmonica, and I got good enough so that when I was fourteen, I got hired for a band in town with some other kids from the local high school. And we started getting some gigs. We played school proms, some fraternity houses on the weekends, local bars, whatever we could come up with. I wasn't great, but I was good enough to get hired.

JC: Did you enjoy playing harmonica?

SH: I did, actually. The only thing that got me switched off of it was that me and the guitar player in this band I was in began to listen to more jazz records. We listened to Lester Young and Charlie Parker, Count Basie and Duke Ellington, all sorts of different things. And I started to really want to play the sax, which I already knew a little bit about. I played a little piano, I tried to play the guitar, I tried to play the drums. So I thought that if I was going to get serious about things, fifteen or sixteen would be a good time to do. I got ahold of a tenor sax and began really studying more earnestly.

JC: Were you taking lessons?

SH: No. I had some clarinet lessons when I was eight years old and then again when I was ten from a very good local teacher in Providence, a guy named Frank Marinaccio. He gave me some very good background in fingering and how to blow the thing properly. I got a good grounding from that so that when I picked up the sax, I was over that hump already. I was playing gigs the first week I had it. I wasn't good, but there were no other kids around to play. Also, I was the bandleader, so they weren't going to turn me down.

JC: I did the same thing! Were you starting to play jazz?

SH: Yeah, we played a lot of blues, and we gave it a stronger beat because we had to play for dancers. And we'd play for places like the Rhode Island School of Design, which had a taproom where you could go and pass the hat around and make ten or fifteen dollars apiece if you did well. Brown University had a bar as well where we could play on weekends. There were a lot of clubs in downtown Providence. Very often you risked not getting paid, but if you chased the guys around enough you could sometimes get your money.

We also did weddings. They'd be very disappointed when we showed up at the wedding and didn't play "Alley Cat." We were the worst wedding band ever. And people were outraged. I know there are some people, somewhere, who got married with our band there, and they're saying, "Can you believe it? See this band? They made CDs!"

JC: I was hired for a wedding once, and they wanted me to play that ridiculous tune, "Evergreen." I thought, "How hard can it be? I'll just get the music and sight-read it." But I couldn't do it. I hated the tune so intensely that I was incapable of learning it. Musician friends started saying, "Don't make Judy learn a tune she hates. She'll get her 'Evergreen Headache.'"

SH: We used to do the same thing. There'd always be a little guy at these things, sort of like the maître d' or something, but he was used to working with really professional wedding musicians. Guys who knew the routine. He'd come up to us and have this look on his face. He'd say, "The father of the bride and the bride are going to dance, and they want to hear 'Daddy's Little Girl.'" We'd say, "Well, we don't know that." We'd never heard that song before. I'd never been to a wedding before in my life. He said, "Well, what about 'Feelings'?" "Ah, we don't know 'Feelings.' We don't play that." He'd say, "Well, what *do* you know?" We'd say, "Well, how about 'Laura'?"

"Oh, God, O.K." So he announces, "And now the father is going to dance with the bride and they've requested '*LAURIE*'!" And we'd be playing away, and I think people just figured, "Well, we can't get another band at this late a date. And these guys have already eaten."

JC: Hilarious! That old finger-snapper, "Laurie."

SH: And I never understood why "Alley Cat" was supposed to speed up as you play it. What was that about?

JC: I never understood that either. Some things are meant to remain a mystery.

Tell me, what's your favorite combination of instruments to play with now? Or do you have a favorite?

SH: I do. For the last fifteen or twenty years I've really enjoyed working with just the quartet. That's really what makes me happy. Whether it's a pianist or a guitarist doesn't always matter, although I find that with the piano, I'm generally happiest. I love working with the organ, too. A good organ player, that can be a real nice situation. It doesn't mean that I don't enjoy other things. I do. But for the most part, I find that if I have less to do than I do in a quartet that I'm leading, I often don't get enough exercise. Sometimes my playing isn't up to the standard I'd like it to be because I don't get enough time to play.

I found at one time I was working in a lot of larger bands—three or four horn players—and I found that my playing wasn't up to the standards that I'd like it to be, even physically. I'm not a good practicer. I don't have the discipline to do it myself. But if I'm working in a quartet where obviously I need guys that I can depend on to carry a lot of the load, still, a lot is on me. But I enjoy having that responsibility. For some reason I do better that way.

JC: Talk about your CD with Duke.

SH: That was fun. I got a chance to record again with Duke Robillard, who's a really old friend and a guy whose playing I've loved for many years. And Chuck Riggs, of course, another favorite of mine. We got to do it at Rudy Van Gelder's studio. I'd never been there before, and that was really exciting.

JC: Talk about why he's so special. And he never ages. He must be 200 years old because he's done every single record known to man.

SH: That's the thing. The oddest thing about it is that I've made records at other studios that sound much more like Rudy Van Gelder records than the one I did in his studio. I'm not sure what to make of that. Unfortunately, I wasn't able to be there for any of the mixing. I had to go back to Europe. So Duke went down and helped out, but even Duke wrote to me later and said, "What happened to the famous Rudy Van Gelder reverb? Where is it?" So I don't know what he had in mind, but it's different.

JC: How did you set up?

SH: Duke and I and the organ were in the outside, and then the drums were in a booth. We had that fabulous room with the cathedral ceiling.

JC: It looks like a Frank Lloyd Wright.

SH: Somebody said it was one his of disciples who built the building. But most impressive, I thought, of all, was the sound of the room. It's the nicest studio I've ever played in. I felt so good when I was playing in the room. But none of that, other than the good feeling, I'm sure, comes through in the recording. Once again, not that I'm complaining, I'm quite happy with it. I did like the vibe of being in that place and thinking of all those records that had been made there.

JC: Most people don't realize, because most people aren't recording musicians, that very often we're in a very small, very unattractive space that feels sort of claustrophobic. Maybe your drummer is way over there, maybe somebody is over there. And that really struck me, just how lovely it was to be next to each other in a beautiful room that feels good and sounds good. It's like you're doing a gig, a good gig.

SH: That's true. Lately I've been looking in discographies and things on the internet and seeing how many things were recorded in Nola Studios on West 54th Street in Manhattan. I've done several records there, but I hadn't realized how many things were done in that place, even not under the name of Nola's. A lot of the Charlie Parker records from the forties were done there when it was called something else, but it was the penthouse on top of Steinway pianos.

JC: Good history. Someone who just recorded there who's another favorite piano player of mine is John Bunch. I know you've recorded with him.

SH: John got me into the studio for the first time when I moved to New York. He was the first guy to talk Harry Lynn into letting him use me and Warren Vaché on a recording that he made. We were in A&R studios on Seventh Avenue. That was the first time I ever made a record.

JC: What do you want to hear behind you when you play? What makes John's playing so special?

SH: The reason John has always been so popular is because he's rhythmic and very spare. He's never been interested much in technique, really. When I first met John, he said, "Look, there's a million pianists out there that can do things that I can't do." And he named a number of guys who were very popular. Then he said, "But there's a lot of stuff that those guys can't do that I can do. One of them is playing in time with the right rhythm. It's amazing how few people can do that."

I noticed when I first came to New York, everybody was hiring John. He was the most popular pianist in Midtown Manhattan because he gave everybody what they wanted, which was very simple and very direct.

When John first started playing in my group with Chris [Flory] and Phil [Flanigan] and Chuck [Riggs], I started calling John to do record dates because he was the pianist you could call for a record date and you knew you didn't have to wait for him to warm up. We'd have a very short amount of time, but with John it was no worry. He came ready to go. Over the years we must've done eleven or twelve albums with that same group, and it just got better and better.

JC: I have to ask you about the Benny Goodman experience because I know you guys were all there, and you were all really young, except for Benny, of course. Who was in the band?

SH: I worked with Benny twice. I worked with him in the '70s with Warren Vaché, John Bunch, Michael Moore, Connie Kay, and Cal Collins. And then I was fired. I was rehired again in '82, and I worked with him for about a year. And that time it was pretty much my band except for Mel Lewis on drums instead of Chuck Riggs.

We did a European tour. Warren Vaché was also in the band, plus myself, John Bunch, Chris Flory, Phil Flanigan, and Mel Lewis. We did a tour of Europe with Benny that year where we played six or seven different festivals and almost all of them did television broadcasts, so there's a lot of videotape of that group. It was a good group, a really good band.

JC: And people can see it on YouTube. Keywords Benny Goodman and 1982.

SH: It was a terrific group. Benny was not in great health at that time, but he played with so much power and feeling. It was very, very exciting.

JC: The fact that he was still playing, that's what I think about. We've been at this long enough to have seen some of the people who originally inspired us to play, like Count Basie. I admire the ones who just kept going. No matter how bad Basie's arthritis was, he still played great. It was like, "I don't need to play all those notes I used to play. I'm going to play this one note." Then other people didn't age so well. You could tell they weren't happy that they couldn't play all the notes they played when they were younger. The fact that Benny was still out there doing it is wonderful.

SH: Benny was so natural, and he was such a force of nature and such a natural-born jazz musician that he wasn't inspiring only because he was Benny Goodman and someone I'd listened to since I was three years old. He was inspiring on every level.

JC: You've played so many different festivals. Do they all just blur together? Are there certain things about festivals that you like? I have to ask you about Ascona too, where we are now. It's a real jazz festival that doesn't have rock with Elton John down the street from the jazz stage.

SH: That's right. That's unique, I think, these days. I know that some of the French festivals have changed so much in the last twenty years, they're nothing like they were when we first played them. You get younger people producing, and the older guys are all dying or leaving the business. You don't have the names you used to have in our kind of jazz. The stars are all gone, a lot of them, most of them. You also have the fact that these younger promoters have never heard of any of these names. They've certainly never heard of us, and they're looking to sell ten thousand seats. So, they need somebody that can sell ten thousand seats. It's a different world today.

But it's almost like the old days here. It's a beautiful place at the foothills of the Alps. It's actually a more beautiful place than any of those festivals were, in a sense. This is kind of idyllic. I think this is one of the few festivals that people can go to these days, another one being maybe Brecon up in Wales, that are still primarily a jazz festival, where people who like jazz can actually go out at night and still hear a lot of the music that they like. It shouldn't be so difficult, but it is.

Fred Hersch

(b. 1955)

Jazz pianist/composer/activist.

Interviewed in 2009

Fred Hersch, whom *Vanity Fair* calls "the most arrestingly innovative pianist in jazz over the last decade," is passionate about both classical music and jazz and is known for his inspired synthesis of the two. He's received fifteen Grammy nominations and numerous other honors, and for the past four decades he's served as a faculty member of the Jazz Studies program at the New England Conservatory.

I met Fred in 1985 when I recorded in his SoHo loft/recording studio in Manhattan. Today everyone in jazz knows and celebrates Fred Hersch, but in 1985 he was known largely by people hipper than I was, so I thought he was just a guy with a recording studio you could rent at a reasonable price.

Everything imaginable went wrong that unusually hot September day. The producer got cranky because Fred had his own ideas on how things should be recorded. I got cranky because my headphones didn't work. My horn player got cranky because his flask ran dry. And the air conditioning broke so we all got even crankier, not to mention sweatier. Ironically, this recording is now one of my favorites.

FH: I'm from Cincinnati, Ohio, which is not a bad jazz town, or it wasn't back in the '70s. In fact, it was pretty good. I remember sitting in—way in advance of when I should've been sitting in—with the local tenor sax legend, a little Irish guy named Jimmy McGary. The only tune that I knew was "Autumn Leaves."

JC: *Well, you've got to start with one tune, and that's a good one.*

FH: Right. So, I played "Autumn Leaves," and I made many of the mistakes that an inexperienced player would make. It was my first time playing with a professional rhythm section, and I was trying to do too much. I probably blew the form of the tune, all that kind of stuff. So McGary took me in the back room of the club—they had a little portable phonograph— and he played me Duke Ellington at Newport, with Paul Gonsalves's famous twenty-six choruses. And he looked me dead in the eye and said, "*That's* time. Now if you want to play jazz, it seems like harmony is not a problem for you, and I can tell that you can play the piano. But you have to understand rhythm because rhythm is how jazz players musically shake hands with each other. And if you don't have that sense of rhythm, then you're never really going to be an authentic jazz player."

So I took his advice. I was thrilled and honored but also confused. So I went shortly thereafter to the local used record store, Moles Record Exchange, and I went through the jazz bin A-Z, and I bought every record that had "Autumn Leaves" on it. I wanted to see how other people had done it. And I think I bought about a dozen albums, everything from Miles Davis and Bill Evans to Ahmad Jamal and Oscar Peterson. I think there was Sarah Vaughan with strings. You know, all these different versions of "Autumn Leaves." And it was kind of an epiphany. "These are all great," I thought. "And they're all different."

So I got the message that, yes, you have to learn the tradition—you have to have your rhythm together, you have to have tunes together—but the idea is for you to sound like you and not like somebody else. But like most developing young musicians, I had people who I probably imitated, and

Wynton Kelly was certainly one of the first. Wynton Kelly has what I call a "happy beat."

JC: Explain that. I know what you mean, but I like saying it that way.

FH: His rhythm is just impossible not to tap your foot to, but not in an Oscar Peterson sense. It's lighter and a little more forward moving.

Some friends played me the first jazz album that really made me want to play: Miles Davis' *In Person: Friday and Saturday Nights at the Black Hawk, Complete.* This was recorded shortly after *Kind of Blue,* so it was basically the *Kind of Blue* band with Miles, Paul Chambers, Jimmy Cobb and Wynton Kelly, although Kelly was on only one of the *Kind of Blue* tracks, Bill Evans played the others. And Hank Mobley replaced Coltrane and Cannonball. Just to hear the way Wynton accompanied Miles, the sense of space, that beautiful beat, and the fact that it was live in a club, you really felt like you were there. That was very exciting to me, and I just devoured that record.

JC: I'm happy that you brought up someone talking to you about time and time feel, especially as somebody who studied classical music, where the time sense is so different. Two things struck me when you talked about Jimmy McGary playing you Paul Gonzalves at Newport and having you hear jazz time. First, that he took the time to do that and second, that you were honored to receive that information and took it to heart. Jazz musicians are always talking about time, but it's a hard thing to explain, which is why he played you something to have you hear it.

FH: Yeah. I came from classical music, but I always improvised. I picked up Beatles tunes and James Taylor tunes and Joni Mitchell tunes by ear and would kind of play them my own way, but it wasn't jazz. Jazz for the most part is a very specific language. It's language-based. And if you want to play with other people or converse with them, you need to know certain things You need to know conventions, intros, endings, how to accompany, how to build a solo. These are the building blocks of a language.

I work with a lot of young musicians, and I find that they have lots of stuff going on, but they don't tell a story. The equivalent might be, if you use a thesaurus and get lots of ways of describing a particular article of clothing or somebody's hair but don't know how to tell a story with it. So the other thing that I learned—not just from jazz but from classical music—was storytelling. In classical music, it's not so much about time, it's *timing*, how you build a piece, where the peaks are, using the composer's intent but making it sound like it's coming from you. So my earliest influence, certainly as a pianist, was Glenn Gould playing Bach. I've been a lifelong admirer of Gould's playing, and when I have time on my hands, I sit and play Bach. I think it's great for the soul, great for the fingers, great for the ear, endlessly interesting. For me, Bach in classical music is the equivalent of Monk in jazz. You can play Monk tunes indefinitely and they're always interesting. They're always little puzzles that you can fit together. And Glenn Gould was a player who not only had timing, but he had time. You really felt the rhythm. Partitas are dance suites, and all of his playing has this life rhythm, this dance rhythm that's really so beautiful.

I brought a recording of one of the movements of Bach's Partita No. 1 in B-flat major for you. The thing about Bach is how he got so much from so little. So much of Bach is two or three voices, at the most four. One of the things I'm known for is my ability to play spontaneous counterpoint. I used to do it when I was a kid and then I thought, "Well, why not bring that into my jazz?"

And it's a very interesting process to improvise two voices and focus half on one side and half on the other. Or to completely focus on my right hand and let my left hand go on autopilot and see what happens, or vice versa. And you know that pianists have a unique viewpoint from the piano bench. We get perfect stereo. When you're away from the piano, it's mono, it's coming from one place. You don't want to mic it the way that you hear it but if you mic it the way the audience hears it, it sounds strange to you.

And I'm a big fan of music from other cultures. The example of my counterpoint that I wanted to play is a live take from a solo album that I did in Amsterdam at the wonderful Bimhuis, a legendary club there. It's a composition by Jobim, "O Grande Amor," a tune I first learned when I played with Stan Getz, and I think you might find interesting parallels with the Bach partita.

JC: I know you're a great fan of Thelonious Monk. Talk about the challenge of putting your own stamp on the music of such a distinctive composer.

FH: That's another reason I say that Monk and Bach, who you'd think would be unlikely bedmates, are closer than you might realize. You can take Bach's music and play it on a synthesizer or a bunch of glockenspiels or a brass choir, and it still sounds like Bach. Monk, who is arguably the most significant composer of small-group tunes in jazz, everything that he wrote fits on sixty pages of paper. He didn't write much. With Bach, it would fill a room. But each one of Monk's pieces has what I call a particular secret or a puzzle that always keeps you interested. And so as a pianist I play a lot of Monk. Obviously, I'm not of his generation. I'm a different kind of person, and I come from a different kind of place. So the challenge is for me to be me, to tell Monk's story with my own language. And that's what I try to do.

I also had the great fortune of studying with Jaki Byard, who was an underrated master of the piano, a fabulous stride player, and a fabulous soloist. He just didn't have it together in the way some of his peers did, like Tommy Flanagan. Also, I think he suffered from being almost too creative. People couldn't figure out what he was. He was unpredictable. Which is great artistically but not that good for your career.

Another person who influenced me as a pianist is Ahmad Jamal. To me, the Ahmad Jamal Trio with Israel Crosby and Vernel Fournier was one of the two great trios, the other being Bill Evans, Scott LaFaro, and Paul Motian. And the Ahmad Jamal trio was all about arrangement, groove, and space.

When I listen to young musicians, or anybody, one of the things I want to know when they're playing, say, a standard, is why *that* standard. Why that standard, in that tempo, in that key? It's like, did you pick that tune just because you thought you were supposed to play it or is there any deep meaning to it? Do you know the words? With Miles Davis or Sonny Rollins, the tunes that they chose were chosen for a reason. Likewise, with choosing a great composer. Whatever wackiness Beethoven got into at the end of his life—being deaf and who knows what else—he did his music for a reason, probably trying to communicate s*omething* out of his misery.

And with jazz musicians, there are lots of tunes out there, but you can only play so many tunes in a set or so many tunes on an album. So I like to feel like there's a connection between the performer and the tune. Sometimes a little arrangement will help, but I think it's what my piano teacher calls "emotional rhythm," that feeling of just being hooked up with what you're playing, and it makes it much easier to play. Sometimes we play things over and over, and it starts to get a little stale. Or you feel like you're repeating yourself, or you've got some tricks that you do, and they work and everybody loves them, but it's not so much fun anymore. So, you know, play it up a whole step.

JC: *Make yourself start thinking again.*

FH: And make yourself start hearing and feeling again. Or, if it's a fast tune, play it as a ballad and see what that does for it. I'm a big person with keys. I'm very key sensitive. I don't play a lot of standard keys. I like to look at the tessitura, the range of the melody. For example, a tune like "How Deep Is the Ocean?" that all jazz guys play, usually as a swing tune in C-minor. I play it as a very slow ballad in E-flat minor, and somehow for me that has a magic to it.

This Sonny Rollins tune I brought you is a great example of a work by somebody who not only picked a tune for a reason but also has a tremendous sense of humor. I'm sure I'm influenced as much by Sonny Rollins as by any other piano player. To me, Sonny Rollins is what jazz is; his virtuosity, connectedness, intellect, sound, humor, command, and, above all, just that deep, deep rhythm that is kind of vanishing. This tune, by the way, is "I'm an Old Cowhand" with the great Ray Brown and Shelly Manne. I love listening to sax trios.

JC: How is your health?

FH: Well, my health is a pretty big subject. I'm fifty-three now and I've had HIV for more than twenty years, and in 1993, I put together the first-ever benefit CD, with the proceeds going to a wonderful organization called *Classical Action--Performing Arts Against AIDS*. It's run here in New York, and it raises money for AIDS services and education, not for research. I asked my friends who owned studios and I asked my engineer and I asked musicians I know, and of course none of us can write a big check, but I asked, "Can you come and play one track?"

The theme of the album was ballads. So we called it *Last Night When We Were Young: The Ballad Album*. I shouldn't have been surprised, but George Shearing, Kenny Barron, Mark Murphy, Bobby Watson, Jane Ira Bloom, Toots Thielemans, just really A-list players, all showed up and played beautifully.

And at that time, I decided that I should go public about my situation. So with the help of a friendly pro bono publicist, I decided to tell the world that not only am I gay but I have HIV. And it was quite something. I found myself in *Newsweek* and on CNN and in all the jazz magazines, gay magazines, talking about this project which raised—this is pre-internet—$150,000 just from an 800 number. I found myself sort of the trailblazer for gay jazz artists and gay musical artists.

Back then, because the medication was not as sophisticated as it is today, many more people were dying. Many people told me that if I came out about my situation, my bookings would fall off and people would be afraid to hire me because I might not show up. But none of that proved to be the case. In fact, from an artistic point of view, it was very liberating not to feel that I was in any particular kind of closet, even a jazz closet, and that my music could expand and embrace all of the musics that are part of me, classical music, Brazilian music, my own creations.

JC: And jazz is a very macho business. I think that's something our audience should realize. I know the prejudice I encountered as a slim, blonde woman. It was all anybody would talk about, "How does this little girl play this music?" Which has always been ironic because I'm not little. But I'm little compared to Fats Waller. So I know what it's like, even with the little bit of prejudice I've experienced. For you to do this was incredibly courageous, especially back then.

FH: Well, one thing I've noticed, and anybody who's hung out in a jazz club knows, is that jazz musicians are generally very affectionate. It's always a hug, never a handshake. I'm sure that over the years people have said things behind my back, but I've received nothing but support. I feel like, the kind of music I play is my music now, it's Fred's music, call it what you will. And if you like it, I'm thrilled, and if you don't, well, I don't like lima beans.

JC: [Laughs] I think that's the first-time lima beans have been mentioned on this show.

FH: In this past year, I've had serious health crises with dementia. I was in a coma for about seven weeks, and I lost the ability to walk, to swallow, and to play the piano. I had gallbladder infections and throat surgeries to repair a paralyzed vocal cord. I've been pretty much off the grid in 2008, but now I'm coming back, I'm playing dates, I'm back on the road.

JC: You just did a run at the Village Vanguard. That's a long gig.

FH: Yup, and the standards are very high. You don't phone it in in a place like that. So things are picking up again, and I feel like I'm over the hump, and I'm very fortunate to be here and to be able to continue to do what I do.

As anyone who's been ill knows, sometimes with people who are ill who have children, a motivation for them is to get well so they can be a parent again, to watch their children grow up, or see their grandkids graduate from college. And I think that my motivation is to continue to make my music, which I think, without being fat-headed, has evolved to a place that's fairly unique. And while I certainly have a lot of influences and I certainly put myself more in the jazz world than any other world, for me the carrot at the end of the stick was to be able to get out and play a week at the Village Vanguard, to be able to go to Europe with my trio, to get some commissions, and to continue to write music. And thank God for modern medicine and fantastic doctors. And thank God I had health insurance.

Anyway, I've continued to raise lots of money and awareness. Also, I've been a mentor to a number of gay jazz musicians who for various reasons haven't come out. Sometimes I get emails or phone calls, and they say, "Gee, what was your experience?" And for me, I think it's nothing but good because if you're going to be yourself as an artist, you need to be able to be comfortable with yourself as a person. You know, you're Judy Carmichael, you're not Fats Waller. Despite the weight differences, you play your music with your accent and I play my music with my influences and my accent.

When I go to a jazz performance, I want to see something that's happening uniquely then, right at that moment. I don't want to see a rehash of the recording. I don't want to feel like every detail has been smoothed over. I'd rather go and see somebody go for it, even if they crash and burn. Although I feel bad for them if it falls apart, in a way that's much more gratifying. It's more interesting. Jazz is often now in a concert setting so it's not really the kind of gritty environment we came up in.

JC: Yeah, the club gig that creates that feeling of looseness, where you feel you can get a little bit wild and fall off a cliff. And, again, I feel this is a great metaphor for life, about accepting who you are, going for who you are, not in an attitude of "okay, this is all I can do," but to continue to go for it. I just said this to someone the other day that years ago, when I was on some concert stage with a bunch of guys, I thought, "Why do I ever worry about what they're going to think of me because the minute I play, I'm naked anyway. They know everything."

FH: The more that we think about "what is somebody going to think?" the less we're able to do what we do. Some people find creativity in cooking or gardening or other activities. When you're doing something like that, time kind of stops, and you're completely involved in the activity. And if we're improvising music in front of an audience and we're thinking about the critic in the second row or about what so-and-so might think of it, then we've taken away from our ability to be as present as we can with what we do. All these are lessons that we all keep learning. And I'm grateful that I'm here and able to continue to do what I love most.

Penn
Jillette
(b. 1955)

Magician, actor, musician, inventor, author and
half of the magic team of Penn & Teller.

Interviewed in 2003

Penn Jillette is the speaking half of the celebrated magic duo Penn & Teller. In addition to Broadway runs, television shows, acting gigs, and other appearances, Penn & Teller currently perform in Las Vegas at the Rio, the longest running headliners to play at the same hotel in Las Vegas history.

Penn is an intense presence who focuses the same energy he's brought to his magic and juggling to his passion for jazz. While others in Vegas work to shorten their time on stage, Penn comes early to play bass for his pre-show, with Mike Jones on piano. Penn and Teller's most recent Broadway run included jazz throughout the show, an expansion from what I saw when Penn and I first met in Las Vegas to record this episode of *Jazz Inspired*. Though I rarely fly to someone for an interview, the chance to see Penn and Teller in action, in Vegas, and to record there, was too good to resist. A mutual friend, the magician Todd Robbins, encouraged Penn to be a guest on *Jazz Inspired*, which is how I managed to slip through Penn's handlers.

Penn started off by discussing his juggling pursuits and how his progress changed after a certain point, as happens with any practiced skill.

PJ: You get better really slowly after you hit a certain point. You work up to juggling five clubs, but to get to six is gonna take years. You're also getting older and you just don't get the gratification you did in the beginning. I got to be forty-five and I wanted to do something I didn't know how to do. So that inspired my pursuing jazz bass.

We were doing a TV show called *Sin City Spectacular*. I've been playing rock and roll electric bass forever, but I never studied. I could read music but not well. We did a thing with the Smothers Brothers, and I became one of the three people to ever be straight man to Tommy Smothers. It was Dick Smothers, Jack Benny, and me. We were going to play "Jimmy Crack Corn," and I had to have an upright bass. I had to play a G and a C; that was it. But I got to hold an upright, which I'd never done. I got to use Dick Smothers' bass, or I guess the bass they rented for Dick Smothers, which I'm calling Dick Smothers' bass because it makes it much more romantic.

I touched the bass, and it just felt right. You hear artists talk about enjoying touching the paint, you hear guitar players talk about enjoying the feel of the guitar, but I never had that at all. I never enjoyed touching the juggling props. I never enjoyed touching much of anything really.

When I was twelve, I just lived to practice, with juggling, with cards. Teller loves to rehearse, hates to practice. I love to practice, hate to rehearse. Teller would like to do all of his practicing with people, I would like to do all my rehearsing alone.

And this is an awful thing to say, I found that I could not understand either the intellectual or the visceral side of jazz without playing it. When I started changing from playing rock and roll every week in my home to playing jazz, everything changed.

JC: What kind of jazz?

PJ: Straight ahead, right outta the Real Book [a compilation of sheet music of jazz standards], and just reading that. And I got musicians to come over

248

to play. Then I realized that if I got two women friends of mine to serve beverages topless, more jazz guys would come over.

JC: I assume that's always an essential element to a jazz experience here in Vegas.

PJ: Well, I said it jokingly. I said, "What can I do to make it more inviting?" Because I never had a drug or any alcohol in my life, there's never been a beer in my home, never any drugs.

JC: But there have been topless women serving drinks.

PJ: Those are not the same.

JC: How did you find Mike Jones?

PJ: There's a cat named Mike Close in town who's a wonderful close-up magician and also a jazz piano player, kinda like Todd [Robbins]. He has that same kind of piano and magic thing Todd does. He read some liner notes on an Oscar Peterson record that said, "The only guy who can play like Oscar Peterson is Mike Jones in Vegas." So Close kinda did some stalking. He called the musicians' union and lied, saying he wanted Mike for a gig, and asked where he was. We found out that he was playing at this restaurant here in town, just a lounge, and we went up there and sadly, but honestly, people weren't really paying attention. It was background music.

I was so new to jazz, I said, "Jesus, he seems really good." And Close said, "I've never heard someone better in person." And he's playing while drinks are clattering.

JC: He needed those topless waitresses.

PJ: He sure did. So, I say to Mike, "You're really, really underpaid here, and you should be a superstar. I have an idea." I thought Mike and I could do pre-show music.

The last person in Vegas who had live pre-show music was Frank Sinatra. Everybody else puts a CD on. I talked to Teller and to the rest of our people and said, "A CD costs $12, and it's a one-time expense, and you put it on, and that's your pre-show." But I kept thinking that being in a casino, it would give you a kind of class to have *live* pre-show music and take you away a little from the slot machines and the feathers. I lobbied hard for this and, of course, told Jonesy that he'd be grotesquely underpaid but paid more than he was making now. As you know, that's what happens in jazz all the time now. You're not gonna get what you're worth, but we'll give you a little more than you're getting now.

Jonesy was very happy to have people listening to him, and now he has 1,200 to 1,300 people who are waiting to see Penn and Teller and listen to him. And they really listen. It's a remarkable pre-show; it's almost an hour. And he has some little stuff he does during pre-show, joking, having people come up and check out the props, and so on. The good news is Mike gets to work here. The bad news is, he has to play with me. I play the first forty-five minutes with Jonesy.

You know the joke, "How do you make a million dollars as a jazz musician? Start with two million." Well, I have the money to play jazz. With Jonesy every night, six nights a week playing forty-five minutes, I've gotten good enough, I think, to not be noticed. In art, your first goal is not to be noticed. Your *next* goal is to be noticed. You can't do those out of order.

JC: How has performing with him changed your show?

PJ: I want to immediately go to the deeper, more pretentious answer, but if I go to the superficial, the answer is, there's more jazz in the show.

JC: Now give me the deeper answer.

PJ: There's a bit we put in, kind of a floating handkerchief thing, which is an old, hackneyed horrible trick that we did a version of twenty-five years ago that I loathed. Then I started thinking about it freshly. My dad loved it, and he always wondered why we took it out of the show. I started thinking about my dad and what he might have liked about that, and what it would be like tying it with the music. We decided that instead of having the carney voiceover on tape, which Todd Robbins helped us write, we'd do it live and have Jonesy do it. And since he was sitting at the piano, he would play accents at certain point on his piano.

So now this piece that was a verbal piece with the carney background has become this elaborate 20th century classical virtuosic piano piece with a voice-over and a magic trick. There's another where he plays behind a gorilla. So Jonesy has gone from just doing pre-show to being more involved during the *main* show. People come out afterwards and they've just seen us catch bullets in our teeth and all these miracles, but they'll be going, "Jesus Christ, what's that piano guy playing behind that gorilla thing with the floating handkerchief?"

[Laughter]

I think I lack all sort of natural talent and inclination for music. But by working on it, I've been able to enjoy and experience a whole aspect of art that had been lost to me. It's also a very interesting, emotional, and accepting thing. When you take up something at twelve, thirteen, fourteen, whether it's violin, juggling, golf, baseball, somewhere in your fantasy you can consider being the best in the world. If you take up bass at eight, you could be Mingus or Ray Brown. We don't know. Maybe, if Ray Brown is your teacher, you'd know you have a better leg up, but you don't really know where it will go. When you take up something at forty-five, you know you're not doing it to be the best in the world, and you know you're not doing it to be famous. And without seeming horribly unpleasant, when I started doing card tricks at twelve, I could have been the best in the world. Now, you know, the race has been run and I'm not. But I could have been.

I was an astonishing juggler in the early '70s, part of the best club passing team ever, Michael Moschen and me. We were the best. We were the first to do nine clubs. When I started doing comedy, I could have been Lenny Bruce. When I started jazz bass at forty-five, it is, by definition, more of a personal growth type thing.

JC: And that's a relief on a certain level.

PJ: And for my personality, that was a huge thing to accept. It's that moment when you realize you're not going to be on the Supreme Court so they can take naked pictures of you in group sex. There's that moment, when you say, "O.K., I'm not going to be on the Supreme Court, I have this power. I'm not going to be Ray Brown."

I got to see Ray Brown four nights in New York City right after 9/11. And I've got to say this, because I want this on record. What I'm about to say, I want pulled and put as a WAV file on the website because it's one of the proudest moments of my life. And I'm lying about this, which is what makes it great.

I saw Ray Brown, and afterwards, one of the guys in the band says, "Do you want to meet him?" Ray Brown is backstage, and I walk in and say, "Oh, it's amazing to hear you play." It was an unbelievable experience. I don't think I'd seen many people that good at anything. Ray Brown doesn't do any tricks. He never plays anything fancy unless it's exactly what it needs. So I was just in awe.

Then he said, "Hey, Penn! You're a really heavy cat." And I said, "Why, thanks." He said, "You're some sort of symphony dude, right? Some sort of symphony bass player?" I said, "No, I'm not a symphony guy." "But you're a very heavy cat." I said, "I'm actually a magician. I work with an act called Penn and Teller." He goes, "Yeah, yeah, yeah. It doesn't matter. The guys in my band said you were a heavy cat. That's good enough for me. Doesn't matter what you do. I know you're a heavy cat." And then he went on to say that he'd never had the guys in his band be more excited about someone in the audience.

JC: That's great. And also, very funny.

PJ: I just loved the fact that it didn't matter to him what I did. On some sort of level that was okay with Ray. So, I've thought that if I ever get to put out a bass record, I'll put on the back, "Penn Jillette: A Very Heavy Cat"— Ray Brown. Doesn't matter that he wasn't talking about bass playing, but Ray Brown said, "Very heavy cat."

JC: [Laughs] Your show has a jazz feel, but it can't have much improv, I would think.

PJ: The show is pretty rigid, and we're trying to do it perfectly, so it's not really improvisational. An advantage when you have a two-person group where you have complete power is that Teller and I both have a hundred percent control. We've been together so long that if Teller gets a nutty idea, I push him. No one holds him back. I don't think you can do that with a four or five-person group, but you can certainly do it with two. If the group's gonna work for twenty-seven years, you're gonna be able to do that. When I said, "I'm learning to play bass," Teller was like, "Well, we gotta put a bit in the show with the bass because you look so good with it." And that's Teller's point of view. "You're six foot six, 270 pounds, stand next to a bass. That'd be good."

JC: I thought the same thing. If ever there was a person who should play the bass, you're the man.

PJ: I look good with it. We had Gary Stockdale and Maury write a bass piece that I could learn and put in the show. It's about a minute and fifteen seconds and covers a big escape from a box that Teller's doing. They wrote it brilliantly. It was written exactly to what I was O.K. at. It was written just beyond where I was when we wrote it. So now there'll be two upright bass bits in the show. Of course, you have to remember how much I must be loving this. I mean, Teller gets into a theater by 8:45 p.m. I get in at 7:45 p.m.

Every other performer in Vegas is trying to get his shows cut down. Lance Burton is trying to do seven shows a week instead of eight and he's trying to cut down everything.

JC: And they show up at the last minute.

PJ: Celine Dion, of course, doesn't even go on stage, which makes it a lot easier. There's a big TV.

JC: Do you mean she's not here?

PJ: Oh, no, she's actually here but only for a minute or two, not so you'd notice.

JC: Did you make her disappear?

PJ: We can only use our powers for evil. That would be doing good for the world. But I'm actually finding a way to make a ninety-minute show run two and a half hours.

JC: I know you have another project that to me seems like a jazz project, your documentary.

PJ: Yes. I can tell you the pitch. We've got eighty-five comedians filmed by just the two of us, Paul Provenza and me. I called up Drew Carey and Robin Williams and all these comedians and said, "You know how you always hear jazz musicians blow over the same changes, you can hear everybody do a blues, you hear everybody do that? And you never hear comedians tell the same joke?" There's something wonderful about being able to put on, "You Don't Know What Love Is," by Sonny Rollins and then put on Coltrane's version and hear how they each approach it. You never hear comedians do that, so we wanted to film every comedian telling the same joke.

It started out small. I thought we'd probably get twenty of our friends to do it. Then I talked to George Carlin and when I said, "You know, George, you hear jazz musicians blow over the same changes, but you never . . ." And he jumped in and said, "Ah, Penn, you aren't smart enough to get this idea. You're gonna do comedians doing the same joke! Why *you*? Why couldn't someone *smart* think of this idea? O.K., it's yours. What can I do to help you?"

They got it, they understood it. Before I finished the pitch, they understood where I was going. So we had proof of concept instantly. People who know jazz will tell you they can hear one chord on the piano and tell who it is. And it's not from recognizing what the musician does when he first sits down, it's just the sound. And we really wanted that with comedians. So we had them tell this absolutely filthy joke called "The Aristocrats." It's a joke that people tell backstage, whether it was Myron Cohen or Lenny Bruce. The whole idea of it is how dirty you can get. It's a competition to see how nasty and dirty you can get. And it goes back forever, and it's never really told to the public.

We didn't know how it was gonna work. It's amazing because now we have eighty-five comedians! We're gonna edit it down into ninety minutes. So, no one is telling the joke, right? But all you need is that snippet., like that one recognizable note. We did the Smothers Brothers. They tell the whole joke and it's beautiful, it's very, very funny. But there was a moment when Tommy turns and looks at Dickie, and Dick turns and looks at him, that is the entire Smothers Brothers' career. You don't need anything else. And this is not in any way diminishing what they've done, it's actually saying that's how great they are. And you get Robin. Robin out on the beach behind his house, who just goes, "You know, a guy . . ." And you're there, you already know.

JC: You asked that I include in this show Jerry Lewis' spoof of a jazz singer from the film The Nutty Professor *because this was your first view of jazz before you took your deep dive into playing. Fun to end with this.*

PJ: Jerry drinks the potion and comes off as Buddy Love and sings, "Up at dawn and sleepy and yawning, still the taste of wine." I love that song. That lounge-type stuff was in some way—obviously, I wasn't that stupid— but in some way, that was a big part of jazz to me. So when I found out that you obviously can't get the Jerry Lewis version—and you wouldn't want to—but I found out from a web search that Mel Tormé had covered that song from *The Nutty Professor* and thought, "Well, I gotta have this." So, that's the reason I brought you this. First of all, yes, Mel Tormé is great, but it's a little bit of a joke because that's the Jerry Lewis song where he drinks the potion and becomes Buddy Love, and sings, "I've Got a World That Swings," with the lyric, "Atom bombs, Cape Canaveral and false alarms, half the universe is up in arms." What the hell are they talking about?

And Mel Tormé, in a bid for petty honesty, changes "Cape Canaveral" to "Cape Kennedy." The phrase "Cape Canaveral" is a swinging phrase; it's a *jazz* phrase. He changed it to "Cape Kennedy." Why? Because he doesn't want people to think he recorded it before the Kennedy assassination? Come on, Mel! So when you hear Tormé's version, change "Cape Kennedy" in your mind to "Cape Canaveral." "Cape Canaveral," much better.

JC: Absolutely.

Billy Joel

(b. 1949)

Singer-songwriter, composer, pianist. Over 150 million records sold worldwide, twenty-three Grammy nominations, five Grammys. Inducted into the Songwriters Hall of Fame in 1992 and the Rock & Roll Hall of Fame in 1999.

Interviewed in 2000

Billy Joel, an ardent jazz fan, is exactly the kind of guest I love to have on *Jazz Inspired*—someone popular for something other than jazz who can discuss why they love the music, how it inspires them, and can convince the uninitiated to give it a try. Normally, it would be almost impossible to get to someone of Billy's level of fame, but he and I live near each other in the Hamptons, we're both Steinway Artists, and I thought I might get lucky. Happily, I did.

    Dan's Papers, a popular Hamptons magazine, has an annual readers' poll called "The Best of the Best" where everything from the favorite Hamptons restaurant to the favorite Hamptons chiropractor is voted on. Billy and I met in 2000 shortly after we'd tied for the honor of "Best Hamptons Entertainer." I spotted him at a reception at our local theater and introduced myself. I mentioned some mutual friends, hoping he'd pick up the thread on one of these connections. He didn't, so I said goodbye and walked away. Halfway across the room, I heard him call out, "*Wait, Judy, come back!* Didn't we just win something together?"

    I took advantage of this funny moment, explained the concept of *Jazz Inspired,* and asked if he'd be willing to be a guest. He agreed on the condition that we do the interview over lunch. Earlier during our initial chat, we had bonded over our mutual love for long, European-style, afternoon meals, which gave him this idea.

We met the following week at his favorite spot in Amagansett, an elegant restaurant frequented by well-dressed ladies who lunch. Billy wore a T-shirt, jeans, and a baseball cap. I wore the same, minus the cap. Billy knew what he was doing by choosing this meeting place. No one even glanced in our direction.

Billy spent serious time preparing for our conversation. He brought a list of songs he'd written that were specifically inspired by jazz and detailed his original concept for each, essentially producing the show for me.

We started our lunch like an awkward blind date and three hours and three bottles of wine later, we were two, somewhat inebriated musicians hanging out. We talked, we ate, we drank, we talked, we ate, we drank. This lunch was shortly before New Year's Eve. When we finished, Billy asked where I'd be gigging that celebratory night.

"I'm playing at a little club downtown called Knickerbocker Bar & Grill."

"How late are you there?"

"Until 2:00 a.m."

"I love Knickerbocker. I'm off a little after midnight, so that will work. I can bring the band. They'll love you."

"Thanks, Billy. That would be great. Where are you playing?"

"The Garden."

"Of course."

JC: Talk about your studies with Lennie Tristano.

BJ: I don't know that I'd call it "study" exactly. I took some lessons from him. It was only for a few months. I was playing with a teacher in Queens and living in Levittown, Hicksville, on Long Island. The woman I was studying with at the time knew that I was frustrated with the whole route of being a virtuoso pianist and studying classical music. I love classical, but I wasn't gonna be Vladimir Horowitz.

JC: How old were you?

BJ: About fourteen. I'd been taking lessons almost ten years. And I was really frustrated with reading the Mozart and the Beethoven and the Bach, I didn't want to read anybody's dots anymore. I wanted to know how to mess around the right way because I messed around anyway. There's a right way to mess around. There are things you can learn to help yourself with that.

This teacher was very insightful. I feel terrible that I can't remember her name. She said, "There's a guy named Lennie Tristano. You should study with him." This was like 1963, '64. He was always mad at me because I didn't practice. I didn't pay enough attention. Now I could kick myself because I didn't realize what a maestro this guy was.

JC: Were you practicing with your classical lessons? Were you religious about that?

BJ: No. I was starting to drop out of the whole rigmarole. I just wanted to go my own way. I think I wanted to be a writer more than I wanted to be a player.

JC: And you already knew that at thirteen?

BJ: Oh, yeah. I knew that as a little kid.

JC: And were you already doing your own melodies when you were younger?

BJ: I was making up my own classical music when I was a little kid. My mother would be listening for me to practice a Mozart piece, and rather than play the dots I would just make up something in the style of Mozart. And my mother knew Mozart, so I got good at this. She'd listen and say, "That's pretty good. You're learning that quickly." And I'd said, "Yeah, this is easy."

The next day I wouldn't remember what I'd played the day before, so I'd play something different, but also in the style of Mozart. She'd say, "What's that?" "Uh, it's the second movement."

I liked improvising and mimicking their styles. You learn more about a composer by knowing his essence, his attitude, his spirit, more than dot, dot, dot, dot, dot. The dots are for the eye to follow, but the ear and heart are connected more, I think. By the end of the week, I wouldn't know the piece I was supposed to have learned. The teacher said I was wasting my mother's money. I kept wishing I could play what I wrote for my teacher.

JC: You never played it for her?

BJ: No. She didn't want to hear that. She wanted to hear the dots. Nobody wanted to hear what I was doing, but *I* wanted to hear what I was doing. So this teacher, sensing my frustration, sent me to Lennie Tristano. I learned a lot about substitutions, about improvisation, about synchronicity. A lot of good stuff. The little bit where I paid attention, I got a lot out of.

JC: You're a big jazz fan, clearly, and also classical, but what else?

BJ: You name it, I like it. Mixing it up. Typical American.

JC: I think a lot of our younger listeners don't realize that jazz was once the popular music and had a huge influence on all that followed. I'm fascinated by all this music you loved and how it influenced you.

BJ: Well, there was more jazz played on the radio when I was a kid. I lived closer to Manhattan when I grew up, so there were a number of jazz stations where I got to hear all the great stuff. Now jazz doesn't have that many places to live on the radio, which is why I think a lot of younger people don't even know about it.

JC: Were you able to hear a lot of live jazz when you were growing up?

BJ: You had to go into Manhattan to hear good jazz. There were a couple places in Queens, the Bronx, but mostly Manhattan, downtown. We were also going to see rock and roll. We were going to hear folk music, and if there was a great jazz artist playing somewhere, we just went. I remember one night I went to see Bill Evans, and I was thrilled. I mean, I was *that close* to Bill Evans. You could only do that in a jazz club. Some of the big bands would come through, too. Jimmy Smith, we used to go see him with Kenny Burrell and Grady Tate.

JC: Was it considered cool among your friends to be listening to jazz?

BJ: Very cool. Way cool. Jazz was for the hip, the intellectual, the guy who wanted to be not exactly a playboy, but somebody who was sophisticated. You actually had to have some education to get jazz. And for my generation, a lot of guys found out how to dress, what to listen to, and what to play your music on, from *Playboy* magazine.

JC: Everybody used to say they bought it for the articles.

BJ: [Laughs] Well, we bought it for the pictures, but it did teach us how to be cool. They had articles on great stereo equipment for the "man about town." None of us had the money for that equipment, but we did have the money for the recordings.

Jazz was always kind of a mystery, like an insider's music. There was a popular era of jazz which was more the '20s to the '40s. In the '50s it got very esoteric. In the '60s it was very inside, and by the '70s it had become very distant from the mainstream.

JC: And it evolved into a lot of the rock.

BJ: Yeah, there was jazz rock, jazz fusion, blues, a lot of dovetailing. Things got electrified. A lot of people were pioneers, taking it to a whole other place.

JC: Did you like where jazz went, or did you prefer the jazz you came up with?

BJ: I like some of it. Some of the stuff Chick Corea and Herbie Hancock were doing was great. But I think I always preferred standardized jazz, the jazz that was based on standard compositions. Oscar Peterson, Bill Evans, Art Tatum.

JC: A lot of the jazz musicians I know don't like much of the contemporary pop/rock scene, but they love you and always talk about your melodies and the great chord changes in your music. The jazz musicians you're drawn to seem to emphasis those same things.

BJ: Yeah. Even when you're not on the melody and you're playing jazz, you're dealing with the chords. If you just sit for too long on one chord, or two chords, you get bored out of your skull. And the real playing is done when there's a lot of movement with chords. But the chords in jazz are cool. There's a progression that makes sense, so even if you get lost you can find your way home again. I never really liked the kind of rock and roll or jam kind of music that's just based on one or two chords. It drives me crazy. I like interesting progressions. I like something that's got a cycle of chords, that's based on some form.

Think of how many times "My Funny Valentine" has been played, how many different ways. Everybody loves the chord progression and the melody, but that's a melody that changes as the song goes along. Jazz guys love stuff like that. I think I base my style of songwriting on more of a standard style of songwriting.

JC: Do you remember the first jazz musician you heard?

BJ: When I was a little kid in the '50s, some of the great big band singers were still having some hits, so I remember hearing Sarah Vaughan, Peggy Lee, and Margaret Whiting on the radio. By the time I was figuring out who was who, things were changing in jazz.

I do remember the first jazz album I bought, *Time Out*, the Dave Brubeck Quartet. I heard this time thing, 5/4 time. I thought, *what is that?* How do they know when to change? Some people won't know what we're talking about here, but standard music is often written in 4/4 time, four beats to a measure, each quarter note gets one beat, 5/4 meaning there's *five* beats to the measure. You don't walk like that. You don't dance like that. It's actually one-two-three, one-two. I was fascinated with what he did with time. And that "Blue Rondo à la Turk," which is in 12/8, I think. So, I had to figure this out. This was a great mystery.

When I was taking lessons, it was a very technical approach. I wanted to know how to improvise, how to make chords sound cool, like Bill Evans's. I wanted the inside knowledge. Jazz musicians had those secrets. It's interesting that there's been a resurgence in big band music and swing. A lot of young people love this stuff.

JC: *Why do you think that is? It seems that every few years swing gets popular again.*

BJ: Number one: it's great music, for whatever era it's heard in or played in. The guys who played it were great, the guys who arranged it were great. The songs that the arrangements were based on were fantastic. And it was danceable and fun for young people. And a lot of the dancing that was done to that kind of music was extremely athletic, so young people *should* click with this stuff.

I think there's a hunger for good music these days because there isn't a lot of it being composed and recorded and played on the radio for the younger age groups. They don't know what they're missing, and when they *hear* what they're missing, there's an immediate yearning and a hunger for it.

My daughter, who's thirteen, is very cynical about this. She doesn't think there's a lot of good pop and rock and roll. She says, "How come it was so much better when you were a kid?" She likes jazz, she likes Broadway, she likes other kinds of music, but she recognizes pop as being kind of disposable.

JC: Are there any of your songs in which you feel your jazz roots obviously influenced the writing?

BJ: Yeah, there's a track on *The Bridge* from 1987, called "Big Man on Mulberry Street." I had writer's block. I had a little, well, not little, this *huge* space on top of the Puck Building just south of Houston Street. I rented the whole top of the Puck Building. It's a very cool building. It was something like 10,000 square feet of open space. And I set up my little keyboard in one little corner. I would play all night, and if I didn't come up with anything, I'd bop down Mulberry Street to Little Italy to get some food. And I made up this persona. I'd picture myself with this big city walk. And I became this fictional character, all made up in my head. "Yeah, I'm a big man on Mulberry Street." Film noir, you know? I was black and white!

[Laughter]

One of the great things about jazz is that even when it was the popular music form of its time it was still on the outside. Jazz musicians were always looked at suspiciously. These are the guys who were smokin' that reefer, who were the wrong color, who you didn't want dating your daughter. And the women singers, they all had loose morals . . .

JC: It's still looked at that way, I think.

BJ: Absolutely. But in a way, that kinda kept jazz very cool. Jazz has always been that outside thing, that other planet, that other orbit, that different drummer. College students *should* be able to relate to this very easily. They feel disenfranchised from the norm with where they are in life, and jazz is the perfect music to find a different satellite, a different orbit, a different place. That's where we musicians live anyway, but the jazz guys more so than anybody.

In the old days, the mainstream establishment music was classical music. The new establishment mainstream music is pop and rock and roll, which is very controlled, very demographic, where all the money is made and where all the record companies live. It's where all the fat cats rule the roost, and the guys who are really on the outside, as usual, are the jazz guys. But now it's becoming more and more the classical musicians. I know guys who are the age of my brother, Alex Joel, who's a conductor who lives in Vienna. He's twenty-eight . . .

Oh, you know what? We're in a restaurant, so a little break here. [To the waiter] I'll have an espresso.

JC: [Laughs] Yes, I'll have an espresso as well. Thank you.

BJ: Alex and all his friends are bohemians. They live this very wild, underground kind of life. Classical musicians don't make two nickels. They devote their entire lives to learning the music, and unless it's government-funded, there's little chance of making any money, so where rock and roll used to be on the outside and the outlaw business, now that's a bunch of baloney.

If you sign a record contract, right now, chances are, even if you stink, even if you only have one hit, you're gonna make a ton of money. You've got record companies behind you, TV shows ready to play you, radio stations ready to play you, marketing people in place . . . the machine is ready to go. It doesn't work the same way for jazz or classical guys. In a way, classical music might become very cool because it might be in the same orbit as jazz.

JC: That's interesting. I don't think people realize that, though. I know that if people find out I'm a jazz musician, they'll think that's cool, but I don't think they realize that it's quite as outside as it is. I think people think that jazz and classical musicians make more money than they do.

BJ: I agree. I think people tend to lump musicians into the "music industry." Well, it's only the music industry in the lucrative aspects, which is mostly pop, teen idols, flavor of the month, the artists that get the most radio play.

JC: *Do you like recordings that are done live? If you picked up a record and it was Oscar Peterson live, would you prefer it to a studio recording?*

BJ: Well, it's too bad you said Oscar Peterson because with him it doesn't matter. But I have learned these days to never trust a studio recording because in the studio you can correct anything, and you don't hear the edit. And they do this with vocals too. I don't want to mention any names, but there are big stars who can't sing at all but get the big fix in the edit.

With someone like Oscar, live and studio are so similar, it doesn't make a big difference, although with a live recording, you get the adrenaline factor, which does juice it up a bit, so I might like that even more.

JC: *You've worked with some great jazz musicians—Ron Carter, Freddie Hubbard, Phil Woods, Toots Thielemans. What does it do for your music to have a pure jazz musician come play with you, someone like Phil Woods?*

BJ: I feel very reverent. We look at these guys as the gurus, they're the wizards, they're the sorcerers, we're just the apprentices. It doesn't take a whole lot of talent to play rock and roll. I'm sorry, but that's the truth.

My album *52nd Street* is an album that was kind of an homage to jazz. 52nd Street is in Manhattan, and it is now named "Swing Street." And they had all these jazz clubs there, back in the '40s and '50s. We played a track called *Zanzibar* where Freddie Hubbard played the trumpet, and he broke into this kind of free-form jazz improvisational solo. When we finished that recording, we all looked at each other and said, "Now we're grownups."

Darlene Love

(b. 1941)

Pop music singer and stage and screen actress. Her best-known film role was playing Danny Glover's wife in the *Lethal Weapon* series. In the '50s and '60s she sang with everyone from Elvis and Dionne Warwick to Sonny and Cher and the Beach Boys.

Interviewed in 2007

Darlene Love embraces life with an enviable gusto, and remarkably, she seems to only look and sound better with age. As a minister's daughter, she grew up listening to gospel music and considers her early years of choir singing a major influence on her musical development. She went on to become a first-call studio singer and featured artist. In 2011 she was inducted into the Rock & Roll Hall of Fame and is ranked No. 84 in the *Rolling Stone* list of the 100 Greatest Singers. She has known great success and great disappointment and feels that it all adds depth to what she does today. We met for the following conversation while she was starring as Motormouth Mabel in *Hairspray* on Broadway.

JC: *You've told me that with every musical performance your goal is to tell a story.*

DL: I feel that all music is great music, whether it's jazz, blues, gospel, or even country and western. The most important thing is that it tells a story, and the more the song tells a story, the more it grabs you. The music will grab you, but then you start listening to the story that people are telling on the records. Jazz and blues and country tell stories about life, whatever it is.

JC: I just saw you in Hairspray *last night and was amazed by your chops. You'd do something unbelievable and then raise the bar five times. Do you enjoy singers with less of that virtuosic range, someone like Alberta Hunter?*

DL: Yes, because they're true. I love Alberta because she's still doing what she wants to do, and always has, whatever her voice sounded like. At seventy-something years old, to still be able to sound great, and I mean really, *really* great, is fantastic.

JC: I saw Sippie Wallace, who sang with King Oliver, Sidney Bechet, Louis Armstrong, when she was in her eighties at the Hollywood Bowl. They had to help her walk over to the piano, this little old lady. But then she started singing, and she was the sexiest woman alive. Seriously. She transformed before our eyes. This reminds me how sexy Alberta Hunter was, even as an older woman, which was what she was when I saw her. What is it about these women that when they're singing, they're ageless and just plain sexy. How do they do that?

DL: They take on the life of the songs. That's why I know acting and singing go together, because even though I never acted before I did my movies, I act while I'm on the stage singing. You put yourself into those songs, no matter how old you are. If you're singing something about life, most of the time it's something that you have lived, something you have been through. You can get sexy because you get sexy within yourself and people see it. And most of the time that's exactly what happens. I am so thankful to God that I still have my voice at sixty-five and I'm able to do what I do, eight shows a week. It's not something that's just gonna happen. You have to get to the place where you take care of yourself, get your rest, drink water, and do all those wonderful things.

JC: Someone took me to a church in Connecticut when I was in my twenties for me to hear the music. We were the only White people in attendance. The friend who took me had gone previously with friends of his, so he knew this place. What struck me was that all the hymns were the same hymns that I'd sung when I'd gone to church as a kid growing up in Los Angeles, except that in this church, there was a jazz pianist and an organist, and the same hymns were sung and played but with the emphasis on the second and fourth beats instead of on one and three. All I could think was, well, no wonder everybody thinks Blacks swing more. They grew up hearing everything on two and four!

DL: That's right. Blacks always say, "We clap on two and four, and the White people clap on one and three." And as you think about it, we've always had music in our churches. I remember back in the days they say they used to have washboards. Sometimes they tell me they even had pots where they used to bang on like to keep the beat.

Well, if somebody is keeping the beat, you're gonna sing on the beat they playin' on. And we've always had a swing organ and a swing piano. And when we go to White churches, they mostly had those huge organs with the pipes. I've never seen anything so beautiful in my life as all that, but they can't get a beat on that. But the whole idea is when you come up with that kind of music in your church, and that kind of music in the White church, that's what really makes the difference.

A minister said one day, one of the most segregated days of the week is Sunday. It should be the day that everybody, White, Black, orange, yellow, Indian, anything, comes together. But I think that also had a thing about, you stay where you are, and I stay where I am. You do what you do, and we do what I do. But as the years are evolving today, you see a lot of Blacks in White churches and a lot of Whites in Black churches. Which is amazing and wonderful.

JC: Talk about Joe Turner, because he's someone I can't hear without dancing around the house.

DL: When you hear his music, you just wanna go with him. Wherever he's taking you, you wanna go with him. It's not about, "Let's just sit here listening to him." No. You go with Joe Turner. You know what I'm saying?

JC: I do!

DL: He has that kind of music. He has that authority in his voice, "Come on, ya'll, you're all going with me." And all of those great blues singers back in those days were like that. One of the songs by Alberta Hunter was one of the funniest songs that we remember. Me and my husband, we were listening to it the other night, and it says, "Nobody would know what you are in the dark." I listened to that and I went, *"What?"* And it's true. Nobody knows if you're Black or White or Indian or purple or nothin' in the dark. *Nobody knows what you are in the dark!* I'm just telling you, it's about life stories.

JC: You've done such a wide range of things in your career, backup singing, solo singing. In a deep way, you understand all the parts. You must listen to music differently because you're listening to every part.

DL: Yes. I love singing lead, the step-out person that sings the solos in the front, but my joy comes from listening to the background and hearing all the parts. My sister and I were having a discussion about harmony and she said that she had read this book that people from Africa—not just with the drums—all had a sense of harmony, and they used to harmonize all the time. So, when you think about it, that's been passed down to us. Nobody ever taught me the alto part. I taught myself how to read music.

JC: How did you learn the parts?

DL: Just from hearing. You wanna hear a really funny story? Back in L.A.—that's where I was born and raised, too—the Blossoms, the three girls that I started singing with, we all had great ears and we had an unbelievable sound. We could sound any way you wanted us to sound. We could sound Black, White, country, blues, jazz, whatever. And that's what

I did for almost ten years. I was a background singer in the recording studios in L.A. And what they would do with us, they would put us with what they called "the readers," the White groups who could read—and they would put us with them to make their sound bigger, to embellish their sound. And they would be reading the notes, and we'd be singing right along with them, singing their parts.

JC: Would you arrange what you were going to sing, or you would just double up on their parts by ear?

DL: Well, most of the time when you had a reader session, the music was written out for us. We could tell you the note it was, we'd follow the notes, we'd go up, go down. And then sometimes, which was really funny, we'd sing the notes that we heard, but it wouldn't be the note that was written on the page, and one of the readers would tell us, "You're singing the wrong note," because that's not the note that is written. And I'd say, "Well, that's the note I hear, and let's go and ask the conductor what it's supposed to be." And nine times out of ten, it was the note we were singing, because the copier had written the note wrong, but we were singing the right note, and they were singing the wrong one, because they were singing the one that was written.

It got to the point where arrangers would call us to go to a session they'd say, "Well, here's the song we're doing girls, let's sit and listen to it and see what you can come up with." So we actually were arranging and didn't even realize it. I found out a few years ago that singers are charging now for arranging, which we did for free. It was for the love that we did it.

JC: You should have been paid!

JC: Seeing you in Hairspray *last night, knowing you were wearing a fat suit . . . I want to come up with a euphemism for that, but it's a fat suit. You've talked about that pressing on you and what that does to your singing, but I wonder if being in that character of a big woman makes you sing differently.*

DL: It really does. We were laughing about this the other night. I had just gotten my hair done, and I wear it very curly like yours, only shorter. Nobody knew my hair was this long because when I went to get my hair done the other day, she flat-ironed it, and pressed it out. She said, "Oh, you need to wear your hair on stage, like that." I say, "Yeah, but then I won't be 'big blonde.'" The curly hair makes you big. So you have to sing with the attitude, act like you're a big woman. That fat suit puts you in a whole different attitude. You become the mama of the group, and you become a nice, healthy, big woman. And that's what I am in that show. I'm a big woman.

The girl whose place I took said, "Don't let them make you wear the fat suit." I said, "Honey, I weigh 125 pounds. I have to be fat. The song is "Big, Blonde, and Beautiful." 125 pounds is not big." I would never sing that song in public without that fat suit on.

JC: Talk about Aretha Franklin.

DL: I met Aretha when she was sixteen years old. I know her from the gospel days when she used to travel with her father and sing. And the first song I ever heard Aretha sing was "Never Grow Old." At sixteen, she was like a bullet shot out from a cannon. Amazing. And I love Aretha when she sits at the piano and plays for herself and sings. I told Aretha, "Honey, you don't never have to stand up in front of no mic. Just sit at the piano." The way I sing, I can hold the mic, and I love it. But her whole groove is sitting at the piano playing for herself, 'cause she gets in a completely total groove when she plays for herself. You can see it. That girl, when she sits at the piano and plays, she's a whole different human being. It's like something comes over her.

JC: As a fan of great singers, I often think some singers choose the wrong material. With writers, they say write about what you know. Singers need to be true to themselves. They may have a great voice, but they often don't sing what's appropriate for their voice or personality. For instance, I'm not going to go all Billie Holiday on a blues.

DL: Well, that's what's happening with the singers today. They're twenty years old, what could they possibly know about some of the songs they're singing? Mind you, let's say they got it together, and they sound great and it's fabulous, but please, man, "The Man I Love," and "The Man That Got Away," you're just singing the words, not the song, because you have not experienced that. I think that's why I got into Billie Holiday toward the adult end of my life, because when we were growing up, we weren't allowed to listen to that kind of music at home. My father was a minister, and we were the children of ministers. I would listen to rock and roll and rhythm and blues.

JC: That was O.K. to listen to?

DL: No, not at home, at our friend's house. That's how we knew what was going on. We listened to the classics, Nat King Cole, Ella Fitzgerald, things like that. But that other stuff wasn't allowed in our house.

JC: Do you think that singers of your generation, who came up listening to jazz, had that influence their rock and pop singing?

DL: Yes.

JC: I don't know that the generation now is listening to jazz.

DL: I don't think they're coming up listening to anything. They probably are, but I don't know what they're listening to. I know, we say, especially our generation, "Where are they going?" Are they gonna be able to do like we're doing, listen to Ella Fitzgerald and Nat King Cole and Aretha twenty years from now? I don't know, because they play their music so loud, it only gets them worked up. Our music got us in the mellow moods. We could sit back, have a glass of wine, and just sit and talk and listen to our music, you know.

JC: I agree. The music that we both love, the songs that inspire you, that you wanted to play today, also make me feel great. They relax me, but also excite and cheer me. That's a tricky combination.

DL: The perfect combination.

JC: *Another question. What do you say to young people in the business? I know you've had, like all of us in this business, ups and downs, but your positivity is inspiring. I feel you refuse to be bitter.*

DL: You really do have to. You cannot take this business personally. You have to audition, or you have to go and do things you don't really wanna do. We still have to do things today, our generation, that we really don't want to do, because you say to yourself, "Honey, I've been out here forty-something years. I know how to do this," but you can't have that attitude because people will think you're pompous, or they'll think, "Who does she think she is?"

You have to have that power within, and that's what young people have to have. I have children, and I can tell you, you have to really continue to express that to them. Tell them, "Hold on a minute. Nobody owes you nothing. You still have to go out and get what you want." Nobody has given me anything. I have fought for everything, and you do have to choose not to be bitter. No matter what people do to you. And I tell people all the time, "God gave me this talent, and man can't take it away. I don't care what he does, what he says, it's still a gift from God to me. And it's mine." I believe everybody has a gift. And it's your gift, and it's up to you to take care of it and use it. And don't let nobody else take it away from you.

When I talk to young people today, especially the ones who come to see the Broadway shows when we have what they call talkbacks, I tell them, if you think you wanna have a career on Broadway, it's a life of its own. You have no life. You go to work six days a week, you do the show, and you go home. In between, you don't have a whole lot of time if you wanna take care of your voice and your health because you have two shows on Wednesdays, two shows on Saturdays, and your only off-day is Monday.

The biggest thing I tell them is, "You have to *choose* to be offended. You have to be persistent in what you want. And don't let anybody take your gift away from you, 'cause they didn't give it to you." And I've had that happen. Phil Spector, who recorded me back in the 1960s, said, "I taught her everything she knows." I said, "Yeah, right. Well, O.K., you taught me. So now, whatever." If you take everything personally, don't get in this business, because it is not a business for the weak.

JC: Your attitude is inspiring and so are you. I learned a lot and had a lot of laughs.

DL: Well, you hang out with me, Judy, and you will definitely get some laughs!

Jane
Lynch
(b. 1960)

Stage, film and TV actress, comedian, singer, and TV host.

Interviewed in 2021

I first became a fan of Jane Lynch watching her hilarious turns in Christopher Guest's films, *Best in Show, A Mighty Wind* and *For Your Consideration*. Although she was initially reluctant to dive into Guest's improvisational approach to character development, she wound up loving the process and now feels that it pushed her forward as an actress. She has since gone on to win multiple Emmy Awards for her roles on the television shows *Glee, The Marvelous Mrs. Maisel* and numerous other programs.

I jumped at the chance to have Jane on *Jazz Inspired* when her press team pitched me about promoting her CD and tour, *A Swinging' Little Christmas*, a passion project where Jane does what she loves most, group singing. *A Swinging' Little Christmas* teams Jane with actress/singer Kate Flannery (Meredith on *The Office*), vocal arranger/singer, Tim Davis, and the Tony Guerro Quintet.

My favorite guests speak with an almost childlike enthusiasm about their creative life. Jane took it to another level when she rhapsodized about harmonizing with others, an activity she considers a spiritual practice.

Jane and I recorded the following conversation in August of 2021 while she was in Vancouver filming the movie *Ivy and Bean*.

JC: *Have you always been a big fan of Christmas?*

JL: Yes. And music has always been a big deal for my family. We played the same albums over and over when I was growing up. It was always a combination of pop music from the late 1950s and early '60s like Bing Crosby and the Andrews Sisters doing their jazzy takes on Christmas music. I also love choral music. So that's what Christmas music is to me.

A Swingin' Little Christmas is like an album that was recorded during that time. Tony Guerro is our band leader. We have his quintet and full orchestra on some of the tracks too. Kate Flannery is my partner in crime in this. We've been harmonizing together for decades. And then Tim Davis, who was our vocal arranger on *Glee*, is our third singer. Kate and I also do a duo show called *Two Lost Souls*. We're all into the same music from that era.

Tim arranged all our vocals. I'm especially proud of our a cappella tunes. One of them is "Carol of the Russian Children," which is real dark and has tons of minor and dissonant chords. We do it lying down on the stage during the stage show because it is so difficult to sing. We lie down, close our eyes, and go into a soft cotton place and do that song.

Obviously, there's some comedy in our show, but we open with the "Coventry Carol," and we do that a cappella as well. My favorite thing in the world to do is to sing with like-minded others, doing tight harmonies where your goal is not to shine separately but to be one voice.

I know that when we did *Glee*—not to give us too much credit for everything that's good in the world—but I know it inspired a lot of kids to join the choir. Kids who were maybe shy or afraid of sticking out saw the popular football player on *Glee* and thought, hmm, he's singing, maybe I can too.

When I was a kid, chorus was my favorite class. I always say that it massages my soul to sing with other people. It's truly a spiritual experience. It's existential. You change from a single person in a world all by yourself and you become one with this thing that is greater than any of us. And it's *beautiful*. It's the most gorgeous thing.

When we were doing *Best in Show* in Vancouver, which is where I am right now, Eugene Levy, Catherine O'Hara, John Michael Higgins, and I used to go into the breezeway of the hotel where the acoustics were amazing, and we would sing a cappella songs. Talk about bonding! It was a transcendent thing.

This was before we filmed *A Mighty Wind*. Chris Guest caught wind of it, and it started his impetus toward writing *A Mighty Wind*. He saw these people who could sing and who loved music so much that he realized he needed to jump on it. Chris loves music, as you know. Chris, Michael McKean and Harry Shearer have played together for decades and have two bands, The Folksmen and Spinal Tap.

JC: I love that you're touring a show like this. I know I keep saying "I love" but . . . I love you!

JL: I love you! See, it's all about love. Music is love. It opens your heart.

JC: We need this now more than ever. Your Christmas show and CD has the spiritual beauty of these songs, the joy and the humor, the fun of it all. Christmas recordings, of the era we're talking about had all of that.

JL: It was a happy accident of fate that we all got together because we had the same musical taste. And when we were on tour in the middle of the summer we said, "Let's do a Christmas album and do it now, so we can get it out by Christmas." Tony Guerro loves this music as much as we do so he arranged most of it. Kate arranged her "Good King Wenceslas" in kind of a Louie Prima way, and it's hilarious. And we did "We Three Kings" in a Dave Brubeck direction. Some of these arrangements are very challenging to sing. We had to work hard on the breathing and deciding *where* we'd breathe.

JC: *Talk about that. The Dave Brubeck-inspired track is very challenging.*

JL: Yeah! Your lungs must be habituated to that, filling up with air and letting it out slowly. We have some phrases that go on and on. The three of us sat down with that song and figured out exactly where to breathe because we had to do it together. The first rehearsals were all about, where the hell are we gonna breathe?

JC: *Plus, the song is in 5/4 time, which adds another layer of difficulty. One of aspects of Dave Brubeck's genius was that he made 5/4 sound natural by splitting up the beats to: one-two-three, one-two, not one-two-three-four-five.*

JL: Wow! I don't know that I even thought about that. No wonder it was so hard!

JC: *Exactly. Everything in you feels music mostly in either 3/4 time, like a waltz, or in 4/4 time, like most standard pop tunes. 5/4 is a combination of those two so you can never really let go because you might lose the rhythmic place and go to 4/4.*

JL: Yes! I've had to work to get it in there so solidly that I don't think about it.

JC: *This is a great way into talking about improvisation, which is a combination of having an improvisational vocabulary, a framework to work within, and then forgetting it all and jumping in, or it doesn't work. It's fascinating to hear you say that in rehearsal you had to figure out the spots to breathe but once you started singing, you had to stop thinking about it or you'd fall off a cliff.*

JL: That's exactly right. I say for acting or for singing, I build myself a little cage and I bounce around freely within it. The cage is the confines of the song. It's the notes, it's the structure, that's the technique. You get the technique down. It's like with a jazz pianist like you. You have to learn your scales and your fundamentals first in order to earn the right to improvise. Correct?

JC: Exactly! I love you saying "earn the right to improvise" because everyone wants to jump right into it without learning those skills first.

I've read that in the beginning you were a bit resistant to improvisation. You liked having the written line. You obviously have a gift for it. I told you earlier that Chris Guest told me that certain people can do this kind of acting and certain people can't. Even when he and I were recording our conversation for Jazz *Inspired, he kept pushing me in improvisational directions to see if I would pick up the thread and do a funny little bit with him.*

Talk about why you were initially resistant to improv and what finally made you change your mind.

JL: I think it's because I'm fearful of a lack of technique. You called it jumping off a cliff, and that's what I thought improv was. I'd go to improv classes and study it when I was in school, and it did feel like people were just making stuff up out of thin air. But I like to work things out. Now, the process is a deeply ingrained habit. I mark out beats, I create an arch, a beginning, middle, and end, and it scared me to just dive into a free-for-all. But when I started doing the Christopher Guest movies, thank God he saw that I could do it, because if he'd asked me, "Are you any good at improv?" I would have said no. Thank God he didn't ask me. I did a commercial with him and we did it very free form, but there was a cage that we were in. Through that, he saw I could improvise.

I was nervous when we started doing *Best in Show,* but then when I saw the end result, I realized that he edits the hell out of it. After a day of filming, I'd think, my God, there's nothing he can use today, but of course there was plenty because we stayed within the parameters of the script.

JC: Your lines are improvised, so what does the script look like?

JL: It looks like a regular script. No lines, but it'll say, "Exterior dog show." "Interior, dog show in progress." And then a timeline description of what needs to happen within that scene. And then you're free to bring your character that you've created into this world with the other actors who've created their character. We've all done it separately. And he just starts rolling the camera. It is very fresh and very spontaneous. I *maybe* stopped being worried by the time we were into filming *A Mighty Wind*.

[Laughter]

JC: What I find fascinating about that kind of acting, in that kind of setting—for me as a viewer—is that because each of you are in character, but don't have set lines, it's almost like psychodrama. For me, you go deeper. It feels like these characters are revealed in a much more naked way.

JL: John Michael Higgins put it this way. I heard him say this at one of our press conferences for one of our films, and I never forgot it. He said we "pack heavy." So before we show up to shoot, we've really figured out our character, top to bottom. It's living in us. We've made the big decisions. We've incorporated the character into our bodies.

Chris sent the wardrobe person to us to ask what we thought our character wears. And the set designer came and asked what we thought our house looked like, so it helped develop this character. I would look at myself in the mirror and have monologues about what I thought as my character. I would opine on something. And always out of that it went deeper and deeper inside me, and by then you've built yourself a real person. You've gone deeper and deeper and deeper, so when you show up on set, you're ready to go. And everybody else with you is ready to go. I bet it's a really fun thing to sit back behind the camera and watch as it happens.

JC: Talk more about being on tour and performing live in front of an audience. I know you've done stage work but most of your work more recently has been film and television. It's got to be very exciting to get back on stage.

JL: It is. I never wanted to do this alone, *ever.* I did *Annie* on Broadway in 2013, the first time I'd been on stage in probably thirty years, and I got the bug. I got it back. I got reinfected. That's when I got together with Kate and Tim Davis.

As I said, the Christmas show is basically a fifties-sixties swinging thing. Kate is more free form than I am. She's will jump off that cliff. And I will pull her back. I'm the technician and she's the free form "drunk," which is funny because she's the soberest person I know.

I basically map it all out to within an inch of its life. I've put in little areas for Kate to just do whatever she feels like doing. It's consistent but it looks spontaneous. We have it so down that we *can* go off. We're protected by the confines of this carefully crafted hour of music and hopefully, laughs. So, when people say we look like we're having so much fun, well yes, indeed we are, because we've built the framework.

Seth
MacFarlane

(b. 1973)

Producer, director, actor, animator, voice actor and singer

Interviewed in 2011

Seth MacFarlane started drawing at the age of two, originated a comic strip for his local newspaper when he was eight, snagged a job at Hanna-Barbera shortly after graduating from college, and *Family Guy*, the television show he created, was on Fox by the time he was twenty-six. *Family Guy* composer Ron Jones calls MacFarlane "the Orson Wells of our time." Seth's myriad talents and prolific output reinforce this assessment.

For the uninitiated, *Family Guy* is a politically incorrect animated series, sort of a cartoon version of the 1950s television hit *The Honeymooners,* except this married couple, Peter and Lois, have three children, one of whom is Stewie, a matricidal baby with an unexplained English accent (even though the family is American), and a martini-swilling talking dog named Brian. Seth voices many of the characters and one of my favorite moments of our interview included these characters jumping into our discussion.

I became a fan of *Family Guy* when I saw the episode *Patriot Games,* which includes a full-length production number of "Shipoopi" from the musical *The Music Man*. Unsurprisingly, it's hilarious. What *is* surprising is hearing the original orchestral musical arrangement in its entirety in this age of sampled music, short budgets, and shorter attention spans. Watching additional *Family Guy* episodes revealed that these extravagant musical interludes are a regular part of the series. This made me determined to get Seth on *Jazz Inspired.*

While arranging an in-person interview with Seth MacFarlane was only slightly less difficult than crossing the Sahara, Ron Jones encouraged me to persevere, insisting Seth was worth the trouble. Ron is a friend, so I trusted his assessment, but the pursuit was a challenge. Seth is not the "biggest" star I've had on *Jazz Inspired*, but he certainly has the thickest firewall. When I met his sister, fellow voice actor Rachael MacFarlane, and told her my experience chasing Seth, she offered, "Believe it or not, this is what we go through getting him home for Christmas."

Seth and I spoke in his Beverly Hills home in December of 2011, shortly after the announcement of his Grammy nominations for his first vocal CD, *Music Is Better Than Words*, and before his debut as host of the Academy Awards.

Before we started, I asked if he'd mind having Stewie and Peter join in, and he said he wished he'd known ahead of time so he could have written something for them to say. This was a revealing comment. As a jazz musician, improvisation is my natural métier, but Seth is a comedy *writer*, so he wished he'd prepared something in advance. Not surprisingly, he did just fine with our spontaneous Stewie and Peter moment.

JC: *I've had a lot of actors tell me they're more comfortable playing a character or working through a character. You're such a great observer of character and mimic, I'd think it would be hard for you to get up and sing as yourself, as you do in your concerts and club appearances.*

SM: Well, that's the challenge. To sing in a character voice is technically simpler because there are a lot of liberties you can take with how refined and technically perfect the presentation is. If Peter or Stewie sounds too good, then it doesn't sound right. With Brian or with my regular voice, there's no character to hide behind.

JC: *I'm struck by the whole gestalt you create when you perform, the suit, the look, the posture, everything. I say this as a fellow performer. Is that an atmosphere you create for yourself, one that makes it easier for you to deliver the music and makes you more comfortable, or is it for the audience? Or both?*

SM: I think it's just sort of an appropriate way to present the music. In these cases, you have anywhere from twenty to forty musicians, which makes it sort of a big night. And if you're gonna put on a coat and tie for a Golden Globes party, you should damn well put it on for forty musicians. For the audience, you want to look like you made an effort to get out there, and it puts you in a more "on your game" frame of mind.

JC: I like it; it's very old school. I came up, as you did, watching these old movies and seeing how they all approached performing. Then, especially in jazz, it went in another direction, where it was sort of cool to not be well dressed, what I think of as a pretentious unpretentiousness, which in a way seems to disrespect the audience.

SM: Well, depending on the night, they're usually pretty well dressed, and even if they're not, they've taken the time to puff out their cheeks and blow out their chops playing for you. So the least you can do is put on a tie.

JC: Were there musicians in your family?

SM: The only musicians in my family were my mother and father, particularly my father, who was more of a folk singer. He played the guitar in a lot of local pubs in Massachusetts, very "Peter, Paul, and Mary" kind of stuff, a very different genre than what I spark to.

JC: One thing I admire is your talking about the art and the craft of great music making. Is it important to you that your audiences understand that?

SM: Well, it's a bonus if they do. I'd like the audience to understand it because I think at one point in popular music, decades ago, they *did* understand it. And we've gotten a little lazy and a little sloppy and a little uninterested in where our music comes from. As a result, that's given the record labels license to put out a lot of crap, which people have, in turn, devoured, so it's kind of all fed on itself. I think that's one reason the industry's having so much trouble. We just don't really care anymore.

You can put something out that feels like it's recorded on a Casio keyboard with a drumbeat and a rap lyric, or a hip-hop lyric, and it'll be a huge hit. And it seems like there should be a little more work put into it. It was more work and more artistry and more high musicality when you were dealing with people like Nelson Riddle, Frank Sinatra, Billy May, and Gordon Jenkins, all these composer-arrangers who were essentially classy and true musicians. They weren't "producers," they were *composers*, and there's a big difference. I think in contemporary music there's been this fallacy of producers being viewed as substitutes for composers, and it's just not the same thing. That's ridiculous. It's the difference between attending Juilliard or going to DeVry, taking nothing away from that fine institution, of course. Their commercials are inspiring. But that's ludicrous to me.

I've always been amazed at how these contemporary producers get away with murder. But even if they don't choose to be interested in how music is constructed, when you hear music that has had a lot of work put into it, it makes a difference, even on a subconscious level. That's why the television shows that I do are all scored with an orchestra. Even if the audience doesn't know that what they're hearing is live music, even on a subconscious level, it somehow makes the content of the show more important.

JC: Were you thinking about music when you were watching animation as a kid?

SM: I was aware of it. At the time I wasn't thinking, "Is this synth or is this acoustic?" because when I was a kid, even the most terrible cartoons, even the crappiest after-school cartoons, were all scored with some orchestra. Nothing was really electronic. Maybe in the late, late '80s that started to happen, but I'd come home in the afternoon and watch *G.I. Joe* and *The Transformers* and *Thunder Cats* and all these shows that were just kind of cranked out as toy commercials at the time, but the music was all fairly legit. It wasn't Mozart, but the music was made with live players. Hanna-

Barbera employed a composer named Hoyt Curtin who did *The Flintstones*, *Scooby-Doo*, and every cartoon they ever put out.

That music sticks in your head when you go back and listen to it. You think, God, they were playing for a cartoon, but these compositions are really good, the orchestra's really good, and it's something that I think makes people know they're hearing something substantive, even if only subconsciously.

This is the only way you can sustain things like a three-minute musical number in animation. If we tried to do the same type of musical numbers on *Family Guy* with the synthesizer that we do with an orchestra, I think people's attention would really wander. For some it already does. I don't think they'd necessarily know why, but there's a power, and a fatness to the sound that you get from an orchestra that's impossible to get from synthesized sounds.

JC: And the length of the number. I got hooked on Family Guy *watching the episode "Patriot Games." I loved the episode and thought it was funny, but what really added this punch was that you had the complete number from* The Music Man, *not an edited version. That was amazing to me. We both know how rare that is. Here on* Jazz Inspired, *I'll play a whole number and have people say, "I can't believe you played the entire song!" Well, yeah!*

SM: In "Patriot Games," that was kind of the first time we'd done that. It was oddly part of the joke. It was spoofing the New England Patriots and the NFL in general, I suppose, but really spoofing the Patriots, who were all about class and no showboating, i.e. when you make a touchdown, you don't spike the ball. And we figured, what bigger way to showboat than with a show tune?

It was also fun to hear the band play those arrangements. Those are dusty old arrangements that were written for the movie *The Music Man* in 1961. I can't imagine they've been played since. They were in a warehouse somewhere near the University of Southern California, and to hear the orchestra play them live and play them so well, it just gives you an appreciation for what great orchestrating that was. It sounded great, it sounded energetic, it's just beautifully written stuff.

JC: Talk about your CD, Music Is Better Than Words, *because this is very exciting, bringing these tunes out, some that people, myself included, haven't heard. You surprised me with some of your choices.*

SM: When Joel McNealy, the arranger, and I looked back at a lot of the old recordings that we liked, there was lots of Sinatra, of course. Sinatra, obviously, never wrote anything. I think there were maybe one or two songs over the course of his career that he had a hand in writing. None of them wrote anything—Bing Crosby, Rosemary Clooney, they were all vocalists.

And the songs that they sang were songs that, for the most part, had been written in the '20s, '30s, and '40s, and they were sort of being reinterpreted by more contemporary arrangers and made into completely new animals. There were a lot of great songs during this period, thousands of great, great songs. You hear a lot of the same ones over and over on those old albums. You hear a lot of "Blue Moon," "Bewitched," "I've Got You Under My Skin," and a lot of Rodgers and Hart. There are so many great songs, but there are also an equal number of great songs that nobody ever recorded.

So, using that model of taking old, old tunes and breathing new life into them with bright unexpected arrangements, which Joel excels at, we were able to put together something that sounded classic but was relatively new. And the songs were deliberately chosen for the fact that they had not been recorded in a pop style. There's no point in doing "Come Fly with Me" because you're never gonna do it as well as Sinatra did. There's no point in doing "Moonlight Becomes You," that's Bing Crosby's tune. It was a deliberate choice to create, quote/unquote, things that were germane to us and that we could lay some claim to.

JC: I've read that Jackie Gleason is one of your heroes.

SM: Yeah, I was a big Jackie Gleason fan growing up.

He was a true showman, and a guy who really understood what it means to put on a show. And just a dynamic entertainer. And Ralph Kramden, obviously. What's not to be amused by with that character? It's hard to find a lot of his other stuff, his Reggie Van Gleason character, which also is so hilarious. But anybody who's ever created a fat, loud-mouthed TV character in some way owes their success to him.

JC: Who of the female singers of that era do you like?

SM: I love Rosemary Clooney, Debbie Reynolds, when she's at her best. And when she's somewhat restrained, I love Nancy Wilson. There are times when she gets, for my taste, just a little too free and loose with the melody; it's a little bit of that Nina Simone kind of thing. It's funny because Ella Fitzgerald would be the other extreme. I'm not a huge fan of Ella Fitzgerald because I feel like she doesn't necessarily do enough with the melody. It's always pretty straightforward.

And Keely Smith I like a lot. I think June Christy is fantastic. So there's kind of a Goldilocks zone of interpretive freedom that, for my taste is just right—and you know, Nancy Wilson has a recording of "Little Girl Blue" that's in my estimation the best recording of that song ever.

JC: It makes sense to me that these are the singers you'd like because you're all about no-pretension, which I think is reflected in your animated shows. You're always sort of squashing pretentiousness. You like the singers who just get to the heart of the tune.

SM: Well, it's also important to breathe life into a tune, but at the same time Cole Porter, Rodgers and Hart, Irving Berlin, and Johnny Mercer, they don't need help. They don't need your help if you're a vocalist. Those tunes work just fine the way they wrote them. That was obviously what Sinatra did better than anybody. He really respected the melody and didn't veer too far from it. At the same time, he acted the story of the song. It drives me crazy when I hear contemporary vocalists playing *American Idol* with these old tunes. It's like, what are you doing? That song doesn't need your Christina Aguilera hand-waving, jackass.

I think that's a fundamental difference between the old style of pop vocals and the new style. And I sound like I'm a hundred years old saying this, but when you watched vocalists back in the day sing these songs, they made it look effortless. That was the whole point. You tried to make it look like it wasn't work. There's beautiful sound, but it's somehow not taking any effort at all, and that, in a way, made the performance about the audience and not about the performer. The performer was there to serve the audience, to entertain the audience.

Now I feel like it's flipped. You have singers who don't really seem to care whether you're watching them or not. They can be singing to their hairbrush and looking at their bathroom mirror, and it's going to be the same thing. You know, I don't want to see how much effort you're putting into it.

JC: *It does seem like it's more about watching rather than about the song and listening. You're talking about the old-style performers who were about* serving *the tune, not* using *it.*

SM: Yes, exactly, exactly! You know, Margaret Whiting never wore a meat suit.

JC: *She didn't?*

SM: I don't think so. [Laughs]

JC: *Talk to me about the reaction of the audiences at your shows. You've sung a lot in public—doing this with Ron Jones' band and obviously with your CD—and your approach is different from the way music is usually presented live these days. Do you think that the audiences are getting it and listening to these lyrics more when they're presented to them like this?*

SM: I have no idea. I mean, I think there's a certain degree of connection that they make with *Family Guy* or *American Dad* that helps bring them in to give this kind of music a chance. You have your *Family Guy* fans, of course, but for the most part I find that the audiences who are there for those shows are mostly people who just like that kind of music and want to hear a band play it well.

It's about trusting the music that can move you. It's the same thing with comedy. When we record an actor for the show or for the movie, if the joke on the page is a good joke, you're only gonna hurt it if you try to put some sort of vocal spin on it. Trust the material. I think that philosophy transcends all these different media.

JC: I'd think that your having such a good sense of pitch and rhythm and a lifelong love of music would contribute to your humor. Just knowing what works.

SM: Yeah, I mean comedy is a very rhythmic, a very timing-specific beast. And sometimes, certainly in animation, the difference of a frame can make the difference in how funny a joke is. Where does the character answer the question, or where does that next line come? Sometimes it really can be down to a frame. So, yes, there's a sense of rhythm to it, of comedic rhythm. And yeah, there's a musicality to it in that way. And I think there are probably a number of subtle hidden connections between singing and comedy that a person with a lot of free time could break down.

JC: I obviously hang out with lots of jazz musicians, and it's interesting how many of them are great at puns, and the puns will go back and forth, and the humor will go back and forth. But it's always building, building, building, snap, snap, snap, because we're improvising. It's almost like it's a practice session. They're keeping their chops up.

When you're writing, with any of your shows, any comedy, and you're working with someone else, is the character in your head? Do you ever speak as these characters, try a line out in character?

SM: Yeah, there's always a tendency to write with my ears. It's something that can be frustrating at times when you're not dealing with an actor who gets it. You write something that's funny if it's read this certain way. But if you don't have an actor who gets it, there's nothing you can do about that. You've got to find someone who understands.

So that's been a really key part of casting the show—who does all of our voices, all of our ancillary voices, right down to the actors who come in to do one or two lines. We have a stable of people that we use who, in a way, know how to read the comedy notes on the paper. That's also a lot of why over the years I've done a lot of my own voices for *Family Guy*, just because it's easier. Rather than having to communicate to somebody, "Here's how this has to be read to be funny." It's just easier to get in there and do it.

JC: As an animation director you live with a voice performance for a while because animation takes a long time to produce, and one performance might seem right when you watch the actor but be a lot different if you're just listening to the voice. Now, directing live-action, you're looking at actors and directing them in a film. You're probably listening to their voices in a different way from other directors.

SM: Yeah, the sounds really do take precedence. If the facial expression isn't perfect but the read is, I'll tend to go with that take, because to me that's where the money is, as far as the laugh is concerned. So, yeah, comedy and certainly dialogue comedy is obviously an audio skill. It depends much more on your rhythms than your physicality. If you're Jackie Gleason or the Three Stooges, it's a different story. But it's all still timing.

JC: I think it is only fair that I ask Stewie and Peter Griffin if they have anything to add to this discussion. I know they'd be angry if you got all the attention.

SM (as Stewie): I don't think your audience is going to know who the hell this is, for heaven's sakes.

JC: I think they might.

SM (as Stewie): All they're thinking about is how much they have to donate to get that little tote bag with Big Bird on it sent to them, right?

JC: Well, that is a big part of NPR.

SM: And slurping your coffee. [Makes slurping noises] Why is there so much slurping on NPR?

JC: We're doing it ourselves! Now give me a little Peter.

SM (as Peter Griffin): Forget it! The last time somebody said, "Give me a little Peter," I completely misinterpreted it and got sued. So I won't be an idiot and walk into that trap again.

JC: [Laughing] I really have to do a better job thinking through my questions before I ask them, obviously. I've learned my lesson, Peter. Thank you for that!

Marian
McPartland

(1918–2013)

British-born jazz pianist, composer,
and longtime host of *Piano Jazz* on NPR.

Interviewed in 2004

Marian McPartland was impressive for many reasons, but what I admired most was her determination and longevity. Her show *Piano Jazz* was the longest-running cultural program on NPR, and her music continued to evolve and expand throughout her life. Marian's sly humor and British accent disguised a no-nonsense toughness and (with certain people) a mouth like a sailor.

Marian and I had known each other for quite a few years when by chance, we were seated in adjacent boxes at Carnegie Hall. I said hello as my eyes drifted to the cast on her wrist that she tried to hide by moving her sweater over it. When I asked what had happened, she made light of it, saying she had a little sprain. In truth, the wrist was broken, for the second time, but she didn't want a fellow musician to see it and possibly suggest to others that she was out of commission. It's hard enough to keep a jazz career going without people thinking you're down for the count, even temporarily. This attitude, along with her ambition and her continuing curiosity about music, made her ageless and kept her going strong well into her nineties.

Shortly after my first record was released, a Japanese entrepreneur approached me about sponsoring a tour for me with Marian and Joanne Brackeen. Women instrumentalists were rare at the time, so he especially loved the thought of a concert with three women pianists from different generations, representing three different styles of jazz. I was in my twenties, Joanne in her forties, and Marian, in her sixties. I called Marian, gushing about this fantastic opportunity to play concerts in Tokyo and Kyoto. "They're going to fly us Business Class, pay (big amount of money), give us two days off in a resort to get over our jet lag, and we'll be the first jazz musicians to ever play Suntory Hall!" Marian dryly responded, "Are you sure we don't have to sleep with anybody?" (I'm cleaning this up.)

It was a huge career boost for me when Marian asked me to be on *Piano Jazz*, which, at that time, was only a few years into its thirty-three-year run. One of Marian's many impressive skills was her ease at playing with anyone, in any style, something very few pianists can carry off as well. My music draws on the style of Marian's husband, cornetist Jimmy McPartland, so duets with me touched an emotional soft spot for her. When we finished recording, her producer came out of the booth and said I should pursue having a show of my own. So appearing on *Piano Jazz* pushed my career forward in multiple ways.

Piano Jazz revolved around Marian's duets with her guests and a focus on musical analysis. In my interview I wanted to zero in on her emotional side and her relationship with her late husband. He was an important influence on her music and career, which in some ways eclipsed his, although he was a significant figure in the early years of jazz, having played with Bix Beiderbecke and other important jazz innovators. Marian and Jimmy split up but eventually moved back in together. I once asked Marian about that, and she said, "We got a divorce, but it didn't take."

JC: When do you remember first falling for jazz?

MM: From an early age, as long as there was a radio playing, I would listen to various jazz bands and play along. It wasn't so much loving jazz as learning to play tunes. Whether they might be nursery rhymes or the pop tunes of the day. Like Bing Crosby singing "Please." You're too young to remember that tune, Judy.

JC: I'm a huge Bing Crosby fan! I've heard a lot of those early things.

MM: Well, we loved Bing, and of course, Jimmy knew him very well. In fact, I have a *Downbeat* cover that I'm very proud of with Bing playing the horn and Jimmy emoting as if he were Bing. Very cute.

JC: Your musical versatility has always impressed me. Your duets with your guests on Piano Jazz *seem absolutely effortless. As a fellow pianist, I know what that takes. And reading up on you, my dear, I read that you were in a four-piano vaudeville act, so you've been playing well with others from the beginning. Is this true?*

MM: Oh, yes, it's true. That was my big start in life. Actually, I had started going to the Guildhall School of Music and was already into playing the jazz classics all day and listening to jazz whenever I could, when I was supposed to be practicing classical music. But I got offered this vaudeville job, and of course, I wanted to drop everything and go. My father offered me money if I *wouldn't* go. But I did go, and I'm so glad, because I think my whole life would have been quite different if I hadn't. Of course, they wanted me to be married to somebody, like a doctor or somebody "nice." That was their favorite word.

JC: But you ran off to vaudeville. How old were you when you did this?

MM: I was about nineteen.

JC: That was a radical move.

MM: Yes, I guess it was. I didn't really think about it until people remind me that that was a very daring thing to do. I didn't think about it at the time. I just had to go. And from then on, I was in showbiz.

JC: Who were the other three pianists?

MM: The owner of the group was Billy Mayerl. He still has a tremendous following in England. He was sort of the Frankie Carle of England. It wasn't really jazz. It was more pop. And the other two people were pianists who worked at the BBC, George Middleton and a singer named Dorothy Carless, who is now living in California. And that made up the quartet.

JC: Tell me about meeting Jimmy. That was such a huge turning point in your life, when you first met him and then played with his group.

MM: When World War II started, I was very busy playing with a group on the pier in a seaside town. They used to call that kind of thing a "constant party." There would be a comedian, a singer, a pair of dancers, a juggler, and stuff like that, and I would be the piano player. Suddenly, all that stopped with the war, and I had to make the choice of either entertaining the troops or going into the women's army, and I certainly didn't want to do that!

I joined ENSO, the Entertainment National Service Organization, which was the English version of the USO. I did that for about a year, and then I joined the USO. Actually, our group was the first to go in after they had the big invasion, and it was just like General MacArthur. We even waded into the water to get off the boat. We had everything except the guns.

JC: Oh, my word!

MM: We had learned how to make pup tents, and actually part of my luggage was an accordion because they were sure that there were no pianos.

JC: You played accordion as well?

MM: I didn't have to, thank God. There were enough pianos around. They had a lot of little spinets. We traveled all through France. It was really terrible when you think of all the horrible things that were happening. We were going through villages that were just a mess of wreckage. We finally arrived in Belgium for a rest period at what they called a rest hotel, which is where I met Jimmy. He was a G.I., but somebody in our show recognized him and pulled strings to get him out of combat and into the USO, so he joined our group. We had a G.I. bass player and drummer, and we toured every morning at the front lines. We were bombed and strafed quite a bit. We were really in the thick of things.

Anyway, Jimmy and I were sort of brought together, you might say. And we hit it off, and then we became very friendly and then we became in love, and then we decided we'd get married. We had to ask permission from his commanding officer, who didn't really like the idea. He said I hadn't known him long enough.

JC: He said that to you?

MM: Yes! We said that really didn't matter, so they let us get married. We were married in Aachen, Germany, in the military government building. The army was very nice to us. They lent us a command car and a driver to go to Brussels for our honeymoon.

JC: How long did you get to take off and have a honeymoon?

MM: A week.

JC: That's a lot! Now, when did you get smitten with bebop and go off in a different musical direction?

MM: Oh, I got smitten with bebop quite early on, before we left Europe even, because we were friendly with Charles DeLaunay (French writer, founder of *Le Jazz Hot*, one of the oldest jazz magazines). We were at his house, and he played a record of Dizzy Gillespie. I asked such silly questions, like, how do they know what to play and are they reading it off the music and stuff like that.

JC: *You wouldn't know on first hearing what was going on with that music, especially with somebody like Dizzy.*

MM: I know. I think the tune was "Hot House." When we got back to the States, we used to go down to the South Side and after our job—we'd be at the Brass Rail playing until three—we'd go to a place that was open until four to hear Jackie Cain and Roy Kral. I always told Roy that he was the person I really admired most as far as being a really good pianist who played wonderful bebop. That's where I got started actually, wanting to play bebop.

JC: *A lot of people don't make that transition from swing to bebop. It's another thing about your playing that I admire, that you're so at ease with either rhythmic underpinning. You seem to effortlessly go back and forth, which is pretty unusual, don't you think?*

MM: Well, I loved playing Jimmy's music. I've got a repertoire second to none. I can play all those tunes, and I love playing them. But that didn't really stop me moving ahead and listening to what other people were doing. Then when we came back to New York, Jimmy kept saying, oh, you must have your own group. And he helped me to get my own group. If it wasn't for him, I probably would not be doing anything.

JC: *It's wonderful that he was encouraging and didn't selfishly keep a great pianist for his own group.*

MM: I really felt that he made a sacrifice by pushing me into having my own group because that meant that I didn't play with him as often. Although we actually played together from time to time right to the end of his playing days, which lasted pretty much all of his life.

JC: *What do you perceive were the challenges for you as a woman in jazz. Were you aware of that, as an advantage? As a problem?*

MM: Well, I guess, the only time it would come up is, some guy would make some silly remark, like how does it feel to be a woman in a man's world? Or you play good for a girl. I still, very occasionally, get that from some guy asking, how does it feel to be a woman in jazz? I say, where have you been all these years?

JC: I can't believe people are still saying this to you.

MM: Well, male chauvinism is still lurking in corners. And nothing can be done about it, I guess, except smile.

JC: Speaking of other great women pianists, we're both big Mary Lou Williams fans. I'm crazy about her.

MM: And I certainly was. And I couldn't wait to try and find her when I got to New York. Of course, I did eventually find her at a little place called the Downbeat on West 52nd Street. She was playing there with a varied group. I introduced myself and of course she knew Jimmy. Jimmy knew everybody, so it made it very easy for me to meet people, and I had always admired Mary Lou. I'm sure you did too.

JC: Absolutely. How did you start Piano Jazz?

MM: It wasn't my idea. Alec Wilder had a show on NPR when his book, *American Popular Song*, came out, which everybody should own, by the way. He had a show that featured singers. He had Tony Bennett, Margaret Whiting, people like that. Then his show ended after about a year, and they were looking around for something else. So I didn't find out until much later that Alec had recommended me to do a show. And a guy from South Carolina, Bill Hay, came to me—I was playing at the Carlisle at the time—and asked me if I'd be interested in doing a radio show. And I thought, what a lovely idea but thought it could only be something that would last a few months. They asked who I wanted to have on, and I suggested having another piano player, which I thought would be the best and easiest way. So that's what we did.

The producing radio station didn't have much money, or maybe not any money, so we would tape the show in the Baldwin Piano showroom in Manhattan. The Baldwin people were always wonderful to us. The engineer would come up from South Carolina, and so would the producer, and we would pull up two pianos side by side and set up the equipment, and we would record right there.

JC: Who was your first guest?

MM: [Laughs] Mary Lou Williams! And it was a bad choice on my part because I think she was feeling a little miffed that I, an upstart English person, was doing a show about jazz and she wasn't. She started out being a little rough and tough, but she sort of got mellow, and she even sang a song on the show. It was very cute. Then we had a quick succession of greats, Hazel Scott, Billy Taylor, John Lewis. I was like a kid in a candy store. I wanted to call up all the people and make the date. I'm still calling up all the people twenty-five years later.

JC: You get to fantasize about who you want to play with and make it happen.

MM: Well, if they agree. I've got a few holdouts, unfortunately. Keith Jarrett isn't really interested in doing the show.

JC: Really? I find that hard to believe. Keith, where are you?

MM: That's what I keep saying.

JC: You're so fearless. I've always admired that you have such a diverse group of guests. You just dive in and play with all of them. Is that from years of playing with so many people? How do you prepare?

MM: I have had guests that you have to drag every word out of them. Then I've had a few that really want to take over. I guess I can mention one name, she's no longer around, Dorothy Donegan. She scared me to death because she really wanted to take over.

JC: *In terms of the interview or the piano playing or both?*

MM: Oh, the piano playing. She almost did me in and at the end of the show I said, "Dorothy, it's O.K., you win." And she said, "I know."

JC: *[Laughs] Years ago, I played four clubs in different countries where we were on the same circuit. She would play for a week, leave town, then I would play for a week. It happened four times in a row. And each piano was destroyed by the time I got there. She was so powerful that actual keys would be missing. She was just like a cyclone coming through.*

MM: Yes, she was. Watching her perform in a club was amazing. She was a great performer. I wouldn't want to be a sideman in that group, though.

JC: *[Laughs] Nor would I! Tell me about Bill Evans. I know you had him on the show.*

MM: I am a tremendous Bill Evans fan. When I was at the Hickory House, he was at the Vanguard a lot, and he finished later. So again, I had the benefit of finishing my gig, then going down and hearing the tail end of his last set. He and I became pretty friendly, and he was one of the first people I had on *Piano Jazz*.

JC: *I love your CD with Benny Carter,* The Songbook.

MM: That was so much fun. I loved Benny. He was just a great friend and a great guy. On the date, he did everything possible to encourage me because, of course, I was a nervous wreck. So, if that date was successful, it was due to him.

JC: *I also admire how you have been creative with your career as well as your music. I don't remember when this was, but it was a few years ago, when you broke your wrist, you then hired another pianist to go out with you to play duets on some of your dates.*

MM: Well, I was so annoyed at having done this, and I thought why should I give up a perfectly good gig and throw the people into panic having to get another group? Why can't I play it myself and hire another piano player? In fact, I was stupid enough to break my wrist twice in almost the same place. So I did the same thing. In fact, I was doing *Piano Jazz,* and I had Diana Krall as my guest and I said, "I'm sorry but I'm only going to play duets with you with one hand. You're going to have to cover for me." And it was so much fun playing two pianos that way I said I'll never use my left hand again.

JC: How about Chick Corea?

MM: He was among my earliest guests and I remember I spent a lot of time learning certain little fills and certain things that he did. He had a tune called "Matrix." And he had a way of playing some of the fill-in parts. I learned how to do a pretty good version of "Matrix" and when he came in, he was whistling "I'll Remember You," and he didn't want to do any of his tunes! He wanted to do all standards. All my work had gone for nothing. [Laughs]

JC: I have to ask you about Art Tatum. I'm sure you heard him many times in person.

MM: Of course, he was one of my earliest influences and somebody I listened to in England. I actually went out and bought a book of his transcriptions, which was a pretty futile thing to do. It was ridiculous, but I did love his playing. I got to meet him when he was playing in Cleveland when Jimmy and I were playing there and went over to hear him. He took us to a speakeasy, and I'd never been somewhere quite like that. It was on a quiet street, in the middle of the night, everything dark, and you went up this flight of stairs and there was this whole big room with blazing lights and a big piano and slot machines, and God knows what all.

He played all night long until about nine in the morning. Jimmy and I just sat there mesmerized. The first tune that took my fancy was his version of "Humoresque." And it was really nice to get to know Art and feel that I had him for a friend. Although, the first time we were playing a gig and he came walking in with his manager, I thought I was going to faint.

JC: I can imagine! Well, Marian, I think you're just fabulous. I am so pleased we've been able to talk and that you were able to take the time to do this.

MM: Well, I'm very happy to hear you doing a show, Judy, and that it's a great success. You have such a wonderful voice. And I love to hear you laugh! I think listening to your show, just to hear you giggle and laugh, that I'd get my money's worth!

John
Musker

(b. 1953)

Multi-award-winning and Oscar-nominated animator,
director, producer, and screenwriter.

Interviewed in 2012

John Musker became fascinated with animation and the music that surrounds it as a child, and he still gets almost giddy talking about it all. He and Ron Clements have been one of Walt Disney Animation Studio's most successful teams, co-directing *The Little Mermaid*, *Aladdin*, *The Princess and the Frog*, *Hercules,* and most recently, *Moana.*

> Animators I've been fortunate to know—and I know many—typically possess a wonderful combination of childlike enthusiasm, artistic imagination, and an ability to concentrate over a sustained period, all skills needed to create an animated feature, which can take years to complete. I met John through a mutual animator friend who brought him to one of my concerts. Afterwards, John handed me one of my books of stride arrangements and shyly asked if I'd autograph it, revealing himself to be a longtime fan and an aspiring stride pianist. It was the beginning of a beautiful friendship.

JM: I grew up in Chicago, big Irish Catholic family. And of course, I'm of the generation that watched a lot of TV as a kid, and that was sort of my education about life and jazz in particular, but through a very circuitous route. There were kids' shows in Chicago, and one of the big shows was *Garfield Goose and Friends*. There were puppets, there was a host, and they'd show Warner Brothers cartoons as part of the show. They had a little theater screen, and Frazier Thomas would sit there and say, "Come in and watch us" and you'd watch these cartoons.

Ray Rayner, another Chicago personality, also had a show back then where they ran these cartoons from the '40s. Sometimes they'd have caricatures of famous actors from the '30s, and I'd be like, "Who's that woman with the big feet?" Years later I realized, "Oh, that was Greta Garbo."

Carl Stalling was the man who composed all the music for the Warner Brothers songs. He literally did like a cartoon a week for twenty-two years! When we're saying Warner Brothers, we're saying Bugs Bunny, Daffy, Porky Pig. I wish I could do the voices for you, Judy. Seth MacFarlane, now he and Eric Colby, those guys can do the voices.

JC: *I have Seth in the other room.*

JM: I loved those cartoons, but musically their scores often had quotes of standards of the day. That's the way Carl worked. So if they mentioned this beautiful woman, they'd play "The Lady in Red" or "A Cup of Coffee, a Sandwich, and You." They'd play all these standards that Warners had the rights to. In 1943, Raymond Scott was this wonderful composer, leader of a quintet. It was actually a *sextet*, but he refused to call it a sextet because he thought that might be too …

JC: *Sexy?*

JM: Yes! It might send people off in the wrong direction, so he called it a quintet. Can you believe that? Anyway, he wrote these great tunes that he sold to Warner Brothers in 1943, and they were quoted in every Warner Brothers cartoon. One of the main ones was "Powerhouse," which was used for any cartoon that involved any sort of assembly line, mechanical factory. When Raymond Scott was writing these tunes, they'd improvise it. And once they got something they liked, he forced them to chart it, and that became the basis for what they'd play. And I think he insisted that when they played in concert, they played it like a concert piece, and it wasn't improv-y at all; it was very much a fixed piece.

And they all had wacky titles. "Dinner Music for a Pack of Hungry Cannibals" was another one. Anyway, those great titles became the basis of my jazz musical education. It was really the Warner Brothers' jazz library that sort of taught me about those pieces of music.

JC: You talk about the wonderful music in these cartoons, which inspired me too. We're the same generation. I remember hearing these tunes, and I realized that there were these inside jokes that I didn't get. My parents would explain them, and that would make the cartoon even funnier. Today we don't have as much shared knowledge of the music, which must make that a challenge.

JM: It *is* more of a challenge. When we did *Aladdin* at Disney, we encouraged Alan Menken to do little musical quotes and jokes, as Robin Williams did when he recorded the Genie. He'd reference things of the day, and we knew it was tricky because Disney films are supposed to be made for all eternity. So if Robin was doing a reference that someone might not get, the question was, will the joke communicate?

Disney films are meant to last fifty years, so even now *Aladdin* is still a popular film, but some of the specific references have ceased to be in the forefront of popular culture. For example, he did Arsenio Hall, who had a talk show around the time we were doing the movie. Robin did sort of an impression of Arsenio Hall, and it was funny because he did the whole sort of dog "woof, woof, woof" that Arsenio would do on his show. When we showed the movie in Japan, the Japanese audiences, which were fairly reserved anyway, laughed uproariously at that. Well, the *Japanese* version of uproarious laughter. Because they said, "Oh, we love the *Pretty Woman* reference" because in *Pretty Woman*, Julia Roberts did Arsenio Hall doing that. So, when they saw that, they thought it came from *Pretty Woman,* and we just nodded and said, "Yes, we're glad you got our *Pretty Woman* reference."

That's the challenge in any sort of a Disney classic, the topicality. But as I was saying, seeing those Warner's cartoons as a kid growing up, I didn't get those musical references. I didn't necessarily know who Edward G. Robinson was, and yet I'd see this guy saying, "Hey, you guys," and all that, and I'd think he was funny. He's just the guy who has a cigar and talks tough.

The same with the musical quotes. They were kind of eccentric and loopy, and I got to know certain pieces of music because they were used often, but I didn't know that that was really "The Lady in Red" when I'd hear that tune. So on *Aladdin,* we took that approach of, "If it's funny on its own right, you don't exactly have to know the reference."

We had a younger staffer at the time, Sarah Duran, who was probably fifteen years younger than we are. Robin did an impression of Ed Sullivan with the, "Right here, very much from the lamp, right here," and all that. We thought it was very funny, so we used it. Sarah, who was our post-production supervisor, had no idea who Ed Sullivan was. So, she said "Oh, he's kind of a hunchback kind of guy and has that funny voice?" Yeah, Ed Sullivan was kind of a hunchbacked guy with a funny voice.

JC: That's interesting. She had a vague notion of him, but it wasn't necessary that she knew Sullivan exactly.

JM: It wasn't necessary, yeah.

JC: Everybody's going to get some things and it's not necessary to get all the references, if it's a funny bit. And what I really find interesting—as you're talking about it, because I've always been into animation, cartoons, all of that—is that I didn't even think about the fact that it was so much about the music. Maybe I was also drawn to the music because, to me, it was all of a piece. Is that how you think of it? You talk about telling the composer to compose it a certain way so you can draw it a different way. Talk about that whole process.

JM: I love the combination of music and animation, and I feel like all animation, even if it has dialogue, is sort of a choreographed dance, and there's a musicality to it. From the earliest days of Disney, the director's rooms were called the "music rooms" because every director had a piano in the room. And the cartoons, the short cartoons, before they did the first feature—which was *Snow White* in 1937—which was long before I started there, by the way . . .

JC: I was gonna say, "You did Snow White, *TOO?" John, I'm even more impressed!*

JM: I know. People used to complain about the "We" disease at Disney, because they say, "Well, when we did *Snow White* . . ." and I'd say, "You didn't do *Snow White*! Those other guys did *Snow White.*"

JC: When I worked at Disneyland, people would quote Walt all the time.

JM: They did?

JC: Yes! They'd say, "Well, you know, Walt was going to . . ." and I'd cut in with, "Did you KNOW Walt?"

JM: Yeah. Did you *know* Walt? Were you on the screen with him? "Well, I watched the TV show. . ."

JC: Exactly.

JM: "I read the book" but . . .

JC: Anyway, continue.

JM: So, the directors' rooms were called music rooms because the short cartoons were laid out musically. In animation, there are what are called exposure sheets, which break down frame by frame what is going to be seen. But they also—back in the days of shorts—had these things called bar sheets. So, literally, the cartoon was mapped out musically before it was animated, and that was mapped out by bars of music. That was transferred to the exposure sheets, so the animators, when they were working on the cartoon, had the music and dialogue all recorded before they did the drawings. So you're really trying to sync what you're doing to those things, and they'd map out musical statements for bits of action. Here's where Pluto gets the flypaper stuck on him, and he runs over here. And, of course, there was "Mickey Mousing," as you'd call it in the music, where they were trying to hit accents in the music that would match the picture.

Even as we did our movies, the ones I directed—*Little Mermaid* and *Aladdin*—the songs were recorded before they were animated, and as we were shaping the songs, we'd talk to the arrangers and the orchestrators and say, "We have a stretch where we really want the fish to swim through here, and there's gonna be this bit of business." So they'd invent little musical bridges and accents and orchestrations that would match the storyboarding we were doing. And in fact, when we did *The Little Mermaid*, it was a throwback to the old system because Howard Ashman and Alan Menken, who wrote the music for that, did a number of the songs that they wrote on the site, in the building with us, in the same way the music was done in the '30s. They were literally right down the hall, and they could walk next door and see the storyboards for it. And they would compose the music, knowing what the storyboard artists were coming up with.

It was a very collaborative back and forth, and it was very much a throwback to the '30s system of producing music, where it was all done right on the site. It wasn't like the composers being 2,000 miles away and then sending you the music through the mail, "Here's my song." It was literally right down the hall.

JC: A live-action movie has all of this production. It has the acting, the script, everything. Then two minutes before it's released, they say, "Write the score." But the way you describe working on The Little Mermaid *is wonderful because it's so collaborative.*

JM: It is. Obviously, in a movie like *Fantasia,* which they did in 1940—where they took classical pieces and animated to those pieces—the music really forms the visuals. When I hear music, I'm thinking visually. So really, it's the marriage of those two things, where you don't know where one begins and the other ends. That's what's so appealing about animation. And the best animation, whether it's at Disney or Warners or wherever it might be, it's that sort of marriage where you can't separate those things.

I also grew up a fan of live action musicals. Again, I got to see them on television and seeing *There's No Business Like Show Business* and certainly *The Wizard of Oz,* which was a staple, a year-after-year event at Christmas, those were so ingrained. But they were part of my kind of pop culture background, the idea that a person, when they were so moved by their emotions, that they could burst into song, and it didn't seem weird. In fact, it seemed *expressive,* and I liked that. I responded to the emotion and the comedy and all, but I went with that sort of convention.

And so, when I was first starting at Disney, the idea of doing musicals where people sang, and sang their inner thoughts, didn't seem odd to me at all. And the wonderful thing about animation is the stylization inherent in it. Years ago, Howard Ashman said, "Live action musicals have kinda gone away because people have a difficult time accepting the convention of people breaking into song in a naturalistic setting." And he said, "One of the reasons I think animation can be a home for the musical is because it's inherently stylized. It isn't real." So, they are drawing—or nowadays, doing computer animation—but that's still not real. And even though it maybe has more semblance of reality at times—because of the lighting and the shading that you can do with computers, it's inherently stylized. So the convention of leaping into song and people singing to each other is more easily accepted.

JC: One thing I've always liked about animation is it's a world I want to step into. I can remember thinking this as a kid with Snow White *specifically, because I loved the rounded edges of everything. You'd see the huts. Everything was so curvy and wonderful and warm and inviting. You wanted to go into that world, something I sometimes used to feel with live action musicals as well. I've never thought about it till this moment—that those early musicals that you and I accepted and loved—that I wanted to step into them.* Seven Brides for Seven Brothers. *I wanted to star in that!*

[Laughter]

JM: Yeah, and have those guys jump on a log right next to you.

JC: Yes! And I think that one of the wonderful things about what you do is that you're in that world. And you get to create that world.

JM: You immerse yourself. You're immersed into the world. There's a producer that I worked with at Disney who once said, which I thought was really a good analogy, "You know what we're really doing? We're building tree houses for people." And in a way, I think that's what you do. Because from a tree house, you see the world from a different vantage point. There's an element of adventure in being in a tree house that's sort of exciting, it's out of the ordinary, and it gives you this other vantage and it's just fun. And so, it's a different world.

John Lasseter, whom I work with now—he was the executive producer at Disney, and I went to school with him at CalArts. He's always big on the worlds of whatever animated film we're working on. What is the world of this? Just like when he directed *Toy Story*, and it was like, "I wanna take people into the inside world of toys. When you shut the door, what happens to the toys?"

And so you're entering kind of a secret world that you haven't seen. For John and for all of us, it's very big. What is the world that we're bringing people to and what is the appeal of that world? You want to create a world that people want to spend an hour and a half in. And that's really what Disney does. *Snow White* was considered Disney's folly because that was the first Disney feature-length cartoon. People said, "Oh, it works for eight minutes or seven minutes or five minutes, but ninety minutes? To have people suspend their disbelief and believe that if somebody dies, they really die?" Like when Snow White's in that coffin. He proved his critics wrong. He got people to emotionally invest in drawings. And it's an illusion. It's all a sleight-of-hand thing.

But music was always a huge part of that. Almost every Disney film was rooted in the emotion of the piece, was rooted in the story, but the story was rooted in song. And the songs told the story and were inseparable from the story. The problem with some musicals is that the story stops when they do a number. You can take the number out and still have the story. Disney was very big on the songs advancing the story or character, and if they don't, then they don't belong in there. At times they cut songs out of movies because they didn't perform that function.

So really that's a part of what we tried to do on *Little Mermaid*, and *Aladdin*, and *Hercules*, and all the musicals we've worked on. The key story points are carried in music and in song. And if you took that song out, the story would kind of fall apart. So that way you're not just stopping to have a song. It's advancing plot and character. Howard Ashman believed in that. And Ron Clements and I—Ron co-directed and co-wrote these films that I'm referring to generally—we believed that as well. That's paramount to being successful with involving the audience.

JC: I think jazz musicians and animators have an interesting thing in common. We both have an ability to imagine and create different worlds and step into them, losing ourselves in improvisation while keeping the story together. I can see this natural connection as we're talking about this.

JM: Exactly. Ron Clements and I wrote these scripts. The first drafts of the scripts for *Aladdin* and *Little Mermaid* and these other films that we've done, we use a slight jazz approach, in that, when we're writing the script, we have sort of an outline. Ron is really good at structure, and I'm more of the improviser, I create bits of dialogue and bits of business, so I go through and in effect I improvise on paper after we have the structure, and Ron takes what I've written and re-edits and adds his own stuff, but basically we're kind of . . .

JC: *Playing together.*

JM: Yes. He's kind of left hand, I'm kind of right hand, and out of that you get this. You can get this kind of filigree where you invent something and maybe just like any improvisation, sometimes you hit a dead end, but sometimes it leads somewhere, and there are characters that may materialize that were only barely sketched in initially that you discover, or a storyboard artist creates some really great bit of business or expression or something, and then you're like, "How can I write to what they've created?"

It's like when you're improvising and somebody takes a solo and they go a certain way, then you jump on board and follow it. I think that's what we do with our storyboarding, in our visualization of the process. One idea leads to another, connects somewhere else, and you're trying to bring it back around, and that's the fun and challenge. There's a playful aspect to jazz, and animation is nothing if not trying to seize that spirit of play. It's ironic, because in some ways animation is the least spontaneous art form in that you're trying to get the illusion of spontaneity but because you literally start with a blank sheet of paper and you have to create everything that's there, you don't have anything to work with, and you're doing it a frame at a time.

And yet when you watch the best animation, it feels like it was tossed off and it flows naturally, just the way the best jazz improvisation works, where you can't believe someone's mind worked that quickly, that they went to that spot and other musicians followed them and then they embroidered that, and they came back around at the end. It's great when you get that kind of counterpoint and interplay of jazz. That's what the best animated films have had, that same process.

JC: *You play the piano. I know other animators who play jazz. So you've answered the question of why this is such a natural fit. But I'm curious about some of the composing for these films. I know that very often in live action films they use a temp score, then they wind up using something else for the completed film. So let's say I'm making a film, and I want something like what Nino Rota did for Fellini. We use that until we write something specifically for my film. Talk about the process with your films.*

JM: I know what you're talking about. When we worked with Howard Ashman as he wrote *Little Mermaid* and *Aladdin*, Howard's style—working with Alan Menken who did the music, Howard did the lyrics—Howard was really the story driver of the songs. He and Alan worked in the pastiche style. So, Howard would give Alan a point of reference for the tunes, the feel of the tunes that he wanted to put in the score, and Alan had that as a jumping off point. So, for example, "Friend Like Me," the Genie song, when Howard wrote the original treatment for *Aladdin*, before Ron Clements and I ever got involved, he wrote a forty-page treatment and wrote five or six songs for it. He was possibly going to direct it. Turned out he didn't wind up directing it, but one of the songs he wrote was "Friend Like Me," which is a song for the Genie. The Genie was a central part of his version of *Aladdin* as it is in the fairytale. But he thought of the Genie as a Fats Waller type. That was his point of reference.

And in fact, his version of *Aladdin* was basically conceived as a Hope/Crosby musical, kind of an old Paramount movie, like *Road to Baghdad,* and the Genie was this hipster Fats Waller, throwing out jokes and wisecracks and that sort of thing. For example, Fats Waller has a huge catalogue, but "The Joint Is Jumpin'" for example, has this breezy feel where he's throwing lines out, he's singing, he's kind of playing, and that became the sort of template for a "Friend Like Me," which was the Genie's big number.

JC: *I know you were an early jazz fan because you were listening to these things and you were getting it from animation, but did it make you immediately think, I want to draw? Were you already drawing?*

JM: There was music around our house, certainly. My mother played the piano, and she was a bobby-soxer, so she had all this sheet music for "Shoo-Fly Pie and Apple Pan Dowdy" and "Comin' In on a Wing and a Prayer." Those are all the songs that were around when she was a kid, and her maiden name was very beautifully hand-written on this sheet music. And we had a piano in our house. She'd play the piano, and she played "Maple Leaf Rag" and all, so I kinda grew up around music. Then, of course, I was taught by the nuns in Catholic school, and that almost destroyed me. I had a few years of piano lessons. I never practiced. I'd go in, and Sister Mary Stella, who was six feet tall and about 250 pounds . . .

JC: *She sounds like a mean cartoon!*

JM: She was kind of a caricature of the mean nun, almost, although she really wasn't, but to a kid, imagine you're a third grader, and there's a woman who seemed like she was like 6'5" . . .

JC: *And wearing the habit.*

JM: And wearing the habit. And you'd go in the basement of the convent, and it was weird because they had pinball machines there. I don't know why exactly, but there was a room there where you'd sit and practice before you went in to see Sister Mary Stella. I'd go in there, not having played a note all week, and I'd be like, "I'm gonna get killed!"

JC: *I'm having a moment of guilt here because you have my music book, and I keep asking if you've been practicing.*

JM: I do have your book. And I feel equally guilty.

JC: *Don't feel guilty. Continue.*

JM: I'm still guilty about not practicing enough, and now I wish I'd practiced when I was young, now that I'm trying to play the piano. But I always drew as a kid. My mother—in addition to her piano playing—painted a little, so I was encouraged when I did that sort of stuff. I do think drawing was kind of an escape for me. I had, as I say, five sisters, and I think even back in the day, I did caricatures of my fellow students and my teachers, and for the school paper. I'd draw the chemistry teacher and the biology teacher and make them Frankenstein. I was sort of known for that.

And I went to the musicals in my high school, and I did some theater stuff as a kid. I was never in a musical, but I'd go to the high school musicals, and I played in these kind of bad comedies, with the sort of church theater group. I really enjoyed the collaborative nature of, "Hey! Let's put on a show!" We'd paint the sets, and I drew the posters and programs. Animation appealed to me, ultimately, as I did draw, and I drew more and more.

One thing that appealed to me about animation—and this relates to jazz, I think—is the collaborative nature of it. You can play solo jazz, but there's something appealing about working on an art form when you're working with other artists, and the thing you're going to produce is added to and reshaped by their input. You're coming up with things, they're coming up with things that you wouldn't have, and it becomes an additive process. You're working with other people, you're not a lonely hermit, off in your room.

I did have kind of a romantic vision of this, which is partly why I'm still trying to learn how to play piano. I'm still terrible, and I don't practice enough, but the romantic version of the solo piano player, late at night with the cigarette . . . and of course, my father died of lung cancer, but despite that . . .

JC: *Hmm . . .*

JM: But there's something about the whole noir-y thing, the lonely piano player in the dark bar, that I still kind of like.

JC: *Is that how you think of me?*

JM: No, no! You have a smoky voice, but I don't think of you as lonely. You seem surrounded by love and warmth and kindness.

JC: [Laughs] You do have a romantic notion about this, John. I like it.

JM: I do have a romantic notion of it, and even the whole film noir-y thing, which had jazz scores and that sort of thing. When I was in college, I discovered the works of Raymond Chandler, who wrote *The Big Sleep* and all those great Philip Marlowe detective things. He's the guy who'd say, *"She stood out like a tarantula on a piece of angel food cake."* And speaking of you, he'd said, *"She was a blonde. She was a blonde that would make an archbishop kick in a stained-glass window."*

JC: [Laughs] Why thank you! And you did the noir-y voice. Well done!

JM: Yeah, so there you go.

JC: What jazz reminds you of that scene? This is like free association.

JM: Well, there was actually a score for the film *Farewell, My Lovely*, a version of a Philip Marlowe story that was done in the '70s. It had been made in the '40s, and called *Murder, My Sweet* with Dick Paul. But this was made with Robert Mitchum. David Shire did the score for it, and it was kind of bluesy romantic, trumpet and saxophone, dark streets, and *"I had a hat, a coat, and a gun. I put them on, and I walked out of the room."* I mean, that's Raymond Chandler.

Anyway, I loved all that and I love David's score. I saw that movie three or four times. But the whole kind of noir-y thing I liked. And there's a comic strip, *The Spirit,* that Will Eisner created in the '40s. He was a private eye, but he wore a mask, so he was some kind of cross between Dick Tracy and a superhero kind of guy. But he did these very noir-y comics, which influenced William Friedkin and people in their live action films.

So I was loving those drawings, loving hearing that music and that whole noir aspect of jazz that I just found romantic and appealing. I'd ride the El in Chicago and the sparks would ricochet off the building as you'd go by. They'd light up the building, and I'd think, "Who lives in that building?" It's an Edward Hopper painting in there waiting to come to life. It was all part of some great big jazzy, bluesy kind of romantic, wistful thing that I imagined. And in the animation, obliquely, I use it. Certainly, Disney films have cheeriness and light, but they also have these darker qualities and melancholia and emotion. And I think I pulled some of that out of the jazz and things that I was listening to through my formative years.

JC: You're an Erroll Garner fan, and I know you saw him on The Tonight Show *back when they played jazz on* The Tonight Show. *I had to get that in there.*

JM: Absolutely. It's weird when I think about that and realize that they don't have jazz guests now, but Johnny Carson was my introduction to the jazz world, and I used to see Erroll Garner, and I'd always be fascinated by him sitting on that phone book, and sort of talking as he played. And then when I tried to teach myself piano in my post-Catholic school years, I got an easier version of some of Erroll's tunes and that had "El Dorado" and "Paris Impressions." Then later I got actual transcriptions of more complicated stuff like his "Where or When," which I love. He uses every key on the piano at least once, and I love the kind of colors that he could create in his music.

JC: Talk about "Down in New Orleans" from The Princess and the Frog.

JM: *The Princess and the Frog* was a fun movie because we wanted to do an American fairy tale. We'd done many traditional sorts of European fairy tales, and we thought, could you do one that had an American setting? And we said, "What city in America seems like where a fairy tale could actually happen?" And that led us to New Orleans. We took the story of *The Frog Prince*, which, as written in Grimms' Fairy Tales, has nothing to do with New Orleans. As it turned out, it's the favorite city in America of John

Lasseter. And we found out after the fact that Walt Disney's favorite city in America was New Orleans.

JC: That's what Walt told me. Back when we used to hang out.

JM: We used to eat chili at the end of the day. He'd have a Scotch and his favorite chili.

JC: And talk about New Orleans.

JM: And the Sherman Brothers were playing in the background, and we would share this banter.

JC: I knew them too, of course. Continue.

JM: Now, we also had heard Randy Newman's tune, "Louisiana" which was about the flood, and Louisiana is a very elegiac, powerful thing, and we thought, "If we're doing this American fairy tale, what about Randy Newman?" Who, as it turned out, spent summers in New Orleans as a kid. So we suggested to John Lasseter that we'd love to use Randy to write the music and proposed it to Randy and he said he'd love to do it. We wrote our script after we'd been down there, after we'd met the voodoo priestess, Ava Kay Jones and talked to various sorts of experts on this and that. We tried to fold it all into the story. Originally, our movie was gonna be narrated by an otter named Gumbo and Randy Newman was going to do that voice, à la Jiminy Cricket. Gumbo would invite us into the movie and say, "Well, this is what's going on," and he'd play a kind of a weird reedy piano that we would use.

Well, the movie got to be too long, so Gumbo went away and actually Randy sort of read for the part of Gumbo, and his acting was . . . a little sketchy. Then when we said, "Guess what, Randy, we're not doing Gumbo anymore." He said, *"It's 'cause of my reading!"* And I'm like, "No, it wasn't your read . . . " "Yes it was! You thought my acting was . . . " "No, no, we *loved* your acting."

But we wound up cutting the character. So, we said to Randy, "Can we do some kind of an opening that's sort of a Valentine to New Orleans? That celebrates all the things we're eventually going to see in the movie?" So, he wrote this tune, "Down in New Orleans." And originally, at one point, he was going to sing it, but I said to Randy, "Dr. John is such an icon of New Orleans. What if he sang your tune?" And Randy, who is a contemporary of Dr. John and loves Dr. John said, "Yes, yes, let's use Mac." So, Dr. John, one of my idols growing up in Chicago, performed this tune, "Down in New Orleans," that sort of has all the colors of the story we're going to tell, dealing with voodoo, rich and poor people, what food means, you know. We're talking about all the things that New Orleanians love, and sort of mashing it into one song. So, this was our sort of Valentine to New Orleans.

JC: I have to ask you before I let you go about "All the Cats Join In." I've been doing that tune for a while, but it's only recently that I saw the animated short of it, which is very cool. People can see it on YouTube.

JM: In the postwar period, they did what's called package pictures where they strung a bunch of shorts together, and they were almost all driven by music, really. And one of them—and it's a great short—is based on "All the Cats Join In" with Benny Goodman playing with a quartet with Teddy Wilson. It's a great swing tune. And they conceived it as a real vehicle for Freddy Moore, a great animator at Disney who drew cute girls, these sort of bobby-soxer or coed types. So this piece involves a bobby-soxer kinda getting ready to go out in a jalopy to the malt shop or something.

And the fun thing about this is that the sets are sort of drawn just ahead of the animation, so they draw a car just in time for somebody to jump in it and they draw a shower for her to use, and a towel for her—just in time, or it would have been the raciest Disney film on record. And again, the piece was recorded, storyboarded, but then animated after the music was recorded, so for every little accent in the music, they found a spot for the animation.

And there's a fun bit where a cop shows up and suddenly the car's gotta slow down, and it works perfectly with the music, where suddenly things go on a little bit of a pulse and then, once the cop leaves, *bang*, it picks up again and off the car goes. It's a wonderful piece, and when I went to CalArts, that was one of our favorite pieces. We'd think, "Wouldn't it be cool to do something, some musical piece like that?"

JC: So you're going to come hear me in a couple of nights, and I'll play "All the Cats" for you! Feel free to jump on stage and we'll swing dance! Thanks so much, John. This was wonderful.

JM: Do my idol Steve Allen's line. "Thank you for having me." And I will thank you for being had. That was his old joke.

JC: We love you, Steve, wherever you are!

Willie Nelson

(b. 1933)

Grammy Award-winning musician, actor,
songwriter, author and activist.

Interviewed in 2021

Willie Nelson is, and always has been, a busy, passionate man. While he is much celebrated for his Country music, he loves and continues to be influenced by the American songbook standards he heard growing up and the jazz musicians he admires. His latest CD, *That's Life,* is his second tribute to his favorite singer, Frank Sinatra, and it's this CD that encouraged his press people to pitch me about having Willie on *Jazz Inspired*.

I've always been a Willie fan. I knew that our mutual love for Sinatra would give us a starting point and that his passion for another of my favorites, Django Reinhardt, could keep the conversation going for hours.

In over twenty years of doing *Jazz Inspired*, only four guests have brought me a gift and Willie was one of them. He sent me his "Willie's Remedy" coffee and tea, his own brand of extremely yummy coffee and tea, both infused with hemp extract which results in a balanced combination of stimulation and relaxation, much like Willie's music. He talked to me from his home outside Austin, Texas over Zoom.

JC: Things have come full circle for me, Willie. This show is just a little over twenty years old, and one of my first interviews was with Jerry Wexler, who spent the whole time talking about Western Swing. I know he was a very important person in your musical life.

WN: He was a great producer who knew what he was doing. He knew me and I knew him and he kind of instinctively knew what I could do. He was the best.

JC: *In* Me and Sister Bobbie: True Tales of the Family Band, *the wonderful new (2020) memoir you and she wrote, you said he was the first producer who let you do exactly what you wanted to do and left you alone to do it.*

WN: That's true. He let me do it the way I felt it and with whatever arrangement and musicians I wanted around me. I've kept going in that direction, and I guess that so far, it's turned out pretty good.

JC: *I should say! In* Me and Sister Bobbie, *the chapters alternate between your point of view of your childhood, life and musical development and Bobbie's, which I found intriguing. It was obvious that you two had a deep connection thanks to your music. Bobbie's played piano for you off and on for fifty years.*

WN: One of Sister Bobbie's heroes when we were starting out was a gal from Waco who played piano. We had a lot of mentors and a lot of people we listened to in that area, especially around West Waco and Abbott. Out West, we had what they called a SPJST Hall, which is a Czechoslovakian dance place. All the guys would go there, play a bit of music, have a beer and a great time. Those are the good old days.

JC: *Something that really impressed me in reading your book was that through all your trials and tribulations—you and your sister have not had an easy life—there's a positivity with no judgment about anything that happened, an acceptance of what life brings to you. Is that something you learned when you were young or is it part of your nature?*

WN: Well, my sister and I grew up together in Abbott, Texas, with what they used to say was "a population that never changed because every time a baby was born, a man left town." I loved it and still go up there and have a lot of fun.

JC: *I guess what I'm getting at is something that has always come across in your songwriting, and certainly in this heartfelt book, is that no matter what you've faced in life or how sad it's been, there's always been a beautiful life force within you that's pushed you forward with purpose and positivity. And I've wondered if that was taught to you or if it's your great faith. A lot of people would have been taken down by what you've gone through.*

WN: I think faith has *everything* to do with it and believing in yourself and believing in a lot of other people, and kinda thinking positive. Just think of what you want and get out of the way and let it happen.

JC: *People talk about self-made people, and they usually mean someone who starts out with no money and winds up with lots of money. But you were conscious of the person you wanted to be, read books on positivity, moved forward with conscious choices and made yourself the man you wanted to be. You are genuinely self-made.*

WN: Well, thank you. I think we all have that ability. It's something we're born with, and you can either do it or not do it. I just kinda knew where I wanted to go and what I wanted to do. I knew that music was going to be my life because it's the only thing I really love to do. And the same thing with my sister Bobbie. We just grew up playing together, and it's been a positive experience for both of us.

JC: *You celebrate your love for Frank Sinatra on your wonderful CD* That's Life. *These are the songs you grew up hearing.*

WN: Absolutely. And Frank Sinatra is my favorite singer of all times. And I read somewhere that I was his favorite singer. So what could be better than that? I love the way he chose songs to do, I love the way he did them and I don't think he ever intentionally did a song the same way twice. Plus his phrasing was fantastic.

JC: *I'm glad you brought up phrasing. Your phrasing is unique, and I think unexpected a lot of the time. You float over the pulse of the tune in a lovely way that* *eludes other singers. Frank did that too. You both just tell the story and phrase the lyrics the way you feel it.*

WN: The secret word you used there is *feel*. If you do it how you feel it, you might feel it different next time, but so what?

JC: *People talk about exposing yourself emotionally, which certainly great lyrics and these great songs inspire, if you're connected to the story. That's something you've always done and Frank too. It doesn't seem like that's been a particular challenge for you, which it certainly is for a lot of singers.*

WN: Yeah, I never tried to keep the emotion from coming through. It's not something that you go in and say, "Well, I'm going to get a lot of emotion in this." It just happens. And then you take it and run with it.

JC: *That's something you and Frank share. You break our hearts . . .*

WN: And love doing it!

[Laughter]

JC: *I'm also delighted that you're giving me an opportunity to talk about Django Reinhardt. People who know you well know how much you love Django.*

WN: I've been a Django fan for many, many years. His guitar playing was fantastic. And I loved it the first time I heard it. I tried to play as many of his songs as I could, tried to get a lot of his licks. Somebody said I was like Django with one finger. I took that as a compliment.

[Laughter]

JC: *It is kind of mind blowing when you think about his playing, that he was injured and managed to do what he did only using two fingers. As Django fans know, in 1928, at the age of seventeen, he was in a fire which badly burned half of his body including his* *ring and little finger. Doctors thought he'd never play guitar again, but Django taught himself to play with two fingers.*

WN: He came back from a lot of problems and went on and said, heck I'm still a good guitar player. So he took these two fingers and went to work.

JC: Talk about your new book, Letters to America. *You say in the introduction, "I like to think that I'm committed to the positive idea of being fine. And to always keep moving forward." I loved that.*

WN: Well, one of my favorite sayings is, "Delete and fast forward." So that's kinda where I'm at. I take life one day at a time, literally, because I don't know what's gonna happen tomorrow. Right now, everything's cool, but in a minute it might all go to hell. Right now, I appreciate what's happening and this is all we have.

JC: We certainly need those thoughts now more than ever. How have you been during the pandemic?

WN: Well, I wrote a few things. I wrote one that I kinda like. It goes:

> *Energy follows thought*
> *Think about what you want*
> *And then get out of the way*
> *Because energy follows thought*
> *So be careful what you say*

JC: I like that a lot. Especially now, when people are not watching what they say a good portion of the time. That's beautiful. How is it being home and not on the road?

WN: I miss it. It's been a year. This is March 1st, so one year ago today was the last show that we played down in Houston and it was great. We had 80,000 people. Since then we haven't been able to do much.

But here's another song I wrote recently. It goes:

> *Live everyday like it was your last one and one day you'll be right*
> *Treat everyone how you want to be treated and see how that changes your life.*
> *Yesterday's dead, tomorrow is blind, the future is way out of sight.*
> *So, live every day like it was your last one and one day you'll be right.*

JC: *Love it! Where are you now? Is that a piano I see behind you?*

WN: Yeah, this is a little farmhouse we have outside of Austin. Behind me is the piano and some guitars. And outside, we've got about seventy-five horses in the pasture. It's great.

JC: *Now we're coming full circle regarding something else besides our Jerry Wexler connection. When he was on the show, I started off welcoming him, and he stopped me and said, "No, I have to introduce you!" So I thought that, in honor of our friend Jerry, I'd have you wrap this up because I know you were a radio man and have a sign-off you used to use.*

WN: Whenever you're ready, I'll throw it at you.

JC: *I'm ready!*

WN: This is your old cotton-pickin', snuff-dippin', tobacco-chewin', stump-jumpin', gravy-soppin', coffeepot-dodgin', dumplin'-eatin', frog-giggin' hillbilly from Hill County, sayin' it's been nice talkin' to you all. Bye, Judy. Love you.

JC: *Bye Willie, love you too.*

Arturo O'Farrill

(b. 1960)

Jazz pianist, composer, arranger and artistic director
of the Afro Latin Jazz Orchestra. Six-time Grammy winner.

Interviewed in 2019

Arturo O'Farrill brings the world together through his music by combining musicians from different cultures and musical influences from past and present. Arturo sees all these elements connecting in an inspiring spiritual continuum, one that he celebrates on his CD, *Fandango at the Wall*. Its release was our excuse for getting together for a conversation in late 2019.

Arturo's father, the celebrated Cuban composer, arranger, and conductor, Chico O'Farrill, helped make music a central focus of Arturo's life from the beginning. Arturo has worked with some of the greatest musicians in jazz and continues to pursue collaborations that inspire him in new directions. His focus is wide and deep.

I found Arturo's attitudes about what we do with music, how we share it, and what we learn from it particularly inspiring, along with his commitment to put good thoughts and actions into the world. Arturo was a rare guest who was a few minutes late, so when I opened the door something inspired me to scold him in a comical way, prompting him to kneel and declare he was groveling at my feet, begging for forgiveness. How could I not love this guy?

JC: *Your energy, which comes through with your music, is so beautiful. You said a wonderful thing just before we started taping. You replied to something I said by saying, "I can tell you don't live in the jazz ghetto in your mind." That was really beautiful. I know what you mean. There is a lot of this jazz ghetto thing. Talk about that.*

AO: Let me begin by saying that I believe very strongly in the concept of jazz. I just don't believe that it's played out as well as it could. When I was a kid, I heard "Seven Steps to Heaven" and when Herbie Hancock first steps off into the stratosphere, unraveling layers of African rhythmic code, my life was changed forever. I have nothing against jazz. But I think that in some ways jazz has stratified, *elitisized* and created this thing in and of itself that is very off-putting. Somehow, we have become less relevant to the world than ever. I saw a statistic showing that we're less relevant than classical music in terms of sales. I'm a jazz musician, but I believe in Kendrick Lamar, the rapper. I'm a jazz musician, but I believe in Gottschalk. I'm a jazz musician, but I believe in Albert Ayler as much as I believe in Charlie Parker.

So for me, the way that we look at jazz has unfortunately sometimes become a way of identifying ourselves as opposed to embracing the infinite. "I'm a jazz musician" or "I'm a jazz enthusiast" or "I'm a jazz historian" or "I'm a jazz scholar." And invariably, you get a description of the 1950s Blue Note era. It's just such a small little slice, a segment of something so huge and infinite and powerful that could never be contained by any label, any institution, any one person. There's no spokesperson who can ever do that. Being open to what jazz could become is so much more important than defining what it is. And this goes for all of life. People who define themselves by what they listen to, what they eat, what they wear, or where they live, are people who live in the ghetto. People who define themselves by what they *are*, by what they could *become*, are human beings.

That's what I mean when I say the jazz ghetto, where people go, "I live in this infinite little point right here." People who are *real* jazz people, people who really love jazz, understand that jazz is a journey. It's not a what, it's a how.

JC: That's wonderful. And so inclusive. This is music that absorbs, reinvents, and reinvigorates itself.

Talk about your wonderful new CD. Talk about inclusivity! I grew up in Southern California, so where you recorded it, how you recorded it, means a lot to me. The whole concept of it is beautiful.

AO: *Fandango at the Wall* became a project that I worked on for many years with the producer Kabir Sehgal, who's one of my oldest friends. What happened is that a board member from my beloved nonprofit, the Afro Latin Jazz Alliance, which performs, educates about, and preserves the music of all the Americas emanating from African and indigenous roots through the entry point of jazz, sent me an article from *The New York Times* about a wonderful man named Jorge Francisco Castillo who twelve years ago founded a festival called Fandango Fronterizo. He was a retired librarian who had just gone through a divorce, so his life was in upheaval. To focus on something positive, he volunteered to clean up the beaches of Tijuana. At that point he didn't realize that the border wall juts right into the waters. There's literally a wall right into the Pacific Ocean. At that point he'd also started being interested in son jarocho music, which is a regional Mexican folk music style. It occurred to him that this spot would be a great place to have a festival of son jarocho music. He gathered a bunch of folks from the United States and from Mexico and they literally met at the wire mesh wall at the border. A lot of people don't know what that wall is like. The actual two legal borders don't touch. They're actually forty feet apart. The wall in Mexico is forty feet from the wall in the United States, and in the space in between is a park called Friendship Park.

Periodically, the border police would let people come to the park on weekends to celebrate birthdays or weddings or whatever crazy stuff they want to celebrate. So Jorge said, "This is a great place to have a fandango." A fandango is traditionally a celebration of life with much dancing, much drinking, much singing, much guitaring. He managed to get all his friends from all over the United States and Mexico to meet at that point when they opened the door to Friendship Park, right at the mesh. So you have, literally, musicians on either side of this mesh wall performing together. When I read about this, I thought, "My God, this is such beautiful, pure activism. This is the spirit of real activism. Taking the very elements which oppress, hurt and enrage you and turning them into the very elements that unify you, that give you license and draw you in to celebrate humanity and life. I've gotta meet this man." We contacted Jorge and he invited us to visit him.

I'll tell you a funny story. I went to his house to visit him and stayed a couple of days. I've met all kinds of important, heavy people, but I was just in awe of this man and of his vision. We went and met with Jorge and learned about the music. The jaranas, the different guitars, the different functions of the different songs at siquisiri, which opens up every fandango, and we cautiously asked him if we could join the celebration. He was a little wary about the idea because they love that thing and don't want it to become a big publicity stunt. I really respect that. In all the cultural diplomacy I've ever done, it's never been about visiting a country or the people and going, "Hey, we're jazz musicians. Look how great we swing. Yay!" All the cultural diplomacy we ever do is about entering silently with great love and respect into the countries we visit and saying, "You are amazing. Show us how we can serve you."

So that's what we did. Jorge went back to the committee of organizers that run the thing and they invited us. We came to sit alongside our Mexican brothers and sisters, not to take presents. There was no buying, no selling. We just stood side by side with our Mexican brothers and sisters and sang at the top of our lungs across this wire mesh.

We brought quite a cast. We brought Regina Carter, the Afro Latin Jazz Orchestra, the Villalobos Brothers. We brought Sahra Motalebi and Rahim AlHaj.

JC: I couldn't believe it when I read all these names.

AO: Antonio Sanchez was there too. And it was such a celebration of life. I felt so affirmed as a human being in the presence of chicken wire and border guards with machine guns. And that's a miracle because it shows you that this thing, this moment in history, this aberration that is taking place in our lives right now, is actually a cue. It's actually a clarion call to join together in a stronger way than ever and to become more convinced that what we need to do is respect the right of every human being to exist, to be fed, to be clothed, to be loved, to have a job and an educational opportunity across the world. And when we still live on a planet where three people have everything and the rest of the world has nothing, we have a lot of work to do. That's what I learned in Tijuana, watching people celebrate with the greatest joy you could imagine. I've learned this lesson over and over. It's not what you have. It's not what you wear. It's not where you live. It's who you are and how much of yourself you give to those in front of you.

So many times, the act of performing for someone is a demonstration of sorts, and very few times do we really enter into a performance situation where we invite the audience in.

JC: I look at it as an experience that's all together, the audience and performer. The connection is everything. I do look at that when I go out to perform. I consciously don't want it to be a voyeuristic exercise for the audience. I want that communication.

AO: You know exactly what I'm talking about. We love it when people interact, give us energy, and return love, but I think it goes deeper than that. I get the feeling that you understand the idea that the difference between performer and spectators is a construct. And no matter who has what expertise, or who does what, when you enter into a relationship with somebody who's listening to you perform, that's a holy relationship.

And holy relationships cannot take place in the guise of hierarchy. So on some level what you want as a performer is to stop being the expert and to take someone by the hand on this journey with you. In the process you have to be as open to what they have to say as what they have to offer to that moment of performance. I have an old trick that I do. I've been doing this for a thousand years. I have an orchestra and trios and quintets and octets almost every time that I perform. I'll make a nice, tidy little set list, and I'll have a game plan, and invariably I'll depart from it.

And my band members will look at me like I'm nuts, 'cause I'll start improvising and going in a completely different direction. They have no clue what's going on, and you know why I do this? Because it equalizes the playing field. Because the audience doesn't know us, and they're at a disadvantage. The audience doesn't know what we're doing, or who we are, or what we're about. We know, we got the papers in front of us. We've all played a thousand times together and that's a hierarchically unfair relationship. So once we equalize that by taking great big risks, we really enter into a fairer playing field. Maybe the audience doesn't know that I've just changed the game plan. But they sense danger.

JC: Which to me is the great thing with jazz. If you're doing it the right way, and you're always walking on that edge and sometimes falling off, the audience loves it. They're constantly talking about that, and I know it's happened to you that audience members have said things that relate to this. One person says, "I loved seeing you order your band around," or "I loved looking at your feet tap," or "I loved looking at you directing the action. I didn't know what you were doing, but I loved it when you pointed at one musician and then another." They're involved in that whole process, and they can see that it's improvisational, that it's spontaneous.

AO: Because we all inherently understand that we have to put our lives in danger, so to speak, to really experience life. We have to try that which we've never tried before. But it's safer to do it in the presence of people who are also taking that chance with you. So audience members who feel that you are exposing yourself, that you're vulnerable, you're taking a chance, you're jumping off that ledge with them, are more willing to go with you. And that to me is the sacred responsibility. That's so different from what we're taught, isn't it? What we're taught is to have control, to know what we're gonna play, to have a set list, to have our shtick and to know how to unravel it. It's interesting, because I think that the real purpose of art is to equalize, and in so doing to liberate.

JC: That's lovely. To equalize and liberate. That's profound and beautiful.

Now talk about jazz education. That's changed a lot over the years.

AO: When I was growing up, the only place that had a jazz program was North Texas State and UMass. The way I learned to play jazz, I had to go down to a club on Eldridge Street on the Lower East Side of Manhattan and sit around while a bunch of older musicians—Tommy Turrentine, Jimmy Vass, James DuBois—they'd just "stand around and play music, man." You'd be like, "Hey, man, how'd you play that turnaround?" "I'm not telling you, man. Go get me a beer."

And then, if you got them enough beers and nickel bags they'd eventually say, "All right, I'm gonna tell you once, only once." God forbid you should not get that turnaround that one time he shows you, 'cause he will never tell you that again.

That's how we learned. We learned by asking our elders to please divulge the secrets. But the part that doesn't get taught is that we had to hang with our elders. We had to look at them. We had to understand them. We had to live side by side with them and see their socioeconomic position, who they were, their character. You can't get that in a classroom or from a YouTube video or from a book or from somebody who's in a nicely pressed, pristine suit or whatever, saying, "This is the turnaround for this and that. These are the tertiary dominants and this is the tri-tone substitution . . ."

JC: Can you imagine me hanging out in those clubs when I was twenty? I took my life in my hands. And some of those places in L.A.? It was more dangerous when I was coming up in L.A. It was harder for me to go to a club there because I had to drive to some dodgy area. But I learned a lot, just the way you're describing. I watched and listened.

AO: But you are a hero. Because women took their lives in their hands to learn to play this music. In fact, my first boss was the amazing Carla Bley. I spent three years touring with Carla Bley, and it was the most unbelievably important part of my life because I understood that jazz is not a gender issue. Jazz is not a sexual preference issue. Jazz is a journey inside. And in order to get there, you have to be willing to stand in places where you may be subjected to gender derision. And if you're gonna learn this music because you love it, nothing will stop you, nothing. I love my people, but it's really lost on students who just sit in the classrooms and get taught.

JC: Talk about "On the Corner of Malecón and Bourbon."

AO: I'm gonna do my best Rod Serling here: *Imagine a place where jazz and Latin are neither jazz nor Latin, but both are one, and both are the other. You've just entered "On the Corner of Malecón and Bourbon."* [Laughs] That was such a bad Rod Serling. I want everyone to please forgive me.

JC: I loved it! That's exactly what I felt listening to this. This song is a beautiful blending of styles and music. I loved this piece because you had so many different things going on. It's absolutely delightful.

AO: Thank you. "On the Corner of Malecón and Bourbon" is basically about how Latin music and the music of jazz are irrevocably intertwined. And we know that from the fact that New Orleans was actually kind of an African village as Havana was, and both of them are the same place. If you think about it, New Orleans and Havana are very similar.

J C: A lot of people don't know that. They know about the French influence but not the Caribbean influence.

AO: It's a port city. And the port that had the most trade with New Orleans was Havana. They were within spitting distance of each other. And a lot of the inhabitants of New Orleans had Hispanic surnames. Cargo Park was filled with people from Central and South American and the Caribbean.

So the birth of jazz was irrevocably intertwined with the birth of Latin music, and you really have to call both places Africa. The stuff that I love about that piece is that I directly take some of what Scott Joplin did, specifically the stride aspect, the brass band aspect, that kind of jagged rhythm of the syncopated right hand, and I compare those to the guitar-type rhythms that take place in Latin music because there were no pianos in the mountains of Cuba. Somehow, I sensed that these two worlds are so interconnected, which is one of the tragedies of having this incredible embargo against my people. It's a tragedy.

JC: I think that's why I was so tickled with this piece, because you make that rhythmic connection obvious. It's beautifully illustrated and I really hadn't put that together before I heard this. I guess I know it in my bones, but I was hearing all these different rhythms playing all together. It was fantastic.

AO: One of Louis Armstrong's earliest big hits was "The Peanut Vendor." And Dizzy Gillespie was the father of Cubop. And there was Duke Ellington. Let's face it, all the really great and visionary creators of what we call jazz—which is a word that I can't tolerate—are actually people who understood that the journey of this music doesn't originate in St. Louis or Kansas City or New Orleans. The journey originates in West Africa, and then it comes up through all of the Americas, the Caribbean, Central America, Mexico even, and then it lands in the United States and becomes what it becomes here.

But even as it's becoming what it's becoming here, it's becoming other things throughout the rest of the world. Calling jazz "American's classical music" is like calling classical music "Austrian music." It's just too small. That's the message of "On the Corner of Malecón and Bourbon." It's about fluidity. It's about understanding that the rhythms that we call ragtime were rhythms that were taking place at the same time in Havana. And the other thing I love about "On the Corner of Malecón and Bourbon" is that I get to pay tribute to my heroes starting backwards, because I'm a little bit . . . What do they call it when you do things backwards?

JC: *Ginger Rogers?*

AO: [Laughs] Dyslexia! I'm a little bit dyslexic, but I don't do it on a micro-scale. I do it on a macro-scale. The whole structure of "Malecón and Bourbon" is the history lesson from Cecil Taylor backwards to Scott Joplin, and along the way we visit Hamiet Bluiett. We visit Charles Mingus. We visit Charlie Parker, and we visit Louis Armstrong. And when we finally get to the beginnings of what we call jazz, which is this kind of raggedy thing that I made up to mimic ragtime, there's a moment where the pianist just goes, "Oh, that's interesting. It sounds just like a montuno." And before you know it, they're off on this crazy swinging Latin rhythm thing. I think it's about fluidity.

JC: *These things make me tear up.*

AO: The things that make us cry are so important because they reflect something really, really strong. They remind us of how brief this beautiful experience is. And how giving over to it with abandon is the most important thing that we can do because this is such a gift. This is such a gift, and we don't know what happens after. Well, some of us think we do, or some of us know we do, some of us know we don't. Whatever you know is nonsense because this moment *is the moment.* And so the natural response is to tear up, and if you're in touch with the reality that this is fleeting, there's a sense of loss and a sense of gain from recognizing that moment. If you realize that, it will also affect the way you respond to others. Because if you realize how little we have, how short it is, then you're going to want to give yourself away.

JC: *Gracias, mi amigo. I loved every bit of this.*

AO: What a pleasure. What a privilege.

Paula
Poundstone
(b. 1959)

Standup comedian and author.

Interviewed in 2018

The best comedians and jazz musicians have great timing and an ability to capitalize on the unexpected in brilliant ways. The comedian Paula Poundstone improvises a major part of her live shows by interacting with her audience the way jazz musicians play off members of their band. As any fan of the NPR show *Wait Wait...Don't Tell Me!* a weekly current events quiz, can attest, Paula, a frequent panelist, can endlessly improvise hilariously on a level few comedians can match.

My time with Paula was one of the rare *Jazz Inspired* conversations that wasn't taped in person. I feel that a better connection is usually made face to face, but Paula jumped right in with such tremendous focus that I felt as if we were in the same room, even though Paula was at NPR West in Culver City and I was at NPR's studios in Manhattan. I told her that I'd seen her onstage a number of times and saw her process as very similar to that of a jazz musician. She immediately connected with that thought, and off we went.

Three months after our chat, I went to see Paula's live show, hoping to finally meet her in person. I stood outside her dressing room talking to a friend when the door opened and a woman peered out and said, "Is one of you Judy Carmichael? Paula recognized your voice. Come on in and say hello."

I talked with Paula shortly after the release of her book *The Totally Unscientific Study of the Search for Human Happiness.*

JC: I've always thought that comedians perform in a way that is similar to the way jazz musicians work in terms of timing and improvising, even if they have a set program. You improvise a good portion of your live shows with audience interaction. Other stand-up comedians, who have a set monologue, often have some interaction with the audience too, whether they want it or not. But you, in particular, seem like a jazz musician on stage because so much of your show is obviously a spontaneous back-and-forth with your audience that can take you in a number of unexpected directions. I'm curious about your process and how that approach developed.

PP: Well, firstly, thank you. That's good company, being with you jazz musicians. When I first started in Boston, around May of 1979, I was doing open mic nights, which is sort of the college for stand-up comics. The comedy scene was really developing at that time and there were still probably many more comics than there were slots to go on, so the open mic night was red hot. The premise of an open mic night being that anybody who wanted to go up for five minutes could. We'd have a raucous crowd on Wednesday nights at the Ding Ho in Inman Square in Cambridge. The audience would sort of peak at nine or ten at night, and it dwindled exponentially with every act that went on, so people were very touchy about their five minutes. I had a tendency to lose track of what I was doing, and I could hear the knives sharpening in the back. I would often stay on stage just to protect myself from the angry comics.

So when I started out, I tried hard to write out a five-minute set and I'd practice it in my rooming house room where I lived, and I'd time it. Then I'd go on stage and I was scared, so I'd get nervous and sort of forget what it was I meant to say, regardless of how much I'd memorized it the week before. I bussed tables for a living back then, and if you looked closely, you could often see my lips moving while I was bussing tables because I was memorizing my act. But I'd go on and forget what I was gonna do or I'd get distracted by something that I saw on the way up or something that the last comic said, and I'd respond to that. Next thing you know, I wouldn't know where I was in the five minutes.

And so my original take was that this was very unprofessional, that saying things that I didn't plan on saying was bad. I don't know at what point it occurred to me that a lot of times the funniest thing I said the whole night was stuff I hadn't planned to say. And when I finally realized that, I cut myself loose. I went towards the fun stuff.

I've been doing this job for thirty-nine years. I do have an act. Somewhere in my head, thirty-nine years of material is rattling around, but my favorite part of the night is just talking to the audience. I do the time-honored, "Where are you from? What do you do for a living?" and in this way, little biographies of audience members emerge, and I kind of use that from which to set my sails. Seems to be working so far.

JC: I'm thinking about jazz musicians I know, myself included, who are almost incapable of doing the same thing the same way, and that's what I'm getting from you, that that was really hard for you.

PP: It was. And it gives me misery. In television, when you do those late-night shows—in the old days, anyway—they used to want to know what you were gonna say so I'd write out exactly what I was gonna say and I'd try like hell to stick to it. And in almost all of those sets, I cringe when I see them. Part of it was I'd get so nervous about having to say the same thing that I'd written. It was an effort to remember it, but also, it's just not me. And finally, on Craig Ferguson, when he was doing his really terrific *Late Late Show*, they used to make me write out what I was gonna say so they could give it to the censors. Then they'd go, "Say whatever you want." Once I was unbridled, it was much better.

And here's a little-known fact about me: I'm a drum student. And a very bad one. For the last couple of years, I've taken drums. I started because my son—who played for ten years—had this terrific teacher. He didn't continue his lessons because he sadly succumbed to, through no fault of his own, electronics addiction, which is a real thing and a very serious problem. He got to where he just wouldn't do anything anymore, even get out of bed. So I said to the drum teacher, "Look, come anyway because you can talk him into taking the lesson." That worked a couple of times, but then it became clear that it wasn't gonna work anymore so I told the teacher that I'd take lessons because we had six o'clock on Wednesday nights, and I wanted to keep that spot open for him for when he recovered. Sadly, he never did, and that was probably three years ago. I still take drum lessons at six o'clock on Wednesday nights. I'm still waiting for my son to come take over. I'm so bad, it's embarrassing.

JC: Do you have a full drum kit?

PP: Yeah. Ask my neighbors. You'd think that my neighbors would pitch in and pay for my drum lessons just to make their life better.

JC: Yeah, the better you get the less they suffer.

PP: Exactly.

JC: They haven't offered?

PP: No. But summer's coming. It will be worse when the windows are open. Part of the reason I've continued is that I love the idea of being able to sit down and do something even though I won't be a real drummer. Also, I believe it helps the brain. I volunteer in a nursing home a couple of mornings a week, and the connection between music and the brain is an astonishing thing. With some people I lean down to their wheelchair and I say to them, "Do you have children?" And they stare at me for a long time, and then they go, "I'm not sure." Then I'll put on some Pete Seeger CD, and by golly, those lips are moving.

JC: My fantasy is that you'll play drums next time you do The Tonight Show. *In the old days, they'd have Buddy Rich tap dance or somebody else bring out some unexpected talent. You can sashay over to the band and sit down and play along.*

Anyway, regarding the connection between comedy and jazz, I think of you as a jazz comedian and not just because you're a jazz fan but because I see similarities between your process and the process of jazz musicians.

PP: I see that from my drum lessons. In one of the books, they had me do something called, is it "Call and Answer?"

JC: "Call and Response."

PP: Yes. And what's weird about it is that I can play one bar of something and then the next bar makes sense, but I don't know why. Even if I play it just once, I know what the next thing will be. In a way, stand-up is similar to that. There are times where it's the timing with which you said something that makes it work. It almost doesn't matter what you said if the timing is right.

JC: Exactly. That's very much like jazz.

PP: If you just get in there and throw something in at that right moment, it works. I remember one time, many years ago, when I was on *Wait, Wait... Don't Tell Me!* and I think the guest was like the head of the FBI or something. He was on the section of the show called "Not My Job," and my boss, Peter Sagal, was asking him a question. The man was explaining something, how he worked with George Bush Jr. He was trying to say something but couldn't get it out correctly. He said, "Well, George Bush didn't think . . ." and he paused the wrong amount of time. I swear this all happened in the blink of an eye. Peter and I looked at each other, and we were like Harry Potter in *The Goblet of Fire* when Harry and Cedric Diggory see the silver cup at the same time and start to run for it.

So the guest goes, "George Bush didn't think," and I pretty much, not literally but figuratively, shoved Peter Sagal out of the way to take the joke myself. We both had the same thought at the exact same time. And the thing is, if you didn't say it quickly enough to fill that quarter note, so to speak, you'd miss it. It wouldn't work.

JC: *Exactly what we do with jazz.*

PP: And so, what I learned about myself from that, is that I don't care who gets hurt.

JC: *[Laughs] I've heard you a lot on the radio, but I've seen you in person as well and watched how you go in one direction, then an audience member says something, and you grab that and take everything in another direction. That's exactly what jazz musicians do. If you're playing solo, it's one thing—which is what you're doing—but if we have a group, we might be headed in one direction with our improvisation and then somebody else joins in with an idea and you grab that and go off someplace great or you play yourself into a corner. Then it's all about how you get out of that harmonic corner.*

PP: I've certainly done that. But I don't consider myself a solo performer exactly. I depend on the things that the audience brings to it. My manager tells people all the time, "Well, Paula knows who to talk to in the crowd." That is such a load of crap. I have absolutely no idea who I'll zero in on. I sometimes talk to people because they're in my sight lines. Sometimes an audience member says something, then adds in a word or two as they were laughing or whatever, and that will attract my attention, so I'll focus on them. Or sometimes somebody's got on a hat or they're sitting funny or whatever.

Once I've begun to talk to somebody, that little biography starts to develop. In some ways, I feel like a conductor, where when I return back to that person, I'm sort of bringing up the strings again, and then you go over to the horns. But the truth is, it can be anybody. It doesn't matter. You get somebody talking for a couple of seconds, a few minutes, and they're fascinating.

JC: *One of the most appealing things for me about watching you in action is you are genuinely curious and interested in these people. I think that would be a hard thing to fake.*

PP: There's one thing, though, where I do glaze over a little bit. When I say to somebody, "What do you do for living?" and they go, "I'm a software developer." I'm like, "Oh, my God!"

JC: Where do I go from here?

PP: Exactly! And then I quickly say, "What do you do in your free time?" Or I'll ask them, "What's the software supposed to do?" And it's always like, "Well, it's the software that goes into developing the software for the software . . ." You really gotta move away from that.

JC: I have to bring up Vince Giordano because I was delighted to learn that you love the music in the TV series Boardwalk Empire *and that you have the soundtrack from it.*

PP: I used to avoid TV. I'd stopped watching any prime-time television, really, since Radar left *M*A*S*H*.

JC: That's a long time, Paula.

PP: It's a very long time! I've never seen *Seinfeld*. I've never seen any of those shows everybody talks about because I have OCD, and if I start watching, I can't stop. When I'm in a hotel room, though, I watch the news or look for an old movie or an old sitcom. I was in a hotel one night, and I stumbled across *Boardwalk Empire* mid-season. First of all, it's so beautiful, even though it's very violent. But at the same time, it's a period piece, it's about the Irish mob during Prohibition, and it's so well done that you cannot take your eyes off of it. I decided to avoid my obsessiveness by buying it on DVD and only watching it while I worked out. That worked really well for a while. I'd be in a hotel and bring my little DVD player down to the fitness room and walk on this silly steppy-thingy with the headphones on. Then, because it's that kind of serialized show where they leave you hanging, I'd get hooked.

So I'd lower the bar. First it was only while working out. Then it was only while eating Butterfingers. Then it was only while driving. The next thing I knew, I just watched it over and over. But part of the life's blood of this really brilliantly done show is the music. And thanks to you, I now know it's Vince Giordano and the Nighthawks.

JC: Tell me about your book, The Totally Unscientific Study of the Search for Human Happiness. *You experiment with everything from Taekwondo to swing dancing to discover what can not only make a person happy but keep them that way.*

PP: My book is a series of experiments, doing things that I or other people thought would make me happy, and every chapter is written as an experiment, with the hypothesis, the variables, the conditions and field notes, etcetera. But the real question for me wasn't whether I'd enjoy doing something. The real question was what I could do that would leave me with a boost, so that when I was done doing it, when I returned to my regular life, I still felt good. To have an umbrella, so to speak, for the inevitable on and off rains of one's daily life. There's an analysis section of each chapter. I check back in and see if whatever it is I'm experimenting with is rubbing off on my regular life, of raising a house full of kids and animals and being a stand-up comic, and just being stuck being me twenty-four hours a day.

JC: One of your pursuits to happiness was swing dancing.

PP: I was out one day on the Third Street Promenade in Santa Monica, one of those areas of town that has street musicians and that sort of thing. I noticed this group swing dancing to recorded music. I watched for a few minutes, and it looked like so much fun. It's this wonderful upbeat music, for one thing, and the people were really good at it. It wasn't a dance troupe. It was just regular people who knew there was a dance thing there at that time, and they came and joined in. I asked one woman how she learned to do it, and she said, "Well, there's a woman named Rusty Frank who teaches swing dancing all over Los Angeles. She has a night in Marina Del Ray, a couple of nights a week where she turns an Elks' Lodge into Rusty's Rhythm Club, and she trains people to swing dance and then they have these social dances."

So I decided I'd put that on my list of things that might make me happy. Plus, the music is upbeat, and that tends to lend to one's happiness. There's the physical exercise of the dancing, and there's social life. All these people with big smiles on their faces doing this great thing. So I sign up for these group lessons. Unfortunately, I was so bad that I was slowing the group down. I had to switch to private lessons, so there goes the social life. And then I was still so bad that my teacher couldn't use the upbeat music. I swing dance to the blues. I do the Charleston to "Fire and Rain."

JC: Hilarious!

PP: Well, eventually I'd go to Rusty's house for lessons. I'd take as many lessons as I could in order to write this chapter. And somewhere along the way, I noticed some tap shoes in her studio. So she started teaching me, and now there's two kinds of dance that I don't do well.

Part of the joy of it is the music. Now she comes to my house. She has it all on her iPhone, and she brings a little portable speaker. She pushes that thing on and away we go, and it's turned me on to all sorts of great music, actually. Rusty says all the swing dance music is either about food or love.

JC: Well, what's not to like?

PP: Exactly. We always warm up to this song, "Could'ja," sung by a wonderful guy named Todd Murray. So one day we're at my house in what I refer to as "the ballroom" although I have a teeny house. We're in front of my coffin-bookshelf where Rusty puts her music, and we're on the little space of wood floor, dancing. She walks over to her music setup, pushes a couple of buttons, and says, "Isn't this odd? I can't get the Todd Murray song to play the right way." And she keeps pushing it, and it's coming on with just the instrumental, not the vocals. Anyway, she puts it on and we start dancing to just the instrumental. And then the doorbell rings. She goes over and answers my front door, and there stood Todd Murray, in a tuxedo! There stood Todd Murray, and now he's singing with the instrumental of "Could'ja." He came in and serenaded me.

JC: Fantastic! Was this a birthday present?

PP: No. Rusty is just one of those people. She was Facebook before Facebook was invented. She knows everybody, and she delights in hooking people up.

JC: *That's such a beautiful story. And I have to quote you to you. I love your saying "Happiness is like a rogue piece of eggshell." Talk about your "get wired" experiment, where you tried social media.*

PP: The words lonely and tired were in that chapter more than in any other, regardless of how challenging my life was during writing the different parts of the book. And as it turns out, what helps make us happy is a lot of the stuff that our parents told us; go outside, get some exercise, call a friend. Those things work. The first chapter of the book is the "Get Fit" chapter. I took Taekwondo and self-defense with this guy, and I have no passion for Taekwondo or self-defense. I did it because it was the closest workout place to my house.

I remember at one point, as I was taking notes, I'd go to a class with this guy and then I'd come home and write more notes so that I could write up the experiment properly. I remember one time thinking that the class was a little pricey, and I thought, I don't wanna tell people you have to spend a lot of money to be happy because I don't think that's true. And I said to myself, *O.K., mostly what I do with the guy is a lot is calisthenics.* So I thought, *What's to stop me from doing that at home?* So the next day I go to the guy again, and he says, "Do 500 rope jumps," and I did 500 rope jumps, and he says, "Do thirty push-ups," and I did thirty push-ups, and he says, "Do 100 sit-ups," and I did 100 sit-ups, and then I rolled over ready to either cry or throw up. Finally, he said, "Get up." And I thought, *that's why I go to this guy.*

JC: *Well then, there you have it. For happiness, it's exercise, get enough sleep, get outside, call a friend. Your parents were right.*

PP: Yeah, and I hate to ever say that my parents were right about anything.

JC: *But were they right?*

PP: They were right about that. I have to say, that with my kids, I'm right about a lot more things than my parents were. It's not a race, but I'm winning.

JC: Have you pointed that out to them?

PP: I try not to, because they're in that young adult phase where you'll lose them if you point it out too much.

JC: They'll realize it eventually. When they're on NPR, doing their interview someday, they'll say, "You know, I've realized that my mom got it right more often than my grandparents did."

PP: Yeah. That's my hope. And maybe that's not a *noble* hope, but . . .

JC: It's an honest hope.

PP: It's after world peace, alright?

Paul
Prudhomme

(1940–2015)

Celebrity chef and author of eleven cookbooks who popularized
Creole and Cajun cuisines through his restaurants,
culinary products, and television appearances.

Interviewed in 2007

The Louisiana chef/entrepreneur/restaurateur Paul Prudhomme was one
of my most inspiring guests. His attitude, his creativity, and his commitment
to others were a wonder to behold. It is especially touching for me to think
back on this conversation since Paul Prudhomme's famous New Orleans
restaurant, K-Paul's Louisiana Kitchen, closed permanently in July 2020
due to the pandemic.

Chef Paul grew up the youngest of thirteen on a farm near
Opelousas, Louisiana. The meals his mother cooked for this brood were
made from what the family grew on their farm or caught from the nearby
swamp. Prudhomme believed that his Louisiana childhood formed his
approach to cooking, and he maintained that music and food capture the
imagination and bring joy to one's life like nothing else.

I was fascinated by Prudhomme's tremendous success, especially
considering his humble beginnings. Jamie Roche, a Louisiana native who is
my publicist and occasional co-producer, managed to arrange an interview
with this spectacularly busy man, which took place about two years after
Katrina, the hurricane that wrought such devastating damage in and around
New Orleans.

Chef Paul was interviewed frequently during his long career, and I could tell that he wasn't particularly excited about yet another conversation about Cajun cooking. Once we got into the deeper meaning of music and food though, he brightened considerably and grew progressively more enthusiastic. We met at his 120,000-square-foot plant outside New Orleans, where we were surrounded by seductive aromas from his test kitchens. During our conversation, I was offered delicious samples of every imaginable goodie and was sent home with a variety of his famous "Magic Seasonings."

JC: It was fantastic walking into this incredible space and immediately being greeted by all these wonderful smells. It's just overwhelming. My publicist is with me, along with Carter, her two-year old, who looked up from his stroller and started sniffing the air the minute we walked through the door.

To me, there's a connection between aromas and music in how they both can immediately bring you emotionally to a memory or event. Those two things will take a person to a place quicker than a visual image, quicker than a painting, quicker than any other kind of creative endeavor.

PP: I think you've gotta include a third one. Think about when you put something in your mouth and consider the smells and the emotion of what's happening. Most people go through that but never recognize and focus on the emotion of it. They miss something wonderful.

People eat something and say, "Oh, that was good," but they often miss so much. If you really focus on what your body can tell you is happening in your mouth, especially when it's fresh, when it's good, it's fantastic! A fresh piece of fish that's only one day old and it's got seasoning on it and it's cooked well, it's just amazing, the flavors and the emotion that you feel from it. People never think about eating. I mean, we just do it so often we take it for granted.

People say, "Man, that was good!" But it's sort of a passing thing. Somebody says that to me at the restaurant, and I'll think they really understand. But then I'll start questioning them. I'll say, "Did you get that flavor?" I've sort of stopped doing that because there were so many people who were just so excited about being at the restaurant and getting food that was new to them and having that be the focus, that I gave up. They didn't understand if I got into the depth of the emotion of it because very few people think of food as emotional.

JC: I wonder how we can help more people appreciate that. It's a joke among traveling musicians that food is important to us because we travel so much and are deprived of good food. But I think it's a focus because we're all creative and sensitive and appreciate great cuisine.

It can be comical to get a group of, in my case, jazz musicians, talking about food because we go on and on in detail and get very emotional about it. I've had people listen to these conversations and say it's like we're talking about sex. I've had exchanges like, "Do you remember that place in Switzerland that we played with that incredible strudel?" And I won't mention the piano or the audience. But a lot of people don't take the time to taste, to appreciate anything. They're missing out on a huge sensual, emotional experience.

PP: I agree. I've heard musicians do just what you're saying, and as a matter of fact, a lot of people here in Louisiana do that too. One of the things we'll say frequently—I've been saying it all my life—is that it's better than sex because you can do it more often.

JC: [Laughs] I'm going to use that! I like that a lot. And I think you do have a culture of food appreciation here. Any time I play in Louisiana, it's mostly about the food. When I arrive for a concert, the first thing I hear, before I'm told where I'm staying, when the sound check is, before I get the rehearsal time, is, "We have breakfast planned at a tiny place on the river, then lunch at this old Cajun joint, and dinner will be at this amazing crawfish shack." At first, I thought it was just this one presenter who hired me in Lafayette, but then it was that way in every town I played. And I can tell you, it's not that way in the rest of the world. Unless you're in France, of course.

PP: You're right. It's our culture. We just absolutely love to excite people with food, and whether we cook or not, we want to take you to our favorite restaurant. Some of the best restaurants in the city, especially before Katrina, were hidden in small patches of a neighborhood, and I always felt that they didn't get enough tourism. But now I think that's good because tourism would destroy them. They'd have to make the place bigger. They've got one or two people cooking in the back. It's usually women and they own the restaurant, so it couldn't get bigger.

One of the greatest restaurants in this city is Dooky Chase. And Dooky Chase is in a Black neighborhood. It's a Black restaurant, and it's run by Leah Chase, who is married to Dooky Chase, who runs a bar. She runs the restaurant, and he runs the bar, but in the same building. And her restaurant is just incredible. It's one of those places where the gumbo is a cherished thing. Not only cherished by the customers but by everyone inside the building. The cooks feel that this is a special gumbo, a "zeb" gumbo. Zeb means herb. They use all kinds of greens, and they use the herbs in their culture. They use the greens as an herb. It's wonderful to be a part of that culture.

JC: How do you manage your huge outreach with your herb business, the cooking, the cookbooks, the television, all the things that you do to try to convey this message to people to take the time and savor these things? It's got to be a challenge, especially in America. We know you have this appreciation in Louisiana, where everybody's excited about a great dish. But how do you do it in Wichita?

PP: Well, it's simple. You can't do it in Wichita. But you can help get it to another level in Wichita. And that's the reason that you see this huge building that you're sitting in that's devoted to herbs and spices, because it's one of the best things I can do. I know I can't feed everybody in America, but I know that I can produce herbs and spices that will make their food better. And it won't be Louisiana food, it won't be New Orleans food, and it won't be Lafayette food, but it will make their food better, in Wichita or wherever. I know it will, and I've heard it a million times, a billion times, from customers over the last thirty years.

It's such a joy to be able to run a company where our whole life is devoted to making people happy and to giving them joy within their body. I believe that herbs and spices are one of the essentials that the body needs. It's one of the best things that you can put in your body, and for centuries herbs and spices were the medicine of every culture. I feel very good about what we do. I mean, it's a business, and you've got to run it as a business, but every once in a while, you get this little moment that says, "Look what I'm doing, man!"

I've always wanted to feed everybody, and now we're putting out enough seasoning that we're getting close to a lot of people. Each year we reach more, so it's exciting. When we can get to any kind of restaurant, no matter what the size, if we can get great seasoning in there and give them an idea of how to use it, it's not going to magically be what we do here, but it's going to be better. And it's going to make the customer feel better. And you're putting great herbs and spices in that body.

JC: I feel the same way about music, that if you reach people with it you can enhance their lives. The challenge is getting them to sit down and listen to it and let it touch them. Did you listen to a lot of music growing up?

PP: I listened to French music a lot. I grew up without gas or electricity, and we had a battery radio. There was this huge—and I mean gigantic—battery. We couldn't afford to buy it, but every now and then—like every three years—we'd have it. Each member of the family got to use it in turn. It got better over the years since I was the last of thirteen, so as my brothers and sisters got married or left the house, I got more time with the radio.

I used to have the radio half an hour a week. That was my time, and I'd listen to *The Lone Ranger*. And then it got to where I could listen to music. We had three stations that we could reach, and that was it. Just three stations! One was KSLO in Opelousas. I'll never forget KSLO.

They did everything. They had French music on, but they also had local music that was considered rock 'n' roll. And one of our MC's was Rod Bernard. He and I grew up together. He was an MC on the radio, then became a musician. Now he's in television, but he was one of the rock stars of our city. He played great stuff.

JC: When you mention rock, I think about a figure that was a great transition figure between jazz and rock, at least to me: Louis Jordan. I know you're a fan. I'm a huge Louis Jordan fan too.

PP: His music sort of makes you float. And I don't think of it as floating off my chair; I think of it as floating out of my head. I let it drift out there, and it just feels so wonderful. It feels so good inside.

JC: There's music everywhere here, and now it's almost time for Jazz Fest, where everybody descends upon New Orleans.

PP: We're going to have an incredible number of musicians in the next twelve or fourteen days in the city, and that's great. All my life, music has been a part of it. Of course, food is first, but music has been a part of it. And when we started talking, it reminded me of how special the area is and how much musical diversity we have, like our food diversity. We have a band in front of the restaurant every night now. We swap from a great jazz band to a band from my area, a French band, a Cajun band.

When I came back from running away from Katrina, I went into the French Quarter and couldn't open the restaurant, even though it hadn't been damaged. I went to my house, which is on the same street but twenty blocks away, and it hadn't been damaged either.

Every time I'd go to the restaurant, though, I wouldn't hear the same sounds from the French Quarter that I did before the storm. In the French Quarter, you go down the street and you're gonna hear some stuff. Somebody doing something you recognize. So we decided when we re-opened the restaurant to put a band out front for two or three weeks. It was such a hit with our customers that literally every time we would not put the band out front, people would start calling in before they'd make the reservation to ask if there was a band.

It's just so amazing, the emotion of the city. They love their food, and they love their music. If they can come to a celebration where there's both, they're gonna do it. Whether it's an anniversary, or a before-wedding dinner, a kid's graduation, all these things, the music and food go together in New Orleans. And I don't know of a restaurant in the city that has music that's live that's silly enough to pay for it.

JC: You're saying that to a working musician! You can't say that!

PP: No, it's like, we didn't think of it as being essential, but we do now. I think that it's incredibly essential to us to continue satisfying the locals. Not only the food does, but the music does, too. And you know, if it's a birthday or an anniversary or something, we'll send a band in. They'll do a special song for them. And I think that it's really helped our business, and probably because of it we get closer to break-even than other restaurants. So the musicians have made us money instead of taking it away.

JC: I love that. And you saying the word "essential" here reminds me that many years ago, when I was just starting as a professional jazz musician, I had a physical therapist I was seeing say, "It must be hard to be in a business that isn't essential, that people don't need." She knew people needed PT but not music.

It never occurred to me that music wasn't essential, that people didn't need it, because I think it is essential. It's part of my life every day. I know for a fact that people are happier and lead a richer life if music is a part of their existence, if it's genuinely a part of their life.

I ask people if they're music lovers and if they say, "Oh, I like all music," I know those are the people who aren't real music lovers. Music is kind of this vague background noise to them. People who genuinely care about music say, "Oh, yeah, I'm a big fan of Stan Getz," or "I'm crazy about Cajun music." It's the equivalent of you knowing that great food, nourishing food, is essential, as opposed to being satisfied grabbing a fast-food burger. It's knowing that fresh, nutritious food does change your life. So I love that word, "essential," and I love that you are now aware that you need music at your restaurant.

PP: A huge percentage of my Saturday mornings is my time for music. The company gave me a birthday present of a little speaker that you put an iPod in, and it gets really loud. It's got Cajun music on it, it's got Doug Kershaw, it's got Johnny Cash, it's got all kinds of stuff. I put that on Saturday mornings, and I turn it literally all the way up. I can hear it throughout the yard, throughout the house. I don't think about it, I just do it every morning. I get up, get coffee, put it on, and let the music rip.

JC: So that's your time to sort of replenish yourself too.

PP: It feels good. I'm listening to our local music, which I love so much, and it's like when it's real loud, I understand some of the loud stuff that I didn't before, because it starts to get inside of me if it's really loud, you know. The neighbors also hear it. The neighbors are listening to Cajun music with me, man. My house isn't isolated, but it's far enough from my neighbors that I can really crank up my music. It's a wonderful Saturday morning ritual. It started after the storm, and I'm still doing it.

JC: Back to food: Can you tell me one great cooking tip?

PP: I'll give you one really simple example: fresh fish is better than frozen. There's a better smell to it, and there's a huge difference in the taste. You put seasoning on it, it makes it even better. What most people do, or a lot of people do, is cook food too long. And when you cook it too long, you take the moisture out. I feel like the reason our restaurant is popular, the reason it's still going for almost thirty years, is because we've learned that. We teach the people who work with us that when you're cooking, you don't take away the moisture that's naturally in whatever you're cooking. And I don't put oil in the pan, I put oil on the fish. And then once you put the oil on the fish, you add the seasonings and that makes the seasoning stick well, but also, that's enough oil because one of the things that happens when you put a lot of oil in the pan, is that where there's no steak or fish or vegetables, or whatever you're cooking, that oil is super-heating because where it is on a piece of vegetable or a piece of flesh, where it is, it's going to be cooler. So, you're super-heating it in between those things and you're actually giving the oil a taste that's going to affect the dish.

JC: That's great information! I'm going to cook entirely differently now. And when I put a band together, it's all about the musicians. Those are my ingredients, just like cooking with great ingredients.

PP: It's essential. Just like the way we buy fish. The first thing we do with every piece of fish and every ingredient that comes into the restaurant is set it down in the kitchen and someone from my staff opens it up, looks at it, smells it, and weighs it to make sure that the weight is right but also to make sure that the freshness is right. If it's not right, we'll just say, "We don't want it." At times we've turned back fifteen or twenty percent of everything that comes through the back door.

JC: I have to ask you, thinking about growing up with a family of thirteen kids—that seems like running a restaurant! There must have been skills you learned. Was your mom really into cooking, or was it just, I've got to get these kids fed?

PP: Well, it's the reason why I'm here, because of Mom and the culture. Mom was a great cook. And she really believed that if you do all of that food and if you do great-tasting food, it would be good for the kids. They grow up stronger and better. It was part of a philosophy.

We didn't have gas or electricity. So when she wanted fish, she'd say, "Go get me some fish." We'd go out to the swamp, which was two blocks away, and throw a line in the water, and within a half hour, forty-five minutes, we'd have enough fish to feed everyone. We also had chickens in the yard.

Everyone in the neighborhood would butcher animals, beef and pork, and they'd do it once a month. Everyone would get a piece of that animal because nobody had refrigeration.

So, most months we'd get a fresh supply of meat. Everything we ate, we had to shoot or catch. We had to chase it down. The chickens, we had plenty of them in the yard, so that was simple. All the vegetables were grown. We produced everything we ate.

When I was growing up, the only thing we would buy was flour and sugar. We didn't buy cornmeal. We'd take ten hundred-pound sacks of shelled corn to the mill, and Dad would give them two sacks and the guy would take the other eight sacks and grind them up for us so we had cornflower and cornmeal. And with sugar cane, we'd take three wagon loads of it and go the sugar cane mill, and they'd take it and squeeze the juices out into this gigantic tank.

So that was the way we lived. There was no other way since we didn't have money. Then at the end of the year, after the harvest was done, with the money crop, like cotton, we paid our bills. We'd usually have $200, maybe $500 left. My Dad carried it in his pocket, and that was the money we'd have for the next year.

I believe that it was the best way to grow up and so much better than now, because you didn't have the influences from the outside, which could be good, but could also be very bad in a lot of ways. We didn't have radio, television, and all the other media. And we played within the neighborhood, and when we had time, we would go out into the swamps. That was the neighborhood. It was Black, White, it was everybody you knew, and it was a wonderful way for a human being to become an adult.

JC: It had to be a leap to come from this kind of background to do what you wound up doing.

364

PP: It took my business starting to grow and being on the *Today Show* to realize how wonderful my life has been. And you know, it's sort of like, well, that's what we do. So it ain't no big thing.

JC: You wanted to do this, you went for it, and you just kept going and didn't think about it being difficult or impossible?

PP: No, I think I failed the first four restaurants in a row, and it didn't bother me.

JC: Do you think that coming from those difficult childhood circumstances made you more resilient?

PP: I think the only way I can answer is that my life has shown me not to be afraid to die. It's a waste of time. Eventually you're gonna die. Don't be afraid of it.

JC: You've inspired me, Paul. Do I look inspired?

PP: Actually, you look hungry.

JC: I AM! And it's your fault!

Robert Redford

(b. 1936)

Actor, director, two-time Oscar winner, and the founder of the
Sundance Film Festival. In 2016 he was awarded the
Presidential Medal of Freedom.

Interviewed in 2005

Robert Redford was at the top of my wish list for *Jazz Inspired* from the
beginning. I'd heard him mention on NPR's *Fresh Air* that jazz had inspired
him throughout his life and influenced many of the programs at his
Sundance Institute, so I knew he'd be a perfect guest for my show.
Additionally, I'd grown up watching his films and admired the fact that so
many of them had a broader message beyond their obvious appeal as pure
entertainment. I inferred from this that his conversation would go deeper
than the usual celebrity chitchat and that he might welcome an opportunity
to talk about inspiration and process.

    In 1980, when Redford was in his early forties and already a major
star, he could have taken roles capitalizing on his leading man looks.
Instead, he turned to directing and won his first Academy Award for
Ordinary People, a study of the disintegration of a seemingly perfect upper-
middle-class family after the death of one son and the suicide attempt of
the other. In 1981, Redford started the Sundance Institute, which operates
in several locations in Utah, to help support independent filmmakers.
Redford used his celebrity and money to take on new challenges, develop
and grow artistically, and support and stimulate other artists.

I was determined to get him on *Jazz Inspired* but scaling the multiple levels of handlers that guard big stars can be like climbing Mount Everest. It was no different with Redford. To my delight, in 2005, after years of fruitless pursuit, his people called my people, meaning his office called me.

"Hi, Judy, this is Ray Grant. I'm calling for Bob Redford, who asked me to reach out and see if you'd like to be part of the Sundance Film Festival next year. We're having four jazz trios play concerts for the first time during the festival, and Bob would like yours to be one of them."

I took advantage of the moment and asked if I might interview "Bob" for *Jazz Inspired* while I was at Sundance. Yes, I now call him Bob. And as I suspected, because of Redford's interest in the creative process and his love of jazz, he said yes.

The Sundance Festival is held in January in Park City, Utah, and at the much smaller, Sundance Resort, an exquisitely beautiful Shangri-La of cozy rustic cabins, larger villas, a glass-walled/two-story barn-like performance space (where my group performed) with a sparkling stream gently flowing around it, a spa, a ski area, hiking trails, and a main lodge. One of my jaded, road-weary musicians, upon arriving and taking in the scene, threw his luggage to the ground, waved his arm toward the surrounding snow-covered peaks, and declared, *"I can't work like this!"*

Once we settled in, I called the office to ask where I could set up for the interview. I wanted to do a little recon before my Redford roundup the following day.

"Bob has a little cabin/office in the woods he thought would be perfect for the two of you to spend some time alone," the person who answered the phone replied.

I'm not making this up.

Robert Redford has been both famous and gorgeous for years, of course, and observing the various ways he negotiates the reaction his appearance elicits is telling. Some ridiculously beautiful people seem to have an invisible curtain around them, a protection of sorts from years of people staring at them. Others use their looks to manipulate. Redford does everything possible to ignore the fact and attempts a normal interaction. It's impressive.

We met for the first time right before our interview. He came in fresh from a day of skiing, introduced himself, and apologetically said he needed a few minutes to make a call. "Wait here, Judy," he said. "I have something for you."

He returned, handed me a postcard with a picture of Stan Getz on it, smiled, and said, "This is how we'll begin our conversation. I'll be with you in a bit." I've always thought he did this to give me a few minutes alone to collect myself, in case meeting him stunned me into silence, or to give me a starting point for the interview in case I was unprepared. Whatever his reason, it was a generous move.

When he returned, he said, "Turn off the tape recorder. Let's talk for a bit and get to know each other."

After an hour of surprisingly personal anecdotes and comparing notes on our respective Southern California childhoods, I insisted that we start the interview so I wouldn't take up too much of his time. We spoke for another two hours.

JC: *Did you grow up listening to jazz?*

RR: My mother and father were very interested in music. I wouldn't say we were dirt poor, but we were on the lower end of the register in a working-class neighborhood that was mostly Mexican. I had a paper route. My parents were very young and loved music and dancing. It was in the day of the big bands, so they were dancing to swing music.

In Santa Monica, where I grew up, there was a place called the Aragon Ballroom. My parents went there one night to dance, and it just so happened to be the end of Benny Goodman's tour that year. The story I was told was that he was getting tired of playing his regular tunes and was exploring this new concept, which eventually became "Sing, Sing, Sing." He and his band had worked it out and had decided it was sort of where Goodman wanted to go. But it was not being accepted on the tour.

They played Cleveland, Baltimore, Milwaukee, wherever. They kept trying to do this in addition to their regular menu, and it didn't fly. Goodman was getting more and more upset about it. And he got to the end of the line at the Aragon Ballroom. It was walking distance from where we were living. My parents happened to be there for this incredible moment in history that was recorded. It was the famous version of "Sing, Sing, Sing."

JC: What was your first defining experience with jazz? The moment that led you to become a fan.

RR: For me, personally, the moment came when I was about fifteen. There was an older woman that I was connected with.

JC: Ah, I like this part of the interview.

RR: Yeah, well, I would have liked it better had it been more on my terms. [Laughs]

There was this twenty-year-old woman, and I was fifteen. She was very, very hip. She loved jazz, and I was crazy about her. I think that as far as she was concerned, I was this cute mascot or something.

She talked about jazz, and I didn't know what that was. At that point in time, it was almost like this strange transitional time with the big bands that had gotten to the end of the line—Les Brown, Ray Conniff, and all those mainly dance bands. Of course, you had the Dorsey Brothers and, on the sides of it, Dixieland and ragtime. They were reappearing on the scene but not very forcefully. You had Ben Pollack. You had the Firehouse Five Plus Two.

Then suddenly she says, "I want to introduce you to something." And of course, it was jazz. We went to this little place in L.A. across from the old Ambassador Hotel. We went in there, and it was really weird. It was small, like a bunker. And it had a lawn across the front. It was a tiny, tiny place. The lights were blue. Everything was dark. People were wearing dark glasses. There was a lot of smoke. It was teeny, teeny. And there was Gerry Mulligan, Chet Baker, Hampton Hawes on piano, Red Mitchell on bass. It meant nothing to me. Absolutely nothing.

But then I got so hooked on jazz, I went on a rialto for music. I went to Howard Rumsey's Lighthouse, which was a shack on the sand right near Long Beach. Then there was Sardi's, where Sarah Vaughan got really cooking. And suddenly something else was happening. I was told it was happening in San Francisco. So I said to my friends—we were just in high school—"We've got to get up to San Francisco." So we went up to San Francisco on a very illegal trip in a stolen car. [Laughs]

We got up there to look for jazz. I didn't know San Francisco. We were young. We were kind of living like outlaws at that moment.

We stumbled into a place that I thought was a jazz club because of the way people looked. And it was small. It turned out to be a Beat poetry reading, which I also knew nothing about. It was concurrent with jazz. Michael McClure, Kenneth Rexroth read. Kerouac was in the crowd there and looked kind of like a bouncer. There was Gary Snyder. And it was the same thing. It had the same impact to me. What is *this*? This is new. This is really exciting stuff! It's out there.

Putting those two events together—they were almost simultaneous—had such an impact on me. I think I carried that throughout my life. I just got completely interested in jazz and followed jazz groups and went to various places to hear jazz. I'd go anywhere to hear jazz, especially when I went to New York to become an actor.

It started when I was pursuing being an artist in France. I went to France around 1957. You had Eartha Kitt there, you had the Modern Jazz Quartet there, you had artists who couldn't do well in America who were finding a home there. You had some very interesting jazz because Paris was totally taken with Dexter Gordon and people like that. So I just kind of kept following it. I suddenly started seeing it from the perspective of Europeans who had enormous interest in jazz. And then I came back to America, to all that was happening there.

JC: You were in France at a very interesting time for jazz. And when you came back to America and to New York it was also a fascinating time for jazz.

RR: Oh, yes! That was 1958. I got into what was going on there and became a Gerry Mulligan fan and a Chet Baker fan, and I remained one for the rest of my life.

JC: What's special about them to you in particular?

RR: I think I've gotten to this place in my life where I can look back on something and be able to define it, which I don't think I could have at the time because I was too busy living it. I didn't even think about defining what was special about it when I was younger, but now I can look back and it's a little easier to define.

I think it had to do with taking chances. I think it had to do with always being interested in something that was on the edge, that was going to go somewhere new, and my being interested in change. I saw change as positive. As a young actor I was very drawn to improvisation. I think that came out of me being impressed by jazz. These artists were looking for some new way to go. There were new voices about to emerge.

I think art is always going to have new voices. Now that I look back on it, I realize that jazz has always been a vehicle that can float with change. It's always going to be doing new things and have this improvisational element to it.

I remember being in Washington, D.C., and going to a place called the Senate Lounge and hearing Charlie Byrd when he was just returning from Brazil. He had this whole new bossa nova thing. It was jazz and bossa nova combined, and suddenly, that whole style took off.

Jazz has always moved around. It's always exciting. I can equate it to the art I've been involved in because I'm constantly trying new things and combinations and using different art forms to inspire each other. So jazz has played a huge role in my creative life. And poetry, and particularly new forms of poetry, have played a huge role as well. That's why it's become a main part of Sundance. I'm sure it's affected my work both as a filmmaker and an actor. You hear music in your work. You hear rhythms.

JC: Do you listen to music when you're working on a role?

RR: I don't listen to music to inspire a performance in a specific way, I just listen to music. While I'm thinking about a part, I don't study too much because that can lead you to get locked up in ways of doing things. You want to be loose. You want to be free. You also want to allow for what the other person is going to do. If they're going to be there with you and dance with you, then you have to allow for what they're going to do. You have to be loose, just the way jazz is loose.

JC: That's exactly what jazz musicians do. I can't play a tune too many times when I'm recording. When I do a session, I really like to do a first or second take, because if we keep doing it, we all get locked in. And we almost stop listening to each other as much as we did when we played the song through the first time.

RR: Well, you're the real thing. I'm not a jazz artist, but I'm a person who supports and respects it. And I've probably been so impacted by it that I've used it in my own work and life. But you're the real deal. I'd be curious why, aside from what your gut is feeling good about while you're playing, what else you're thinking about while performing. For me it's like pushing the edge.

I'm very excited that we're developing these programs with jazz at Sundance. It's a chance for me finally to go back to my origins and do something about it for others. Someone said that jazz is really America's classical music, which is a wonderful idea, because it did start here.

JC: I think jazz could only have started here, in America, where we have these different nationalities influencing each other. You and I grew up in areas of Los Angeles where we were the minority. That's made me think about these things. America's various cultures influence, reinvent, and reinvigorate each other, which is what happens with jazz all the time.

I see the same process here at Sundance. You bring various great thinkers from different disciplines together to talk about their ideas, which at first glance might seem unrelated but are connected and mutually inspiring. You might have an astronomer and a tap dancer, but somehow if you put them together something interesting is going to happen.

RR: I love contradictory elements coming together because you never know what's going to happen. Jazz comes together like that. "Hey, just ride with me on this," or "Why don't you do this, and we'll see what happens?" There is nothing more exciting when something happens. You're in a rocket ship.

When we started Sundance, I was very interested to see what would happen if you put film and dance together. Cross them over. With dancers, their feet and body are alive, but their faces are dead. They're frozen. A lot of actors don't know how to move. They act with their faces. When you force the actors to get with the dancers and the dancers to get together with the actors, maybe something will happen. And maybe there will be a new form of filmmaking related to the exposure to dance. Sure enough, we ended up with this experimental project where this guy got on roller skates, and while the dancers were going through their works, he skated in and out of them with a handheld eyeball camera. It was some of the most exciting footage I've seen because you've broken through the proscenium look. You got in and out and in and out, and suddenly it's very organic.

Those are the kinds of things that get me excited, and that's what Sundance is committed to. Jazz is the perfect model for that, the perfect vehicle. So we're always going to be interested in jazz.

JC: It's very much the American philosophy. As Americans, we grew up with the thought of being unique and creative, that being an individual, an independent voice, is something we're supposed to pursue as Americans. That's what makes America inventing jazz make sense to me.

I've always thought that being a director is very similar to being a jazz band leader, in that it's your film, your vision, your tune, as it were, but you have to choose actors—as I choose musicians for my band—who will realize your vision but have their own individual sound. They have to actualize their character but realize your vision of the story. I told Frank Gehry that it was like getting everyone in his office to play with him.

RR: Yes! And you're raising an interesting point about rhythm. There's the overall arc of the film that's going to have its own rhythm. Then there are many arcs within. That's like when actors are together in a scene. I was always led as a director by music and as an actor, although it's a little harder when you're performing because you can't be as broad, you can't look at yourself. At least I can't. You're just in it. You're *doing* it. But your gut can tell you things. It can't tell you whether the scene is any good or not, but it *can* tell you when it's organically working as a rhythm. You can feel it. Just like when you're dancing with somebody who's with you and dancing with somebody who's not. Then there's the larger arc of the film. Technology has pretty well pushed things forward here, faster than we can cope with.

It's interesting to me that technology is now being used to create the rhythms with the ability to cut and edit. So that's a new kind of rhythm that can be created technically. You could take a performance from one week, and if it's out of whack with the next, through editing you can try to shape it. That's one way to get a rhythm in a film. For me, when I work, I want to make sure that the rhythm is in the scene to begin with, that I won't have to rely too much on editing later. I want to feel, if I'm working with actors in a scene, that the scene has the rhythm I think it needs at that time.

For example, there are some scenes that are full of anxiety, pressure, and tension, and the meter is ticking, and you need that accelerated rhythm.

That would really be like hip-hop or something like that. Then you want those moments where silence plays a big role, where it's a whole other rhythm. You become conscious of rhythms within the larger one. One can be technically or mechanically manufactured, and the other has to come out of you. That fascinates me.

JC: *It fascinates me too. It's all about listening. When I was coming up, I got to know Count Basie, and I went to him and asked, "What's the answer? What should I do?" And he said: "Listen." And I said, "And?" He said, "Just listen."*

Acting is all about listening, isn't it? You can't get that rhythm if you don't have actors who are listening to each other.

RR: That was one of the biggest things I focused on when I became an actor, because I thought I was starting in the business from the real disadvantage of never having wanted it all my life, for one thing, and for another, not thinking I was qualified. I didn't have any training. So I was probably a little self-conscious about vocal training and knowing Shakespeare and all that. One thing I was sure convinced of was that listening had to be part of the deal. It made me crazy, particularly when I was a young actor, to be working with actors who didn't listen.

I remember working with one actor where I just about hauled him off and hammered him. We were working on a scene, and I would listen to him carefully because that would help me be there. How can you be there if you're supposed to be listening and you're not and you're just artificially listening to the other actor in the scene? Maybe it became a life raft for me because I didn't have anything else to rely on. At least I would make this real for myself. So I would listen to the other actor. And then when it was time for me to respond, I noticed his lips were moving. I thought, *What the hell is that?* I realized he was mouthing my words for his cue to come. It made me furious. So, yes, listening has its own rhythm.

JC: I'm thinking of the musicians you've mentioned whom you really love. They're all great listeners. Some musicians forget to listen, just as the actor you mentioned did. Musicians can sometimes go on autopilot.

As a director, how do you work with actors who love to improvise and say, "Let me try this scene this way, I want to do something entirely different?" Are you open to that?

RR: Totally. What's interesting is that most of the time it doesn't work. [Laughs] Including my ideas. I've said that to directors. "Can I just do it my way?" And they say, "Fine." And it's terrible. But I love to hear it. I love for an actor to say, "Hey, can I try something?" That's music to my ears. Of course, I would never deny an actor that choice. Even when the meter is ticking, and you've got some guy looking at his watch in the back.

JC: You once said something to the effect that you wouldn't like yourself as an actor if you were the director, and you wouldn't like yourself as a director if you were the actor.

RR: I think I know what I meant. What I think I meant is that as an actor I have a certain joy zone where I really love it and really appreciated it. I really love being left alone. I love doing it my way. I love having so many choices you can play with. I love playing with those choices. And I love letting the director make the decision on which choice to use. I also shut out most of what is around me except what's supposed to be around me in the scene with the character in whatever environment the scene calls for.

And for me, it's always easier outdoors, because you're out there in a real meadow with real trees. When you get inside, with the set in a studio location, where it's artificial, it's always harder for me. But to be out where things are real, and you can allow yourself to be in that space and not think about the lights and the camera—though you have to think about it a little bit—it's much easier. Now that I've directed, I think I act better for a director. But I always liked being free. And being free in a space. So I made it almost a professional point not to learn the language of the camera. Not to learn too much about what else was going on. You shut out the noise, and you almost go into a Zen place.

As a director, I realized that two things were coming together that I hadn't realized, which was a career that I thought I was destined to have, as a painter or an artist. When I gave that up and became an actor, I thought that was gone. But I realized that I was basically putting two things together—performing and painting a picture, which is very much like being a conductor as opposed to a musician. I suddenly realized how much I loved conceiving the whole thing. I loved having the idea, then filling it in like a painting. The tools were mine and everything was mine, so I would pay attention to everything.

As a director I enjoy every part of it. I enjoy detail. I enjoy watching everything that's going on with the actors, the background. I don't like watching a monitor. I like to watch the actors and trust them. But I have very strong feelings about how the whole thing should look, so I find myself going in and working with the actors and sometimes maybe saying a little too much. No one has ever turned to me and said, "What are you talking about?" But I don't know that I wouldn't have liked that as an actor. Just leave me alone, you know. Not that I won't listen to what you have to say or won't do what you want me to try to do as an actor. But don't talk too much. It's like learning a sport. Don't tell me too much. Just show me and let me follow.

So, I guess that's what I must have meant. I love acting and I love directing, but I don't know about mixing the two. I've done that once and it was hard. Because as an actor I was isolated and as a director I was involved with everything, the mise en scène, and I love it.

JC: *You use everything when you're directing or acting. Your being a painter gives you a sense of composition, and music a sense of rhythm.*

RR: And sport. I was an athlete. If you're an athlete, you have to have rhythm.

JC: And you've done it all here at Sundance. Do you think your interest in individual creativity and how creative people inspire each other drew you to jazz? Or did jazz stimulate that interest in you?

RR: It's like one character in search of an author. Which came first here? I clearly was, at a fairly young age, wanting to move out of where I was to new places, and always in an exploratory mode. When I locked into this, I didn't think about it at the time, I just thought, *I've stumbled onto something great.* That's all I thought about. If I look back now, let's just say that I was certainly susceptible to something like jazz.

JC: And you understood it right off.

RR: I think I did. I didn't know what was going on, but I sure liked it. I couldn't have liked it, if some deeper part of me didn't understand what was going on. Even though intellectually I couldn't have explained it, I was able to go with it. But then I think from that point on, that informed the things I did. It was sort of a tandem deal.

JC: I have to say, personally, that I'm thrilled to a part of the first presentation of jazz here at the Sundance Film Festival.

RR: Sundance has expanded in many ways, using the seed of success in one thing to generate other avenues. Jazz is meant to come in as well. You're taking these things and bringing them into this thing called film but using that to create a broader platform so that people will say, "Ah, look at how film and jazz can work together in a different way than we thought." It's not just scoring a film. It's much deeper than that, in the filmmaking process. Let's share that with people. Let's do something with that. Let's have artists here to maybe talk about film. Let's have Judy Carmichael here and talk about films that she's been impressed with. Let's go the other way.

I'm very excited about that because this is the first year where we're moving out in that direction and we're able to promote it. We've got Cyrus Chestnut, Bill Charlap, Marcus Roberts and then *you*!

JC: *I'm excited about playing here and being juxtaposed with the films, like an aural sorbet, between all those visuals.*

RR: With some of these films, you may be more than a sorbet. You may be the main event!

JC: *[Laughs] You create all these wonderful opportunities for artists. And you've done that for me as well, both musically and with this conversation.*

RR: My pleasure, as you can obviously tell.

Hannah
Rothschild

(b. 1962)

British writer, philanthropist, documentary filmmaker.
In 2015 became the first woman to chair the
Board of Trustees of the National Gallery in London.
In 2018 was appointed Commander of the Order of the
British Empire (CBE) for services to the arts and to charity.

Interviewed in 2009

Hannah Rothschild grew up listening to early jazz greats Teddy Wilson and Fats Waller thanks to her grandfather Victor's love for swing music and his own Wilson-inspired piano playing. Hannah's introduction to bebop came much later, when she discovered in her family tree an unknown great-aunt, Baroness Pannonica (Nica) Rothschild de Koenigswarter. Mysteriously, this relative was never mentioned by the family, although on further exploration proved to be a much-beloved patron of the American bebop world and a close friend of Thelonious Monk and Charlie Parker, two of the style's greatest practitioners. Nica had twenty-four jazz songs written for her and became known as the "Jazz Baroness." Hannah Rothschild's exploration of Nica's life and close relationship with Monk inspired her 2008 documentary *The Jazz Baroness*.

In 1948, on her way to the airport to join her diplomat husband in Mexico, after a visit to New York, Nica stopped to visit Teddy Wilson—a friend of her brother Victor—who played her a record of "Round Midnight," by a then unknown jazz pianist named Thelonious Monk. Unable to believe her ears, she listened to the record twenty times in a row and was bewitched. Having missed her plane, she never returned home. Abandoning her husband and five children, she moved into a suite at the Stanhope Hotel in Manhattan and set about trying to meet the musician who had made this extraordinary record.

I met Nica in 1984, the same year Hannah did, when the great jazz pianist Barry Harris came with Nica to hear me at an Upper East Side club called Hanratty's. At the time, I was the new kid from California who was making a splash and getting good press. Nica and Barry wanted to check me out and make their own judgment. Nica commented that her brother Victor would love me since he was the family's swing music fan, so she bought one of my records for herself and another to send to Victor in England. Soon after, Victor called me from London in the first of what would be a series of long-distance chats about swing music. Coincidentally, I also met his son Jacob Rothschild some years later. When I was pitched the idea of having Hannah on *Jazz Inspired* to talk about *The Jazz Baroness*, I realized that Hannah must be Jacob's daughter and Victor's granddaughter.

HR: I discovered Nica by looking at our family tree. My grandfather, Victor, who you knew, had spent a lot of his life compiling this very exhaustive family tree, which he'd traced back through several generations of Rothschilds. While looking through it, I found a very close relation with this glorious name, Pannonica. I thought, "How bizarre. Why have I never met her?"

Over the years, bits of information came out. For example, that she flew Lancaster bombers during the war. That Charlie Parker died in her apartment. That she lived with a jazz musician called Thelonious Monk. I thought, "Thelonious and Pannonica, now there's a match made in the heaven." You can't find two more strange and wonderful names than that.

She lived in New York, which seemed incredibly cool to me, and she used to wake up after midday and drive downtown to have a Brandy Alexander for breakfast. She also lived with cats. In terms of the romance, I had finally found a really cool relative. I can't tell you how excited I was. But I had to wait to meet her till I came to New York when I was in my twenties and I was working for the BBC, which sent me here on an assignment. I looked her up in the phone book, and there she was. I rang her up, and said rather nervously, "I'm your great-niece." And she goes, "Wild!"

We arranged to meet, and she said, "Come to the club at twelve o'clock." Her being a great-aunt, I assumed that she kind of meant a cup of tea at noon. Not a bit of it; she meant whiskey in a teapot at midnight. I asked, "How do I find the club?" The club was on 23rd Street, not that cool of a place to hang out as a single girl in the '80s. When I asked her how to find it, she replied, "Just look out for the Bentley." Then she hung up.

So I'm trying to explain this to this perfectly charming taxi driver, who, like many cabbies in New York, could speak about two words of English, "Just look for the Bentley," I said. Eventually, we find this car, and in the back were two drunks. And I'm thinking, "What are they doing in the car?" And one of the first things I said when I met her was, "There's a couple of bums in your car." She goes, "Marvelous, that means no one will steal it." I'd lived a fairly sheltered life in England and wasn't really expecting to find a relation like this.

JC: Had anybody given you any warning about her at that point?

HR: No! As I said, there were the rumors. I think anyone who flies a Lancaster bomber in Africa in 1942 . . .

JC: Sounds pretty exotic to me.

HR: Yeah. I thought that was pretty cool. Anyone who lived with a jazz musician . . . Charlie Parker, I didn't know very much about him, but I knew enough to know that it's probably not the best idea to have him die in your apartment.

JC: *Probably best not to have* anyone *die in your apartment.*

HR: Well put. I don't want to offend any relations of Charlie Parker.

JC: *I was telling a musician friend that I was very excited about our meeting, partly because of my own earlier connections with Nica and with Victor. And I said, "You know, the British just do eccentrics better than we Americans do. We pretend to it or posture it, but it's usually just bad behavior and pretension." Seriously, I've met more true eccentrics who are British. And certainly, your great-aunt was an eccentric.*

HR: Yes, I think so. There are whole books written about British eccentrics. We're a race that celebrates differences, and I think that's one of the great things about being British. We don't mind people being different.

JC: *One of the things in your film that I loved was that you went back and forth visually between her life and his life. Some of the things in their backgrounds which, if you take away Nica's great wealth and just look at how isolated both of these lives were, they have that childhood isolation in common. Neither of their lives were the norm.*

HR: I think one thing people find difficult to understand about the story, myself included, is how this intense connection would develop between two people who ostensibly came from the most different backgrounds you could imagine. She came from an intensely European background, great wealth, great privilege; she'd been brought up in incredible isolation. She couldn't even go to the loo without a servant going with her. It was unthinkable that she'd walk down the road carrying her own purse. They had their own railway carriage when they traveled. There was always a footman standing behind the chair. She wouldn't have known how to boil an egg, let alone clean her own shoes. Every weekend there would be kings and queens, shahs and politicians and presidents who would come and stay. In theory it was a huge contrast to Monk's upbringing. Monk was born in North Carolina, three years later than she, and came from a very impoverished background. Came to New York, lived in the San Juan Hill area of New York's Upper West Side, in a tiny apartment.

His mom worked mostly as a cleaner. He had a good education, and certainly she had a poor education. He had one skin color, she had another. He was a Christian; she was a Jew. So there wasn't really anything obvious that would unite them. But when they met, there was clearly a very deep connection. So what I was trying to do in this film was explore the differences, because that's interesting, but also try and see if there were similarities.

For her, above all, there was something in Monk's music that profoundly touched her. I almost feel as if she was waiting her whole life to find a kind of emotional connection with something. And I think it's been proven that music more than any other art form can touch people emotionally and transform people emotionally. No other art form, painting, writing, nothing does it. But music can get to us. You hear a song and it transports you that second back to a place. You put on another record, you burst into tears. You put on still another one, you feel ridiculously happy.

JC: *I once read that the place in our brain where smells are recognized is right next to the place where we recognize music. Which made complete sense to me. And it's a very primal place. For me, nothing can take me instantly back to a memory like a smell or music, a memory you don't even know you have.*

What I'm interested in is Nica's ability to focus and her desire to focus on the importance of this music and to be ahead of her time, as it were, because you emphasized that too in the film. It's common knowledge in jazz circles that it took a long time for people to appreciate how valuable Monk's music was. But she got it right away.

HR: Yes, she did. I was reading Robin Kelley's biography of Monk. He was reiterating how unappreciated Monk was. "'Round Midnight" is, to most of us, a fairly easy record to understand, with its beautiful melody and fairly conventional harmonic structure. But even when it came out, it was lambasted by the critics. Nobody got it. And people like Leonard Feather, the great *éminence grise* of that day, said, "This man can't play. He just can't play music." To hear that now, it seems extraordinary because he's *Thelonious Monk*. Benny Golson, the bebop saxophonist who I interviewed for this, said, "She could hear it ahead of her time."

JC: *Teddy Wilson was the one who mentioned Thelonious Monk to her. She knew Teddy through her brother Victor?*

HR: Well, her brother Victor was a very keen amateur pianist, and at one point, Teddy Wilson, one of his great heroes, came to London and gave piano lessons, odd as that might seem. And he gave a piano lesson to Victor who really, really loved jazz. Victor took Nica to see Duke Ellington at Streatham Town Hall in the '30s.

JC: *I don't know that he ever told me that he took those lessons. He never played for me. We'd talk on the phone, and I'd lay the phone on the piano and play for him. Barry Harris brought Nica to hear me, and then she said, "You have to meet my brother Victor because he loves this style of piano. He'll love you."*

She came to hear me a number of times, but of course, her great passion was bebop and Victor's was swing piano. We had many transatlantic phone calls that would just go on forever. I kept thinking, "Who exactly is this person with the beautiful accent? And does he know how much this call is costing?"

HR: [Laughs] I remember him playing very clearly. I remember as a child going to stay with him. He lived in Cambridge, and he was quite a big guy. He had a pet owl that used to live in his study. Very Harry Potter. And this poor owl had to listen while Victor bent over his piano and basically beat the hell out of it.

JC: *Another eccentric! Did you like jazz when you were you younger?*

HR: I loved it. Also, I had another cool aunt. Here's a terrific name-drop coming up. Peggy Ashcroft, an aunt by marriage. She's a very distinguished British actress, and she had a long affair with Paul Robeson that caused a huge scandal. Of course, I love Paul Robeson. And then my grandmother, my mum's mum, knew Louis Armstrong pretty well and liked to pretend that she might have had a little bit of a dalliance in the dressing room.

JC: *See, you come from a long line of scandalous people.*

HR: A long line of groupies!

JC: *Talk about how Monk and Nica originally got together.*

HR: I'm surprised that it was one record that caused such mayhem. She hears "'Round Midnight" and doesn't go home! So the story right from the start was pretty surprising. And I think that what both moved me and surprised me was discovering their similarities. I discovered, for example, that both of their fathers had suffered from mental breakdowns and were incarcerated—Nica's father actually killed himself as a result of both depression and getting the Spanish flu, a very common and terrible thing that happened after the First World War. And they both spent a total of only about seven years with their respective fathers and were both brought up by very, very strong women. Nica's mother was a Hungarian called Rozsika, and Monk's mother was Barbara, who was an incredible, dignified, matriarchal figure. So behind the obvious differences I started to see all these similarities. I love the idea of exploring why we're drawn to people. Why does X like Y, and Y likes Z? And how do you meet someone across a crowded room, and what's all that about?

JC: *Has it changed the way you think about things, exploring a character so deeply like this, and someone who's a relation? Do you feel as if you're likely to have more courage in making some sort of radical decision?*

HR: Oddly enough, it's almost the opposite. I almost feel like she's done it for me. That there's something almost freeing in knowing her story. I feel I've spent most of my life trying to accept who I am. I'm a terrific homebody. I love home. I'd hang out there with the kids and never move. So in a way, I'm very much not like her. And I suppose there's part of me that thinks, "God, wouldn't it be great to be that free?" And I feel very dowdy and dull by comparison, that somebody could be so transported by a song or believe so passionately in a cause or lay down basically everything safe to protect a certain amount of people. I wish I had a little more of that in me. On the other hand, if I felt that every time I turned on the radio, it might cause a seismic shift in how I live, I think I'd be a little nervous.

JC: I would too. Although I heard a Count Basie record that made me want to drop everything and learn how to play like that. Which is what I did. I was young—twenty-one, twenty-two—but it was late for a jazz musician to get started. Musicians that I knew who were serious about being professionals were already playing professionally in their early teens. I was playing some ragtime, but I was a German major and not planning on a music career, even though I had gigs. But someone played me an early Count Basie record, and that was it. I was determined to play like that.

HR: Do you remember which one it was?

JC: "Prince of Wales." It was when Basie was with Bennie Moten's band. I was already playing piano, but not much. It was an artistic epiphany that inspired me to learn how to do what he was doing. I thought, "I'm going to sit in a room, listen to this record over and over, and teach myself how to play like this." So I know about that kind of thing taking over your life. But what I find interesting is that this continued for the rest of Nica's life. For me, this was six months of craziness at a young time in my life when I decided I was going to do everything I could to learn how to play like Basie, but then eventually I needed to pull my head up and make some money.

I did become a musician though, but I couldn't just be focused on this great love that I had. I had to start thinking practically and decide how I could make a living while pursuing that love, so that record did change my life. I find Nica's incredible focus fascinating, which is what I get from the film—and even from the little bit I knew her—that focus to the exclusion of everything else.

HR: Monomaniacal, if there's such a word. She was forty-something, forty-one, I think, at the time. Although she'd had this very privileged young life, then the Second World War broke out, and a lot of her relatives, including close relatives, perished in the Holocaust. She'd gone to Africa, she'd fought in the name of freedom, and she'd come back, and of course the whole world had ripped apart at that point. What the Second World War did, of course, was totally uproot everything. And by enlisting in the Free French Resistance, she had the opportunity to actually have a job, have a life, do something different. Immediately after the war ended, she was expected to go back and be the perfect little housewife again. She couldn't do that. I think in a way that jazz and the very nature of bebop, the fact that it's improvised, the fact that it's free form, the fact that you never know where it's going to go to next . . .

JC: It's very rebellious.

HR: Exactly. It seemed to kind of tap into exactly what she was looking for, and I think that was part of it. It seemed to underscore her emotions, but also it gave her a cause. She hadn't fought for freedom just to go sit back and watch her newfound friends be pushed around.

JC: How did the musicians feel when you talked to them about her? How did they feel about this woman who wanted to help them? Were they willing to take the help? Were they suspicious? Did they accept her because she was already close with Monk?

HR: Without exception, the generation that was around in the early '50s were just really pleased that somebody liked the music and was prepared to stick up for them, that she was there to lend a hand. Through the '60s and '70s it obviously became a much more political subject. But in the '50s, I think they were just delighted that someone—I don't think it mattered what their skin color or gender was—took it seriously and loved it. I didn't meet one person who was anything other than thrilled that she was there for them.

Most jazz musicians were not in it for the money. If you want to get rich, jazz is not necessarily the first thing you choose. I think some people did very well, but on the whole, you do it for the love of the music and hope to get by. I've made films and I've interviewed people over the last twenty-five years in lots of different artistic fields. I've never ever met a group of people who are as intelligent, as articulate, and as generous as jazz musicians.

JC: A lot of fans think that good jazz stopped in 1942, an opinion that is helped by the fact that they don't listen to anything recorded after 1942. But you've obviously enjoyed all of it. What in particular do you like about bebop?

HR: Bebop took me a long time to get into. I didn't suddenly go, "Oh, great, bebop, I get it." When I first heard it, it was like, "Oh, God. What is going on here?" I was having real trouble with Monk, for example. And one of the musicians I met said, "Go buy *Monk Plays Ellington*. That's your way in." So I trotted off and bought the album, *Thelonius Monk Plays Duke Ellington*. And I think it was "Caravan" that was the first track I heard, and that was my way in. Gradually, once you kind of understand it—it's not rocket science, you know—you enjoy it. I think I was trying to be too intellectual about it rather than just let it wash over me. And after listening to Monk now for fifteen years, no one for me comes close to him in bebop.

You can't get bored of it. There's always something that you haven't heard, so even "'Round Midnight," which is not terribly complicated as tunes go, even that gets you emotionally. Even before we started, I was thinking, if I were to pick lots of Monk recordings, you can't really say that "Dinah" is like "'Round Midnight," or "Hear My Song" is like "Abide with Me." It's all so different. I don't think you can say, "That is typical Monk." Or can you?

JC: I think for me what makes Monk so interesting is that he's so distinctive, so no matter what he plays, you know it's Monk because of that crazy approach. Even the way he touched the piano was very different.

HR: And you hear the stride influence, the gospel.

JC: Your bringing up stride reminds me of something special about the players of that era. The great pianists Tommy Flanagan, Barry Harris and others grew up listening to the history of jazz. It developed right in front of them. Jazz has a short history, so they were listening to Fats Waller and the people who invented jazz as they were each developing their own styles, as was Monk. Then they evolved into these bop players. But you hear the roots, the stride, swing, all of it in their playing.

I play stride more smoothly, more like Fats or Teddy, but when Monk strides it's very childlike, like everything he does, like in "Dinah" or "Lulu's Back in Town." You have to say it's bebop, but he's striding.

HR: And the other thing, Monk comes here, he's still a young man, but they've got the whole series of classical music going on in the park. His mother pays for him to have lessons with a really good teacher. He goes on the road with a gospel choir for two years. Also, living in New York at that time, you'd only have to walk around the corner to hear calypso, you'd go around to hear big bands. The kind of cross-fertilization between all these different types of music in New York at that time were endless. I can't believe I'm pretending here that I know about music. I'm a complete charlatan.

JC: You've convinced me! [Laughs] Another thing that struck me in your film is you didn't over-romanticize the jazz life. You went deep into these characters. You discuss Nica knowing Nellie, Monk's wife, and that as far as everyone knew, Monk and Nica weren't lovers, but they were very, very close. God forbid, we actually think of a friendship that doesn't have to do with sex. I'm curious, as a filmmaker, making a documentary, how you approached that, or if this was just an exploration and then it unfolded the way characters do for a novelist.

HR: I didn't know when I started whether they'd had an affair or not. I assumed they probably did because we live in an era where you can't even see an advert for ice cream without it coming down to sex. But of course things don't necessarily come down to sex. I really did ask every single person who spent a lot of time with them. Did they or didn't they? And every single person who spent time with them said no, they didn't.

And I can assure you, had I thought that the answer was that they had, I would have said so. I wasn't trying to protect anybody. I genuinely didn't think they did. Do I think she loved him? Yes. And I think you only have to look at one photograph, let alone all the photographs of them together to look at her looking up adoringly at him. She loved him; of course, she loved him. Did he love her? I don't think he loved her like that. I think he was really thrilled and grateful that she got him and that she got his music and she understood it at a time when lots of people didn't. But I genuinely think he loved his wife, Nellie. I think it was that simple. He wasn't the best husband, but Nellie kept them together. And Nica made their life a lot more comfortable.

The other thing that you were talking about earlier is the jazz story. Everyone loves to make out that jazz comes out of the whorehouses, and then everyone becomes a drug addict and that's jazz. Well, of course, it's not jazz. It's a ridiculous and rather offensive way of describing jazz. Yes, there were a lot of casualties along the route, a lot of alcohol and drugs. But it's much more complicated than that. And there were lots of jazz musicians who never touched drugs. For example, you don't look like somebody who's *ever* touched a drug. Well, not recently anyway.

[Laughter]

JC: No. I'm addicted to tennis. I'm very square.

HR: Blooming health would describe you.

JC: Thank you! And I just love that you gave a broader picture of jazz and these individuals. As a filmmaker, I thought you really captured that whole era and gave insight into Nica's very unusual upbringing and the world of all these jazz musicians.

HR: I hope so. I think the achievements of musicians in that era were phenomenal. You talk to someone like Quincy Jones, who now lives in a ginormous house in Bel Air, and it's almost impossible to imagine that's the same Quincy Jones who was in the back of a tour bus, going through the South, never enough to eat, doesn't know where he's gonna sleep. It's a big journey these guys made. And I think one has to feel nothing but respect for their integrity and determination. The vast majority of musicians put in hours and hours of hard work, practice, love and disappointment. To be creative, as you know, you've got to get knocked down a lot more times than you're picked up.

JC: *And you really captured it all. How long did it take to put the film together?*

HR: About fifteen years. But I got so lucky. I got to meet those incredible people and to explore one of the most fascinating periods of history and listen to some beautiful music. Talk about lucking out.

JC: *Well, I'm thrilled that we were able to meet. Who would think? I keep meeting Rothschilds!*

HR: You've known three generations. So now I have to introduce you to one of my kids so you'll know four.

JC: *Then I can say, "I remember when I used to play piano for your great-grandfather!"*

Nadja Salerno-Sonnenberg

(b. 1961)

Classical violinist, educator, and author.

Interviewed in 2019

Nadja Salerno-Sonnenberg has been a powerful force in the world of classical music throughout her career. When she was eight, she moved from her native Italy to America to study at the Curtis Institute of Music in Philadelphia and later with Dorothy DeLay at the Juilliard School. In 1981 she became the youngest-ever prize winner in the Walter W. Naumburg International Violin competition and in 1999 was awarded the Avery Fisher Prize for "outstanding achievement and excellence in music."

Nadja's explosive stage presence and passionate musical interpretations brought her international acclaim, recording contracts, awards, and a nonstop touring schedule. Additionally, back when television shows featured musicians of sophistication rather than the current pop star, Nadja was a frequent guest on *The Tonight Show Starring Johnny Carson*, *Sesame Street*, *Live from Lincoln Center*, and many other programs. All this success came to a crashing halt in 1994 when she sliced her little finger while making dinner for friends. Still, she pushed forward. During the six months it took for her finger to heal, she refingered pieces for three fingers and continued to tour and perform.

Eventually, exhaustion and depression set in, culminating in a suicide attempt and a serious re-evaluation of her life. Now, in a move that surprised all but her closest friends, Nadja has jumped into a new life in New Orleans, teaching at Loyola University College of Music and Media and plunging into the Louisiana scene. Although she continues to perform, her main focus is her teaching and her New Orleans adventures. Souvenirs from Nadja's many Mardi Gras celebrations are displayed around her house, and when I dropped by the day after our interview for a quick hello, she was on her way to a Saints' game dressed in the team's black, white, and gold colors.

Nadja and I are close in age, and her go-for-broke style and ferocious stage presence thrilled me when I was coming up. I was never anyone's vision of a jazz musician and was always the lone woman instrumentalist at every festival I played. As for Nadja, when other women violinists were wearing strapless gowns, she often wore pants and played with a fervor that spoke to a different kind of passion for the instrument. In her own words, people either loved her or hated her. I loved her.

JC: Everyone thinks of New Orleans, your new home, as a jazz town, but you're known for your classical music. Were you a jazz fan when you were younger?

NSS: I listened to it my whole life. My household had such a different array of music going on constantly, from Led Zeppelin to opera. I was listening to Ella Fitzgerald way before I knew who Ella Fitzgerald was because my mother loved her, and she had the albums. I listened to Jascha Heifetz because my mother loved Heifetz. It wasn't until I was maybe seventeen, eighteen, that I started buying my own stuff and making my own decisions about what I wanted to listen to.

JC: That was fairly common with our parents' generation and their parents. Our generation seemed to zero in on their own popular music to the exclusion of other music. You were very fortunate to be exposed to so much.

NSS: When I came to the United States in 1969, my grandparents lived in the same house as we did, so you had three generations under the same roof. My grandmother was listening to Sergio Franchi and Domenico Modugno and all these great Italian kind of soul singers. That's the music of our blood. But my mother was a classical pianist, so she introduced me to classical music. She also loved Broadway and jazz and things like that. My grandfather introduced me to opera, which was probably the biggest musical influence for me because I was listening to opera singers when I was teeny. My entire career, people have told me that I play like a singer. That's what I knew. And my brother was listening to Led Zeppelin. So this was all in the same house. It was phenomenal.

JC: We know what the accessibility of music through different platforms has done to hurt the record business, but in a positive way, it has created a generation of kids who are open to all different kinds of music because it's so accessible.

NSS: It is. When I mention something in a class I'm teaching, within an hour they've already heard it. Everything is right there for us. So in that sense, yes, it's good.

JC: Are your students open to all kinds of music or just focused on classical?

NSS: They're open. The minority of my students are performance majors, so music is not even what they want to do when they graduate, but they love it. And Loyola has an unbelievable jazz department, as you can imagine, and an incredible opera department. These kids go on to sing at the Met. There are phenomenal choirs at the school, and then there's orchestra. And I have my string orchestra that doesn't have a conductor. I lead it. And I head up all the chamber music groups.

The kids are so varied. Sometimes they don't want to play classical music. They want to learn their instrument better so that they can go play jazz. You have to convey to them that whatever you're going to play, we're talking about twelve notes. And those twelve notes, if you play them well, are going to serve you well in jazz, bebop, classical, whatever you choose to do.

JC: You're an Ella Fitzgerald fan. You brought me a track that was very specific because she's recorded "Mack the Knife" a number of times.

NSS: It's impossible to pick five tracks that have inspired me, which you asked me to do. But I had to put Ella in there. This is a track I grew up with. That's why I love this particular one. It's not just Ella singing that tune. Everybody sang it, right? But she sang it so many times in so many places. This is a recording that my mother had, an LP, *Ella in Berlin*. I can just see it. It was black and white on the front. It's from the concert that she did there, which is the version I love.

JC: You're fortunate that you had a family that played music, that had passion for it. I know loads of people who didn't have that, who haven't been exposed to the profound joy music can bring. After a concert recently, an American couple in their mid-fifties thanked me for introducing them to Gershwin. I didn't judge them. They just weren't lucky enough to have somebody who had introduced them to Gershwin. I do judge the fact that the American educational system doesn't guarantee that we're introduced to Gershwin.

So I love that you teach future professionals and amateurs. Music major grads often tell me that their teachers never talked to them about what exactly it takes to pursue a career in music. Do you talk to the ones who want a career about how to create a career and stay inspired?

NSS: I think that whatever vocation one pursues, everyone wants to be inspired. I feel fortunate that I can inspire people when it comes to music. I can instill inspiration and excitement and vibrancy in these kids, whether or not they want to be in class.

It's a very different world now. There are two things I notice about the generation I'm teaching. One, they're incredibly entitled, and that's really frustrating for me. Also, they've got it a lot harder than I ever did. They're saddled with more emotional problems than we were, but they don't understand the concept of working and failing and continuing to work. If a student has too many absences, and I say, "Look, you're missing too much; it's gonna affect your grade," the next thing is not the student coming to class more. The next thing is I get is a notice from social services at the school saying, "This student has blah-biddy-blah condition and needs to be excused from class."

So, as a teacher, what do I do about that? Whether they're going to go on to a life in music or not, I want them to know that music is always going to be something that will help them, that they can rely on, and that the discipline that's needed to make music, especially classical music, is something they can carry with them the rest of their lives. Discipline is a good thing.

I've been teaching for a while now, so I have my own, very unorthodox, very not PC way of teaching. I'm surprised that I haven't been fired yet. But I believe that my kids love me because they know that I love them, know that I want them to reach their potential. They'll play something and go, "What do you think? How'd that sound?" And I respond with, "You think that's ready to go on stage and perform?" I totally embarrass them. That's been working.

JC: I would think so! [Laughs]

NSS: One thing I remember from my teacher, Dorothy DeLay, was that she taught us how to teach ourselves, and there's nothing more valuable than that.

JC: Talk about the conductor-less approach. To me, that's jazz. My view about classical music is that you work, work, work so you can be on stage and make it sound like it's all spontaneous. With a jazz musician, we work, work, work and get all our ideas and our technique at a level where we can express whatever we can think up at the moment and hope it's constructed so beautifully that it sounds as if it were written ahead of time. Jazz musicians will transcribe great solos to study them because they're so well composed, even though they were composed on the spot.

NSS: Yes!

JC: *I've read what you said about the conductor-less group, that the members have to come to that place on their own where they listen differently because they're not looking at a conductor. These are all the things that jazz musicians do when they play together. Is that common, to have a conductor-less group?*

NSS: I'd say about twenty years ago there were fewer conductor-less ensembles, but they've been around for a very, very long time; they're just very rare. I think the main thing is that they train the ear. You have to look at your music whether or not you have a conductor. If you're a soloist, you've got it memorized. But if you're a member of an orchestra, you've got to look at your music. So let's say there's a conductor up there. How many times do you look at that conductor? If you're driving, how many times do you look at your rearview mirror? Because you have to focus on another spot.

If you're looking down at your music, you can peripherally see these hands waving around and very quickly you can look up. But if that's not there, if you don't have anything there, then what? Who's guiding you? As music director of a conductor-less ensemble, believe me, I lead them. But I lead them more emotionally and in rehearsal, to prepare for this spontaneous performance. There's no ear training more powerful than that.

I grew up in Rome, in Italy, and pretty much everywhere in Europe but especially Rome, I think, there are like eight streets that come into one piazza, and there's like one guy there with a whistle. You have so many cars, and what if that guy wasn't there? You'd have to use your common sense and know instinctively, "That guy looks like he's gonna go." I know that the guy three cars ahead is going to change lanes. So again, everything has to be so heightened. All of your senses, including visual, because you're looking at everybody else on stage, not just the one guy or woman up there in the front. It's a phenomenal, vibrant way of making music.

JC: *It is. And that's what jazz musicians are thinking all the time. Because we're looking at each other, feeling each other and listening intently.*

NSS: Jazz, at least in traditional jazz, you've got the tune. The tune is exposed, everybody's playing the tune. Then everybody takes their solos. So in that period of time, most of the musicians are not playing, or maybe you've got little support playing going on. But basically, is that not just time off? Because you know instinctively when the 16 or 30 measures are done and when you're supposed to come in.

JC: It depends on the musician. For some musicians, it is time off, but it shouldn't be. Time is the big thing we talk about in jazz. There's correct time, but there's a lot that you can do with where you hear that beat. And lots of musicians think, well, we're all following the bass player and the drummer. They're the ones setting the time. The beat. But for me, I want every member of my band to have a similar view of where that beat is. So, yes, it's time off when they're not taking a chorus. But if they're really listening, they might do a little riff behind you that picks you up or pushes you forward, or they hear you fall off a cliff with your improvisation and they jump in with something. They're involved throughout. So even when they're not playing, I want musicians who are still engaged so I feel their support.

NS: Well, that's chamber music.

JC: I ask my guests to bring me tracks that either inspired them initially or continues to inspire them. And I loved that you had things that were very emotional and also some that were upbeat, like Pete Fountain.

NSS: Pete Fountain is kind of new to me since I moved here. However, I was on *The Tonight Show* with him. I would have hugged him and not let him go, but I didn't know better back then. I was fully immersed in a soloist's classical concerto career. But I knew who he was, that he was a famous jazz clarinetist. I didn't know him, but now I do, and he's become a very dear friend. And now Pete has opened up to me and he's pretty much the only clarinetist I can listen to. He's just phenomenal. And then I remember, my God, I was sitting right next to him on *The Tonight Show* with Johnny right over there and I totally missed the opportunity to pick his brain.

JC: You've said that coming to New Orleans radically changed your life. You talked about the different focus on your career at different times in your life, how you felt in your twenties, your thirties, your forties, your fifties. People who take the time to look at these things and make conscious decisions about their life are the people I admire the most. So many people have no idea why they're doing what they're doing. It's sad to me.

NSS: Those are people who continually float, and sometimes that's their choice. But the secret is this: You need time to think about your life in a serious way, and by time I don't mean a week. You need time, and you need time alone. And I'm not talking about taking time off from work. I'm talking about emotional, depressing time alone, where you just look at yourself in the mirror and say, "What the hell is going on?"

And you have to try to figure out the answer to that. It's like, O.K., let's just have everything that's important in your life go to shit, and you sit alone on your couch for a year and see how you feel about that. Nobody wants that, but that's when you learn, when you really discover. That's what I mean by the kind of time to figure out what am I doing. I literally made lists, things I loved and didn't love, the people I loved, and asked why do you love this person? Why do you not love them? Well, I kind of like them . . . "O.K., so you can take a half hour of this person." Really pick yourself apart. I always did it in the mirror, because it was like I became the therapist looking at somebody who really needed a lot of help.

In my twenties, I could not wait to get on stage. And then afterwards, woo hoo! In my thirties, I looked forward to going on stage, but I felt differently afterwards. I felt gratification. I felt proud. In my forties, I was not so happy to get on stage anymore because I started to dread it. But when the concert was finished, I felt just pure, serene happiness, not like "yay" kind of happy but just, "I have used the gifts that God gave me, there is nobody on stage that's disappointed with that concert, there's no manager of the orchestra, nobody in the audience, everybody was pleased. I can get on the plane and go home knowing I've done what I was put on this Earth to do." But I dreaded going on stage.

Then in my fifties, it was not even that. After the concert I just felt empty. And yet I was the busiest I'd ever been in my life, between forty-five and fifty-five, because I was carrying on a full-fledged solo career, and then I was music director of New Century Chamber Orchestra in San Francisco, and I started my own record label, and then everything else that life throws at you, all the personal stuff. And that's a lot of work. That's a lot to juggle. And I'm just gonna say it, *menopause*.

I'm sorry, but that was a tough ten years, for me and for everybody around me. Also, in your fifties some health issues start to arise. And you sit down and think, "What are you doing? You have some time left; I hope. What would you like to do with that time? What is it that you love the most about music?" And for me, it was putting the piece together, rehearsal. It had nothing to do with putting mascara on, and heels, and going on stage. I had gotten more than enough standing ovations in my life. It really wasn't about the performance anymore. It just meant nothing anymore. But how can you just walk away from music? Of course, I can't do that.

I started to realize that I love getting together with people and rehearsing. I sort of tailored my life in a way where I could have that. And something else that was infecting me was this overwhelming desire to expunge all the knowledge that I have. So what better way than to teach? Like, "Y'all are gonna hear more than you wanna hear in this hour."

And I chose this city. I've always loved this city. I knew I was going to leave New York. The city changed. Nobody was more in love with New York than I was, but I changed, and it became a very lonely place, a very angry place, a way crowded, way expensive, very noisy place. I didn't wanna be there anymore. And this city was beckoning. And I thought, "Do it." I made a decision to move to New Orleans in April 2018, and I was moved into this house that you are sitting in in August.

And I will tell you this—and I am not exaggerating—I enjoy every single day of my life. Every single day. It's not like bad things don't happen, or

I'm not cursing about something. But every day there is joy in my life. Something beautiful.

JC: And the fact that you're able to pass on your knowledge and change people's lives is spectacular, because there aren't enough good teachers. Inspiring teachers are essential.

NS: A teacher has to have three elements. They have to have the knowledge of whatever it is that they're teaching. They have to have the commitment to do what they're supposed to do, but go the extra mile and have a very, very strong commitment. And that commitment covers a big range. Figure out how to communicate to each student individually with what they need. Here comes Ms. Delay again, who's really superior at speaking to you, to your brain, and what you specifically need. If she said to me, "Sugar plum, I want you to practice this this way and come back next week and play it for me," that would not sink in with me. What she said to me was, "So-and-so, a friend of mine, played it so beautifully for me yesterday. Let's see what you do next week." So psychologically, this is what I mean by commitment.

The third element is that you have to be wildly—especially these days—inspirational. I've taught so many students, master classes, my whole life. All over the world. And the kids, they know how to play, but then I say to them, "Do you feel anything when you're playing this movement?" And to try to draw it out of a kid in a master class, what do you have? Twenty minutes, thirty minutes? But it occurs to me that this idea was never even introduced to them. "What do you feel when you're playing this? You've learned the notes. Your sound is beautiful. Everything is just sounding beautiful, but I'm not *feeling* anything. What do you feel when you play this?" I don't think these students were ever asked that question. Because you can see a difference if you ask this question. In thirty minutes, you see.

Roy Scheider

(1932–2008)

Stage, film and TV actor, best known for playing Police Chief Martin "We need a bigger boat" Brody in the movie, *Jaws*.

Interviewed in 2004

Roy Scheider was known for the sensitivity and intensity he brought to the characters he portrayed. A lifelong music lover, Roy first fell for the heartfelt songs of country music and later for the joyful sounds of New Orleans jazz. Roy felt that life *is* music, and in particular saw a special connection between the art of acting and jazz.

I met Roy in 1999 at a party at the Sag Harbor home of the novelist, E.L. Doctorow, who encouraged Roy to be a guest on my new radio show. Doctorow was a friend and one of my first guests on *Jazz Inspired*. I hadn't known that Roy was a jazz fan and was delighted with this discovery. I followed up on this suggestion over the next few years, but Roy always had an excuse for turning me down.

In a delightful if unlikely turn of events, we found ourselves seated next to each other at physical therapy, waiting for our respective ice packs after our treatment. Roy leaned over and said, "You're Judy Carmichael, aren't you? I listen to your show all the time and love it." I raised my hand and replied, "Talk to the hand! I've been chasing you for years to be on *Jazz Inspired,* and you've ignored me." He laughed and admitted that he didn't think he knew enough about jazz to be a guest. I said I'd forgive him if he finally said yes.

When we met to record, Roy asked if we could listen to some music before we started, something no other guest has suggested. "What's your pleasure?" I asked. "Louis Armstrong." We listened for a while and he eventually said, "I think we're ready."

We began by discussing how music can bring a person to emotional truth.

RS: Musical artists cheat; they have an instrument. They have a quicker way of getting to you and tearing you apart than an actor does. Shakespeare knew that the quickest way to anyone's emotions was through music. And you talk to any of your friends. If they hear just two bars of a certain piece of music, it takes them back thirty years, and they know exactly what happened at that time or what was going on in their life then.

JC: You mentioned Shakespeare. There's obviously someone who had a lot of music in their writing. Talk about other playwrights who have that quality.

RS: I think that each playwright, in his effort to capture the mystery of the human voice, has a voice of his own, and he brings that to how he sees other people act. He takes their emotion, mixes it with his, and presents something that isn't quite realistic but has great truth in it. It's very powerful, whether it's *Long Day's Journey* or *Hamlet* or Pinter's *Betrayal.* And as an actor, you don't get a play the first time you read it, and you don't get it the second time. You may get it the third or fourth time, and you'll get it even better when you sit down at the table and just read and listen with other actors.

If you're patient and your ears are open, the playwright will tell you how the scene should be played because you have to listen to the music; you have to study the music. It's like what you do when you study a piece for the piano. You have to play it over and over and over and over again, and then the day comes when you say, "Oh, now I've got it. Now I know." And then you go and play. You're probably playing the closest thing to what was written, but it took you that long to get there.

JC: *It's a very similar experience playing through something with my band. We have the notes, but we haven't made music yet.*

RS: Right. We have the words, but we haven't added the humanity yet.

JC: *So you're listening for the different musical voice of each playwright as you approach the material.*

RS: Yes. And the play is not alive until it's performed. It's just something in a book or written down. It's only alive when people say the words. For instance, I remember when we were in rehearsal for an Arthur Miller play called *Incident at Vichy* at the ANTA theater in Greenwich Village. I was watching the rehearsal one day, and Miller was in the third row. In the middle of one scene, he got up and started walking back and forth, back and forth. When the rehearsal was over, I went up to him and said, "Mr. Miller, why were you walking back and forth like that?" "I was listening to what that actor was saying, and what that actor was doing with my words," he said. "What he was doing is not what I wrote. What he's doing is *better.*"

JC: *That happens with music all the time. I've done that in a recording session, where I do what I think is an outtake, then I listen to it and like it better because it wasn't what I had originally intended. And the surprise of it was delightful and gave something extra to the performance.*

RS: Last night I was watching a wonderful documentary on Channel Thirteen on violin players. One of the moderators was a Frenchman who was commenting on a particular violinist and saying that what made him so remarkable was his ability, or his willingness, to go flat whenever he felt like it. He said, "Now, listen to this," and they played a piece of his music, and the last draw on the bow was as flat as could be. But he did it deliberately for an effect. It had nothing to do with the rest of the music. I said, "Oh, my God, it works!"

JC: *Interesting. Did you grow up listening to jazz? Was this something you came to early?*

RS: No. I grew up in New Jersey. My brother and I listened to only country and western music when we were ten, eleven, twelve, because that was easily accessible to our life and to our times. All that moanin' and groanin' and havin' the blues. Then when I was about sixteen or seventeen and we could steal somebody's father's car and drive over to New York, we started to go to places like the Stuyvesant Casino and Central Plaza and Nick's and Eddie Condon's and go listen to jazz. And when I heard that, it just blew me away. I mean, when I heard original, really great New Orleans music, I said, "That's me, that's where my heart is." So for two or three years we constantly went to these clubs. We spent our time and money listening to this music.

JC: Because of the emotion of it? Is that what hooked you in?

RS: And the amount of empathy you could have. There were great White musicians, but most of them were Black. And if you understood and knew anything about their history and where they came from, the fact that they were up there playing with such dignity, such elan, such mirth, I was transfixed. I thought they were the most charming, elegant men I had ever seen in my life.

JC: You thought about that at that age? You thought about that issue, about them being Black?

RS: I knew they were different from, say, my father and his friends. There was like a secret club. I don't know, maybe they all smoked marijuana. [Laughs] I don't know what their secret was, but there was an unsaid language amongst musicians and an unsaid sense of appreciation of what the other musicians were doing. And how they would slide in together, and they would play with their brother, and then their brother would play this. [At this point Roy teared up.] You see, when I talk about that, it gets me very emotional. There was a kind of peace and harmony in those musicians that I didn't find in my own family, that I didn't find in my life. Later, I found it on that stage.

JC: That's so beautiful. That kind of cooperation and empathy, that's what touched you. Me too, when I first heard jazz musicians. That's what made me want to be a jazz musician.

RS: Yeah! I wondered, why can't I be like that?

JC: That's beautiful. And it's just about the music. Everything else falls away, and it's about this pure experience.

RS: Yes, that we can do this together. We can make a beautiful thing, and this beautiful thing will protect us from all the ugliness.

JC: Do you feel that in the theater in the same way?

RS: Yes. It doesn't matter whether the play is a tragedy, or the music is deep and dark like Wagner, there is still beauty within the darkness that is uplifting. But in a play, no matter how many people are strewn about the stage at the end, *Hamlet* is never a play that distresses me because there's always the one element of this man who represents unguided reason, but he's a man who is sympathetic, loving, is incapable of being in love, but he is loving.

JC: I've never thought about that until right this minute, but that's always appealed to me too. The first time I saw any actors on stage, or any stage experience, that communication and that empathy that they have was something I wanted. I wanted to have that experience.

RS: I didn't do anything in high school other than the high school play, but the college that I went to—Franklin and Marshall in Lancaster, Pennsylvania—had a theater. And the first play I saw there was a play inspired by Herman Melville's *Billy Budd*, and it just blew me away because of the sense of playing that was going on on the stage. They are called plays because everyone is *playing*. I thought that was a very powerful thing, and I wanted to be part of that.

I found a home in the theater. I lived in the theater. I did my academic work, but my heart was always in the theater. And there was no question in my mind about what I wanted to be because I'd found something that I liked to do with people like me. That kind of acceptance, it's like music. It was my music.

JC: *What other musicians got you excited about jazz?*

RS: Well, it was the early piano playing of Jelly Roll Morton. Then I moved on to Armstrong and Sidney Bechet, then Jack Teagarden, then into the moderns with Lester Young and Johnny Hodges, then on to Sinatra, and then when bebop came, I was completely confused.

JC: *Everyone was confused.*

RS: [Laughs] I used to think, "What is this stuff?" I feel a little differently now.

JC: *Talk about Frank Sinatra.*

RS: Frank—I mean Mr. Sinatra—he was probably the finest acting pop singer that we've ever had. One piece that I thought was really special was him singing *Angel Eyes*. It's so melancholic and so blue and so down and out, and he just exemplifies unrequited love. He's the Romeo of all singers, and it's easy to see why both men and women adore him the same way.

Most people don't necessarily have happy love lives. They just don't. And so a singer like Frank, who's a great musician and has a great ear for phrasing, can take a song and break your heart.

JC: *Do you think his being an actor made him a better singer?*

RS: No, I think his being a singer made him a better actor. Because he started as a singer and what he tried to do, even when he played with Tommy Dorsey or he sang with those early bands, what made him different was he wasn't rushing through the song, he was sitting on notes and caressing them and caressing you. He's saying, "I'm like you. I feel as you do, and it makes me sad." That's the basis of his acting, and the good directors knew that.

JC: I've heard you say that everything in life is music. Do you use music as an inspiration for you? If you're working on something, would you listen to music? Like before we started talking now, I love that you wanted to listen to some music to get you in the mood.

RS: Yes, some authors, some playwrights make you want to listen to discordant music, music that's not comfortable to listen to. It's twisted, it's perverted, it's strange. And others want you to listen to something very soft and very lovely. With Chekhov, I can't imagine playing New Orleans music to that, but I can imagine *Swan Lake* or something very simple and beautiful like that.

JC: Do you have an all-time favorite tune?

RS: Jack Teagarden's recording of "A Hundred Years from Today." The lyrics go something like this, "Don't save your kisses, pass them around. You won't need them, because a hundred years from today, who will know, who will know?" I mean, I forgot the lyrics now, but I just find them so moving because it's saying, don't hesitate to love, don't hesitate to be warm because a hundred years from today who's gonna know? Who's gonna care?

JC: I got to hear Norma Teagarden, Jack's sister, years ago in San Francisco. She plays piano. She used to play for him, sometimes. And it was so moving for me. Here was this woman in her late seventies, missing some notes because she had a little arthritis, but it was the real deal. I could hear the history of the music with every chord and phrase. I started crying right there at my little table in this little café where she played. I was probably in my early thirties, and I was mesmerized by this and went up to her and told her how much it meant to me, that I'd gotten to hear her in person. That ability to connect immediately to the heart is what we're all trying to do. And so many people can't do it, especially now. It seems like it's harder now because everything's so glib, ironic, commercial...

RS: And fast.

JC: The opposite of what you were saying about Frank Sinatra, where he caresses the notes and listens, which, for an actor, is everything. You feel some actors aren't even listening to what they're saying.

RS: Exactly.

JC: Did you want to be a musician growing up?

RS: No, I never felt that I was musically talented. Both my mother and father sang. My mother had a lovely alto voice, and she could harmonize anything. And I grew up listening to her singing every popular song of the '30s and '40s while she ironed. She sang the words, and she knew them all. So there was always the sound of her singing. I never had that natural ability to sing. And I was always shy about that. My wife, Brenda, has a beautiful voice, and it's one of the reasons I married her. I complain a lot that she doesn't sing enough.

JC: Did you take piano lessons or anything like that?

RS: No. No. It wasn't encouraged in my family. It never even occurred to me to say, "I would like guitar lessons," or anything like that.

JC: And acting was something you took off on your own.

RS: My mother was from the Irish section of New York, and my father was from the German section. And when they went to get married, my mother's priest refused to marry her to my father, a German Protestant. So they took their witnesses and they drove to Manhattan, and they got married in a little church, St. Malachy's, which is the Actors' Chapel on West 49th Street. That's my only connection.

JC: That's a wonderful story! Do you still go out and hear music?

RS: Not much. I live out here in Sag Harbor, but I do go to jazz concerts now and then and listen to this station. *And* I listen to you!

JC: *[Laughs] Thank you! Do you still listen to any country and western?*

RS: Oh, yes. Hank Williams can still tear me up.

JC: *And those great song titles. You told me a song title you liked.*

RS: My favorite is "It Drives Me Crazy, But It Keeps Me from Going Insane."

JC: *My favorite is "When the Wrong One Loves You Right."*

RS: Oh *yeah!* Great!

JC: *A friend of yours, Blythe Danner, is a big Bill Evans fans. Are you?*

RS: Evans is genius.

JC: *When you said sweet but melancholy...*

RS: Yes, genius.

JC: *How about Tony?*

RS: Tony Bennett is wonderful. Still a wonderful singer. And I remember when he was a laughingstock. My friends who thought they knew all about music used to laugh at Tony Bennett.

JC: *Why was that?*

RS: Because he was this kind of lowbrow, a nightclub singer. He had no particular appeal, seemed like a third-rate Frank Sinatra, but then he developed as an artist and he began to take his time and he began to sing jazz, sing more songs where he was the actor and not just the singer. He'd learned a lot from Frank, and he learned a lot from all the other singers around him, and now he has his own inimitable style.

JC: It's interesting, coming into his own happened relatively late.

RS: I watched that whole career. I watched him make the turnaround. And now you say Tony Bennett, you go, "Oh, yeah. Tony Bennett, big time, big time."

And you know what? I heard Plácido Domingo being interviewed once on NPR, and they asked him who his favorite singer was. My thought was he was gonna name some opera guy from Hungary or something, but he said Frank Sinatra. And the interviewer said, "Well, why do you like Frank?" And Domingo said, "Because he has a remarkable ability. When he sings, he ends a phrase, but it doesn't really end, the silence continues. He continues in the silence." That is very strange, but that's what he hears when he listens to Sinatra. He hears that emotion continue.

JC: That's what you'd strive for as an actor.

RS: Yes, yes!

JC: Exactly. Otherwise, it would just be line readings.

RS: Yes. It's that he hits the emotional notes that just lay in the air. And that's what Domingo loved about Sinatra. It's like when they asked Baryshnikov who his favorite dancer was, he said, "Fred Astaire." And the interviewer said, "You'd rather dance like Fred Astaire than the way you dance?" He said, "Of course. And so would every dancer I've ever met. They all wish they could dance like Fred Astaire." Using space and silence, even in dance.

I never went to any acting classes per se, but I went to some late-night scene study classes that Harold Clurman used to have in the Stella Adler studio. And I remember one night, Harold was talking about times on the stage when you do nothing, when you are in repose. I don't know if that's the correct word, but there are times in your life when you don't move, and you don't say anything; you just listen. You make a special kind of music when you just listen; you provide a space for the other music to come through. Also, we don't move and act all the time. Sometimes we're just still.

Sometimes I've gone to the theater and watched friends of mine act, and I mean, they're really close friends that I can go backstage and they'll ask me what I think about their performance and I can really intelligently say how I was affected by it. I'll say, "What does this character look like when he's in repose, when he's not doing anything? I think you need a few more of those." And Harold would say, "You don't have to act all the time. There are times when you don't act, you don't have an inclination to *do*. You have an inclination to stop and listen." And that's important. They talk about actors who know how to listen because they know that listening is part of the music of life.

JC: That's got to be very difficult.

RS: It's hard because as a young actor you want to be active. You want to be acting. You've got to have your intention and you've got to do that, *do*. But sometimes you don't "do." You just stop.

JC: Ginger Rogers was great at listening.

RS: She listened like crazy. She allowed everything that was being said to register on her face and she did nothing. She'd just let it all come into her. She was a gem.

JC: That seems like it would be very difficult, to have someone sing a tune to you.

RS: Well, in motion picture acting, that's the other half of your performance, how you react to what's being said or done. That's the other half of the performance. You gotta be able to listen and have the audience see what you're thinking. They'll see if you really listen. Little things happen to your face, and they know you're hearing it.

JC: What are you listening to now?

RS: If I feel a little despondent or if I feel a little depressed or I don't like the way things are going and I perhaps am not too pleased with myself, I can take any of these pieces of music and put them on in the living room and take my shoes and socks off and just dance for an hour alone.

JC: That's wonderful.

RS: And it's very refreshing and it gets me out of everything. It's my kind of yoga.

JC: That's so lovely. I feel sorry for people who aren't music fans. They don't understand that they can get this kind of joy from it. I'm so glad we finally did this, Roy.

RS: I was scared to death, but I'm glad I came.

Diane Schurr

(b. 1953)

Two-time Grammy Award-winning jazz vocalist/pianist.
In 2000 was awarded the Helen Keller Achievement Award
by the American Foundation for the Blind.

Interviewed in 2017

Diane Schurr carries on the tradition of two powerhouse singers who inspired her, Sarah Vaughan and Dinah Washington. She is a bundle of enthusiasm and creative energy and brought that spirit to a guest appearance on *Sesame Street,* where she explained to Elmo how a blind person can learn to use other senses to adapt in the world.

I talked to Diane after the release of her CD tribute to two of her other biggest inspirations, Stan Getz and Frank Sinatra. Her CD, *I Remember You: With Love to Stan and Frank,* commemorates the support—musical and otherwise—that she has gotten from both of these towering figures.

JC: *We both have a soft spot for George Shearing.*

DS: Well, George and I met when I was about eleven when mama took me to the Edgewater Inn in downtown Seattle, Washington. It was really a thrill to be able to meet George and of course his guide dog, Lee, who was obediently under the piano bench. I auditioned for George. I did "Portrait of Jenny" and some other things. He talked to me about Braille music, which he had used, of course. Most of it was classical music which I studied when I was a little girl. He suggested that I keep doing the Braille music and I did for a while, but then I just kind of eased out and continued to play by ear because that's how I'm most comfortable.

JC: So many people on this show have told me that they started out reading music, then they just went by ear.

DS: Yeah. And with Braille music, you can't just glance at it. You have to read it with one hand or just read it and memorize what you read. For instance, when I do a recording, especially if it's relatively new material, the lyrics are in Braille, so I can just fly across the pages with my fingers while I'm doing my deal, so it's kinda cool.

JC: I love your latest CD, I Remember You: With Love to Stan and Frank, and the fact that you celebrate two big inspirations who are men, Stan Getz and Frank Sinatra. Women singers usually celebrate other women singers.

DS: I remember when I was a little kid listening to Stan on "The Girl from Ipanema," which as you know was a big smash. So that was a big influence when I was a girl. With Frank Sinatra, one of my favorite songs was "Young at Heart." I remember listening to that when Mama was feeding me oatmeal and chicken noodle soup when I was two or three years old, in my highchair. My memory goes that far back.

JC: Music really does connect with memory. I read that the place in the brain where we register music is right next to where we register smell, and they can both take us instantly to memories.

DS: It's so interesting that you mention that because I used to go to the Washington State School for the Blind, and whenever I'd get sick, I'd have to go upstairs to the infirmary, and the smell that pervaded the infirmary was Merthiolate. And I would hear music like "A Summer Place" by Percy Faith. It all connects in a memory. I know that's a weird analogy, but what you just told me, it's just kinda like, "Wow! I get it." You know what I'm saying?

JC: Of course. And I read that when you were at that school, they played Dinah Washington in the halls. I wish my school had been that hip! My school years would have been a lot more fun if I'd been listening to Dinah Washington between classes.

DS: Mama and Daddy would send me some of my favorite things, Dinah Washington's albums, *Unforgettable* and *What a Difference a Day Makes*. They'd send me these things. And of course, back then it was vinyl, and it was just so wonderful to get that big box, to grope inside, and have the smell of the vinyl and the cover.

JC: Ah, the smell!

DS: And everything. And then my house parents would put it on the record player, which was in an office somewhere, and the speaker would be hanging from the ceiling in the playroom. So that was something I really looked forward to. And, of course, *After Hours*, that album by Sarah Vaughan, they also played that, and they played *The Best of Bostic*, Earl Bostic, I mean.

JC: I'm telling you, that's a hip school!

DS: Well, it's just stuff that I really loved, and it really helped to keep me from being so lonely because it was tough. I started going to the school when I was four and a half, and it took me a long time to figure out, "Why do I have to go to this place?" But they didn't have any public schools for people with the kind of disability that I have until I got into the fifth grade, and then I started going to public school.

And I have a funny story behind that! In public school, where the sighted go, to be called on you've got to raise your hand. Well, at the school for the blind, you didn't have to raise your hand because everybody was blind. So when I got to public school, I got in trouble for just shouting out my answers.

JC: That's hilarious!

DS: The teacher said, "No, no, you've got to raise your hand to be called on." I thought, "O.K., this is weird." [Laughs]

JC: *It's crazy that no one prepared you for that. Getting back to the records your parents sent you to play at school, I would think that you'd feel like you knew those singers in a deep, personal way because they were the people who took care of you and were with you at a very lonely time. At least that's what I'm inferring from how you describe those years.*

DS: All I'll say is that it just wasn't easy. I don't think that some of those house parents were specifically trained all that well in dealing with people who had disabilities. That's all I'm gonna say on that subject.

JC: *I love to ask someone with a voice like yours what you hear with a singer like Sarah Vaughan.*

DS: Well, I think she had perfect pitch. She could be like an instrument, just like people like Ella Fitzgerald and so on. Sarah's voice was also like an instrument.

JC: *That's how I feel with you. That's how I felt about Dinah Washington too. Singers who are another instrumentalist, who just happen to be using their voice.*

DS: Although Dinah didn't scat. I've never heard her scat.

JC: *I don't mean it specifically with scatting. I mean that they just sing and do what they want with this instrument that happens to be their voice.*

DS: Exactly. It's almost like overkill with some singers, the way they use their voice. There's a big difference with people like myself, and Sarah, and Dinah and Ella and a couple of others, because we know how to place the note. We're thinking what we want to sing. It's in our minds in a nanosecond, and then we just go for it. And that's what jazz is all about.

JC: *Talk about what's so special about Sinatra. Do you think of him as a jazz singer?*

DS: He's not just limited to jazz. He was a great crossover artist in his day. "Nice 'n Easy" was played on a lot of crossover stations. "That's Life" was played on a lot of crossover stations. Plus, "All the Way." All these tunes were crossover in their day.

JC: I've never thought about it that way. When I hear you—and I can't describe this any other way—I always think "clean singing," and I don't mean that in contrast to some people who have stuff on their voice, which I might like too. But you just have a clean intent, clean execution, and it just feels so good. So with Frank, what did you want to capture with this CD? Because tribute CDs can be tricky.

DS: What you just said is exactly what I wanted to catch with Frank, because he delivered in the same way that I deliver, in a clean, honest, forthright, no BS kind of way. But it's a forthright way of being able to deliver both a melody and a message.

JC: Talk about Alan Broadbent. He's one of my heroes. What was it like working with Alan?

DS: Brilliant pianist. And a really nice guy. And what we did is, we'd get on the phone like once a week and work together on these arrangements of the *I Remember You* tracks, and it was really fun and that's how we did it. He'd play, and I just listened to what he played, and we'd talk about it, and that was that. We'd spend about an hour and do a couple of the things, and then the next week we'd do some more.

JC: People always say to me, "Oh, I envy your piano playing" and I know they say the same thing to you: "I wish I had a voice like that." But what I think is one of the great blessings of a creative life is that we can work through things in our life through our work. We also relate to everything in a different way and connect with people in a different way.

DS: I think so. I really do. We have a gift of being able to just, whatever we're going through, be able to communicate that, whereas a lot of people find it a little bit more difficult.

JC: *I hope that people can learn from these conversations and maybe be a little more open to that kind of thought, because even just coming in here today, I feel as if you and I have known each other forever. Now I have known your music forever, so that helps. But we had an immediate connection.*

DS: I agree.

JC: *And who has influenced your piano playing?*

DS: Well, we were talking about George Shearing. He was a big influence. Peter Nero was a big influence. I actually have a recording done in 1963 called *Frankie Carle, Floyd Cramer, Peter Nero - 3 Great Pianos*. All selections from each of these players. Incredible stuff.

JC: *And singers who play piano. I realized recently that many of my favorite singers were piano players.*

DS: Dinah Washington was a piano player. Sarah Vaughan was a piano player.

JC: *And Ella played harmonica. Maybe Billie Holiday didn't play an instrument. I don't know. But so many of them that we're talking about played piano. And what do you think that brings to it? Think about the young singers who are out there listening, who think, "I don't need to learn piano." Tell them why they should.*

DS: Piano or guitar or whatever instrument a person chooses to play just makes everything a little bit more precise. Being able to do chords underneath, to embellish what you're already doing with the voice, is a really cool thing to do. Like, I listened to a lot to George Benson in my younger years, with his scatting, along with the guitar and everything, and I started doing some of that kind of stuff myself. It's really fun.

JC: *What do you tell musicians in your master classes? Give me a little mini master class.*

DS: One of the things I try to impart to the students at any of these colleges is that no matter what's going down in the world, don't give up on your dreams.

JC: Well, enough people are going to tell them the opposite.

DS: It's really a travesty. I don't think that's right. It's kind of like being spiritually wounded.

JC: They'll find out soon enough if they can't continue. People project their own fears onto others and tell young people not to pursue their dreams. How dare they?

DS: I think you're absolutely right about that. I don't like the word *should* anyway. I think it implies inadequacy. Like it says, in recovery programs, twelve-step programs, whatever. "Don't *should* on yourself."

JC: [Laughs] Talk about the change in the recording industry. It's very different now from when we came up.

DS: I miss going into Tower Records and being able to even buy my own product! I used to do that on the day that it was released. When I lived in Orange County, California, we'd go into Tower and look for it and make sure they had it on the shelf. There was this wonderful guy named Bruce, and we'd play the record—you know, in the back of the store—and crank it up so the whole store could hear it. It was just a blast.

JC: That's fantastic! I'll tell you a comparable story. Here in Manhattan, there used to be a Tower Records on Fourth Street and Broadway in the Village.

DS: I know. I've been there.

JC: My office was right around the corner, and my apartment was on Broadway, so I'd walk south, then turn left on Fourth to go over to Lafayette to my office, so I passed Tower Records every day. I would go in just to look at my CDs because I was so thrilled they were on the shelf. I was right there by Benny Carter because they were alphabetized, so that was also nice, being next to Benny. If I went late in the day, I'd have to leaf through the CDs to find mine, but if I went in the morning, there would be a row of my CDs—about ten of them—displayed across the top above all the other CDs and moved to the front of the row, in front of CDs that should have been in front of mine. I thought, "Somebody at Tower loves me," but I found out later that a number of my friends who lived in the neighborhood were going to Tower Records early in the day and pulling out my CDs and putting them in front.

DS: Well, God bless them for doing that. That's the generation we were in. That's what's so fabulous about being able to talk about all this with you!

Allen
Toussaint

(1938–2015)

Award-winning New Orleans musician and record producer
in multiple genres from R&B and soul to funk and blues.

Interviewed in 2007

Allen Toussaint worked in nearly every area of the music business and brought
his wide-ranging tastes to every project he undertook. He was inducted into
the Rock & Roll Hall of Fame in 1998, and in 2013 he was awarded the
National Medal of Arts by President Obama.

Toussaint felt his biggest inspiration was his beloved New Orleans,
and although this Big Easy native was temporarily living in New York City
when we spoke, because of the devastation wrought by Hurricane Katrina,
he made it clear that New Orleans was always in his heart and influenced
everything he did.

Allen and I met in Laguna Beach, California, at an annual dinner
that Steinway hosts for its international piano dealers where he was to
perform. When I found out he would be the surprise pianist for the event,
I arranged to interview him that same evening. Allen was fascinated by my
interest in stride piano, like many of the older jazz musicians I've met over
the years, so I made a point of playing for him before our interview. This
gave us an immediate connection.

JC: What was your first introduction to jazz?

AT: My brother had introduced me to Dave Brubeck's quartet with Paul Desmond. Desmond's solos were just so melodic and so wonderful. It all seemed like it had been done before, even though a lot of it was improvised. It was so pure and organized, I couldn't help but just love that. It was so easy on a young ear.

My brother was a guitarist. However, he tricked himself out of a whole career because he liked all of the bad cats out there so much that he thought he just wasn't worthy. Everyone has their own signature, and he has a beautiful signature. But he had so much respect for everyone out there, he was just a guy who would play at home. But he still has a very sweet touch, and he knows enough to play his own signature. He just doesn't think it's enough for the world. I understand that. Don't agree, but I understand it.

JC: Growing up in New Orleans, I think most people would think you were listening to jazz from day one. That's what people who don't live in New Orleans think. What were you listening to as a child?

AT: Well, early on I heard boogie-woogie, like "Pinetop Boogie" and also Albert Ammons. The early hillbilly music was very soulful as far as I was concerned. I hadn't learned that there were specialists. I thought whoever played piano played everything that a piano played. So anything I heard, I thought everyone knew about it except me, whether it was blues, hillbilly, or jazz.

I remember my mother buying an Emerson record player. And during those days they used to give you some lagniappe when you bought something. Like if it was a record player, they'd give you two albums. So we got two albums. One of them was what we'd now call easy listening music, and the other was light classical. Well, not as light as light can be, but classical. And I remember one of them had Grieg's "Piano Concerto in A Minor" on it.

I had this old upright, of course, that they had sent to my house for my sister to play. She didn't wind up playing because they started her out with a teacher who smacked her hands when she made a mistake, so she immediately hated the teacher and the piano.

I loved the piano because I guess I didn't have a teacher that early. Of course, this piano was old, and a half step out of tune, and not totally in tune with itself. But I remember hearing Grieg's "Piano Concerto in A Minor" and I figured, well, I have to learn this because piano players are playing this—all except me. It hadn't dawned on me that it was Grieg's "Piano Concerto in A Minor." I just knew it was this classical music. So I had to play in B-flat minor to make it sound like A minor on the piano, since it was a half-step off. So I learned Grieg's "Piano Concerto in A Minor" off this record in B flat minor. A most humbled version, as I got to know later.

But I did the best I could with it. It's quite an extensive piece. It's not a verse and chorus and out. It's a whole piece with movements and all. And I must say that I did learn the whole piece by ear and in B-flat minor. And I had a good time with it. I also listened to Paul Weston's orchestra playing stuff, and I learned other pieces. Also, Benny Goodman's "Love Walked In." There was also this trombone duet. All from those two albums that my mother got with the Emerson record player, which sent me off to another world of learning these pieces.

Then I began to hear other pieces in categories like that. So it was no longer just boogie-woogies or just "Nola" and "Doll Dance." My mother liked things like "Nola" and "Doll Dance" and "Moonlight Serenade." When company would come, she'd have me come play "Nola," play "Doll Dance." She made sure I heard those pieces.

So those are some of the things that I went through coming along. It was much later that I heard pianists like Art Tatum, which was a shocking situation.

I had met the sounds of Professor Longhair, which I consider the strongest influence in my whole life, as far as people on record playing the piano goes. I had been playing the boogie-woogies and the shuffles as I heard them on radio and on some records.

Then I heard Professor Longhair and his stuff wasn't like any of the things I had heard. I learned everything I could and waited for the next thing that would come out on record. One of the other kids would hear about it and he'd say, "You know there's another Professor Longhair record out," and we'd wait for it to come on the radio as many times as we could, then find it at a record shop. Because things weren't nearly as easy to get to as they are now. And I didn't have even the money to get the records back then. Many times, you'd wait until you heard it on the radio to learn another part.

But when I heard Professor Longhair, that really stomped on my life, the extra liberties he would take with the form. Even though the old blues guitar players took those extra liberties too, like rather than things having to be four bars, eight bars, etc., they'd change when it got ready, when they felt like. It didn't follow the regular form. Professor Longhair did that as a pianist, so that was very good for me to hear. It didn't have to stop when it come down and make the dominant seven. It didn't have to be just *that bar* to the four; he would play an extra one if he wanted to. I just thought that was absolutely wonderful.

JC: To have that kind of freedom?

AT: I didn't know that was freedom. I didn't call it anything but Professor Longhair. And I didn't apply it to anything else I played. I just figured this was Professor Longhair music. I hadn't developed any of my own philosophies about anything.

There was a gentleman named Ernest Penn who came through my life when I was about twelve. He used to be a banjo player during the jitney days in New Orleans. He came from the era that if you played a string instrument, you played everything that had a string on it. So he played banjo, mandolin, violin, bass, and piano. He came from a whole group of musicians for whom that's how they felt about it. He didn't feel it was unique that he did that. Most of those guys who played a string instrument thought that if you didn't play other ones, "well, you not ready to be here tonight."

By the time I met him, his gigging days were over, he had no instrument, and he'd come to live out his days with his old mother and aunt, or his aunt and grandmother. They lived across the street in College Court where I lived. He was a master pianist. But he was an outcast from wherever he had been. Something in his life had gone dreadfully wrong.

One day he heard me playing piano in my house, and when I came outside, he said to me, "You know, I'm a string man, and I play everything with a string on it, and I was a master banjo player." He was a very spicy man and had no teeth in the top of his mouth and very few at the bottom. My parents hated him. But anyway, when he told me that, I invited him in to play. He began to play what I call butterfly piano, where the hands float over the keys like a butterfly. The piano suddenly got to be—this piano that had been sitting in the house all that time—suddenly got too big for the room as he sat there and played. He was just trilling with the right hand and was happy and vibrant and very definite. I just fell in love with that style of playing.

Again, my parents, my mother especially, didn't want him around because he smelled of very strong alcohol all the time. He was a very spicy little man who talked fast and plenty. He was annoying to everyone, but I would wait till he'd wake up every morning and bring him over to the house to play and show me some of this butterfly piano and these old songs. He would play things like "High Society," and when it comes time for the clarinet solo, he played that clarinet solo note for note on the keyboard while he was going, just happy and looking around.

He was very patient with me with this kind of music because there was so much going on. He would have to slow it down for me because I wanted as much of this as I could get. He would slow it down for me to see what it was. Anyway, he added tenths into my left hand. He added tenths into my whole life! I will always be grateful for that. However, when it's time to think of him, I think of him right in that form and nowhere before or after because he was so very, very complete. He came also from the philosophy: *Don't show anybody your stuff because they'll take it, and they won't let anyone know it was yours.*

JC: *But he showed you.*

AT: Of course! How about that? He was the greatest influence I had as a human being sitting next to me at the piano.

Professor Longhair was my influence on record because I didn't meet Professor until much later, as an upper teenager, which was wonderful. And I had him down so pat it was like he was meeting himself.

JC: *What was his reaction when he heard you play?*

AT: Well, he had known about me because people had been telling him about me from time to time because I became a session musician around fifteen and a half. And he'd hear me being Professor Longhair on a record sometimes. Or *trying* to be Professor Longhair, because it's always—don't care how close you think you are—when the real person sits and plays it, it's different. You say to yourself, "Oh, yes. Whatever I *thought* I was doing this is really it." Even Fats Domino with his triplets. Sounds so simple and everyone can do that. But when he sits and plays, it's just, "Oh, yes, that's how it goes."

JC: *I always think a great example of that is Basie because he can play that one note and somehow if you play that one note and try to sound like him, you don't. It's not complicated, but it's so special and so specific, the way he got that special feel and where he placed that one note. No one sounds like him.*

And I like you describing that butterfly piano. I've never heard that phrase before. I mean, I'm here watching you gesticulate and illustrate what you mean, and that's a wonderful term for it, sort of stride piano with both hands and with great delicacy.

AT: Of course, some of it is chunk-a-chunk, but the other was butterfly, and he was just a master at it. He played with such bravado and such wonderment. And it was just he and I sitting there. When he'd play, he'd get to the last tune, "Duh duh, duh, duh, *bump!*" and when he'd do that, he'd jump up and say, "Hot de mighty, Sam!" Just the two of us there. In fact, he would frighten me sometimes when he would jump up from the piano when he'd get through playing.

JC: It's such a gift when you get next to someone who's that enthusiastic about teaching. It really takes off like a rocket for a young person to get to be that close to an inspired soul. A lot of piano teachers are present, but they're kind of bored and just get through the lesson with no enthusiasm or real engagement. What you had was really special.

Now I want to ask you about living in New York. How has being here changed your focus on music? You identify with New Orleans so much. It's so much a part of who you are. And people who know New Orleans identify it with you. Has there been anything about living in New York that's inspired you, that's made you think in a different way? I know it must be terribly sad with all the different things that have happened with Katrina, but have there been some aspects of living in New York that surprised you, that influenced your music? Have any projects come out of this?

AT: I don't know what words I'd use, but it's very exciting living in New York for a while. I've been coming here since I was five, so I've seen the skyline. But an extended period, yes, this is the longest I've ever been away from New Orleans at one time. I still consider this just an extended visit.

Being in New York hasn't changed my life, but it's certainly inspiring where I am, because wherever I am, I figure that there's so much New Orleans in me I don't have to worry about carrying it. I can't leave it anywhere. It's like carrying my hand or my elbow, that all comes with me. So I'm pretty much rooted in New Orleans. Wherever I am, the largest part of me is New Orleans there with me. I'm being inspired from a New Orleans perspective about everything I see. I'm seeing it from the eyes of New Orleans. That's not confusing to me. I eat it up.

Like, I don't go to New York looking for New Orleans cuisine. I'm not looking for the New Orleans restaurant in New York. I don't need to. I want a New York restaurant in New York, and I want a French restaurant in France.

We're all reflections of whatever we take in. I wouldn't want to miss New York making an effort to think on New Orleans. It's already me. I assume that that'll always be there, even if I was trying to do something else

And I must say, the buzz in New York is buzzing constantly. I make notes wherever I am and have all my life. And I've been doing this since I was a little boy, writing on little scraps of paper or pulling off the side of the road to write something down. It's not just the plot of a tune but where you were when you saw it in your head and how you felt when you saw it.

I am highly inspired by New York since it's so massive. How many windows in New York? And how much life is going on in all of those windows? And then you disappear in a hole in the ground. These two parallel universes operate. It's just amazing how massive it is and that it works. And the yellow streak, I mean metaphorically, the taxicab. To stand on the corner and just don't look at anything in particular, just take that in and see how that feels and what it means because it's always moving. I wouldn't want to miss any of that.

It's extremely inspiring to be any place, but especially New York because of that movement. The very best is expected. And the very best, whoever fattens the livestock, takes it there. When they give you a drink with a straw, it may have half of the straw taken off and they've twisted the little top to make it pretty. Put a little straw on top there. Just for you to take that off and throw it away. That's amazing.

JC: I'm constantly aware of the fabulous mix of cultures when I visit New Orleans and all the different kinds of music, and I would fantasize that someone who grew up in New Orleans would be very open to mixing things up. Many people I talk to immediately want to compartmentalize. They'll say, "It's that kind of music or it's that kind of art or it's this." I would think someone from New Orleans would be open to thinking, "Oh, it's a little bit of this, it's a little bit of that." It's the whole gumbo metaphor. I would think you're well suited to absorb all of these different aspects of New York and be very open to what would result. You're shaking your head yes.

AT: I'm sorry about that. I forgot we're on radio. I'm involved in you right now, Judy.

JC: Thank you! How has your early jazz experience or boogie influenced your work?

AT: Well, for one thing, my mother liked this stuff like "Nola" and "Doll Dance" and the likes. And on Sundays I heard operas. Let me say we were poor as Job's turkey, but my mother, for some reason, thought she was highfalutin. I don't know what made her feel that way. But I would hear operas, and I remember loving operas even though I had no ambition to be going in that direction. I remember hearing this on Sunday evenings, and I began to associate Sunday evenings with these beautiful performances. I think I liked that as much as I liked the boogie-woogies.

But I think that my music, even though I'm pretty much noted for a lot of funk because New Orleans is very funky and very jazzy, a lot of it is not extreme or funk from the gutbucket. But I think by being so diversified in my tastes coming up, I think without being conscious of it, all of that's mixed in there in some sort of way. I've never thought of it as a problem because in producing various artists—that's been my forte, and most of my life has been spent in the studio producing artists—it wasn't like they came to me for a certain thing or a certain kind of funk.

Whenever they came, it was a fresh slate. It wasn't because of what they heard me do with Lee Dorsey and they wanted *that*. Whether that's a curse or a blessing I don't know. But I'm glad that so many different artists have come to me. The marriages that I've had with them caused me to get some vibes out, get many different colors that wouldn't have been released if I would've been just polarized in one direction.

JC: *Talk about this CD,* The Jazzity Project.

AT: It's the only one of its kind that I've made. *The Jazzity Project.* I call it "Jazzity." It's not a cop out, but it's calling it something not quite jazz but "Jazzity." And if I can coin that phrase in this case, it's just that I have ultra respect for jazz musicians who've paid the jazz dues. And of course, it's hard to say what you call jazz and what you don't call jazz.

I remember my father telling me once, if a person spells their name B-O-X and pronounces it "John," they have a right to do it. So, whatever a guy calls his own music, if he wants to do that, he has a right to do that. But I have so much respect for jazz musicians. I think it takes the same kind of devotion as the highest form of any music to do it well and to get the avenues to express yourself because we all really have something to say. Some of us just don't have the streets and avenues. And for some of us, the streets are so bumpy because of our chops development. But you can hear who really has something to say. Well, jazz musicians seem to not settle for less than what is required to say what they have to say.

JC: *That's nicely put. I like that.*

AT: And that's a whole life. I want to respect the jazz world enough to not say that out of all your life you can come along now and you're playing jazz. No, I'm playing "Jazzity."

I feel so strongly about good jazz that I felt I didn't have a right to be in that number at the time. I don't feel badly or sorry about it. That's quite all right with me. It's like I told myself, "Know your place, son."

I do think it's a wonderful thing, in the ladder of evolution, how a person perceives things, and when they bring it to you with their perspective. Any kind of way someone hears and moves the music forward, I think that changes things and moves to the next step in evolution. Even some people who think they're sounding just like Lou Rawls and you love the way they sound, but you didn't know they thought that. That's what I mean by everyone hearing differently. They don't sound anything like Lou Rawls to you, but they're thinking they're sounding just like him. And you hear a whole new thing that sends you off to do something great that he and Lou Rawls never thought about.

JC: That leads me to a very interesting thought. As a producer, if someone comes in and wants you to help them do a Lou Rawls thing, do you point out to them that they don't sound like Lou Rawls? Or do you let them sound just like Lou Rawls in their head because that's what's inspiring them?

AT: Now, if a person told me they wanted to do a Lou Rawls thing, I would see what that means to me in terms of their style and how I would produce it. I wouldn't imagine that Lou Rawls is here and make his music. I'd just hope that whatever I did—and had a good time doing—would be all right.

JC: So that's really the focus: How are we going to have a good time and get the best result.

AT: Of course, that may cost you sometimes, but it may be worth it. I must say this booking agent, Katrina, did a lot of things by booking me out of town, here and there, and connecting me up with other collaborations.

And one of the most important collaborations in my whole lifetime is with Elvis Costello because he is so self-contained, for one thing. And he is such a prolific writer, thinker, liver, mover, everything. He's a hands-on guy, and he does his homework immediately. Every part of him is to the moment. There's nothing left home under a drawer. So, to be working with someone like that was, and is, really outstanding. And I say "is" because we've toured earlier on and we're going to do it again at some point in the near future, so I like to speak in the present tense.

JC: *And you're enjoying the touring, I can tell. Your whole face lights up when you think of it.*

AT: It's a different thing because my life is spent with the red light—"You ready in there? You ready to roll it? OK, take two, take three, whatever." Even "tune the guitar!" When you're gigging, which I haven't done a whole lot in my life, with everything right there in front of you, it's instant gratification, or instant whatever you gonna get. But instant gratification is the meat of the matter. So you really find out a lot. It's about human beings in front of you. There they are. And here *we* are!

Neil deGrasse Tyson

(b. 1958)

Astrophysicist, author, science evangelist.

Interviewed in 2006

My guests for *Jazz Inspired* are usually creative people I've admired for years whom I discover or know are jazz fans. In contrast, I knew nothing about Neil deGrasse Tyson when we met.

For years I played in a softball game in Sag Harbor, NY where I live, and was left fielder a few times in the celebrated "Artists and Writers Game" in East Hampton. I decided that I wanted a game that was less about celebrity and more about sport, so in the late 1980s I started my own Sunday game. My game had its smattering of celebrities, but the lineup was mainly comprised of local folk from various professions whose work we seldom discussed. I was often the only woman in the game but occasionally, one or two other brave women would drop by. Trash talk and maximizing our meager skills was the focus. *"YOU RUN LIKE A TURTLE, CARMICHAEL!"* You get the picture.

One Sunday morning, a tall, handsome man wearing a spectacularly colorful Hawaiian shirt ambled onto the field. The newcomer said very little, and no one claimed him as a friend, so he remained a bit of a mystery, especially with that shirt. I haven't seen somewhere wear a Hawaiian shirt with such élan since I left California.

I make it a point never to ask people what they do for a living, since almost every other New Yorker I know does just that. This time, however, I couldn't resist. As Neil and I set out toward the parking lot after the game, discussing the mighty battle we'd just endured on the field, I said,

"I usually don't do this, but something inspires me to ask what you do for a living."

"I'm an astrophysicist," he replied.

"*Really?* I *love* astrophysics! My father got me into it when I was a kid. Please tell me you're a jazz fan. I've been dying to get a scientist on a radio show I have on NPR where I talk with creative people about jazz and how it inspires them. I'd love to discuss the connection of math, science, and music. Please tell me you're a jazz fan?" I'm afraid I gushed.

"I'm big into blues," he acknowledged.

"Good enough! Can you give me your number?"

"Google me, you'll find me," said the man who, at that time, had more than one million Twitter followers, had appeared frequently on *The Colbert Report, The Big Bang Theory* and other shows and was recognizable, apparently, to everyone but me.

This very busy man gave me loads of time when we finally met up a few months later at his office at the Hayden Planetarium in Manhattan.

JC: *Talk about the connection between music, math, and science.*

NDT: There's a lot written on that subject. Perennially, there are people who explore the universe looking for the music of the spheres. Some of that I think is a little overwrought. The universe has its own agendas, and it doesn't necessarily include music. I think what's more fascinating is the number of scientists who have a deep, long, and significant interest in music, either as performers or as very serious listeners. By far the largest collection of classical music I've ever seen under one roof—that was not a radio station—was a colleague of mine who had an entire room devoted just to his albums, with thousands and thousands and thousands of them. I asked, "How long will it take you to listen to all of these?" He said once every ten years he listens to it all, and it takes him about a year or so just to remember everything that is there.

This was an astrophysicist. You wouldn't have guessed that. So perhaps there's some overlap between that which stimulates the mind when you think about music and that which stimulates the mind when you're thinking about the frontier of cosmic discovery.

JC: I know lots of medical doctors who are big into music. They're always coming up and telling me that they were going to be a career musician or that they made their way through medical school playing gigs. Do you play yourself?

NDT: No, I don't, not well. [Laughs] So, the answer is no, a flat-out no. I wish I were good at it. At least then I would sort of entertain myself with it and not always have to listen to other performers. But other performers are professionals at it. And for ninety-nine cents or a few dollars you get to hear them. I'd rather listen to them than my poor attempts to imitate them.

JC: You're extremely passionate about music. When we first met and began talking about music, you lit up. Did you grow up in a musical household or were you drawn to music on your own?

NDT: My parents always had music of all kinds on in the background. It was jazz and classical and sort of pop singers of the time or at least singers from their generation. That would have been Sinatra and Harry Belafonte, folks like that.

There's this gap between that music and my coming into my own style of what I like. Eventually I returned to what they liked. So I find myself listening to all the tunes that they'd played while I was growing up between age zero and twelve. Now it's come full circle. I can claim their generation of music. My parents are now pushing eighty. Back when they were in their social prime, when they were in their teens or twenties, I now claim a lot of that music as part of the portfolio that I carry around on my computer and listen to.

JC: Do they feel vindicated?

NDT: Definitely. They say, "Oh, he's finally coming around." It's funny, I'll just learn a fresh tune that's an old standard and if they hear it, they'll just start humming along. Plus, they know the words. I used to think they were just making it all up.

JC: You're a big blues fan. I haven't had a lot of people talk about blues on this show. They've scratched the surface of blues but you're heavy into it.

NDT: Well, heavy not in terms of how much blues I own but in terms of simply its effect on me when I hear it on the radio or when I play it on my own system. If I'm driving a car and stumble on a radio station that's playing the blues, particularly the kind of blues where you're feeling the pain of the person singing, I've just got to pull over into the right lane and go real slow. Or maybe pull off the road entirely and listen to the entire song because it's so emotionally wrought with pain that you can't do anything but commiserate with that pain. For me, that's what music *should* do. It should take your emotions to places that maybe you can't get to yourself or you're already there and you seek a resonance with the music.

I rate myself as a pretty happy guy, so why would I even like the blues? It's because it's a deep reminder that not all the world is sunshine and blue skies. Without that reminder, you lead a deluded life, a completely misrepresentative understanding of how most people in the world live.

JC: It can also remind you how far you've come. Maybe you've had your moments that weren't so happy. It sort of puts you back in that spot, and then you think, "I remember what that was like."

NDT: Definitely. As is true with most music, you're transported either to a moment when you first heard the song or at a time when some event in your life was most resonant with the themes or the emotions of that which is played.

Let me put it this way: When you do science, there's emotion when you make a discovery, when you're hot on the trail of some new idea about how the world works. But for the most part, there's a lot of bookkeeping to make sure your data is sound and you're not making mistakes.

So there's a lot of science that thrives only because it is done *without* passion, without emotion. Because emotion is one of the strongest forces that interferes with your ability to evaluate and understand and interpret data. That's why the stereotype of most scientists is that they're dispassionate. It's a fundamental part of so much of what has to happen for a person to be a good scientist.

So there are times when I'm doing that. And then when I'm done or I'm ready to take a break, I've got to reach out and feel what it is to be alive again. Nothing does that for me like the blues.

JC: I'm struck by the similarity of jazz and what you do. You talked about collecting data, having all of the structure there, all of the knowledge. Then if you're really working towards discovering something, you have to have all of that in place, then completely let your emotions go, or your sensitivity, to create something or be open to what you're trying to discover. This is definitely what happens when you're playing jazz.

NDT: That's a perceptive point. Of course, the notes are there for the taking. How many notes are there? Not that many. Yet not everyone can put them together into music. And there's a lot of data out there, and not everyone can put it together into an actual acute understanding of how the world works.

Most of my colleagues, myself included, when we're at observatories—which is becoming a less common thing to do, to take a pilgrimage to the observatory to get your data—nowadays the telescopes are operated by a single telescope operator. When we do get to do this, we plug the business end of the telescope into the computer, and we can be anywhere on earth and be connected to the telescope.

But that pilgrimage is less frequent. One of my great regrets is that there are many fewer trips to mountaintops now. There were times when I'd be living through the night, nocturnally, as astrophysicists will do, because the stars come out at night. One star will come out during the day; it's called the sun. But you don't need a big telescope to see that. Sometimes you get sleepy, and sometimes you need a pickup. Good music will always do it. So we'd always compare the portfolio of music that we'd all bring to the telescope dome. The telescope dome has this acoustic resonance, and no matter how bad your playback device is, the sound comes out much richer because of the geometry of the telescope dome itself. It's just you, the music, and the cosmos.

JC: I always hear music when I look at the stars. I don't know if that's just me being a musician, but it's all a great symphony to me.

NDT: Well, of course in space there's no air. As the movie *Alien* said, "In space no one can hear you scream."

JC: Are we going to take that path?

NDT: [Laughs] Not only can no one hear you scream no one can hear you play music, either. So the music has to be all in your head as you see the planets undergoing their stately journeys around the sun. Not only do planets move around the sun, the sun, among other stars, moves around the galaxy, and galaxies move in the universe. So it's quite a symphony or one might even call it a ballet, choreographed by the forces of gravity.

JC: That's wonderful. And when you were talking about experiences that you've had and music bringing things like that up, I'm thinking of your story about "Texas Flood" which you told me earlier.

NDT: I spent a few years getting my master's degree at the University of Texas at Austin. So it's my first year there, and then I come home to the Bronx for Christmas vacation. And I turn on the news and they said,

"Heavy rains and severe flooding in Austin, Texas." I run to the TV, and outside my apartment building there are pianos floating down the street. Apparently, this little creek had overflowed, and it took out this entire bank of stores. One of them was this music store, and so these pianos were floating down. I said, "Oh, my God."

The storm eventually subsided, but I thought, "My gosh, this was devastating if you were here." Sure enough, eight months later Stevie Ray Vaughan comes out with an album called *Texas Flood,* and I said, "I feel your pain, Stevie Ray." And it was my first firsthand encounter with something that inspired a blues song, and it just made you that much more connected to the event.

JC: Talk about Buddy Guy.

NDT: Buddy Guy is by far my favorite musical performer. In fact, I heard him in a small club in Austin. I knew nothing about him. He was just at a nearby club that I went to. I was just forever moved by his voice and his command of the guitar. I don't even want to overanalyze it. Let me just simply say that I felt his music. I believe every word that comes out of his mouth when he speaks of pain, even when he speaks of joy contrasting with the pain. One of my favorite lines is his woman had done him wrong and his dog left him or whatever, but it was, "Honey, if I never see you again, that's too soon for me."

JC: That's hard. He even lost the dog!

NDT: Exactly! So blues ought to be that which makes you a part of that experience; otherwise there's no communication going on. It's just Muzak.

JC: I love you talking about the feeling of music because it's something you're always striving for as a musician. At least, I think people are. I know I am. And trying to be more and more honest. We always strive to get to what we're feeling at the moment we're playing. When I play with my trio, it's always interesting to me what audience members say to me about my musicians. I will know how my musicians connected by the emotion the audience picks up from them.

My guitar player, Chris Flory, is a wonderful blues player, and people always come up—because every note is kind of ripped from his heart—and say, "Did he just break up with his sweetheart?" And he's not singing. They get this from his great emotional playing. But that's this blues feel, exactly what you're saying. He connects with these people because there are no histrionics. He just sits there and plays guitar with honest feeling.

NDT: If you're not connecting, then go home, because we're wasting each other's time.

JC: *Absolutely. You've mentioned Miles Davis to me, and you said you loved the space between the notes, which is something I'm very interested in. Talk about that.*

NDT: Before I got into blues and jazz in general, I spoke with a friend of mine in college who was the jazz announcer for the college radio station. And I said, "Give me a list of albums that the jazz aficionados would praise, just so I can start where I need to start, if I'm going to gain an appreciation for this." On the list was Miles Davis's *Kind of Blue*. I played it first, and it was O.K. but I didn't think much of it, and I thought, "Well, I wonder if there's anything more exciting on these other albums."

So I thought, "All right, let me put it on a tape and just play it in the background while I'm cooking dinner. You know, just maybe there's something I'm missing." And then one day I was making eggs or something, and I dropped the spatula because the music had finally penetrated this wall I'd had up that prevented me from understanding or hearing or listening or feeling what was out there, what these performers were trying to tell me. Trying to tell *me*, right? Because he wrote it for *me*. Because when I dropped my spatula, those notes were communicating with *me*. Not only were the notes communicating with me, the space between the notes were communicating with me, particularly in "Flamenco Sketches." I turned off the burner, and I sat down on the couch and I just listened.

The world is not solely a juxtaposition of objects. It's also a juxtaposition of the space between objects. And in some cases, the space matters more than the objects themselves because, of course, you *live* in the space. I found myself living in the space between the notes of "Flamenco Sketches."

JC: People always talk about the acoustics in a hall, but for me, as a performer, I feel the quality of silence that that audience gives me. I play very differently depending on the silence, and I know other musicians do too. I play with the space differently if the quality of silence is really juicy and inviting, because I want those notes to linger in all that space.

NDT: At the risk of overstretching this sentiment, the universe is mostly empty space, punctuated by remarkable expressions of nature, be they exploding stars, colliding galaxies, comet impacts on planet surfaces. The space is the stage, and the objects within the space are the actors. So when I get into a deeply performed jazz piece that takes full advantage of what the silence can do, I'm transported out in space.

JC: That's beautiful. And poetic. You're also a McCoy Tyner fan.

NDT: Well, actually one of his albums, *Manhattan Moods* is a favorite. I grew up in the Bronx, but now I live in Manhattan, so when I moved back to New York I said, "Well, *Manhattan Moods*, I wonder what he's got going there? What is he saying? What does he mean?" So I bought the album, and I just played it and looked out my window while the music was playing. Out my window there's the park, there are lights, there's the street, there's people walking. It is the soul of Manhattan captured in those pieces on that album.

You're transported from the dark, wet, street. It had just rained. It's two in the morning. The hotel light is flashing. The subway rumbles underfoot, and this music is playing. It's the music you'd want here if that scene had a biographer. So any time I want to feel Manhattan again, I just run through *Manhattan Moods*.

JC: Talk about Milt Jackson.

NDT: I first got into Milt Jackson in college, by accident. Somebody was playing one of his Montreux albums, and there was this xylophone or vibraharp, whichever one it was at the moment. I don't even know if they're the same instrument. But it was as though someone took a piano and then dipped it in velvet, dipped it in butter, I don't know . . . [Laughs]

JC: But something good and smooth!

NDT: Yes! I don't know what velvet butter is, but if you could do that to a piano, you'd get the notes that come off his hands when he plays the vibraphone.

JC: You're very interested and active in bringing science to a broader audience, as I want to do with music. How does one do that, in your case, with science but also with music? We're talking about jazz and blues, this music that we're passionate about, that we know people would love if they heard it, not all of it, but certainly some of it. How do we do that?

NDT: I don't have any secretly successful ideas about that. What I do know about the universe, when I try my best to bring it down to earth, one of the tactics that enables it is ensuring that any time I'm in a position to do so, I'll make sure that I have one foot in my scientist's camp and another foot in the camp of the listener. Then I'm a temporary conduit between the frontier of discovery and your living room. What that means for me as a communicator is, I'll put on my communicator's hat and say, "Well, what matters to the people?" So I'll make sure some part of my day I watch the TV shows that are popular, I'll watch the Super Bowl, even though I don't really like football. I'll watch it because everybody else is watching it, and they'll be talking about the commercials or about some play.

Your access to the frontier of popular culture is no less important than the access of the frontier of your field if you want to connect the two together. You have to know where the public is at all times. It's your objective to bring the music to them. So find out what matters to them, and see if you can tap into that. Then they'll come running. They'll beat a path to your door.

JC: Now Neil, I have to mention "Fly Me to the Moon" because that's such a perfect tune for you.

NDT: "Fly Me to the Moon" is one of these jazz standards that I'm sure is on everybody's jazz standards list. But I was just reminded of how the song, written before we landed on the moon, could be so popular and so upbeat and so forward looking, yet still tell about love. It mentions Jupiter, Saturn, and Mars. This is real Astrophysics 101 going on in this jazz standard. I never cease to be impressed by the extent to which cosmic discovery has penetrated pop culture. The true measure of that is not whether it gets talked about in the news, it's whether artists take ownership of it. Because the moment an artist claims it as his or her own, it's part of your culture.

JC: You should be playing that song here as we walk into the Hayden Planetarium, you know like the Basie band or something. Can't you see that? This is my suggestion.

[Laughter]

JC: You're laughing—I'm serious here!! Well, I can tell that this suggestion is just not going to be taken seriously.

NDT: I'll consider it.

JC: This meeting is here in your office, so I want to at least know that my suggestion is being considered.

NDT: It's considered. [Laughs]

JC: Yeah, yeah, then ignored, obviously. I'm looking forward to walking in next time I'm here and hearing "Fly Me to the Moon" blaring over the speakers. Do I seem too aggressive in lobbying for this? You're laughing, but you know this is a good idea, Neil, you just don't want to admit it!

Loudon Wainwright III

(b. 1946)

Singer-songwriter, humorist and actor.

Interviewed in 2020

Loudon Wainwright III is a witty, engaging storyteller, whether acting or in his main gig as a singer/songwriter. The *New York Times* critic, Stephen Holden, says, "Wainwright wrings more human truth out of his contradictions than any other songwriter of his generation."

Loudon enjoyed setting his songwriting aside to celebrate his favorites from the Great American Songbook on his new release, *I'd Rather Lead a Band,* an upbeat, swinging collaboration with Vince Giordano and the Nighthawks, with whom he's collaborated previously on the soundtracks of *Boardwalk Empire, The Aviator,* and other films.

This was my first interview during the pandemic, and as my good luck would have it, I discovered that Loudon lives on Shelter Island, just across the water from my home in Sag Harbor on Long Island. We recorded in his front yard, keeping an appropriate social distance. At one point, we were interrupted by his cats meowing away, and ended with a UPS man interrupting our conversation with a delivery.

JC: You're my first interview during this present adventure that we're going through. How are you doing with all that's going on?

LW: I'm fine. I mean, relatively speaking. We've been here since March 15. We have an apartment in the City which we've been to once and didn't like when we went. So this has been great. It's so beautiful out here, and the island is pretty sparsely populated, even now. So it's a great place to shelter.

JC: Do you miss travel and being on the road?

LW: Well, I haven't really liked traveling for about twenty-five years, and I've been doing it for fifty years. I miss performing, I miss standing up in front of a bunch of people and playing my songs. That I miss. And the money too. But going to LaGuardia or renting a car or schlepping to a Holiday Inn, I don't miss any of that.

JC: I was delighted when I got your most recent CD, especially since it's with my old pal Vince Giordano. I think it's the perfect CD for the time we're in because it's happy and it's fresh, even though these are songs that were written a long time ago.

LW: Vince and I first worked together in 2004 on *The Aviator*, the Martin Scorsese movie about Howard Hughes. There are several scenes in nightclubs with bands, and I was one of the band singers. Three out of my four kids are singers, and my son Rufus and my daughter Martha were also in *The Aviator* being singers from a different era. I think I was from the '30s and Rufus was from the '20s and Martha was from the '40s. Anyway, that's when I first started to work with Vince, and then we worked together again on the music for *Boardwalk Empire*. I sang on a couple of things, and Vince was the main band for that TV show, so I was a vocalist on some things. We've known each other and worked together for about fifteen years. And Randy Poster, who's a music supervisor and producer and was involved in those projects, said, "You guys should make a record together."

An old friend of mine, a great producer named Stuart Longman, has worked with me on a couple of records and also works a lot with Vince. So Randy was our producer/music supervisor and Stuart pulled together a record deal with this great new company called Thirty Tigers. We got a budget and cut the record last September in three days. He had a twelve-piece band, so we did it in a big room at the Electric Lady Studios on West 8th Street, and it's called *I'd Rather Lead a Band*, which is the title track. That's an Irving Berlin song.

JC: You mentioned growing up listening to your dad play his records and your parents dressing up to go out and seeing them dance. That reminded me of something that the singer Ann Hampton Callaway said to me years ago. She said that watching her parents dance and hearing this sophisticated music made her want to be an adult. I loved that thought, wanting to grow up to have that martini and dance with your sweetheart. A lot of people go, "Oh, that's old-fashioned," but there was an elegance and a romance in that time that was really beautiful.

LW: Right. In the liner notes I wrote for the project, I talk about how we consciously, or perhaps unconsciously, loved the music that our parents courted to and made out to, that we were conceived by, that we were created by. You like to think, "What were they listening to that special night?" My dad had a great record collection. He liked a wide range of music, so I heard a lot of these songs when I was a kid.

JC: Lots of pop stars have made these standard recordings, some successfully and some less successfully. But this music is really in your bones. You feel this music and love it, and it shows.

LW: Well, as a song*writer*—never mind the music, the changes, the chords and the beauty of that, and then the beauty of the players that Vince assembled and uses, those great, great musicians—the writing, the lyrics are, I mean, we're talking about Rodgers and Hart and Frank Loesser and Irving Berlin, you know, the poetry in the songs. Because I'm primarily a singer-songwriter, the lyrics are what really grabbed me a lot on these songs, that informed a lot of our choices. It wasn't just the musicality of it, it was the lyric writing.

JC: The uninitiated who don't know the Great American Songbook, they'll say, "Why do you call it the Great American Songbook?" And I'll talk about the construction of these songs, the way the lyrics work, how they speak to the bigger picture, to these deep feelings that we all feel. Even the songs that are very upbeat and sort of tongue in cheek are speaking to something that we've all felt, which you really capture. One of the songs that I was delighted to see included here is, "I'm Going to Give It to Mary with Love." Now, I have to say, people talk about songs today being sexy or dirty or . . .

LW: Or both.

JC: Or both! But some of the sexiest songs were written in those days. Think about "Do It Again." I think that's one of the sexiest songs ever written.

LW: Some of those lyrics in "Bewitched, Bothered, and Bewildered" are pretty out there. "Those ants in my pants," if you'll excuse the expression.

JC: Exactly! But "Give It to Mary" is hilarious. And as I was listening to it, and your interpretation of it, I was thinking, "Can I play this on NPR?" Talk about this track.

LW: Well, the original version of this song was recorded in 1936 by the incredible Cliff Edwards, also known as Ukulele Ike, and most famously known as the voice of Jiminy Cricket.

He was a jazz-er in the '30s, a great ukulele player, and he had a whole bunch of these kind of risqué songs, including "I'm Going to Give It to Mary with Love." There was one he had called "I'm a Bear in a Lady's Boudoir." In my own work, I come up with novelty songs every once in a while, so I can really appreciate a good novelty song.

JC: Your whole jug band experience.

LW: Right. I was in boarding school back in the '60s, and I was in a jug band. It has that kind of a feel to it, too.

JC: What got the jug band thing going during that time? What sort of started that trend?

LW: Well, the original music was in the '20s and '30s with the Memphis Jug Band Stompers, groups of Black guys in the South using conventional and homemade instruments.

JC: Right, but I'm thinking about what you're thinking about with those '60s jug bands.

LW: Jim Kweskin and the Jug Band were the most successful. When I was in school in the '60s, they were very well known, and they had wonderful people including Maria Muldaur; Geoff Muldaur, her husband; Kweskin of course; the guy who played the washtub bass in the jug was a guy called Fritz Richmond, and, maybe most interestingly, Mel Lyman, who later became a kind of guru and a cult figure in Boston. I loved the Jim Kweskin Jug Band. They did those original songs. And I developed my penchant for that kind of music.

JC: You mentioned Geoff Muldaur, and I didn't know his version of Bix Beiderbeck's "In a Mist," and I love it. It was a surprise to me and a delight.

LW: Yeah, this is a great album. It was made in 2003 when I was living in L.A. and I've known Geoff, aside from being a huge fan of his when I was a kid. We got to be friends, and we did shows together. Geoff is a serious musician, a great clarinet player, and a wonderful arranger. He had this concept of taking the music of Bix Beiderbecke, recording some of the songs that Bix did with different singers, and then arranging some of these piano pieces that Bix wrote, some of which were never recorded before. So he got together this project. I sing on it. It's called *Private Astronomy*. And my daughter Martha sings on it, and Geoff's daughter Jennie Muldaur sings on it. It's just a real interesting record that Geoff made, and it's one of my favorites.

JC: Along the lines of the elegance of that earlier era when these songs were written— and something that always strikes me—is how unadorned the singers' performance style was. They don't have to do anything histrionic because there's so much substance in their interpretation of the song. That's something that really appeals to me.

LW: Right. A lot of the great, great singing is unadorned.

JC: Like Lee Wiley, whom I know you love. I'm a big fan as well.

LW: Well, I love singers, great singers. And, I mean, I knew about Anita O' Day, and I knew about Ella Fitzgerald and Billie Holliday and Mildred Bailey. But I didn't really discover or hear Lee Wiley until my girlfriend Susan played me a Lee Wiley CD. And I was just blown away by the simplicity, the elegance. She was from Oklahoma, which you don't think of as an elegant place particularly. But her delivery and her phrasing and the relaxation. She's just a great, great singer.

JC: With the really great singers, you feel that the work has already been done and it's internalized, so they don't have to overdo the presentation. It's sort of like, when somebody knows what they're talking about, they don't have to raise their voice.

LW: Right. Well, to use an acting term, they don't push. They tell the story of the song. They don't scream it at you.

JC: Exactly. And I think it's a lot sexier that way because of the confidence of it. It seems like, "I know what I'm talking about, and here it is." Nothing sexier than that.

LW: Well, I love her version of "A Ship without a Sail," which is a Rodgers and Hart song that we recorded for our album. I mean, there were some things we heard that we liked, and I decided that I wasn't going to try to do it because the definitive versions had been done. We thought about "I Can't Get Started," or some Louis Armstrong things. It's just too solid and you can't mess with it. Lee Wiley's version of "A Ship without a Sail" is so beautiful, but I figured I could do it differently. So we didn't feel threatened by trying that.

JC: What do you listen to during the day? Do you listen to music?

LW: I listen to music when we start to cook dinner. I'm a musician, but when I go to a restaurant, the first thing I say is, "Can you turn down the music?" I can't stand music in restaurants unless it's really good music. But I listen to old jazz. I don't listen to singer-songwriters, I'll tell you that much. I listen to kind of non-threatening, great jazz.

JC: [Laughs] I'm sorry to laugh, but I totally get it. If you listen to singer-songwriters you'd be working.

LW: Right. But we were listening to a Stevie Wonder record last night, and Thelonious Monk. I mean, I can just name-drop cool people.

JC: But you listen at the end of the day. I do the same thing, when I can have it as a background while I'm cooking dinner. I listen to things that are different from what I do. It's my reward at the end of the day. But I like it that you say you don't listen to singer-songwriters.

LW: That would be my idea of Hell: to be on an island with a record player and have to listen to John Prine and James Taylor records, or Jimmy Buffett. I would blow my brains out.

JC: [Laughs] Talk about "A Perfect Day."

LW: "A Perfect Day" was actually a hymn. It was written in 1907 so it's probably the oldest piece of material on the CD. The lyrics were written by a woman named Carey Jacobs Bond. I heard it when I was watching the Turner TV channel, and there was a Barbara Stanwick, Fred McMurray movie. It wasn't *Double Indemnity*, it was a goofy Christmas comedy [*Remember the Night*] but at one point, Barbara Stanwick sits down at the piano and pretends to play, and this wonderful character actor starts singing this beautiful song, and it just reduced me to tears. So I tracked it down and Paul Robeson recorded it, country singers have recorded it, Irish singers have recorded it. It's a really interesting song and, again, there's a lot of poetry in it.

JC: You've told me that you like the subject of death in terms of songwriting or discussion. What do you mean by that?

LW: Well, it's an interesting situation we're in here: we're going to die. I was writing about getting old and dying even when I was a young guy.

JC: How young?

LW: In my twenties, when I started writing.

JC: Why was that?

LW: I don't know. I suppose, morbidity on my part?

JC: I'm curious because when I was very young, around ten or so, and my parents would say they'd known someone for twenty years, I remember thinking how wonderful it would be to know somebody for twenty years. So, I was thinking in terms of length of time, which was unusual for a ten-year-old because our time frame is so different at that age. But I don't know that I was thinking about death. So continue. It's a good time to talk about death because it's on everyone's mind.

LW: Yeah, well, you know, it's just a predicament and a reality. "The Angel of Death" is one of the songs that I suggested we talk about. I'm friends with John Scofield, who is known primarily as a wonderful jazz guitar player, though he plays for the Grateful Dead, too. But he made this wonderful record called *Piety Street*, which is the name of a recording studio in New Orleans. It was produced by a guy called Mark Bingham whom I actually grew up with in Westchester. It's a Hank Williams song called "The Angel of Death," and they kind of deconstruct it and make it into a moving gospel song. It's just so great. And scary and spooky. When I think of it, it reminds me of those . . . there's this famous painting by Edvard Munch, the Scandinavian painter...

JC: The Scandinavians are good on death.

LW: They are. And it's this family gathered around a deathbed. And that's what the actual lyrics are: "When the lights all grow dim, and the dark shadows creep, and then your loved ones are gathered to weep. Can you face them and say, with your dying breath, that you're ready to meet the angel of death?" So it's a happy-go-lucky thing, perfect for a pandemic. [Laughs]

JC: Is your process the same, going in to record this way, besides the fact that you're not playing guitar?

LW: No, it's quite different. I've made a bunch of different records over the years, different kinds of records. But on this record, I'm just a vocalist. When I'm making a record of my own songs, I bring all the emotional baggage of that. You know, "These are my songs," and so I have attitudes about them, some of which are probably a little screwed up. I'm not objective because it's my own work. On the other hand, I know what I want. But with this, it was just a question of picking great songs, going into a vocal booth, putting on the cans, and singing with the band. It was such a relief to not have to be Loudon Wainwright III, weird, kooky songwriter. I was just a singer. I kind of approached it like it was an acting job, actually.

JC: Because you're acting the story of these tunes.

LW: You have to inhabit the songs. It's like a role. And it's like what we just talked about, about not pushing. You have to own it and inhabit it, and hopefully that happens.

JC: Just in a practical sense, talk about moving forward with your career and touring these days. People will ask me, "When are you doing a concert I can see?" And I'm like, "What part of this are you not paying attention to?" Because concert halls are the last things that are going to open up. So how are you planning, or what are you doing?

LW: Well, I've done a couple of virtual things where I've just gone down into my basement and streamed, played a little thing with my guitar, and people have watched it online. That isn't really a lot of fun, without an audience there. But it's something. As far as the record goes, the record is going to come out in October, and we're talking about doing a virtual thing. Maybe take Vince's band and whittle it down to about four pieces, and maybe do something safely distant that would be streamed at the Village Vanguard or something, so that people could actually watch it on Zoom. But, yeah, everything is turned upside down. And it's really tough for musicians. Are people going to go back to the opera? I don't think so, not for a while, anyway. Or small clubs. But we're here now and doing the best we can.

JC: Are you practicing? Are you still playing a lot, writing a lot?

LW: Well, my primary job is to write songs, and I've written a couple songs.

JC: And do you find this time good for that? Different?

LW: Well, if we're talking about "The Toilet Roll Blues," that was inspirational.

JC: I really liked that song.

LW: Oh, good. I can't say that I'm super-inspired by this nightmare that we're living through. I've referenced it in the songs that I've been writing. But do people want to hear songs about this madness? We'll see, I guess.

Acknowledgements

Thanks to Lee Mergner for inspiring me to write this book, Peter Goodrich and Steinway and Sons for supporting *Jazz Inspired* from day one, Chris Flory for his intelligence, consideration, and good grammar, my editor Connie Rosenblum for being a shining light during the pandemic and for helping me push forward with this project, Sheila Gerzoff and Felix Contreras for their sage advice in the early years of *Jazz Inspired*, Mark Sendroff, Nina Healy and John and Jill Walsh for allowing their homes to be my "studios," and to all the fascinating, talented *Jazz Inspired* guests who have shared their thoughts on how and why they do what they do.

About the Author

Steinway Artist Judy Carmichael is one of the leading interpreters of classic swing and stride piano. She received a Grammy nomination for her first recording, *Two-Handed Stride* and has been featured on numerous TV and radio programs in the States and abroad, including *Entertainment Tonight, A Prairie Home Companion*, NPR's *Morning Edition*, CNN's *Business Unusual*, CBS *Sunday Morning,* and shows for the BBC, Australian Broadcasting Corporation and film and television in Brazil. Judy's memoir, *Swinger! A Jazz Girl's Adventures from Hollywood to Harlem* was published in 2018. Judy continues to tour internationally and when she's home, which she seldom is, she's usually on a tennis court in her beloved Sag Harbor, New York.

www.judycarmichael
www.jazzinspired.com

Made in USA - North Chelmsford, MA
1336495_9798986487502
10 12 2022 0840